FLORENCE
NIGHTINGALE

VAL WEBB, who has degrees and career experience in fields as varied as theology, business, public relations, art, and microbiology, says her goal in writing is to make contemporary theology and religious thought accessible to thinking, often disenchanted people. Inspired by Florence Nightingale's many theological writings, especially an 800-page manuscript on religion, Webb seeks to introduce readers to the woman she met in her research:

> *I was fascinated with [Florence's] demand for a moratorium on the term* God *because of the theological baggage surrounding it. I was stunned by her relatively unknown "scream" against Victorian expectations of women.*

Born and educated in Brisbane, Australia, Webb has degrees in both science and religion from the University of Queensland, Australia, and a Ph.D. in systematic theology from Luther Seminary, St. Paul, Minnesota. She is on the adjunct faculties of the University of Minnesota and Augsburg College, and is a visiting lecturer at Whitley College, Melbourne, Australia, and Murdoch University, Perth, Western Australia. She is the author of four books, including *In Defense of Doubt: An Invitation to Adventure* and *Why We're Equal: Introducing Feminist Theology* from Chalice Press.

FLORENCE NIGHTINGALE

THE MAKING OF A
RADICAL THEOLOGIAN

VAL WEBB

CHALICE
PRESS

ST. LOUIS, MISSOURI

Biblical quotations, unless otherwise noted, are from the *New Revised Standard Version Bible*, copyright 1989, Division of Christian Education of the National Council of the Churches of Christ in the United States of America. Used by permission. All rights reserved.

Cover art: Reproduced by permission of Mayo Historical Unit, Mayo
           Foundation, Rochester, Minnesota.
Cover design: Wendy Barnes
Interior design: Elizabeth Wright
Art direction: Elizabeth Wright

This book is printed on acid-free, recycled paper.

Visit Chalice Press on the World Wide Web at
www.chalicepress.com

10 9 8 7 6 5 4 3 2 1   02 03 04 05 06 07

Library of Congress Cataloging–in–Publication Data

Webb, Val.
   Florence Nightingale : the making of a radical theologian / Val Webb.
      p.   cm.
   Includes bibliographical references and index.
   ISBN 0-8272-1032-9 (alk. paper)
   1. Nightingale, Florence, 1820–1910. Suggestions for thought to the searchers after truth among the artizans of England. 2. Nightingale, Florence, 1820–1910—Religion.   I. Title.
   BL50.N473 W43 2002   2001004461
   230'.092—dc21

Printed in the United States of America

Contents

PART II: The Evolution of a Theologian

Dedicated to two great women:
my mother, Joan Woodcraft Skerman,
and JoAnn Dunn, a good friend,
who died the day this manuscript was completed.

*You say that "mystical or spiritual religion is not enough for most people
without outward form." And I say I can never remember
a time when it was not a question of my life. Not so much for myself but for others.
For myself, the mystical or spiritual religion as laid down by John's Gospel,
however imperfectly I have lived up to it, was and is enough.
But the two thoughts which God has given me all my whole life have been...
First, to infuse the mystical religion into the forms of others
(always thinking they would show it forth much better than I), especially
among women to make them the "handmaids of the Lord."
Secondly, to give them an organization for their activity in which they
could be trained to be the "handmaids of the Lord"...
When very many years ago I planned a future, my one idea
was not organizing a hospital but organizing a religion.*

FLORENCE NIGHTINGALE

Preface

How much right does a biographer have to interpret somebody else's life,
to put his (her) own truth on it, to guess at "the real reasons"?...
Can the biographer trust his (her) objectivity after years of round-the-clock
living with a saint who turns out to be only human?...
The relationship between the biographer and his (her) subject
is the most intimate one in the world of letters,
both affectionate and adversarial, as delicately strung with tensions
as a long marriage.

WILLIAM ZINSSER[1]

Our earthly immortality depends on someone remembering us. How this is done determines whether we become famous, infamous, or forgotten. In an African tradition, the deceased is part of family discussions (and arguments) as long as someone—a grandson, neighbor, or great-grand daughter—can remember the person alive and "recreate" him or her for others. When this is no longer so, the departed spirit becomes unreliable, causing mischief as well as blessing. The importance of this is lost in our society's overabundance of written words and visual images, but in a community dependent on oral history for its collective memory, the one who remembers ensures continuity. Without firsthand witnesses (and sometimes *because* of them), our memory succumbs to the mercy of those who describe us, having never experienced the squeeze of our hand, the twinkle in our eye, or the spring in our step.

I realized this when my father, Dr. Percy Skerman, died. As his phenomenal memory served him less well in his final weeks, we made a photo album of important people in his life. By showing him pictures and talking about these people, we remembered *with* him. After he died, the extended family shared their memories of him, each adding stories others had forgotten or never known. My children, who have lived in a different country from my parents most of their lives, now have a larger memory of my father from this communal recollection, and their children, who did not meet him, will "remember" by our remembering him *for* them in the future. There will come a time when no one who knew my father "in the flesh" remains, and his memory will depend on the two-dimensional prison of text and image. Although his life was well documented, gaps will appear where we forgot to ask and record. Patterns and continuities must then be teased from between the lines, and as contexts and history change, it will become progressively more difficult to "remember" him as he was. An Indian play, *Naga Mandala*, has, as its lead character, a "story." Personified as a beautiful young woman, the story pleads with a jaded writer to "write her" so that she does not die. As he procrastinates, she becomes frantic, knowing her life or death lies, *literally*, in his hands.

This task confronts a biographer with the challenge to make a "story" come alive from a bunch of written facts—or fiction. Unfortunately, biographers sometimes create people with frighteningly little likeness to the original! After Florence Nightingale's colleague Sir Sidney Herbert died, his biographer requested of Florence his many letters to her. Since theirs had been a candid exchange between two people maneuvering for radical reform under great opposition, Florence shared her horror with his widow: "Honor has departed from the face of the earth in the matter of biographies ... 'A new terror is added to death.'"[2]

Negative articles surfaced posthumously about Sir Sidney's political record, so Florence published her *own* account of his work in order that *accuracy* might prevail. The executors of Florence's will were ordered to destroy her private letters, and she wrote *destroy* or *burn* across many she sent to friends. Fortunately for us, she recanted in her final days. Perhaps she outlived enough contemporaries to see their biographies and realize the importance of accurate records.

What does *accurate* mean when applied to a life? William Zinsser says:

> A biographer must also have the insouciance of a psychiatrist or a priest—a talent for being unruffled by quirky behavior—and the patience of a detective. For if the trail is often faint, it's because the trailmaker made a compulsive effort to keep it that way. [3]

And if the *trailmakers* fail to sanitize their own memories, relatives and friends perform the task, destroying priceless records for fear that a less than saintly image will emerge of the diseased. J. P. Morgan said, "There are two reasons why a man [or woman] does anything. There's a good reason and there's the real reason."[4]

The biographer's task is to find the *real* reason—which is rarely at the front of the file cabinet but is hidden in a paper mill of letters and jottings ranging from philosophical treatises to dinner menus. Often the dinner menus give the better clues! What is *omitted* sometimes reveals more than what is included. Anyone dabbling in genealogy knows those dark family branches that defy investigation—an illegitimate child, a prison term, or the sibling no one mentions.

Why would a biographer give up several years of life to ensure that someone *else's* life is documented? Aside from a rare lucrative cash deal, most persevere because they identify in some way with the person or their cause and feel the need to further interpret them to the world. If many biographies have been written, a new biographer might feel the subject has been misrepresented, idolized, or demonized. Extra information may have come to light that better explains a life or challenges previous conclusions. One thing is sure. The biographer chooses to write about one character over others, and interprets the material from his or her perspective and experience. Biographers hold people in their hands to do with them what they will, to prove a theory or recreate a character. They expand on the "truth," which may never be fully grasped, in the hope of pulling the veil a little further away from a face. Sometimes the research acquires a life of its own, leading down unimagined paths and ending with conclusions different from the initial hunch. A new biography does not necessarily supersede earlier ones, even though some *need* to be superseded. Instead, it adds to the accumulated knowledge and expands the conversation between the subject as revealed in life and writings, previous biographers, new information and scholarship, and the *new* biographer standing at a new place to tell the story.

Fresh biographies are needed because there are "fashions" in biographical writing. Nineteenth-century biographies were commissioned by families to embroider for posterity a noble sampler of a life—the "two fat volumes" as Lytton Strachey called them:

> Who does not know them, with their ill-digested masses of material, their slipshod style, their tone of tedious panegyric, their lamentable lack of selection, of detachment, of design? They are as familiar as the cortege of the undertaker, and wear the same air of slow, funereal barbarism.[5]

Strachey shattered this mold, urging biographers to move from rigid chronology and glorification of a life to lay bare the facts as they understood them. In his iconoclastic book *Eminent Victorians,* Florence was transformed into a driven, obsessed woman determined from birth to be a nurse regardless of who or what stood in her way. While the "lady with the lamp" myth *needed* challenging, Strachey simply created a new myth.

Remembering great *women* brings additional problems because rarely were their lives recorded or their writings published. Old masters hang from millions of hooks in art museums around the world, but where are the old mistresses? We have measured the progress of nations by founding "fathers" and military heroes as if the male pursuit of conquest and control singularly accounted for the continuity of a society. The women who married these men, gave them birth, or disrupted their lives and history, such as Cleopatra, Pandora, and Helen of Troy, peep through only as hints—names dropped in male conversations or through women's diaries consulted for glimpses of their famous men. The inventory of multicultural, multiskilled, wise, creative, and ordinary women over the last two thousand years still awaits publication to complete the picture. Nothing is more frustrating than a five-thousand-piece jigsaw puzzle with a missing piece. No matter how much we admire the finished puzzle, our eyes see only the space. And if a puzzle piece is retrieved from under the living room couch long after the puzzle has been dismantled, the piece makes no sense on its own, nor can we be certain which puzzle this piece fits.

This is how I felt when I discovered Florence Nightingale had written an eight-hundred-page manuscript on religion she called *Suggestions for Thought*. I was holding a puzzle piece that did not fit the picture of Florence on the puzzle box of history, treading her saintly way between wounded Crimean soldiers. There had to be *another* puzzle into which this piece fitted. Why had her theological writings never been published or even mentioned, despite her fame? Why had I, a feminist theologian, heard nothing of her surprisingly modern ideas on women, referred to in John Stuart Mill's famous book *The Subjection of Women*? When my lonely puzzle piece finally found its place in the revised picture of Florence I share in this book, I discovered she privately printed a few copies of her manuscript at the same time that the controversial *Essays and Reviews* was published addressing the same issues. *Essays and Reviews* challenged the theological elite of the Church of England, suggesting a "reasonable" theology for a disheveled Church in an age of science.[6] Florence's *Suggestions for Thought* offered a "reasonable" theological alternative to atheism or blind belief for the *working class* displaced by the Industrial Revolution and ignored in Church squabbles. Florence's ideas were not idle speculations of an educated, upper-class woman with time on her hands, but something she felt competent and compelled to share from her experiences with poor villagers. Many of the working class were without *any* religion, but were seeking one. Others retreated behind bankrupt doctrines:

> Multitudes of conscientious and feeling persons, terrified at the work in which the mind of the age is engaged, in sifting opinions long taken for granted as true, fearing that, if those opinions were lost, all religion would be lost, are ceasing to reason, sheltering themselves under authority.[7]

Is the situation so different today? Aren't you a trifle curious as to what Florence recommended as a solution? I was, especially since I live in a town where the Mayo Clinic and its medical facilities employ one third of the population. If anyone should know about Florence, it should be someone living here. Yet I did not discover her "reasonable religion," finally published in the 1990s in two edited editions, in the medical library but in a book sale catalog mailed to me. As I asked one health professional after another if they knew of Florence's military reforms, her advice on Aboriginal deaths in Australia, her Poor Law reform, her sixty years of bedridden seclusion after the Crimean War, or her theology, the universal response was surprise or disbelief. How could so famous a person be so little known? Thus began my personal journey to understand Florence Nightingale from my perspective as a theologian and a woman. I was fascinated with her demand for a moratorium on the term *God* because of the theological baggage surrounding it. I was stunned by her relatively unknown "scream" against Victorian expectations of women who "have passion, intellect, moral activity— these three—and a place in society where no one of the three can be exercised."[8] I empathized with her frustration and guilt at the "murderer" she had become by disturbing her wealthy family's peaceful existence:

> What am I that their life is not good enough for me? Oh God what am I?…why, oh my God cannot I be satisfied with the life that satisfies so many people?[9]

Florence's first biographer, Sir Edward Cook, called her manuscript *Suggestions for Thought to the Searchers after Truth among the Artizans of England* a "by work," filling her distracted mind while she waited to become a nurse. However, this *by work* addresses in erudite depth the concept of God, Universal Law, God's will and human will, sin and evil, family life, spiritual life, life after death, and reincarnation. Even Cook wrote of her:

> She was not "the lady with the lamp." She was the lady with the brain—one of those rare personalities who reshape the contours of life.[10]

What does one make of this? The more I read Florence's immense literary output, the more I encountered a "God-intoxicated being" whose reform was not her goal in life, but the *consequence* of her religion.[11] Florence cannot be interpreted outside the parameter of a woman in love with, and loved by, God and absorbed with deepening that relationship. After several calls from God, which she struggled to answer despite family opposition and lack of opportunity outside a religious order, she finally established an Order of one, grounded on her inner experience of God and expressed in action for the working class. Her "religious" interests were not side issues or Victorian religiosity, as many biographers have assumed, but the *center* of who she was. Just as nursing research has now rescued Florence from the inadequate "lady with a lamp" image, theological research must restore this theologian of liberation, whose reflections on God came from her experiences of oppression—whether with the village poor, in the stifling upper-class drawing room, or among suffering Crimean soldiers. This is the Florence I will sketch in this book. To see her as any less is to miss her altogether. Like any biographer, *my* experiences will also interact with the texts, but the challenge will be to "hear" her without simply projecting a mirror of my own thoughts and experiences (i.e., if she is like me, she would have thought and felt this and this).

The first chapter explores previous biographies to determine how the "myth" of Florence began and why it has dominated history. Chapter 2 describes Florence's early life moving toward her first call from God and the efforts she made to answer the call against family opposition. Chapter 3 accompanies Florence down the Nile River, watching her theology develop out of experiences with ancient Egyptian religion and culminating in her vows to God at thirty. In chapter 4 Florence realizes her longtime dream—a visit to the Kaiserswerth Institution for the Training of Deaconesses in Germany—and pays for it with her family's anger. As a result, she writes a bitter attack, examined in chapter 5, on the demands of the Victorian family on daughters and the need for a female "savior." Florence finally leaves the family in chapter 6 to become the superintendent of an Institution for Distressed Gentlewomen in London, and from here she is sent to Crimea. Chapter 7 explores her busy years of Army reform after the Crimean War and her continuing efforts to have her "religion" for the working class published. The religious convictions that drove her life—an inner mysticism modeled on John's gospel and the medieval mystic writers, and a passion for the poor played out in the fine tradition of Liberation Theology—are examined in chapter 8. Chapters 9 and 10 examine in detail Florence's theological manuscript *Suggestions for Thought,* with her radical ideas on God, humanity, and the human task of helping to bring in the reign of God. Chapters 11 and 12 are structured around her significant friendship with Benjamin Jowett, a classical scholar and theologian from Oxford with whom she corresponded, often weekly. The letters give shape and life to Florence's ongoing reform and writing, allowing us to meet the witty, passionate, frustrated, and brilliant Florence face-to-face, and follow her until her death in 1910, at age ninety.

Of necessity, an examination of Florence's thoughts requires many quotations from her writings. These also allow us to enjoy her skillful way with words, metaphors, concepts, and humor. Victorian English, however, has words, turns-of-phrase, and punctuation unfamiliar to twenty-first-century ears, together with spellings different from American convention. For the most part, I have left the English spelling and original words and phrases in her quotations, sometimes bracketing explanatory words for clarification. On rare occasions, I have updated the spelling for readability. By adopting these procedures, the dramatic flow of her language and thought patterns is retained. If something strange appears to have missed my computer spell and grammar check, read the sentence through a couple of times using different points of emphasis, and the meaning will emerge, albeit in an unfamiliar format. As a feminist theologian, I am acutely sensitive to her generic use of the masculine throughout. In Florence's era, this was correct grammar, rules a highly educated Florence would follow with care. In her day, most people in public positions *were* male; thus the linguistic inadequacy was not as obvious as it is today. Inclusive language would be a later battle. I have therefore retained *man, his, Kingdom,* and so forth, in Florence's quotations since to adjust so many words would become too much of a distraction along with her difficult Victorian English, losing the impact of her words. If Florence were here today, she could and would make the adjustments so much better!

There are many people to thank for the successful completion of such a project. I would like to acknowledge the help of the Rochester Public Library staff, especially Frank Hawthorne, who winged in interlibrary loan resources from near and far, including a microfiche of the original printing of *Suggestions for Thought,* which greatly facilitated research; Patrick Dean for introducing me to the photo of Florence used on the cover; the Mayo Clinic Historical Section, where this photo resides, for permission to use it; Alex Attewell at the Florence Nightingale Museum, London; and the staff of the British Library, London. The following edited collections of Florence's writings have been invaluable, making relatively inaccessible letters and writings more accessible: *Cassandra and Other Selections from Suggestions for Thought,* ed. Mary Poovey (New York: New York University Press 1993); *Suggestions for Thought: Selections and Commentaries,* ed. Michael D. Calabria and Janet A. Macrae (Philadelphia: University of Pennsylvania Press, 1994); *Cassandra: An Essay,* introduction by Myra Stark and epilogue by Cynthia MacDonald (New York: The Feminist Press, 1979); *Florence Nightingale in Egypt and Greece: Her Diary and 'Visions,'* ed. Michael D. Calabria (New York: State University of New York, 1996);

Ever Yours, Florence Nightingale—Selected Letters, ed. Martha Vicinus and Bea Nergaard (Cambridge, Mass.: Harvard University Press, 1989); *Florence Nightingale Curriculum Vitae: With Information about Florence Nightingale and Kaiserswerth,* ed. Anna Sticker (Dusseldorf-Kaiserswerth: Diakoniewerk, 1965); *Letters from Egypt: A Journey on the Nile, 1849–1850,* ed. Anthony Sattin (New York: Weidenfeld & Nicholson, 1987); *As Miss Nightingale Said: Florence Nightingale through her Sayings; a Victorian Perspective,* ed. Monica Baly (London: Scutari Press, 1991); *I Have Done My Duty: Florence Nightingale in the Crimean War, 1854–56,* ed. Sue Goldie (Iowa: University of Iowa Press, 1987); *Dear Miss Nightingale,* Vincent Quinn and John Prest (Oxford: Oxford University Press, 1987); *The Friendship of Florence Nightingale and Mary Clarke Moore,* Mary C. Sullivan, ed. (Philadelphia: University of Pennsylvania Press, 1999); *Florence Nightingale in Rome: Letters Written by Florence Nightingale in Rome in the Winter of 1847–1848,* Mary Keele, ed. (Philadelphia: American Philosophical Society, 1981); Margaret Lesser, *Clarkey: A Portrait in Letters of Mary Clarke Mohl (1793–1883)* (Oxford: Oxford University Press, 1984). While there are scores of books written about Florence Nightingale, I would recommend three for those who want a comprehensive biography of Florence: Sir Edward T. Cook, *The Life of Florence Nightingale,* 2 volumes in 1 (New York: Macmillan, 1942), a condensed edition of the original two-volume 1913 biography; Mrs. Cecil (Blanche) Woodham-Smith, *Florence Nightingale* (London: Constable, 1950. First ed. New York: McGraw-Hill Book Co., 1951); and Barbara Montgomery Dossey, *Florence Nightingale: Mystic, Visionary, Healer* (Springhouse, Pa.: Springhouse Corp., 2000).

This book began as a collection of *seven* women who contributed to major theological debates in church history but were not recognized at the time. When my research on the *first* woman, Florence Nightingale, rebelliously began growing itself into a whole book, David Polk, my editor at Chalice Press, responded in his marvelously creative way and agreed to accept a full book on Florence as a *prior* project. Thank you, David, for being an author's dream editor. Thanks are also due to my family—my three children, Helen, Paul, and Karen and their families, and my mother, Joan Skerman, for their patience in listening to hours of "thinking aloud" about Florence—she has been an extra sibling for quite a while! My special thanks are always reserved for my spouse, Maurice, who helps write every book, not by tapping on the keys, but with his love, enthusiasm, common sense, and light relief, which make such huge projects possible!

Val Webb

Time Line for Florence Nightingale

1818   William Edward Nightingale (WEN) and Frances (Fanny) Smith marry.

1819   Florence's sister Parthenope (Parthe) born in Naples, Italy.

1820   May 12th—Florence born in Florence, Italy.

1821   Nightingales return from Europe to Lea Hurst.

1825   WEN purchases second estate—Embley in Hampshire.

1828   Test and Corporation Acts repealed, allowing Non-Conformists to hold public office.

1829   Catholic Emancipation Act passed allowing Catholics to hold public office.

1831   WEN begins tutoring Florence.

1832   First Reform Bill passed despite Bishops' opposition. Sir Sidney Herbert elected to Parliament.

1833   Emancipation of slaves. Oxford Movement begins.

1835   WEN fails his bid for Parliament.

1836   Institution for deaconesses established at Kaiserswerth, Germany.

1837   Florence's first call. Leaves for Europe with family. Victoria becomes Queen.

1838   Nightingales travel in Europe. Florence meets Mary Clarke ("Clarkey") in Paris.

1839   Nightingales return to England.

1840   Queen Victoria marries Prince Albert. Florence studies mathematics with a tutor.

1842   Florence meets Christian von Bunsen and Richard Monckton Milnes.

1844   Florence becomes friends with Aunt Hannah Nicholson, refuses cousin Henry Nicholson's marriage proposal. Consults Dr. Howe about working with the poor.

1845   Sir Sidney Herbert becomes Secretary at War. Florence's plan to work with Dr. Fowler at Salisbury Hospital thwarted. John Henry Newman becomes Roman Catholic.

1846   Florence studies hospital reports from Paris. Receives Yearbook from Kaiserswerth. David Strauss' *Das Leben Jesu* translated into English by George Eliot.

1847   Florence goes to Rome with Bracebridges and meets Henry Manning, the Herberts, and Mary Stanley. Clarkey marries scholar Julius Mohl.

1848   Florence takes a retreat with Madre Mother Colomba in Rome before returning to England.

1849   Florence declines Richard Monckton Milnes's proposal of marriage after a seven-year courtship. Goes to Egypt and Greece with the Bracebridges. She receives a second call.

1850 Florence makes spiritual vow of obedience and chastity on her thirtieth birthday in Greece. Visits Kaiserswerth for two weeks and writes a report for them. On returning, is made to spend six months with Parthe. Hilary Bonham Carter studies art in France and stays with Clarkey. Henry Manning converts to Roman Catholicism.

1851 Florence meets Dr. Elizabeth Blackwell. Spends three months at Kaiserswerth, Germany, while Fanny and Parthe are at Carlsbad Spa. Begins *Suggestions for Thought*. Monckton Milnes marries. Religious census taken in England.

1852 Florence goes to Umberslade spa with WEN, then to Aunt Mai's. Considers converting to Roman Catholicism. Finishes first draft of *Suggestions for Thought* and *Cassandra*. Receives call to be a savior. Parthe has a breakdown and Sir James Clark suggests Florence leave home.

1853 Florence goes to Paris to visit hospitals. Receives an annual allowance from WEN. Starts work at Harley Street as volunteer Superintendent. Turkey declares war on Russia. F. D. Maurice forced to resign from King's College for his *Theological Essays*. International Statistical Congress founded.

1854 Florence toys with leaving Harley Street for King's College Hospital, but goes to the Crimean War instead with her nurses and the Bracebridges, arriving November 4. Non-Conformists admitted to Oxford.

1855 Florence at Scutari Hospital in the Crimea. In November Aunt Mai replaces the Bracebridges as Florence's companion. Nightingale Fund established in London. Benjamin Jowett's *Epistles of St. Paul* published, and Jowett asked to resubmit to 39 Articles.

1856 Florence receives General Orders as head over all Crimean nurses. Visits all battlefield hospitals. War ends March 30 with Treaty of Paris. In July, Florence leaves the Crimea, aged thirty-six. Meets the Queen, then settles in London to work on Army reform. Non-Conformists admitted to Cambridge.

1857 Florence analyzes her Crimean statistics, completes her document on Army Health, and the Royal Commission into Army health is established with Sir Sidney as head. Florence declares herself an invalid. Aunt Mai and Arthur Clough assist her in London. Indian Mutiny begins.

1858 Florence continues Army reform, revises *Suggestions for Thought*, and writes *Notes on Hospitals*. Her *Notes on Matters Affecting the Health, Efficiency and Hospital Administration of the British Army* is published. Clough becomes Florence's assistant. Palmerston's government, including Lord Panmure, Secretary of State for War, goes out of office.

Parthe marries widower Sir Harry Verney. Jews admitted to Parliament.

1859 Florence continues her Army reform. Royal Commission on the Health of the British Army in India established with Florence's encouragement. Her *Notes on Hospitals* is published. Clough is made secretary of the Nightingale Fund. Lord Palmerston returns to power with Sir Sidney as Secretary of State for War. Darwin's *Origin of Species* published.

1860 *Essays and Reviews* is published. Florence's *Notes on Nursing* is published. *Suggestions for Thought* is privately printed and reviewed by Benjamin Jowett, John Stuart Mill, and Sir John McNeill. Copies also go to Florence's father, Uncle Sam Smith, and Monckton Milnes. Florence begins friendship with Jowett. The Nightingale Training School for Nurses opens at St. Thomas's Hospital. Florence writes a paper on hospital statistics to be read at the International Statistical Congress. The Madre and von Bunsen die. Aunt Mai leaves Florence and becomes estranged. Hilary takes Aunt Mai's place. Sir Sidney and Clough are ill.

1861 Florence asked to assist in organizing Army hospitals for American Civil War. Her Indian Sanitation work begins. Declines Queen's offer of an apartment in Kensington Palace. Harriet Martineau promotes *Notes on Nursing* in the press. King's College Training School for Midwives established with Nightingale Fund. Prince Albert dies. Sir Sidney dies in August and Arthur Clough in November. The devastated Florence becomes ill. Sir Harry Verney becomes Chair of the Nightingale Fund until his death.

1862 Florence works on Indian Sanitary report from materials gathered from military bases across India. Publishes on the Contagious Disease Act. Meets Jowett in person for the first time. Nightingale Fund begins training in midwifery at King's College Hospital, London. H. B. Wilson and R. Williams tried for heresy over *Essays* but acquitted.

1863 Florence completes Indian Sanitary report (*The Red Book*). Her article "How people may live and not die in India" read at National Association for the Promotion of Social Science Congress. Lord de Grey appointed Secretary of State for War through Florence's influence. Bishop Colenso (South Africa) deposed for his biblical criticism. Jowett charged with heresy over *Essays* but acquitted.

1864 Florence drafts suggestions for British delegation to Geneva Convention that established the guidelines for the Red Cross. William Rathbone asks her advice on nurses for Liverpool workhouses. The Contagious Disease Act she opposed was passed. Her *Suggestions in*

Regard to Sanitary Works required for the improvement of India was sent to all Indian military posts.

1865 Florence begins work on Poor Law reform, plans Liverpool Workhouse infirmary, and moves to permanent home in South Street. Receives another call from God. Her *Suggestions on a system of nursing for hospitals in India* published. Hilary Bonham Carter dies young. Henry Manning appointed (Catholic) Archbishop of Westminster.

1866 First Women's Suffrage petition presented to Parliament by John Stuart Mill.

1867 Florence celebrates thirty years since her call. Continues Indian work. Organizes Sanitary Commission of India Office. Publishes paper on training and organizing nurses for the sick poor in Workhouse infirmaries. National Society for Women's Suffrage formed, but Florence refuses Mill's invitation to serve on board. First Lambeth Conference of Anglican Bishops.

1868 Working on Indian sanitary reform and recognized as most knowledgeable woman on Indian sanitary problems. Writes *Method of improving the nursing service of hospitals*. Joins the National Society for Women's Suffrage but not active. Visits Lea Hurst to help care for her mother, her first visit home in ten years.

1869 John Stuart Mill's *The Subjection of Women* published, quoting Florence. Women get the vote in municipal elections. Vatican I (1869–70) declares papal infallibility. Irish Disestablishment enacted.

1870 Florence advises both sides of Franco-Prussian War on military nurses. Advises National Society for Aid to the Sick and Wounded, precursor organization to British Red Cross. Publishes tracts for Indian villagers on sanitary matters and turns her attention back to the Nightingale School.

1871 Florence interviews probationary nurses to establish quality of Nightingale School training. St. Thomas's Hospital moves to new location. Works with Henry Bonham Carter on Nightingale Fund. Is recognized by both sides of the Franco-Prussian War. Her *Notes on Lying-in Institutions* published. University Test Act passed removing religious test requirement to matriculate and graduate

1872 Florence turns to her writing. Begins *Notes from Devotional Authors of the Middle Ages*. Helps Jowett with Plato translations and *The Children's Bible*. Charles Bracebridge dies.

1873 Continues writing. Two articles on theology published in *Fraser's Magazine*. Jowett's *The School and Children's Bible* published.

1874 WEN, Mother Mary Clare Moore, and Selena Bracebridge die. Florence takes on more responsibility for her mother's care. Becomes honorary member of the American Statistical Association.

1875 Continues with Indian sanitation and villager education for few years and also with nursing and public health reform.

1878 Women allowed to attend lectures at Oxford for the first time, and admitted to degrees at University of London.

1879 Robert Koch (Berlin) publishes paper demonstrating six types of bacteria, proving Germ Theory.

1880 Fanny Nightingale (aged 92) and Uncle Sam Smith die.

1881 Florence reconciles with Aunt Mai after twenty years. Pasteur produces vaccine against anthrax.

1882 Florence inspects Nightingale School of Nursing for *first* time. Organizes a team of nurses for Egyptian Campaign. Dr. William Farr dies.

1883 Florence receives Royal Red Cross medal from the Queen. Sir John McNeill and Clarkey die.

1885 Continues Indian reform work and becomes interested in the First Indian National Congress. Monckton Milnes dies.

1886 Contagious Diseases Act repealed.

1887 Queen Victoria's Jubilee (on throne). Florence celebrates her Jubilee Year—fifty years since her first call. Works against registration of nurses until her death. Nurses Jowett through an illness in London. Her eyesight begins to fail.

1888 Dr. Sutherland retires after thirty years of work with Florence.

1889 Florence opposes British Nurses Association Charter. Aunt Mai dies.

1890 Florence's 70th birthday. She and Jowett plan to endow Chair in Statistics in Oxford. Not done. Parthe dies at eighty-one.

1891 Dr. Sutherland dies.

1893 Florence's final paper on nursing read at nurses' congress of Chicago's World's Fair. Jowett dies in October.

1894 Sir Harry Verney and William Shore Smith (Aunt Mai's son and inheritor of Nightingale estates) die. Florence's memory begins to fail.

1896 Embley sold. Florence makes will, appointing Henry Bonham Carter executor.

1897 Queen Victoria's Diamond Jubilee.

1901 Queen Victoria dies.

1904 Florence receives Lady of Grace of the Order of St. John of Jerusalem Award from King Edward VII.

1907 Florence becomes first woman to receive Order of Merit (from King Edward VII).

1908 Florence becomes second woman to receive the Freedom of the City of London.

1910 Florence dies in her sleep on August 13, aged ninety.

PART I

The Story
of
a Life

CHAPTER ONE

Biographies—Fact and Fiction

Everyone knows the popular conception of Florence Nightingale.
The saintly, self-sacrificing woman, the delicate maiden
of high degree who threw aside the pleasures of a life of ease to succour
the afflicted, the Lady with the Lamp, gliding through the horrors
of the hospital at Scutari, and consecrating with the radiance of her goodness
the dying soldier's couch—the vision is familiar to all.
But the truth was different. The Miss Nightingale of fact was not
as facile fancy painted her. She worked
in another fashion and towards another end;
she moved under the stress of an impetus which finds no place
in the popular imagination.

LYTTON STRACHEY[1]

"Who is Mrs. Nightingale?" the London *Times* newspaper asked in October 1854, echoing the thoughts of a nation. *Mrs.* Nightingale? Since women nurses had never accompanied the British Army to battle before, the least the venerable *Times* could assume was that the leader of a group of women off to care for notorious soldiers was a respectable married widow, not a single woman of thirty-four.

In March of 1854, Britain had aligned with France to prevent Russia's European advance against the Turks, a war to be remembered as "the most unnecessary war in modern Europe."[2] For its attack on the Russian naval base at Sebastopol on the Crimean peninsula in the Black Sea, the British established its hospital base at Scutari on the opposite shore of the Black Sea (across the Bosphorus from Constantinople, now Istanbul), assuming victory would be quick and simple. When Florence and her nurses arrived at Scutari on November 4, 1854, the makeshift hospital was full, and the battle of Inkerman a few days later raised patient numbers to 2,300. Only days after that, several supply ships meant for Scutari were destroyed in a hurricane. On the Crimean battlefield itself, supplies had not reached the troops in time for the disastrous winter approaching, and scurvy, dysentery, frostbite, and starvation engulfed the Army, sending a stream of half-dead soldiers crammed in overcrowded boats with cholera-ridden comrades on a nightmarish trip to Scutari Hospital. While the trip took about five days across the Black Sea, this did not account for the up to fourteen days' wait until the boat was loaded to capacity, or up to a week anchored in the Bosphorus before the sick were landed. Once on the Scutari dock, the wounded were at the mercy of whoever could be enticed to carry their rough stretchers up the steep, long ascent to the hospital. Sidney Osborne, volunteer chaplain at Scutari, described the fiasco:

> It is now a matter beyond all contradiction that the way in which the sick and wounded were brought from Balaklava to Scutari, was in its every detail utterly undefensible. They were put on board in a condition demanding the utmost care; many had fresh severe wounds, some had undergone recent amputation, many were weak to the last degree, the generality of their clothing wholly insufficient; and yet they were crowded together between and sometimes on the decks with not even an apology for a bed; some, indeed I fear many of them were even without a blanket to lie on.[3]

At Scutari Hospital, seventy soldiers a day died, packed together against the cold in unventilated rooms, without clean bandages and clothes. One thousand soldiers died from cholera without firing a shot, and those surviving the boat journey encountered medical staff untrained to handle so many casualties. At first, the British public did not know all this, but, unlike previous wars, it was to learn through an independent war correspondent from the London *Times* who reported not only the horrors but also that the French were better equipped, with numerous surgeons, sufficient supplies, and the excellent Sisters of Charity. An irate letter appeared in *The Times* demanding "Why have we no Sisters of Charity?"[4] Sir Sidney Herbert, Secretary at War and target of this accusation, was a close friend of Florence's and was aware of her skills as the volunteer superintendent of Harley Street's Institution for Sick Gentlewomen in Distressed Circumstances at this time.[5] He realized that she could solve his professional embarrassment, and Florence saw Scutari as her longed-for chance to serve God. Four days after being approached, she was at sea with thirty-eight assorted women and the blessing of the British nation.

Despite its uselessness and tragedy, the Crimean War established Florence. Personally, it provided the "accident," as she called her association with Sir Sidney, to obey her call and prove her organizational, charitable, and creative skills. Practically, it gave her the chance to escape her destiny in the Victorian family. Publicly, it produced an icon for the British imagination—the myth of the gentle, self-negating "lady with the lamp," treading her dainty way among horribly wounded soldiers— that would dominate the future, even though Crimea accounted for less than *two* of Florence's ninety years of life. Acquiring a life of its own even before she returned to England, this image glided through history inspiring thousands of young women to serve others, no doubt a more suitable icon than a determined woman out to change the world, beginning with the British Army! Angel she was, but not the fluffy kind—more like Michael ("who is like God?"), sent to protect and deliver the Israelites at a time of great anguish.[6]

A distraught nation needed something noble from so disastrous a war, and the stories of returning soldiers and the *Times* correspondent gave them Florence:

> Wherever there is disease in its most contagious form and the hand of the spoiler distressingly nigh, there is that incomparable woman sure to be seen. Her benignant presence is an influence for good comfort, even amid the struggles of expiring nature. She is a "ministering angel," without any exaggeration, in these hospitals, and as her slender form glides quietly along each corridor, every poor fellow's face softens with gratitude at the sight of her. When all the medical officers have retired for the night, and silence and darkness have settled down upon those miles of prostrate sick, she may be observed alone, with a little lamp in her hand, making her solitary rounds.[7]

In Florence's absence, a Fund was established in her honor with donations flowing in from rich and poor. The instigators of this Nightingale Fund consulted her in the Crimea about how the money should be used, suggesting that a school for training nurses be established with Florence as its head. Overwhelmed by the daily horrors of war, Florence was not about to make such a decision, requesting it wait until she returned. Even then, she did not want to rush into a half-baked scheme.

> If I had a plan in me…it would be simply this—to take the poorest and least organized Hospital in London, and putting myself in there—see what I could do—not touching the "Fund" perhaps for *years*—not till experience has shown how the Fund might be best available…I therefore must decline making any plan whatever, even if I were not overwhelmed at present, not with plans, but work.[8]

While the administrators of the Nightingale Fund knew of Florence's pre-Crimea idea to create a women's training establishment like the Protestant institution she visited in Kaiserswerth, Germany, they did not know that Florence's experiences in Scutari were militating against such a plan. She had discovered a more urgent mission that she alone could fill—defending the common soldier at war and at home. On returning to England, she requested release from the responsibility of training nurses, relegating the Nightingale Fund to a subcommittee and St. Thomas's Hospital, London, which was eager to house the training school. The school gained her attention briefly when it was opened in 1860 with promises that she might also design a new hospital around good sanitation principles and patient care. However, this did not come about, for while she submitted an organizational plan for the nursing school, it was rejected as too ambitious by the doctors:

> The class of women who now supply hospitals with sisters could not undertake a hundredth part of what you wish to impress on them as essential…It would be impossible to find women capable of undertaking the competitive examination you have drawn out.[9]

St. Thomas's initiated its *own* plan and appointed its own staff under the Nightingale name. When shown the nurses' contract, Florence called it a servant's contract and submitted her preferred specifications before returning to Army reform. Her publications on the care of the sick during this period were based not on the Nightingale School, but on experiences in the villages around her estates and in the British Army.[10] *Notes on Nursing,* published *before* the school was opened, was addressed, not to hospital nursing, but home nursing, the responsibility of all women despite their lack of training.

The Nightingale School's early years had little connection with Florence, and her *first* official visit was twenty-two years after its establishment. In 1872, when administrative and location changes were made, Florence, with her Army reform underway, met with its probationers and staff in her home, and provided an annual address to be read at the school. Even then, she did not focus her efforts there, as she was advising the Army for the Franco-Prussian War, creating drafts for what became the Red Cross, finding herself up to her ears in Indian sanitation reform, editing Benjamin Jowett's translations of Plato and his *Children's Bible*, writing her never-published book on the medieval mystics, preparing monographs on district nursing and home health, and caring for her elderly mother, to name a few activities. The Nightingale School of Nursing established schools around the world, cementing Florence's name as synonymous with nursing, even though it was not the central focus of her career. Others were also caring for the sick poor. Of the thirty-eight nurses who went to Scutari with Florence, twenty-four were from Catholic or Anglican Orders involved in such care. Quaker Elizabeth Fry preceded Florence to Kaiserswerth, Germany, to observe their methods before starting a nursing institution in London. When the Nightingale School opened, twenty-six religious organizations were supplying nurses to London hospitals, a fact that hampered initial contributions to the Nightingale Fund because of sectarian fears it would also be a religious order. Non-Catholics suspected it would be Catholic, and Anglicans feared it would be Unitarian because of Florence's background. Many of Florence's nursing theories were outdated once the germ theory of disease was established, and many ideas attributed to her because of the school were not hers.[11] What Florence *did* contribute to nursing was a professional, nonsectarian approach to patient care with better-educated women, improved organizational structures, and good sanitation principles. These innovations all came from her theological convictions, which will be analyzed later in the book. Contrary to what many in her day believed, Florence argued that health and illness were not arbitrary gifts or judgments sent from God, but were states that humans can and must attain for themselves by cooperating with the laws of God discoverable in nature by observation and statistical analysis.

When I explained my research to a friend who trained at the Nightingale School at St. Thomas's, she was aghast. Despite lectures and memorabilia on Florence as founder of nursing and the Nightingale School, she knew *nothing* of Florence's other reforms, her sixty years of seclusion, her fringe involvement in the school, or her religious writings. "How come we were never taught this?" was her constant refrain. This is a question I also wrestled with, since the information is there in Sir Edward Cook's definitive biography,[12] in other biographies over the years, and in Florence's personal letters and writings.

While no single reason answers the question, many explanations converge. First and foremost, Florence the nurse captured the hearts of the British public before they even set eyes on her. Laura E. Richards' biography, published prior to Florence's death, begins:

A company of military and naval officers met at dinner in London. They were talking over the war, as soldiers and sailors love to do, and someone said: "Who, of all the workers in the Crimea, will be longest remembered?" Each guest was asked to give his opinion on this point, and each wrote a name on a slip of paper. There were many slips, but when they came to be examined there was only one name, for every single man had written "Florence Nightingale."[13]

England sang about "The Shadow on the Pillow," "God Bless Miss Nightingale," and "The Soldier's Cheer," and ships, children, and racehorses were named after her. Returning soldiers caressed her memory, and mothers of dead soldiers wept over letters from her hand describing their sons' last words and decent burials. When Sir Sidney launched the Nightingale Fund in London, the adoring crowd listened to one soldier's letter:

> What a comfort it was to see her pass. She would speak to one and nod and smile to many more, but she could not do it to all, you know. We lay there by hundreds; but we would kiss her shadow as it fell, and lay our heads on the pillow again, content.[14]

As the "lady with a lamp," she was captured in almost divine poses by artists and poets, Henry Wadsworth Longfellow's poem "Santa Filomena" creating the tone and mythology for others:

> Lo! In that hour of misery
> A lady with a lamp I see
> Pass through the glimmering gloom,
> And flit from room to room.
> And slow, as in a dream of bliss,
> The speechless sufferer turns to kiss
> Her shadow, as it falls.[15]

This Florence was installed in the public imagination even before she returned from twenty months in the Crimea. Two Florences now existed, and, since the real Florence virtually disappeared from public sight on her return, the popular image triumphed. Strachey says:

> The name of Florence Nightingale lives in the memory of the world by virtue of the lurid and heroic adventure of the Crimea. Had she died—as she nearly did—upon her return to England, her reputation would hardly have been different; her legend would have come down to us almost as we know it today—that gentle vision of female virtue which first took shape before the adoring eyes of the sick soldiers at Scutari.[16]

Florence indirectly fueled this legend-making by refusing all public accolades on her return. Knowing plans were afoot to welcome her back, she refused a man-of-war vessel, traveling first to Paris then arriving, unnoticed, in London. She made no public appearances or statements despite pleas from politicians, friends, and family, and refused to have her portrait painted. Her mysterious absence simply increased public adoration. As far as the world was concerned, the real Florence disappeared, and, since her name did not appear on her parliamentary reform activities, many people forgot she was still alive. The fickle public opted for the icon, and biographers embellished the Crimean Florence with a childhood in keeping with the image—a heroic young girl preparing for a divine task. Crimea and the Nightingale School of Nursing became the sum of her life and work.

This was the age of the heroine biography, eagerly devoured by young female minds as a vicarious escape. Although called biographies, they were closer to constructed fiction, including only suitable facts about a life within appropriate limits for their young readers.[17] Heroines were courageous, good, and spiritual from *childhood*, characteristics that enabled them to face adversity and opposition in later life. While they might accomplish deeds beyond the scope of the average young woman, they never stepped beyond societal and cultural bounds for long, and they responded to their challenges differently because of their gender. While heroes explored a range of adventures, heroines fulfilled home duties, remained feminine, and shone in public only in nurturing, caring, and service-oriented roles. Grace Darling, the twenty-three year old daughter of a lighthouse keeper on the Northumberland coast, a favorite for heroine collections, rowed out in a raging storm to save nine shipwrecked people. However, on returning, she reassumed the female role of nursing them back to health. Florence, another favorite subject, was depicted, despite her longing to escape her idle home life, as *sacrificing* it and her health for soldiers, serving below her class and beyond her "duty." Although her father gave her a rigorous "male" education—"With him Florence learned Greek and Latin and mathematics, and was extremely quick at learning foreign languages"— the biographer follows immediately with, "The little girls were taught, too, by their mother to work their samplers and do fine sewing."[18] So accepted were these gender rules that the 1873 *Portrait Gallery of Eminent Men and Women* described Florence's *Notes on Nursing* as "feminine in its thoughtful sympathetic insight, manly in its straightforward, energetic utterance."[19]

To foster devotion in boys and girls, such biographies searched for a common thread in a life to show an evolution of heroism from childhood. Without fail, two minor incidences from Cook's biography become central for validating Florence's feminine caring skills from childhood as a "natural" direction toward nursing, even though her first few "calls" mentioned *nothing* about nursing. Florence's sister Parthe *broke* her dolls, but Florence mended them, and gave her own dolls constant care during dangerous illnesses, lining them up in hospital rows "while they were most carefully and tenderly nursed by their little mother, who doctored them and tempted their appetites with dainty dishes until they were well again."[20] In the second story, the young Florence convinced a seasoned shepherd not to destroy his wounded sheepdog. Putting hot packs on its swollen paw, she made the dog comfortable and gave prophetic instructions, a divine foreknowing, about the dog's recovery. When the awestruck shepherd claimed she had worked wonders, Florence instructed him, as Jesus did after raising Jairus' daughter, "You can throw away the rope, for he's going to get quite well now, only you must nurse him carefully, and I will show you how to make hot compresses."[21]

The comparison with Jesus was often hinted at in such biographies, and *his* three years of ministry also spawned birth and childhood stories later to support the revered image of him that developed in early Christian communities. Florence's childhood stories take on a premonition of a great work crowning her life—nursing, of course, not Army reform and Indian sanitation:

> The look of gratitude in the eyes of the dog moved her childish, pitiful heart, but how well was she to learn to know that look in the eyes of suffering men, when the very name of Florence Nightingale meant hope and comfort to the wounded soldiers, and the sight of her face bending over them was to them as the face of an angel.[22]

Florence's volatile relationship with her family and their destructive, controlling behavior that made her rebel could not be part of a heroine story for young women. Most biographers simply overlooked the family tensions for a picture of happy children playing in luxury and beauty, or else stressed Florence's attachment to her father, ignoring her unhappy relationship with her mother. Despite Florence's detailed accounts of an unhappy, restricted, and rebellious youth, biographers W. J. Wintle and Florence Witts wrote:

> Here [Lea Hurst] little Florence spent much of her childhood, and the earliest thing remembered of her is that she was kind and good. The thing which most struck all who knew her, was that she never

seemed to be thinking about herself, but always about those around her and how she could help or cheer them...The little girl had to work much harder than most children [with her lessons], yet we find she was always happy and contented.[23]

The same biography, written while Florence was still alive, admitted her parents did not share her vocational inclinations, but "did nothing to actually oppose them,"[24] a statement that flies in the face of Florence's account, as we shall see later. Those brave enough to mention the tension soften it by describing Florence's "gilded cage," emphasizing her privilege to make her sacrifice even greater—Scutari needed her, and she had unconsciously prepared for this all her life.

Gushing blood and amputated limbs were not the stuff for female sensibilities, so Florence's experiences of raw, grotesque human suffering were only hinted at. Florence is brave, noble, relatively silent, *feminine*, and upper-class, going far beyond her duty. One soldier remembered, "I can't help crying when I see them. Only think of Englishwomen coming out here to nurse us; it is so homely and comfortable."[25] The image of soldiers waiting to kiss her shadow obliterated the moaning, swearing, death cries, and stench of Scutari, as well as the verbal confrontations Florence had with British Army officials as she stood her ground to achieve small victories. The sacred image of Florence was cemented by the often-quoted words of one soldier, "Before she came there was such cursing and swearing, but afterward it was as holy as a church."[26]

What happened to all Florence's *other* achievements? Wintle and Witts, after eighteen chapters describing her life up to the end of the Crimean War, add one chapter called "The After-work" before the "Conclusion." Fifty years of social reform in the British Army, in hospitals, in sanitation, and in nursing, together with her numerous books and papers, are squeezed into one chapter, though they were the achievements Florence called her greatest ones! As Strachey said:

> In Miss Nightingale's own eyes the adventure of the Crimea was a mere incident—scarcely more than a stepping-stone in her career. It was the fulcrum with which she hoped to move the world; but it was only the fulcrum. For more than a generation she was to sit in secret, working her lever: and her real life began at the very moment when, in the popular imagination, she disappeared.[27]

Laura Richards' biography for young women, published the year before Florence died, delivers 160 pages of embellished prose on Florence's saintly life until her return from the Crimea. Then, writing that Florence realized when she returned that she would never be strong and well again because she had sacrificed herself for the cause, Richards puts her to bed at thirty-six and adds three vague pages to sum up the rest of her life. It was not as if Richards did not know what else Florence did— her father was Dr. Ward Howe, the American reformer Florence consulted about her career and reform work.

Florence herself made it clear that her activities at Scutari went far beyond the mopping of brows, "the least important" function into which she had been forced. She was purveyor of supplies when Army rations were tied up with red tape. She negotiated with all and sundry to remove or divert obstructive army regulations, incurring the wrath of those on whose territories she trespassed. She reorganized the kitchen and the laundry, defraying costs from her own funds and those of the *Times* newspaper. She provided clothes for soldiers arriving from the battle. She bypassed red tape to renovate a derelict barrack, hiring and paying the workmen herself. She set up reading rooms and classes for recuperating soldiers and organized a bank so they could send money to families. She spent days on a horse or in an uncomfortable carriage, inspecting hospitals in the war zone, all the while battling jealousy and sabotage from opponents. She was, in reality, an exacting administrator, not a delicate woman volunteer. Despite this, her adoring biographers painted only the angel of peace: "Only a little feminine tact was necessary to bring together the dilatory members of a board and get them to unlock a storehouse."[28]

At the turn of last century, these sentimental biographies sought to inspire young women to serve God in appropriate feminine ways. Ignoring Florence's disenchantment with the institutional Church and its teachings, biographers constructed her as they wished. An 1887 Sunday school biography calls her a devout Protestant who, on return from Kaiserswerth, established a *Protestant* order of Nurses to match the Catholic sisters[29]—a heroine in one's camp was quite a prize! Her work in the Harley Street sanatorium prior to Crimea became a "foreign mission field":

> She bade adieu to the brilliant circles which she was so well fitted to adorn, and, seated beside some sick and perhaps dying governess, soothed her pains and pointed her to the great Physician of Souls.[30]

Florence would have totally rejected this image, given her frustration with those at Scutari who saw a dying soldier only as a soul to save. Yet the biographers also declared the selection of nurses for Scutari a *religious* selection in some biographies:

> It was also necessary that the ladies chosen should be earnest
> followers of the Lord Jesus Christ. Nothing but real love for Him
> would enable them to stick to their posts.[31]

This is not substantiated by reality—the nurses sent out were a strange
mix. Protestants refused to send nurses under Florence because her
religious affiliations were suspect. Many Catholic sisters, recruited
because they already did such work, opposed Florence, convincing her
never to establish a religious order. One children's biography was
amazed at Florence's *heavenly* charity because she called a priest to a
dying Catholic "as readily as if it were her own favorite minister who
was desired."[32] Wintle and Witts deny any volatile sectarianism existed
at all.

> There was to be no discussion or controversies on religious
> differences. Why should there be? It is surely easy enough for
> Christian people to do deeds of mercy and charity, without
> quarrelling about matters upon which they think differently.[33]

If such biographers were at pains to demonstrate Florence's *religious*
convictions, why did they not share her religious writings? Her *Notes
on Nursing* outlining her religious motivations were widely published,
and some articles appeared in *Fraser's Magazine* in 1873 summarizing
her ideas. Wintle and Witts mentioned these, calling her thoughts
remarkable and startling, but they went no further:

> In this article, which extends to ten pages, the writer emphasizes
> man's ignorance and misconceptions of the nature of God, and
> presses for an entirely new basis of moral science. Some of the
> suggestions here given are rather startling, in that they express the
> possibility that what are known as orthodox opinions may be based
> upon a complete misunderstanding of the character and purposes
> of God.[34]

No doubt Florence's image was good value for encouraging young
women into God's service, but her radical thoughts and her nerve to
express them publicly had to be kept under wraps.

Biographies that focused only on Florence's Crimean and nursing
work assured the British public that all was still in order. The folk myth
of the common soldier and the woman who served them exemplified
the ideal Victorian male-female relationship—long-suffering, brave
soldiers and a hardworking, gentle nurse finding complete fulfillment
in sacrificing herself to serve Britain's men. Florence as a sexless, perfect
mother, wife, and daughter reassured Victorian manhood, assuaged the

British conscience over dying soldiers, and offered vicarious hope that women would aspire to such roles without upsetting the male-female balance. A reformer of the Army and the power behind politicians was a very different and dangerous image. Interestingly, after Florence's first visit to Queen Victoria and Prince Albert, Albert was impressed with her "modesty," an appropriate Victorian womanly virtue, while the queen said, "She has a wonderful, clear and comprehensive head. I wish we had her at the War Office!"[35]

Biographies change with culture, reinforcing different "virtues." While the mid-1800s emphasized the devout young woman in the home, late nineteenth-century writings encouraged duty in the wider world, but within feminine boundaries. Suffragist and pre-war days at the beginning of the twentieth century promoted women who were challenging both the injustices of the world *and* limitations on women. By the 1950s, the psychological turmoil of choosing between marriage and vocation—you could not have both—filled the pages. Florence's confusion and angst began to be featured at that time:

> She was morbid, she was self-willed, and a real problem to her parents who could not understand why she should not be as happy and contented as her sister. She became thoroughly out of sympathy with her family, her relations and their attitude to everything. Even before she was a fully grown woman she was conscious of being set apart. She felt that she had a mission to do good in the world: she felt in some way called to a dedicated life, but what this was to be she did not know. It worried her.[36]

Healing sick dogs and dolls took second place to feeling misunderstood, to a consuming passion for the poor, to a struggle to distance herself from romantic attachments, and to the choice of singleness as self-denial and sacrifice for a greater cause. In reality, however, Victorian marriages were seldom as romantic as the 1950s depicted them, and Florence's rejection of marriage, despite family pressure, was fueled by the actuality that marriage would exclude her from her vocation.

In the arena of serious adult biographies, Sir Edward Cook was commissioned to do the two-volume biography that was published in 1913, three years after Florence's death. Cook undertook the commission on condition he could pursue the truth without opposition, no doubt wishing to displace the mythical image. Sorting through thousands of letters and drafts, he covered in careful detail not only her life up to the Crimea but her massive reforms afterward, arguing that the British Army's debt to her, both in England and overseas, was far greater than that owed by nursing. Cook tried to balance Florence's many sides:

> She was a woman of strong passions—not over-given to praise, not quick to forgive; somewhat prone to be censorious, not apt to forget. She was not only a gentle angel of compassion; she was more a logician than a sentimentalist; she knew that to do good work requires a hard head as well as a soft heart...[she] knew hardly any fault which seemed worse to her in a man than to be unbusiness-like; in a woman, than to be "only enthusiastic." She found no use for 'angels without hands.'[37]

Yet he was constrained by the proximity of Florence's demise and many family members' being alive to withhold material and censure the facts. He did not elaborate on problems in the Nightingale School of Nursing so as to protect its reputation as an opportunity for women. Despite this, Cook still remains the premier source on Florence.

Why then did the myth persist with Cook's biography and some 10,000 letters and manuscripts in the British Library and other collections? I suggest a combination of her seclusion after the Crimea, leaving nothing to challenge the public persona; the anonymity of her reform work, with the Nightingale School and her writing on nursing and health the only public exposure of her name; and Lytton Strachey's biography. Why the latter? Because Strachey, using Cook's extensive work, penned a brief but racy sketch of Florence that became the popular version of her life. Strachey described his own intentions:

> If [the biographer] is wise, he will adopt a subtler strategy. He will attack the subject in unexpected places; he will fall upon the flank, or the rear; he will shoot a sudden, revealing searchlight into obscure recesses, hitherto undivined. He will row out over that great ocean of material, and lower down into it, here and there, a little bucket, which will bring up to the light of day some characteristic specimen, from those far depths, to be examined with careful curiosity.[38]

His rules of brevity, wit, and irreverence *caricatured* his subjects by putting them in absurd situations and mocking them. His agenda with Florence was clear—to replace the gentle "lady with the lamp" with *his* image of a possessed, merciless woman who would manipulate even God to achieve her nursing goal: "One has the impression that Miss Nightingale has got the Almighty too into her clutches, and that, if He is not careful, she will kill Him with overwork."[39] Like many others, Strachey "proves" his thesis with the usual stories—sick dogs and dolls. Then by reducing Cook's nine hundred and forty-four pages to fifty-one pages of the "most relevant facts" (all supporting his argument), he fell slightly short of calling her a witch:

> Madness? Mad-possessed—perhaps she was. A demonic frenzy
> had seized upon her. As she lay upon her sofa, gasping, she
> devoured blue books [government records], dictated letters, and,
> in the intervals of her palpitations, cracked her febrile jokes.[40]

Because all his biographies in *Eminent Victorians* were short and vigorous, Strachey's Florence replaced Cook's carefully nuanced but lengthy portrait as the preferred account, especially as it claimed to be an abbreviation of Cook. The eccentric "nurse from birth" became a subsequent definitive image and source for many books and films. The American Nurses' Association endorsed the 1936 film *The White Angel*, based on Strachey's book, as one of "the best known and most reliable sources available."[41] Cook's two volumes were edited into one in 1941, but still relegated to research-only shelves. *Two* myths now existed—Strachey's caricature and the sentimental image, both with little resemblance to Florence.

Rafael Sabatini's *Heroic Lives* opted for the popular myth from the first paragraph. He denied any parallels between Florence and Joan of Arc, a popular comparison:

> One the one hand, we have a peasant girl acting on an instinctive
> impulse, driven and guided by an inner voice which assumes to
> her simple mind an objective character, taking up a task that
> properly belongs to the other sex. On the other hand, we have a
> lady, delicately nurtured and carefully educated, pursuing a
> reasoned course in a province entirely feminine.[42]

Sabatini had misread the comparisons, however. Florence's friends argued that had *she* been in control of the army, as Joan of Arc was, the war would have been won sooner, and Florence used the comparison to explain the depth of her opposition: "There is not an official who would not burn me like Joan of Arc if he could, but they know that the War Office cannot turn me out because the country is with me."[43] Sabatini's Florence was "womanly," working where women could be "most fruitfully active," with selfless devotion to a cause and an ideal so unstinting it could not be daunted by the necessary personal sacrifice:

> She was a gentlewoman, young, attractive, rich and popular, who
> abandoned the ease and luxury into which she had been born to
> render "the holiest of women's charities to the sick, the dying and
> the convalescent, without regard to the danger, toil and horror she
> would have to confront."[44]

Although Sabatini recognized the importance of Florence's call, he assumed it was to nursing from the beginning, fine-tuned through visiting religious orders. While admiring her administrative skills at Scutari, he limited her later work to founding a nurse training school and writing a textbook to raise the standard of nursing and improve conditions for soldiers. To preserve a "womanly" image, Sabatini ignored Florence's massive work after Sir Sidney's early death, crediting her success to a strong man (my italics):

> It was a difficult task for a woman; it would have been impossible to any woman less accredited by accomplishment. To her it was rendered *comparatively easy* by the assistance of her friend Sidney Herbert, who shared her interest in the soldiers' welfare. It was the collaboration between them, in which she was the guiding spirit, he the speaking voice, which gradually overcame administrative inertia and brought about reform.[45]

Just as juvenile biographers turned to psychological and sociological struggles in the fifties, so did Mrs. Cecil Woodham-Smith, an expert on the Crimean War, armed with new material since Cook.[46] Promoted as the first complete picture of Florence, faults and all, Woodham-Smith's portrait showed a passionate, frustrated child, angry at her privileged life and confused about her own character. Her mother did not understand her, so she sought close friendships and approval from her father and extended family members. Florence was beautiful and intelligent, while her sister Parthe was never a student, followed her mother's social ambitions, and was constantly jealous of Florence. To this Victorian hothouse of idleness and emotion, Woodham-Smith attributed Florence's moodiness as she was torn between her psychological and sociological inheritance and her need to escape. Her life became a struggle between upper-class expectations and a passion to help the poor beyond the limits of duty. Sociologists Elvi Waik Whittaker and Virginia Oleson, on the other hand, *credit* Florence's social status and personality for her success. She was not the first to do what she did, but she attracted attention by defying upper-class convention and enlisting powerful support through her social status, far greater than that of her opponents. Crimea captured England's romanticism and emerging social conscience, and Florence captured their love and admiration with her exceptional personality, intelligence, energy, and rare level of education for a woman (or most men) of her day. All this invested nursing with her status and name, allowing it to become a decent profession for all women.

> It is difficult to appreciate the emotional and intellectual impact of her Crimean activities on Victorian England, where women were

essentially second-class citizens, valued for their decorative and entertaining qualities, and for innocence of social and political issues.[47]

In the last few decades, nursing researchers have pushed aside the "ministering angel" and the "woman possessed" to search for the whole Florence.[48] Some have shown that many Nightingale School nursing principles were not what Florence intended, attributing modern nursing as much to its *modification* of her ideas by successors, but without losing sight of her essence—good patient care and an honorable career for women. Others have acknowledged Florence's many contributions beyond nursing. While philanthropy as duty was expected of her class, absorption in poverty or maintaining a public stance against the *systems*—political, social, philosophical, and theological—that imprisoned the working class were not. Florence's nursing reform came from this broader commitment to step beyond her duty and immerse herself in all the problems of the destitute in order to help liberate them.

A few modern biographies have replicated Strachey's iconoclastic approach, highlighting Florence's failures and defects rather than successes, sometimes with very little charity toward her. F. B. Smith's biography, billed as the first "full and alert reading" of Florence's unpublished papers since Cook, makes Strachey look almost saccharine. According to Smith, Florence was manipulative, power-hungry, unstable, and controlling, with an unremitting drive to dominate her associates and opponents "regardless of the worth of her rivals' goals, the cogency of their arguments or the solidity of their facts."[49] Persuading the easily manipulated Sir Sidney to send her to the Crimea for *her* advancement, he found it easier to submit to this "imperious, unstoppable woman," even though others were better trained. Any loyalty Florence excited in others came through her power over them, and those brave enough to oppose her were heroic victims. Smith dismissed suggestions that her collaborators might have shared her reform visions, arguing that Florence prodded people into action after the war for her continuing power gains, and that those who affirmed her writing and work did so to humor her. Her "calls" were merely claims of "divine appointment to know" in order to give authority to her self-promotion. I personally find Smith's analysis unsubstantiated in Florence's extensive correspondence and writings, the weakness, I believe, lying in his lack of serious attention to Florence's religious essence, calling her calls "sacralized egotism" and her conversations with God "flights of fancy." Biographer Nancy Boyd may have had Smith in mind when she wrote, "The victims of history have many murderers. In the clash of knives, it is impossible to tell who struck the fatal blow."[50] People, she says, are never single causes, but complex personalities, and, while we can break people's lives into many categories, in the end we have to guess how these categories and traits are interrelated.

Florence's "illness"—the "T in F" (thorn in the flesh) in her writings—which changed her into a lifelong, homebound invalid at thirty-six, has absorbed biographers for years. This is discussed in detail later, but its causes and consequences have supported a plethora of conflicting arguments about her personality and motivations. While reclusiveness was not out of character with her shyness as a child and young adult and her introverted personality, some biographers have identified specific physical and physiological illnesses with symptoms debilitating enough to make her permanently homebound. Others question a physical illness severe enough to so disable her, yet allow her to work almost without sleep for months on end. "Invalidism," common among upper-class women, allowed a woman to control her life in a way not usually available to them. I will argue that her seclusion and unremitting focus on her work, for whatever reasons, was *also* in character with the lifestyle in a religious order, and that Florence, though she never joined an order, pursued a parallel life of devotion and obedience to God in her own way. I will also argue it gave her an office "like a man" in order to do the "man's work" to which she had been called.

How can so many different opinions come from the same source material? Because, apart from the massive collection already on hand in Cook's day, new letters, notes, and draft papers from Florence have continued to come to light. The British Library's collection exceeds any other personal collection in their charge, and this is only *one* collection among many around the world. Wilfred Laurier University Press, with Lynn McDonald as project director, is currently publishing sixteen volumes of the collected works of Florence Nightingale, many for the first time, which will spawn another flood of books about her.[51] New research always casts new shadows and spotlights old assumptions, revealing different angles and textures of a complex life. Those who argue that Florence was inconsistent and erratic because she changed her opinions throughout her writings say more about themselves than her. Anyone who for more than seventy years of active writing kept up a flow of correspondence, papers, research, and reflection on almost every topic in an age where so many disciplines were in their infancy, does not remain static in her ideas. We find a progression of thought in

Florence, with later ideas contradicting earlier ones as new information came to light. One of the strengths of our postmodern world is the recognition that systematic unity or uniformity of thought in a person, doctrine, society, or life in general is neither possible nor desirable. Biographers, rather than constantly attempting to corral Florence into a one issue–one party candidate throughout her life, have to content themselves with uncovering just another facet to add to the complex diversity that was Florence.

Florence foreshadowed her own biography in an 1846 journal entry:

> It [the care of the poor] satisfies my soul, it supplies every want of my heart and soul and mind. It heals all my disease. It redeems my life from destruction. Everything else that I do, I always feel that I am not doing it well or that somebody else would do it better, or that I am not quite sure whether it is right, whether I am doing it for the sake of God and whether I had not better be doing something else, but this—I know however badly I do it that they would be doing it worse. And besides, there is no one else but I to do it. I want nothing else, my heart is filled. I am at home. I want no other heaven.[52]

CHAPTER TWO

Nurturing A Call: 1820–1849

Live your life while you have it. Life is a splendid gift.
There is nothing small in it. For the greatest things grow by God's law
out of the smallest. But to live your life, you must discipline it.
You must not fritter it away in "fair purpose, erring act, inconstant will";
but must make your thought, your words, your acts all work to the sacred end,
and that end not self but God. This is what we call CHARACTER.[1]

On February 7th 1837 God spoke to me and called me to His Service.[2]

Florence Nightingale was born in Florence, Italy, in 1820 during her
parents' three-year European honeymoon—her elder sister and only
sibling, Parthe, had been born in Greece. Florence's parents were both
from the "upper ten thousand," who were the social, political, and
economic ruling class of titled lineage and newly rich merchants and
bankers from the Industrial Revolution. Fanny, Florence's mother, was
the granddaughter of Samuel Smith, who made his fortune in a London
grocery business. A humanitarian, he contributed money to America's
War of Independence against crown control despite losing his Georgia
investments as a result. Fanny's father, William Smith (1756–1835), as a
Member of the House of Commons for forty-four years, campaigned
against slavery and religious intolerance, and *for* the poor and
disadvantaged. He also advocated against too much royal power, the
electoral boundaries, and the criminal code, as well as other economic

21

and commercial reforms, and worked with William Wilberforce to end slavery.

William Smith was Unitarian, a religious persuasion that emerged in the late eighteenth century when Joseph Priestley (1733–1804), an important scientist of his day, rejected Christianity's supernatural claims, including Christ's divinity and the Atonement, in favor of a religion based on reason. He published his conclusions in *The Doctrine of Philosophical Necessity*, arguing that while Jesus may have taught God's benevolence and human duty and was, in that sense, a messiah or messenger, there was no need for an atonement for the world's sins. How could human action be blamed for the introduction of sin and evil if "the whole series of events from the beginning of the world to the consummation of all things are one connected chain of events established by the Deity"?[3] Instead, Priestley believed that God's spirit was incarnate in *every* member of the race, and that a person's duty was not the pursuit of personal salvation from sin, but to cooperate with God's agenda for the universe through the leading of God's spirit within. Priestley campaigned for social and religious reform, and also for the admission of non-Anglicans to government, universities, and Parliament to loosen the Anglican Church's control. Many agreed with Priestley's *reform* ideas, but were disturbed at his *theological* ideas, punishable by law as heresy. In 1791, Priestley and his followers formed the Unitarian Society, which demanded, among other things, that all be treated with dignity, including the poor and destitute, since God had a universal regard for humanity and God's spirit was within everyone. Unitarianism appealed to many intelligent people with its humanitarianism, but those concerned with its theology, both Anglican and non-Anglican, kept Unitarians alienated socially and politically. Priestley later fled to America, where his writings became very popular—Thomas Jefferson was very taken with his book *The Corruptions of Christianity*. It was Fanny's father, William Smith, who sponsored the Unitarian Toleration Act of 1813, which finally removed Unitarian beliefs from the criminal list, and who also stayed active in every religious tolerance debate up to the 1828 Test Act repeal, allowing Nonconformists into Parliament. Prior to this, an Act of Indemnity was passed annually to pardon the law's violation by Nonconformists serving in Parliament.[4]

Fanny grew up Unitarian amidst her father's struggles as a member of Parliament for the full recognition of Unitarians in government and society. The family home, Parndon Hall in Essex, was frequented by England's cultural and political leaders. Beautiful, extravagant, and strong-minded Fanny was more interested in making it in society than in reform, however, and it is significant that after marriage she abandoned her strong family heritage in Unitarianism for the social advantage of being in the Church of England. She married the younger William Edward Nightingale (WEN) on the rebound when another suitor failed to meet parental approval, a less than perfect match. WEN was from the Shore family of Tapton, near Sheffield in Derbyshire, an industrial center in the north. His father, William Shore, was a successful banker, but WEN changed his name to Nightingale, as per custom, when he inherited his mother's family property. The introspective, liberal-thinking WEN went to Cambridge and, after marrying Fanny, settled down as a country gentleman fond of travel and intellectual pursuits. He built the impressive Lea Hurst on his family property in Derbyshire, but, after one winter, Fanny declared it too cold and isolated for a year-round residence. Embley Park was purchased near Hampshire's New Forest as a second home, close to the "right" people and Fanny's extended family. The Nightingales spent spring in London, lived in Embley Park until June, went to Lea Hurst for the summer, back to Embley Park for shooting season, in London for November, and at Embley Park for Christmas. Florence abhorred this indolent, purposeless life and was most at home at Lea Hurst near WEN's family—his sister Aunt Mai, Great Aunt Elizabeth Evans, and Grandmother Shore.[5]

In a country where the class system held the world rigidly in place with the theology that God had *appointed* each to their slot, whether poor or rich, a righteous person accepted God's wisdom and did one's duty in one's "place" according to strict societal rules. Any challenge to these defined parameters was a sin. This "natural order of creation" was believed to designate intellectual and moral capacity as well, with the upper class more highly endowed in both areas—another reason why class boundaries could not be violated. God created leaders and followers, and, as a member of the upper class, WEN's "duty" was to oversee his estate, legislate in local politics, and care for his workers (but not seek their equality). Such activities did not creatively fill the hours of his day or the passion of his heart, and, throughout her life, Florence was conscious of her father's underlying sense of despair at his unproductive, privileged life, perhaps because she understood such privileged despair herself. Watching him tend to his mail as if it were important parliamentary documents, she wished he had a factory under his care as his northern neighbors did to give him a purpose. Like many country gentlemen, WEN sought a seat in Parliament (or perhaps Fanny desired it for him), standing for and losing Andover when Florence was fourteen. This turned him off national politics, but, as a local magistrate and High Sheriff of Hampshire for a term, he took Florence with him to court. She became conversant with politics, civic duty, local and national issues, and also important political leaders, witnessing firsthand the problems of the poor. Beyond the duties of his estate, WEN resigned himself to learned societies, his library, and the education of Florence "like a son" he did not have—in Greek, Latin, German, French, Italian, History, Grammar, Composition, and Philosophy. After WEN joined the British Association for the Advancement of Science in 1831, the fourteen-year-old Florence also joined when women were first admitted in 1834. She had inherited his taste for intellectual pursuit, writing later:

> I had the most enormous desire of acquiring. For 7 years of my life I thought of little else but cultivating my intellect. And even now, when I think what a human intellect may become by industry, ambition comes before me like Circe with her cup to tempt me.[6]

Florence also acquired WEN's Unitarian social conscience, demonstrated by the way he cared for his tenants, as Florence's description of his funeral shows:

> The funeral is on Saturday: a walking funeral—what *he* would have wished: only the family and the tenants: his cottagers carry him— One of the very last things he did, tho' ailing, was to see after building fresh rooms to a cottage…he was the truest father to all his people and cottagers: not pauperizing them: but wise and careful: helping them to help themselves: even seeing that the wives kept their husbands' houses tidy himself. There was hardly a pauper on his places: May those who come after him do as well for those he so loved and cared for.[7]

To set Florence's classical education in context, most upper-class families educated their daughters just enough to attract a suitable marriage, but not enough to threaten the spouse. Along with relegating the working class to a fixed and inferior position, the divine "order of creation" had also included women in the less intellectually capable department. Society constructed dire theories about the dangers, even to reproductive organs, of too much study for women. During Florence's formative years, women were thus excluded from university education. Only in 1849 did Florence's friend Elizabeth Blackwell become the first woman to obtain a medical degree in America, when her own country refused her. Elizabeth and her sister established a Women's Hospital and Medical College in New York in 1868 when other American universities refused to admit women. Oxford University allowed women to sit for examinations in 1870, and two women's colleges were established in 1878, together with an Association for Education of

Women. No degrees were granted, however, until 1920. Newman Hall for training teachers became a Cambridge University women's college in 1880, and the four women admitted informally to Cambridge all won firsts! Women first *graduated* from Cambridge in 1928, but did not get full degrees until 1948. Unitarian families were less inclined to discriminate against an education for their daughters, which also explains why WEN invested so much energy in Florence, but she still experienced the tremendous frustration of never attending university nor seeing other women gain even a basic education.

Florence inherited her mother's considerable organizational skills, which Fanny employed in running a large household of servants, family, and constant visitors with military precision and entrepreneurial flair. While Parthe followed her mother's interests, Florence was different— brilliant, conscientious, earnest beyond her years, and overwhelmed with a deep sense of justice. She did not see her future in the making of society, as she called her mother's role. Florence nursed a childhood horror that she was not like her family, always petrified this might be exposed. This early dis-ease evolved into a disdain and anger at what she called a life of "frittering time away on useless trifles" rather than useful occupation. When WEN took over his daughter's education when Florence was ten, the family formed around two camps, Florence and WEN in the library, and Parthe and Fanny in the drawing room absorbed with "endless tweedling of nosegays in jugs and a nameless collection of useless nonsense."[8] This separation fueled Florence's lifelong ambivalence toward her mother and sister, longing for their approval yet disgusted with their idleness. Given Florence's evolving religious and humanitarian focus, Fanny's rejection of Unitarianism's intellectual honesty and social conscience for what Florence saw as an ineffectual, socially blind Anglicanism no doubt added to the tension. A family friend wrote of young Florence:

> I see she was ripening constantly for her work, and that her mind was dwelling on the painful differences of man and man [people] in this life. A conversation on this subject between the father and daughter made me laugh at the time, the contrast was so striking, but now, as I remember it, it was the Divine Spirit breathing in her.[9]

As mistress of the Big House, Fanny, with Florence and Parthe in tow, visited the poor tenant families and villagers to deliver soup and advice. Whereas Fanny saw this "poor-peopling" as the *limits* of her responsibility, Florence was overwhelmed with its inadequacy:

> For me to preach patience to them, when they saw me with what they thought every blessing (ah how little they knew) seemed to me such an impertinence and always checked me. I longed to live like them and with them and then I thought I could really help them. But to visit them in a carriage and to give them money is so little like following Christ, who made Himself like his brethren.[10]

She soon learned that her desire to do more was inappropriate to her class, whose advantage fed off poor people's destitution. The Big House became the symbol for her of this separation:

> This house is the embodiment to me of the drainage of the poor to fill the rich, who, upon the plea of a better bonnet and a better dinner, blurt out "truths" to the poor and expect them to be grateful (without knowing their manners, hardly even their language, certainly not their feelings). And, more curious still, they get their expectation, and the poor, in most cases, strange to say, are grateful...I loathe that house, and the means at once to fulfil our desire in ignorance of the feelings of our fellow-creatures. Fellow-creatures, indeed! Is there one of us who believes that they are our fellow-creatures?[11]

Florence's discomfort with the class structure into which she was born was intertwined with her evolving religious experiences. For as long as she could remember, she had an inner consciousness of the divine far beyond the common religiosity of her day: "God has always led me of Himself. I remember no particular sermon or circumstances which ever made any great impression on me."[12] Her "calls" from God were much more than a justification of her need to escape the inane nothingness of her life, as some have argued. She had experienced the mystical life as a child and later found a language for it through the writings of the medieval mystics. A serious, conscientious child, she went to church and read her Bible, along with practicing the piano and learning poetry. In her journal, she had listed her daily goals—reading her Bible, praying before breakfast and at night, and going to church on Sunday if someone could go with her. The eight-year-old Florence analyzed Bible readings and church sermons in her letters, and it is interesting to see the thoughts that were becoming her own. In 1830, she expounded on the minister's comments about Luke 15:10—that it was not in the resolution, but in the *doing* of a thing, that we rejoice. The man with one hundred sheep looking for the lost one, the woman sweeping her house to find the lost coin, and the prodigal son who returned to his father, all celebrated only when the act was *accomplished*.

This vast gap between resolutions and action haunted Florence. From her earliest writings, she deplored her habit of "dreaming"— escaping, even during family drawing room discussions, into a world of her own creation, where she was free to do whatever she was able to imagine, all impossible in real life. It was her only release from boredom:

> When I was a child and was naughty, it always put an end to my dreaming for the time…Was it because naughtiness was a more interesting state than the little motives which make man's peaceful civilized state, and occupied imagination for the time?[13]

This habit accelerated with Florence's increasing frustration at her family prison. She began to worry if she was unstable, especially when her dreaming was interpreted as rebellion against her divinely assigned place in life. She blamed herself for her "sin," both the dreaming and also the pleasure she found in it. Many biographers have misinterpreted Florence's dreaming by not exploring its meaning in Victorian life. Such dreaming was not unique to Florence, but was a condition many upper-class people struggled with, conscious of the appalling conditions of poverty but trapped in a theological and cultural worldview that dictated against their *acting*.

In an autobiographical fiction from that period, *Nemesis of Faith*, J. A. Froude describes his hero emerging from university anxious to do something for the poor rather than assume the comfortable affluence of church orders. The hero's father chides his son for "dreaming"—longing to spend his life ministering among those "rivers of wretchedness that run below the surface of this modern society," to "pour one drop of sweetness into that bitter stream of injustice."[14] Such philosophical wanderings were natural in college, but not in the real world. A man must do the "duty" required of him by his class. The son reflects to himself:

> I have shown talents, [my father] says, of which it is my duty to make use; the common sense of mankind has marked out the best way to use them, and it is worse than ridiculous in a young man such as I am to set myself up to be different from everybody else, and to be too good to do what many of the best and wisest men he knows are doing.[15]

Froude's hero did not wish to dismantle "the lot which, by an irrevocable decree, it has pleased Providence to stamp upon the huge majority of mankind," but rather to move among the poor to assure them in their suffering of a God of *love*, and be "allowed to sacrifice himself to them, to teach them to hope for a more just hereafter, and to make their present more endurable by raising their minds to endure it."Nevertheless, while dreams of making a difference might be noble today, it was *embarrassing* in Victorian England when one's offspring sought to change the way society had always been. Florence's dream was also to work with the poor, but she would dream far beyond Froude's hero by promising them not a better afterlife or strength to endure their lot on earth, but a new religion that challenged the *system*, theological and cultural, that held them in poverty. Cook described her thusly:

> Florence…was not conscious of doing much, but reproachful of herself for doing little. The constant burden of her self-examination, both at this time and for many years to come, was that she was forever "dreaming" and never "doing." She was dreaming because for a long time she did not clearly feel or see what her work in life was to be; and then for yet another period of time because, when she knew what she was called to do, she could not compass the means to do it. Her faculties were not brought outwards, but were left, by the conditions of her life, to devour themselves inwardly.[16]

The year 1837 was eventful for the seventeen-year-old Florence. When influenza swept England, she immersed herself in caring for the sick in her family and in the village, proving to herself and others what she could do:

> I had to nurse 15 servants in bed, my mother and two children of her brother, who were in the house. I had only one assistant, the cook, who was not ill. But soon other nurses were sent for. The Influenza passed away and all was at an end with my practical life.[17]

Being useful and occupied in some practical work had energized her. The only time she really felt happy at home was when visiting the sick or teaching in the village school. But this was also the year she was introduced to London society, the first step toward the destiny of a suitable marriage. The family also planned an extended tour of Europe in the fall and, in the midst of departure plans, Florence received the first of four audible calls to serve God—"On February 7, 1837, God spoke to me and called me to His Service."[18] The call was nonspecific, but assured her that God had a purpose for her beyond the intolerable life she felt doomed to live. She would have three other audible calls in her lifetime—before going to Harley Street (1853), before Crimea (1854), and after Sir Sidney Herbert's death (1861), and through her life she also recorded her ongoing conversation with God, often in dialogue form. Biographers who do not take Florence's calls seriously forget that *she* did, revisiting her calls at several points during her life and celebrating, in 1887, her "jubilee"—the defining moment of God's first call.

In Europe, Florence reveled in her first experience of France and Italy, meeting historians, politicians, and academics who became mentors and colleagues. Her diaries reveal both her eagerness to absorb all she could in preparation for her new commission, and also her inner struggle not to let society divert her from this call. She documented social conditions and political disputes and sympathized with Italian freedom fighters, filling her notebooks with Giuseppe Mazzini's ideas on the effectiveness of people working for the common good.[19] In Geneva, Switzerland, she also met Jean Charles Leonard Sismondi, the Swiss historian who argued, in his *History of the Italian Republics*, that no state could become or remain great without liberty for all. Sismondi had also analyzed the Industrial Revolution's effect on the English class system, and his critique—and also his personal compassion to the beggars who swarmed his door—gave Florence a broader perspective on the problems she intuitively felt and saw in practice in her country.[20] Nothing missed her critical gaze. When the Grand Duke and Duchess of Florence followed the medieval Easter custom of washing the feet of the oldest and poorest, Florence noted that the Duchess washed

> a little place on each of their feet for herself to kiss...it was not much penance, for she had a chamberlain on one side and a lady on the other to help her kneel down and get up before each of the old women.[21]

A highlight was meeting Mary Clarke (Clarkey), a brilliant, freethinking woman whose home in Paris was a haven for scholars.[22] Clarkey and Florence instantly bonded, Clarkey appreciating Florence's intelligence and keen interest in life, and Florence admiring Clarkey's comfortable rapport with intellectual men. Clarkey's friendship, together with her future husband Julius Mohl, provided a lifeline for Florence as she negotiated her future. While Clarkey did not share Florence's passion for the poor, she shared her passion for life, and was helpful when Florence wanted to visit Catholic convents in Paris.

On returning to England, Florence was convinced God had deemed her unworthy because she had not received any follow-up call—had she overlooked God in Europe's balls and parties? As she struggled like a caged bird with petty arrangements, suitors, and "illnesses," a few people came to her support. Aunt Mai persuaded a reluctant Fanny to allow Florence mathematics lessons. Her neighbor Lord Palmerston introduced her to his son-in-law Lord Ashley (later Lord Shaftesbury), who had initiated reforms in mental asylums, child labor, sanitary conditions, and health in general.[23] Through Ashley, Florence gained access to government reports on all types of reforms for the poor, which she compared with her own notes and ideas, determined to be prepared when the moment arrived. Much has been made of the child Florence recording all the illnesses of the extended family as proof of her single focus on nursing, yet this overlooks Florence's fascination with *all* record-keeping. She also made meticulous notes on flowers, birds, and animals, cataloguing and describing them, including where she found them. She wrote detailed letters beyond her years and her autobiography at ten—in French! At seventeen, she filled journals with comments about the art, culture, poverty, and politics of Europe, and analyzed scene by scene every opera she saw. This was more than a *nurse* in the making. It was the woman who would call statistics the "sacred science" that, through observation and analysis, opened the doors to the thoughts of God discoverable in the universe.

During the "hungry forties," Florence saw much in the villages to break her heart. Many a dinner she missed in the Big House, sitting by the beds of sick villagers—she could not eat a grand meal while this was happening. Besides, her life work with ignorance and poverty was unfolding, and she was already transferring her allegiances:

> We think and reason...We dream our intellectual dreams...Where will they be when we are gone? I feel my sympathies all with Ignorance and Poverty—the things which interest me, interest them. We are alike in expecting little from life, much from God...My imagination is so filled with the misery of this world that the only thing in which to labour brings any return, seems to me helping and sympathizing *there*; and all [that] the poets sing of the glories of this world appears to me untrue: all the people I see are eaten up with care or poverty or disease...Life is no holiday game...it is a hard fight, a struggle, a wrestling with the Principle of Evil, hand to hand, foot to foot...The night is given us to take breath, to pray, to drink deep at the fountain of power. The day, to use the strength which has been given us, to go forth to work with it till the evening..."*Thy Kingdom* come" does not mean only "*My salvation* come"...I never pray for anything temporal—but when each morning comes, I kneel down before the Rising Sun, & only say, Behold the handmaid of the Lord—give me this day my work to do—no, not my work, but thine.[24]

The topic of poverty and its repercussions in Victorian England could fill volumes. England had for centuries been a feudal system, with lords who owned the land and extracted rent and other privileges from tenant farmers and their families on the estates. Despite the gross inequities of this system, poor people and their families did have a place and identity in their village community. The mid-nineteenth-century Industrial Revolution, following the advent of steam-powered machinery for the factories, changed England's economy from an agricultural one to manufacturing. Farms were consolidated into estates, and villagers went to work in the factories or migrated to the big cities, deprived of what previously held them together—farm, trade, village, community, and church. Nothing in the cities was set up to cope with the huge influx of people, and cities became huge slums of the unemployed and destitute. Villages were also devastated without their agricultural base. In a feudal system, the lord's duty was to give "charity" to the poor, crumbs from the rich man's table. But with this catastrophic dislocation of people and structures, the class system was in total disorder. Such was unthinkable, however, since this system was considered part of God's divinely ordained order.

The concept of an order in the universe came through the Greeks and was theologized by St. Thomas Aquinas and the medieval church, reaffirmed and reshaped in the Renaissance, further theologized (especially by John Calvin) in the Reformation, and established as a central tenet of the Church of England. The original ordering *principle* was God, and its ongoing activity was God's Providence:

> Not only does [God] sustain the universe [as he once founded it] by his boundless might, regulate it by his wisdom, preserve it by his goodness, and especially rule mankind by his righteousness and judgment, bear with it in his mercy, watch over it by his protection; but also that no drop will be found either of wisdom or light, or of righteousness or power or rectitude, or of genuine truth, which does not flow from him, and of which he is not the cause.[25]

As *The Book of Common Prayer* reminded the Church's adherents daily, *everything* in an unpredictable, often cruel world was in God's eternally decreed plan. Nothing in God's order could therefore be changed, including the "divine right" of kings and queens to rule nation and Church, laws, civil rulers, the Church—and the class system. England's social structures had been ordained to reveal God's benevolence as certainly as the laws of nature. While class privilege demanded a *moral* duty—governance, leadership, noble behavior, and charity—obtaining better wages for the working class, or their equalization in society, was *not* part of the duties. Reformers who challenged the class *system* rather than following their moral duty of "poor-peopling" (giving charity to the poor) were highly suspect, as both anti-English *and* anti-Church.

Florence's struggle with her own lifestyle was not only with the horrible suffering of the poor people she saw around her, but also with a theology that allowed religious people to walk by on the other side or cast a meager morsel in the poor person's direction. During the fall of 1842 in London, Florence met Christian von Bunsen, Prussia's Ambassador to England, and a theologian and scholar. They had much in common. Von Bunsen was interested, as Florence was, in Plato, religion, and the mystics, and he recognized her exceptional nature and intellect, lending her various books to expand her already strenuous self-directed study. She frequented his home in London and reveled in the intellectual and philosophical discussion. One evening she asked him, "What can an individual do toward lifting the load of suffering from the helpless and the miserable?"[26] Von Bunsen told her of a Protestant institution with a school, hospital, and penitentiary in Kaiserswerth, Germany, training deaconesses to work with the poor. Florence was ecstatic. Since Kaiserswerth was not a *Catholic* order, she might one day be allowed to go there. Up until now, her sole opportunity for helping the poor was on her family's estates and in the village. She had taught in the village school but did not feel well enough trained in teaching, even though others did it with less experience and knowledge. Besides, the constant moving from house to house did not allow the continuity that teaching needed. Kaiserswerth would give her training in *many* avenues and also expose her to hospital work, something she had not yet experienced, but had seen in her travels. She could finally get away from the paternalistic smoothing of the pauper's pillow, a mere pretense, and give herself seriously to serving God. Writing later from Kaiserswerth, she said:

> The first idea I can recollect when I was a child was a desire to nurse the sick. My day dreams were all of hospitals and I visited them whenever I could. I never communicated it to any one, it would have been laughed at; but I thought God had called me to serve Him in that way.[27]

Nineteenth-century Protestantism was reviving deaconess orders to allow Protestant women to follow a religious calling. The Kaiserswerth Order of Deaconesses in Westphalia was one of these, offering three areas of service: (1) care of the sick and poor and the rescue of "fallen women" through their Magdalene homes; (2) teaching; and (3) visitation and parochial work. The founder, Theodore Fliedner, was the pastor of Kaiserswerth's struggling Protestant Evangelical Church, isolated in a sea of Catholicism. He went to England and Holland to raise funds for his church and encountered Elizabeth Fry's prison work. On returning, he visited nearby Dusseldorf's prisons, discovering a need for a shelter for women prisoners after discharge. He and his wife converted their garden house for this purpose, later adding a hospital and a place to train women deaconesses as "servants of the sick and poor, and servants of one another for Christ's sake." Although modeled on Catholic sisterhoods, the order's deaconesses did not take vows, and promised an initial service of five years with the ability to leave to marry or return home should their families need them. Fliedner later added an infant school, a teacher training school, an orphanage, an asylum, and a home for retired deaconesses. By his death in 1864, one hundred institutions and four hundred and thirty deaconesses wore the Kaiserswerth label.

With something concrete in sight, Florence was energized in her research of sisterhoods, sick care, and institutions. Clarkey sent reports of French institutions, and von Bunsen obtained reports from Berlin. Dreaming became action in the early hours of the morning before she emerged for breakfast as the dutiful daughter to checklists of crockery, linen, and jams for the next influx of visitors. The seasonal moving still frustrated her, however. Leaving Lea Hurst after the summer of 1843, she wrote:

> There are so many duties there, which lie near at hand & I could be well content to do them there all the days of my life…One's days pass away like a shadow, & how we spend hours that are sacred in things that are profane, which we choose to call necessities, & then say "we cannot" to our Father's business.[28]

Nothing had changed by Christmas, and, with no further divine instructions, Florence was in despair. Her salvation came in Hannah Nicholson (Aunt Hannah), a single woman relative who knew of Florence's unhappiness and encouraged her to sublimate her frustrations in a mystical union with God as she had done.[29] She and Florence spent hours discussing the mystics and comparing ideas. For Hannah, however, mysticism was her way to *accept* her divine destiny as the single woman always available to the family. Her urging of Florence to do likewise further compounded Florence's pain as she tried to subdue her "sinful" ideas and dreaming. So sure she had been called to serve God, she could only conclude, with Aunt Hannah's help, that God's silence was *her* fault—her rebellion, pride, and lack of patience. She told herself:

> The foundation of all must be the love of God…Only think of the happiness of working, and working successfully too, and with no

doubts as to His path, and with no alloy of vanity or love of display of glory, but with the ecstasy of single-heartedness! All that I do is always poisoned by the fear that I am not doing it in simplicity and godly sincerity.[30]

Biographers have wondered at Florence's almost paranoid avoidance of public praise, but she had learned well from Aunt Hannah's rationalization of the role of a good woman. The Bible said that those who sought outward praise were publicly rewarded, while those who did good works in secret received God's praise. As Cook said of Florence's reticence:

When she...was praised and courted by the popular breath, she shrank, with an abhorrence which some may have considered almost morbid and which was certainly foreign to the fashion of the world, from any avoidable publicity. This was no pose or affectation; it was part of her religion. It was a counsel dictated by her earnest striving to dissociate her work for God from any taint of worldliness.[31]

In the spring of 1844, the American philanthropist Dr. Samuel Gridley Howe and his wife Julia (who wrote "The Battle Hymn of the Republic") visited Embley Park, and Florence requested to meet privately with him. "Dr. Howe," she asked, "do you think it would be unsuitable and unbecoming for a young Englishwoman to devote herself to works of charity in hospitals and elsewhere as Catholic sisters do? Do you think it would be a dreadful thing?" Howe replied, "Dear Miss Florence, it would be unusual, and in England whatever is unusual is apt to be thought unsuitable; but I say to you, go forward if you have a vocation for that way of life; act up to your inspiration, and you will find that there is never anything unbecoming or unladylike in doing your duty for the good of others. Choose, go on with it wherever it may lead you, and God be with you."[32] The question Florence asked of Howe was broad—acts of charity in hospitals and elsewhere like the Catholic sisters. Her call was unspecific at this stage, and "acts of charity" encompassed a plethora of needy situations. Hospitals were one such place, dumping grounds for those with nowhere else to go, attended by destitute women, also with nowhere to go. What Florence had in mind was revolutionary—the possibility that educated gentlewomen— single, widowed, or in need of financial independence—could be organized into a salaried profession to care for the poor as Catholic sisters did, rather than being limited to the occasional "goodwill" visit. Why did Florence approach Dr. Howe? Because he and his wife had already formulated such a scheme in America "to make...nursing available, without payment, to any American citizen who was aged and ill."[33] With Howe's encouragement, Florence "dug after" her little plan in silence, knowing it would trigger a family furor.

A year later, nothing more had happened, and Florence was beside herself. Clarkey urged her to try writing, an avenue open to women, but Florence dismissed writing as a substitute for living—feelings were wasted in words when they could be distilled into action that brought results.

> When one thinks there are hundreds and thousands of people suffering...when one sees in every cottage some trouble which defies sympathy—and there is all the world putting on its shoes and stockings every morning all the same—and the wandering earth goes its inexorable treadmill through those cold-hearted stars, in the eternal silence, as if nothing were the matter; death seems less dreary than life at that rate.[34]

Florence also rejected a "suitable" suitor at this time and was saved from the family fallout by leaving to nurse her sick grandmother, an experience that showed her that simply being female was *not* adequate qualification for caring for the sick, despite what society assumed. She needed more training, and was euphoric when Dr. Richard Fowler of nearby Salisbury Hospital, a friend of the family, invited her to train with him. When her mother and sister found out, they were angry and ashamed that Florence would consider lowering herself to hospital work, and her father was frustrated at the waste of his training, calling her spoiled and ungrateful. No doubt they had legitimate concerns about hospitals, which were places of dirt, poor sanitation, windows boarded against the cold, unwashed bodies, and linens rarely changed between patients. A "nurse" was basically a chambermaid who lived, slept, became intoxicated, and cooked meals on the ward, available in all senses of the word to doctors, who were little more than tradesmen.[35] Florence, who had worked hard on her plan with Dr. Fowler, was devastated, seeing her destiny in the family drawing room loom before her. She explained her shattered intentions to cousin and confidant Hilary Bonham Carter:[36]

> [My plan] was to go to be a nurse at Salisbury Hospital for these three months to learn the "prax"; and then to come home and make such wonderful intimacies at West Wellow [her village] under the shelter of a rhubarb powder and a dressed leg; let alone that no one could ever say to me again, your health will not stand this or

that. I saw a poor woman die before my eyes this summer because there was no one but fools to sit up with her, who poisoned her as much as if they had given her arsenic. And then I had such a fine plan for those dreaded latter days (which I have never dreaded), if I should outlive my immediate ties, of taking a small house in West Wellow. Well, I do not much like talking about it, but I thought something like a Protestant Sisterhood, without vows, for women of educated feelings, might be established. You will laugh, my dear, at the whole plan, I daresay; but no one but the mother of it knows how precious an infant idea becomes; nor how the soul dies between the destruction of one and the taking up of another. I wonder if our Saviour were to walk the earth again, and I were to go to Him and ask, whether he would send me back to live this life again which crushes me into vanity and deceit. I shall never do anything and am worse than dust and nothing…Oh for some strong thing to sweep this loathsome life into the past.[37]

Certainly, Florence's family was opposed to her *working*, the very feature that distinguished the classes, even in their names, but they lived with a deeper fear. The family knew Florence was determined to do something, and that staying at home or replicating a drawing room in her own marriage would not satisfy this calling. As Florence had no doubt said to them as well:

I am such a creeping worm that if I have anything of the kind to do, I can do without marriage, or intellect, or social intercourse, or any of the things that people sigh after. My imagination is so filled with the misery of the world that the only thing worth trouble seems to me to be helping or sympathizing there.[38]

They were afraid she would start an order, like Kaiserswerth, which would remove her from them forever, or even worse, she would join a *Catholic* order. She had no income to live independently, and she did not seem anxious for marriage (her current suitor would wait seven years before being rejected). An order was always an open option. Florence was thinking of one like Kaiserswerth, not just for herself but for the many women like her and cousin Hilary, who was also a single woman at the beck and call of the family despite her great artistic talent. Such women's choices were a suitable, often loveless, marriage or a single existence as unpaid "slave" to all and sundry within the family.

The Anglican Church was establishing deaconess orders with vows, like Catholic sisterhoods, to absorb "surplus" single women identified in the 1851 census. These orders gave women a place, but a subservient one, first under a Superior, then under male priests, since God's word needed mediation and God's mediators must be male. Women could write about their mystical experiences, but men officially spoke for God because of the order of creation. As Florence had discovered, this successfully prevented women from following what they saw as God's plan if it was against ecclesiastical and social rules for women. She dreamed of a sisterhood without vows where women could be trained for a paid position, giving them independence and allowing them to serve the poor at the same time.

Why didn't Florence rebel? First, she had no independent finances. Second, Aunt Hannah had counseled her to accept her destiny as God's will, compounding her guilt and sense of unworthiness. This letter to Aunt Hannah reveals the religious confusion engendered by allowing someone else's beliefs to dictate to her inner voice:

> There is nothing I reproach myself more bitterly for, than for my want of faith...Oh if one did but think one was getting nearer to the divine patience, when to us as to Him a thousand years will appear but as a day...alas! a moment of discouragement seems a thousand years...you are afraid, I see, of the "attractions" of London for me! But I assure you, I never was so glad to leave it...I hope, dear Aunt Hannah, that I shall show some day the good you have done me...indeed I think now my pride is falling down about me, like the walls of Jericho, at some unknown voice, & that is worth living for.[39]

Florence would later abandon this theology of the status quo reflecting God's plan when she saw how damaging it was, both to her and to the working class, but for now, she interpreted the failure of her Salisbury Hospital plan as her punishment. Reaching her lowest ebb, the dutiful daughter by day recorded her numbed feelings by night:

> This morning I felt as if my soul would pass away in tears, in utter loneliness in a bitter passion of tears and agony of solitude...I cannot live—forgive me, oh Lord, and let me die, this day let me die...The day of personal hope and fear is over for me, now I dread and desire no more.[40]

Yet she would not abandon her call. During 1846, she pored over government reports—the 1838 report on conditions of the poor in East London, the 1840 report on Health in Towns, the 1842 report on the Sanitary Conditions of the Laboring Classes, the 1844 report of the

Health in Towns Commission, and overseas reports as well. She busied herself with sick tenants around Lea Hurst in the summer and helped in a school near Embley Park in the winter. Convinced that her longing for affection made her susceptible to situations that might divert her, she began to draw back from all relationships. In a private note she wrote, "Oh God, no more love. No more marriage, O God."[41] This guardedness foreshadowed her later withdrawal from family and friends to focus on army reform after the Crimea. When Clarkey wrote of her marriage to Julius Mohl, Florence responded:

> As has often been said, we must all take Sappho's leap, one way or other, before we attain to her repose—though some take it to death and some to marriage and some again to a new life even in this world. Which of them is the better part, God only knows. Popular prejudice gives it in favour of marriage.[42]

Her "Sappho's leap" became clearer a few months later when von Bunsen forwarded the Kaiserswerth Year Book. Not knowing how she would get there, Florence wrote in her diary, "There is my home, there are my brothers and sisters all at work. There my heart is and there, I trust, will one day be my body."[43]

By fall of 1847, with Florence's body no closer to Kaiserswerth, the Bracebridges, elderly family friends, ardent travelers, progressive thinkers, and supporters of Florence, asked her to accompany them to Rome for the winter.[44] Selena Bracebridge would become the true mother Florence never had. Florence later wrote of her:

> I wonder whether she knows what a difference she has made in my life. The very fact of there being one person by whom one's thoughts are not pronounced fit only for a dream not worth disputing, who does not look upon one as a fanciful spoilt child who ought to take life as it is and enjoy it—that mere fact changes the whole aspect of things to one. Since one has found that there is one person who does not think that Society *ought* to make one happy, I have never had that sinking of spirits at the thought of the three winter months of perpetual row. From the moment one ceases to say to oneself that it is a very wicked thing not to be very happy in it, it ceases to make one *unhappy*, and one does then really first begin to take it as it is.[45]

Far from a cheerful companion, Florence hesitated, also worried her plans would be put further on hold, but Selena's invitation was inspired. Florence came alive with Rome's beauty, history, and religion, experiencing "the most entire and unbroken freedom from dreaming" she had ever had, and meeting people who changed her life.[46] More importantly, she honed both her call and her theology among people who understood her passions and recognized the exceptional creature she was. From Rome she wrote home:

> I assure you, I feel more and more every day my gratitude to that father, who taught me all I ever knew, who gave me all the ideas I ever had, who taught me interest in nations as though they were personal existences, and showed me how to look upon all churches as but parts of the one great scheme, all opinions, political and religious, as but accidental developments of the one Parent Sap which comes up oats in one case and oranges in another. I do so feel, and gratefully acknowledge the advantage of it now.[47]

Florence threw herself into Europe's political upheavals, demonstrating the passion for justice that dictated her life. What is striking about her letters home is the centrality of her religious quest, taking precedence over sightseeing, art treasures, and social events. Her thoughts about religion are not scattered here and there, but dictate the subject matter of each letter. Her absorption was made easier by meeting some English devotees of the Oxford Movement who were visiting Rome to decide whether to convert to Catholicism. Florence attached herself to this group, which included Rev. Henry Manning (who would feature in Florence's life), and visited churches, convents and institutions without raising family suspicion.[48] Sir Sidney Herbert and Liz Herbert were part of the group, and this "accidental" friendship would change all of them. Sir Sidney had entered Parliament at twenty-two and had become Secretary at War in 1845. Part of a group of wealthy men who gave a percentage of their wealth to philanthropic causes, the Herberts were building a nursing home for the poor near their Wilton home. Liz served on the Committee of the London Home for Distressed Gentlewomen, where Florence would become volunteer superintendent and from where Sir Sidney would send her to the Crimea.

Florence's notebooks worked overtime. At an institution for orphans, young women were taught a trade and were established in sound marriages, and young men acquired professions—sculpting, drafting, cloth making, hair-cutting. Florence was fascinated with its organization. Department superintendents came from their own number, and older children cared for younger ones. Every item used was manufactured in the place, and many professors gave free lessons, turning out several significant Paris engravers. When students left the institution, half the income from their work, accumulated in a savings bank, was returned to them. She and Liz also inspected a foundling hospital near the Vatican where some three thousand foundlings were taken in annually, the babies put in a cradle in the wall that swung into view when the bell was rung, then swung back again. At a place for incurable diseases, wounds, and surgical cases, where little could be done, Florence was overwhelmed with the daily horrors witnessed by caring nuns, in stark contrast to her elegant evenings with friends. Clearly on her mind was what she could do in a world so needy. Did Parthe catch the meaning when Florence described a waterfall on Rome's Tiber River disappearing underground and emerging again?

> Oh how I longed to jump down with it, to make the great leap, to disappear with the enormous current, and to come up again, purified, calm, having forgotten all my previous life, as it had done, and pursuing my way through the lovely valley, covering my banks with flowers.[49]

Florence was enamored with both Pope Pius IX and St. Peter's Church in the Vatican. She was impressed with the pope's involvement in Italian politics, his personal visits to institutions for the sick and poor, his opposition to corruption among Vatican officials and priests, his legislation against discrimination against Jews, and his spiritual devotion. And if the pope was her spiritual father in Rome, St. Peter's was her spiritual home. After St. Peter's, "no earthly vanity can fill the soul again so as to satisfy it."[50] To her, its dome on the skyline was witness to God's presence in the world—a "landmark of our faith on the long desert solitary line of the horizon."[51] Keeping daily company with others who would eventually convert to Rome (Liz Herbert and Rev. Henry Manning), Florence was no doubt tempted, given the opportunities it could offer her for service. Yet *was* it her spiritual home? St. Peter's was as much the Church of God as any other and the Anglican *Book of Common Prayer* was almost identical to the Catholic missal. Catholicism offered her a religious order to follow her call, and she was impressed with its visual aids for inviting the unseen into the seen:

> How everybody could go out of chapel exclaiming against Roman superstition and Romanist ceremonies, and the purity of square walls and a black gown—I wonder that all this pomp of nature and of sun and purple sunsets, and rainbowed cascades, is not called useless rites and ceremonies. Why did God make so much ceremony? Why did He not build this world simply with four white walls: and put the Sun on a surplice—there is no use in all that expense of crimson clouds and blue sky—Why, but to lead our thoughts from the seen to the Unseen.[52]

She knew Protestant arguments about popery, yet she could accept *this* Pope as both secular ruler and God's representative—sectarianism had never been part of her vocabulary, having learned religious tolerance at her father's knee. A major difficulty however, was something Florence prized highly—freedom of thought:

> No one who has not known and sadly felt the want of freedom in *word* and *action* can tell how to value enough the freedom of *thought* as a privilege for oneself, and to respect it in others, and to love it till it becomes a personal presence...I have known too well the want of Liberty in word and action, ever to forfeit that of thought.[53]

The family must have expressed their concern, because Florence wrote to them:

> Are you afraid that I am becoming a Roman Catholic? I might perhaps, if there had been anything in me for Roman Catholicism to lay hold of, but I was not a Protestant before. Protestantism is confining Inspiration to one period, one nation, and one place, if I understand it right, and within that period, that nation, and that place of inspiration, allowing you all possible freedom of interpretation and thought. Catholicism allows Inspiration to all times, all nations, and all places...but limits the inspiration of God to herself as its only channel. Can either of these be true? Can the "word" be pinned down to either one period or one church? All churches are, of course, only more or less unsuccessful attempts to represent the unseen to the mind, to give form to "things hoped for," intangible. A church rises because it has succeeded in doing this for a certain class of minds, at a certain period. It falls when another mind, or another period, requires another and different representation to give life to its Unseen. [54]

Florence was struggling not only with truth *within* Christianity, but with truth across all religions. She pursued this further in Egypt, but in Rome, encountering her beloved Greco-Roman culture outside her textbooks made her wonder again at Christianity's arrogance in claiming to be the beginning of God's redeeming activity. Can one look on the magnificent bust of Marcus Aurelius, the great Roman Emperor (161–180 C.E.) and philosopher, and claim only Jesus was inspired and declare Aurelius' writings an imperfect Sermon on the Mount?

> Oh who shall calumniate God and blaspheme by saying that he left a whole world without inspiration, without communication with his Spirit, till the coming of his Son (except in one little corner

of it). Do we not meet the Greeks here halfway in the ladder to Heaven, in the struggle upwards to the Ideal of Free Will, that ideal which is to us the bridge, by which our spirits cross the dark torrent of time and earth and sensual things to the Holiness of God—which is to us the Word.[55]

How she relished the freedom in Rome to be "a Pagan in the morning, a Jew in the afternoon, and a Christian at night," convinced that, to know God, one must study the divine in all its manifestations. After attending a Greek Orthodox Church with Liz, Florence wrote to the family, "I have now prayed for you in the prayers of every religion."[56]

Florence had also discovered the Convent St. Trinita di Monta (Trinita dei Monti) of the Dames du Sacre Coeur (Sisters of the Sacred Heart). She began attending daily vespers, then took a ten-day retreat without telling her family. Madre Santa Colomba, the Mother Superior, became her spiritual counsel there as she learned the spiritual exercises and forms of discipline and self-examination. These would shape and organize Florence's daily life from then on through life—she always kept the seventh day of every month, the day she received her first call, as a time of prayer and study. Very little of convent life, operations, spiritual exercise, and theology escaped her ever-busy pen in those ten days, in anticipation that one day she might reproduce some of it in a secular order. The Madre recognized Florence's unique call, and assured her that fulfilling it was the only thing of importance in life—she must "turn her whole heart to God that she might be ready to do his work."[57] Florence no doubt indicated to her an interest in an order, but the Madre, detecting her mixed motives, advised:

> It is no good separating yourself from people to try and do the will of God. That is not the way to gain his blessing. What does it matter even if we are with people who make us desperate? So long as we are doing God's will, it doesn't matter at all.[58]

At the end of her retreat, Florence recorded her conversation with the Madre:

> *Santa Columba:* Did not God speak to you during this retreat? Did he not ask you anything?
>
> *Florence:* He asked me to surrender my will.
>
> *Santa Columba:* And to whom?
>
> *Florence:* To all that is upon the earth.
>
> *Santa Columba:* He calls you to a very high degree of perfection. Take care. If you resist, you will be very guilty.[59]

Afterward, she went to St. Peter's as a final act, but it was closed. Despite her spiritual euphoria, she felt a foreboding at the symbolism, knowing the gates of the holy city were never shut. Had her time still not come? "How long, O God?…sadly and slowly I took my homeward way to earth again…and returned to the land of the stranger and sojourner."[60]

Florence's premonition was not without cause. At home, all was the same, but with the added burden that her strange ideas should have disappeared. Fortunately, the Herberts stayed in touch, and a sliver of hope surfaced with talk of a health cure for Parthe in Germany. Florence might finally see Kaiserswerth! When the trip fell through, Florence was in despair, assuming God had again judged her not worthy. Aunt Hannah wrote to comfort her, assuring her that *anything*, even a house party or dinner party, could be done to the glory of God. Florence replied in anger, "How can it be to the glory of God when there is so much misery in the world which we might be curing instead of living in luxury?"[61] Letters and visits from Aunt Hannah subsequently ceased.

By early 1849, Florence's dreaming was out of control again, with long spells when she could not remember what she had been doing. Questioning her sanity, she tried everything to stamp out her "sin," hating both her rebellion at questioning God and her weakness at being unable to stop her feelings.

At this traumatic period, Richard Monckton Milnes proposed. A popular, charming, well-educated poet, reformer, philanthropist, and member of Parliament, he first met Florence when she was twenty-two. Despite the fact that she adored him and he adored her, that the family approved, and that she had no guarantee of ever following her call, Florence refused him. In analyzing her decision, she wrote:

> I have an intellectual nature which requires satisfaction and that would find it in him. I have a passionate nature which requires satisfaction, and that would find it in him. I have a moral, an active, nature which requires satisfaction and that would not find it in his life. Sometimes I think I will satisfy my passionate nature at all events, because that will at least secure me from the evil of dreaming. But would it? I could be satisfied to spend a life with him combining our different powers in some great object. I could *not* satisfy this nature by spending a life with him in making society and arranging domestic things.[62]

This was not an easy choice for Florence. She was convinced that the highest and truest love occurred when a man and a woman, attracted to each other, united to "throw themselves fearlessly into the universe, and do its work, secure of companionship and sympathy."[63] Despite her affection, Florence knew that marriage, even to him, would hinder her ability to do what God had in mind for her:

> To be nailed to this continuation and exaggeration of my present life, without the hope of another, would be intolerable to me. Voluntarily to put it out of my power never to be able to seize the chance of forming myself a true and rich life would seem to me like suicide…I think that God has clearly marked out some to be single women as He has others to be wives, and has organized them accordingly for their vocation. I think some have every reason for not marrying, and that for these it is much better to educate the children who are already in the world and can't be got out of it, than to bring more into it.[64]

Despite this resolve, she worried that, should she see him again, she would change her mind, but she consoled herself with the single Christ's devotion to the work of God:

> True, there is in this world much more wanting to be done; but is it the man leading a secular life who will do it? He is apt to see nothing beyond himself and the fair creature he has chosen for his bride. And, as with men, so with women. There are women of intellectual or actively moral natures for whom marriage (unless it reaches the perfect ideal) means the sacrifice of their higher capacities to the satisfaction of their lower.[65]

The family was furious with Florence, heaping more coals on her head for hurting *them* as well. Her mother accused her of "godless ingratitude, perversity and conceit."[66] When she did meet Monckton Milnes again, still with no further call, he was casual with her. She had hoped he might be "longing to talk to me, willing to give me another opportunity, to keep open another decision."[67] Later she decided God protected her from accepting his offer, though she was "tempted" after several years of resistance, seeing it as an "easy escape" from her difficulties. The two remained friends. Florence was godmother to one of his children, and another was named after her. When he heard about the Crimea, he sent Florence his blessing:

> Dear friend, I hear you are going to the East. I am happy it is so, for the good you will do there, and the hope that you may find some satisfaction in it yourself…You can undertake that, when you could not undertake me. God bless you, dear friend, wherever you go.[68]

Florence took only three letters with her—one from Fanny bestowing the blessing she had long sought in vain; one from Henry Manning, now a Catholic priest, commending her to the protection, worship, and imitation of the Sacred Heart; and this letter from Richard Monckton Milnes, the man she loved, but not more than her God.

CHAPTER THREE

Finding God in Egypt: 1849–1850

As you look upon these mighty ruins, a voice seems continually
to say to you, And seekest thou good things for thyself?
Seek them not, for is there ought like this ruin?
One wonders that people come back from Egypt
and live lives as they did before.[1]

The Bracebridges rescued Florence once again and took her to Egypt and Greece for the winter and spring of 1849–50. The family hoped it would cure Florence's fantasies, and Florence, riddled with guilt, wrote to her mother en route, "I hope I shall come back to be more a comfort to you than ever I have been."[2]

Florence was already a student of Egyptology, a discipline jump-started in 1822 when Jean Francois Champollion (1790–1832) deciphered the ancient hieroglyphs. The Greeks and Romans had thought Egyptian religion nothing but foolish tales "incredible to posterity," since nothing remained but "words graven on stone."[3] These engraved words became eternal, however, when the Rosetta Stone was dug out of the Nile Delta in 1799 with the engraved decrees of Egyptian priests a few hundred years before Christ in *three* languages—Greek, priestly Egyptian, and the popular dialect. By comparing the Greek with the unknown Egyptian scripts, Champollion broke the codes, writing them up in *Precis du Systeme Hieroglyphique,* which Florence took with her, awed at this "fresh slate" with which to work:

In Egypt every monument is its own interpreter; it bears its own date, its own history, its own faith engraved upon itself. There is no occasion to go, as in Greek and Roman history, to a number of traditions, all of which we know to be false, and uncertainly to grope for the truth only by comparing the false. Would we but study the language, here we have the contemporaneous history of every monument written upon its own self...In every other one gets one's knowledge out of books—here, even we, in our ignorance, feel we have read what we know from the monuments themselves.[4]

With a British presence in Egypt, wealthy adventurers rushed to investigate the hieroglyphics for themselves, encroaching on Egypt's ancient monuments like desert sand. Artists, writers, historians, religionists, and educated travelers landed in Alexandria or Cairo, equipped with various levels of knowledge about Egypt, letters of introduction, and financial means to hire boats, donkeys, camels, and guides to expedite their adventures. Florence's party was no exception, hiring a Nile sail boat *(dahabieh)* as home for three months. Instantly, Florence was entranced with the great river and its ruins:

You feel, as you lie on the divan, and float slowly along, and the shores pass you gently by, as if you were being carried along some unknown river to some unknown shore, leaving for ever all you had ever known before—a mysterious feeling creeps over you, as if it were the passage to some other world, the invisible journey through the valley—not of death, but as the ancients imagined death, a shore where all you have known appears as shades. You feel as if in the power of some unseen spirits, who are wafting you away from all you have ever seen to the far-off land.[5]

Beside her divan lay many books, including works by Egyptologists John Gardner Wilkinson, Christian von Bunsen, and Karl Richard Lepsius; journalist Harriet Martineau's Egyptian travel guide; *Memoirs of Henry Martyn*, nineteenth-century missionary in India and Persia; and Charlotte Brontë's novel *Shirley*, critiquing the futile life of upper-class Victorian women, a theme much on Florence's mind.[6]

The two sources for Florence's Egyptian trip tell radically different stories. Her letters home, meant to be read aloud in the drawing room, reveal the witty, learned, and poetic Florence soaking up smells, sights, and sounds, and synthesizing them with her impressive knowledge of philosophy, religion, history, and language. How the family must have laughed, shaking their heads, "Oh, Flo!" What they did *not* hear, hinted at in letters but shouted in agony in her diary, was the parallel journey of her disturbed heart. Only by superimposing one on the other does Florence emerge, maturing in thought and experience, and solidifying her ideas on religion, race, vocation, spirituality, and women, the basis of her later theological work.

Previously, Florence had only traveled as an upper-class white woman in Europe. Alexandria was a culture shock. She had seen poverty and degradation in England, but was now confronted with poverty and *difference*—foreign people behaving in foreign ways, challenging her British ideas about the human race. While many of her comments offend twenty-first century ears, they reflect the racist assumptions of Victorian England that allowed it to colonize so much of the world. On the boat, some St. Vincent de Paul sisters had given a fearful account of the debasement and ignorance of Alexandria's women—"they have no religion, and are mere beasts."[7] As they berthed, a crowd of noisy Arabs came aboard "frantically gesticulating, kicking and dancing—an intermediate race, they appeared to me, between the monkey and the man, the ugliest, most slavish countenances."[8] At Elephantine Island in the Nile, once home of the mighty Elephantine dynasty (3074 B.C.E.), the women were "like imps, not with movements like human creatures," and their boats would make a "South Sea Islander" ashamed.

> The yells of those children I shall never forget…not shiny as savages *ought* to be, but their black skins all dim and grimed with sand…I heard some stones fall into the river, and hoped it was they, and that that debased life had finished…Is the earth sick, that she can no longer bear any but the distorted monsters she has now?[9]

Even the ruined temples of the nation that educated Moses and inspired Plato were inhabited by "savages." Normally empathetic with the plight of the poor, Florence was deeply perturbed by her reaction:

> I never before saw any of my fellow creatures degraded (thieves, bad men, women and children), but I longed to have intercourse with them, to stay with them, and make plans for them; but here, one gathered one's clothes about one, and felt as if one had trodden in a nest of reptiles…The thieves in London, the ragged scholars in Edinburgh, are still human beings; but the horror which the misery of Egypt excites cannot be expressed, for these are beasts.[10]

The troubling questions and challenges churning in Florence's mind with this new experience of racial and cultural diversity are hinted at in her description of Thebes as the "primaevil, the pre-Adamite world!"[11]

Global exploration and travel had opened European eyes to a world never before imagined, forcing anthropologists, ethnologists, and theologians to explain the *diversity* of a human race supposedly descended from one man, the biblical Adam. The two stories of creation in Genesis were enlisted and the pre-Adamite theory emerged. The first story (Genesis 1) where God created humankind together, male and female, was the *generic* creation of the world's original (aboriginal) people—pre-Adamites; and the second story (Genesis 2) was God's *specific* creation of Adam and his descendants—the Adamites. The Flood was not universal, but destroyed only *Adam's* descendants (Genesis 6). Noah's sons, the surviving Adamites, accounted for the different Adamite strains or races—Hamites, Shemites, and Japhetites. Pre-Adamites, all those created prior to Adam, accounted for Cain's enemies, Noah's daughters-in-law, the builders of ancient Egypt, and the "savage" tribes, to name a few. The emerging science of ethnology *accommodated* this take on the biblical story by agreeing that the "civilized" nations of Europe, Northern Africa, and Western and Southern Asia *did* seem to belong to one race—the Caucasians or Mediterranean nations. To explain this via the Genesis story, the Hamites spread to North Africa, the Nile Valley, and east; the Shemites to Western Asia as Jews, Arabs, Canaanites, and Abyssinians; and the Japhetic family were the Indo-Europeans— the Aryans of the Caucasian slopes, who migrated west into Europe and south into India, interbreeding with the indigenous people.

The exotic people of the Orient and ancient Egypt—pre-Adamites— had long fascinated Victorian England. Pooh-Bah, the snob in Gilbert and Sullivan's operetta *The Mikado*, sang:

> I am in point of fact a particularly haughty and exclusive person of pre-Adamite ancestral descent. You will understand this when I tell you that I can trace my ancestry back to a protoplasmal primordial atomic globule.

And Florence, in mourning the lost glory of "primaevil, pre-Adamite Thebes," admires a nation from 4,000 years ago with a culture as advanced as Victorian England and an idea of God *more* advanced than that of the Hebrews, the descendants of the *later* creation—Adam. The Egyptians taught

> the worship of the one God, the distinct conception of a progression through Eternity, and a philosophy so deep that all which Solomon knew of legislation, all that Pythagoras and Plato guessed of ethics and spiritual theories, seems to have been borrowed from them, and at a time, too (and for long after), when the Jews seem to have

worshipped God the Creator as the God of the Hebrews, the God of Abraham, Isaac, and Jacob, not the God of the whole world.[12]

While the pre-Adamites from China and Egypt amazed Victorian England with their exotic wares and ancient monuments, there was a more sinister racist path down which the pre-Adamite theory trekked, which was also playing on the edges of Florence's mind. The nineteenth-century *Encyclopedia of Biblical, Theological and Ecclesiastical Literature*, after assigning which nations were, or were not, Adamites, concludes that "the Mongoloid nations and the black races do not seem to be embraced."[13] Mongoloids—Malays, Chinese, Burmese, Japanese, Tibetans—were considered "Dusky" as opposed to "Black," and some argued that they were not far removed from Adam's descendants—perhaps from another son of Adam, or perhaps Adam was sufficiently ancient to spawn both Adamite and Dusky races. What was certain however, was that Adam could *not* have parented black races (the "Negroes, Hottentots, and Bushmen, Papuans and Australian Aborigines so primitive in comparison with civilized races"), since the name Adam signified "red" (broadly interpreted as pink or light-skinned). The encyclopedia says:

> Viewing the Black Races from either a psychic, zoological, or an archeological standpoint, we discover evidence that they diverged from the White and Dusky races at a period which, compared with the Egyptian and Assyrian civilization, must be exceedingly remote…therefore the progenitor of the Black and the other races was placed too far back in time to answer for the Biblical Adam.[14]

Black races were pre-Adamite, as were the delectable Orientals and the ethereal Egyptians, but there seemed to be a hierarchy within pre-Adamites based on development and skin color. While Dusky races displaying certain levels of civilization could *possibly* be assigned to Adam with a bit of a push and shove to genealogical lines, so-called Black races were excluded as much on their "primitive" lifestyle, compared with Victorian ideas of refinement, as on skin color.

This civilized/savage Victorian measuring stick asked some further questions. Given the glory of some pre-Adamite civilizations such as Egypt, and the state of "degradation" of the Black races —primitive tools, rough shelters, and the absence of a High God, clothes, or Victorian morals—did the difference result from unfavorable circumstances causing some races to *deteriorate*, or were some races *not* human from the beginning—not part of the pre-Adamite creation of Genesis 1? Were they, instead, part of the animal creation? Those who argued the degradation theory cited Black races that, under favorable circumstances, "civilized" themselves, an impossible feat if not human. Those who argued the nonhuman theory cited tribes running free on good lands in Central Africa with nothing to degrade them, yet who remained "marked by an inferiority as real and almost as great" as those of the disease-ridden west coast, or in Australia and New Guinea.[15] The former theory allowed for improvement in such races, but the latter gave permission to Australia's British invaders in 1788 to declare the land *terra nullius* (uninhabited) because Aborigines were nonhuman in Britain's theological anthropology textbooks. In New Zealand, treaties were made with Maoris because they exhibited "civilized" tendencies— they were warlike![16] This argument had important religious consequences—did the "savage" have a soul to save? If these beings were nonhuman, not in the image of God, they did not. One can see how Darwin's thesis thrown into this cocktail would ignite the Victorian world. Prior to Darwin, more and more theological gymnastics were required to explain the biblical creation stories in light of scientific observation. Darwin would finally voice what lurked in many minds. Should the discussion of humanity begin not with the *biblical* story, but with anthropological evidence in nature itself?

Such racist theories appall today's readers, especially when we have seen the resultant damage to people and cultures, but Florence, an intellectual struggling with such discussions of her day, weighed the various theories as she traveled through Egypt. When she met an Australian aboriginal "bush" child brought by a Catholic sister to be educated in Europe, she described her as "quite tame," and behaving very well. The sister explained how much easier it was working among Australian aborigines because they "had no religion, absolutely none," therefore there was nothing to undo—it was all doing.[17] On the other hand, the "bestial" lifestyle of half-naked children on Elephantine Island and the degraded temple squatters baying "like jackals" were evidence of human and national degradation, given the wrong set of circumstances or, as she would argue, ignorance of God's laws:

> Egypt to an European is all but uninhabited. The present race no more disturbs this impression than would a race of lizards, scrambling over the broken monuments of such a star. You would not call *them* inhabitants, no more do you these.[18]

In an 1878 article by Florence entitled *Who is the Savage?* Florence identified herself on the side of the "improvability" of all the human race made in God's image, something she worked for all her life and which came from her theological belief that God's laws of progress were discoverable in the universe. The startling title of her article suggests a discussion about some "foreign" shores, but Florence discusses instead the degradated state of many of the poor "savages" in English villages through drunkenness, street brawls, and prostitution, far worse than any of the supposedly "uncivilized" Hindu peasants whom Florence worked so hard in her later years to help, even supporting their desire for independence from Britain:

> It is in order-loving, Christian England; the only country untouched by revolution and riot; the home of family ties, the house of a boasted free civilization. And this is civilization — Christian, settled progress, and civilization. If this is to be civilized, we could almost wish to be uncivilized.[19]

Egypt had come to this, fallen from the highest spiritual and intellectual life to a "savage, sensual, childish life." Florence's inquisitive mind was asking, Why do such nations fall, and could it also happen to England? Britain seemed so apathetic about examining its life and success as a nation in the light of history, comparing its actions with those that brought down other great nations:

> It cannot be a law that all nations shall fall after a certain number of years. God does not work in that sort of way: they must have broken some law of nature which has caused them to fall. But are all nations to sink in that way? As if national soil, like the soil of the earth, must lie fallow after a certain number of crops. And will England turn into Picts again, after a certain number of harvest years, as Egypt has turned into Arabs? Or will a nation find out at last the laws of God by which she may make a steady progression?[20]

The idea that individuals and nations must find the laws of God observable in all of human existence, history, and nature, and move toward improvement, would become a central argument in *Suggestions for Thought*. For the time being, Florence painted the idea into a historical fiction, "Vision of Temples," set in the various Thebes temples that she was visiting. In this allegory, she described how each ancient ruler progressed or failed according to his idea of God and his understanding of the task to which God set him in his rule. By extrapolation, modern leaders and nations are called to do the same, and whether a nation progresses or decays depends on whether they diligently seek the laws of the universe that are God's thoughts, and thus allow humanity to progress.[21]

"Vision of Temples" begins with thunderous language and drumroll akin to the biblical encounters with God:

> And the sons of the Theban kings presented themselves before the Lord. And He said, Behold, I send you upon the earth to govern, and raise a nation that I love. Build me a house that I may dwell in. And the sons of the kings said, What house, Lord?[22]

The first son, Thothmes III (Thothmosis, 1458—1425 B.C.E.) imagined God put him on earth to drive out invaders, so he built a temple (Dayr el Bahree) to glorify his God of military strength—and also a bit of his own strength. Egyptian theology believed that the spirit of the kings returned to God at death for purification and, after 3,000 years or less, depending on their purification needs, returned to their land in a different form. Florence therefore, in her allegory, has each king returning to survey the legacy of his reign. When Thothmes III returned, his temple was in ruins because he had mistakenly imagined God as one who loved glory and military might, and had also loved his own human power and glory. God says:

> Didst thou think that the Lord, who hideth himself, whose mighty works go their still and silent course, without wakening one little bird that sleeps under its mother's wing; who has given his children to perform more beautiful works than he has done himself, and who suffers them to think them as their own; who has given to them to create with toil and trouble, that they may have the satisfaction of thinking, "I have done this,"—didst thou really think that He had for his object his own glory, and that his servants were to seek first, not the *"kingdom* of God," but his regalia and his coronation clothes?[23]

Florence had been struck in Thothmes' temple by the similarity with the Hebrew idea of a "God of hosts and battles." The difference was that Thothmes' God helped *kill* the invaders of Egypt, whereas the Hebrew God *led* the invaders. She called this image of God imperfect— a great and universal mistake.[24]

> I always think how abundant must be the vanity of those people who think God is so fond of His glory; but we all judge, each, his own God, by himself, and think He likes what we like ourselves.[25]

The next ruler, Amunoph III (Amenhotep or Memnon, 1417—1379 B.C.E.), conquered the land as far as Mesopotamia, calling himself the Lord of Truth—"I am become like unto God." He built his temple at El-Uksur (Luxor), not to the God of nature, but to nature and law themselves. After his death and purification, he revisited his temple and found it "full of unclean beasts and creeping things…and the vilest of the creeping things and most abject was man."[26] When the king complained, God said:

> Because thou hast worshipped Nature, not me; because thou hast seen law, not the God of laws, in the world around thee; because thou didst think thou couldst become the Lord of Truth by observing truth, therefore I have filled thy temple with what thou didst seek: lo! There is nature and natural life crawling about thy ruins. Thou must be the servant of Truth, not her Lord, and Truth must be thy master.[27]

Florence hated the Luxor temple with its dark chambers, and, though they were anchored a hundred yards from it for three weeks, she went in it only once. In one chamber, the ruler Amunoph was depicted receiving his name, "Lord of Justice," a mistake "as old as the world and as young as our time, to suppose oneself called to a power one has not, to do a thing which is not one's business."[28] God sends leaders, but the results are disastrous if the leader does not know what God wants him or her to do.

God then sent a new race to govern Thebes: the Rameses dynasty from the eastern delta. Rameses I prepared to build a temple for the great God, but hesitated, asking, "How can the Unknown be known? How can the *spirit* find a *place*? How can the Concealed be manifested?" Believing that he could not know what God was actually like, he sought a cool place under the shade of the palms at Koorna, building a house and dedicating it, not to the glory of God, but to the *manifestation* of God—to Nature, the benevolent mother. The Egyptian rulers have now moved from God as force and military strength, to nature as a replacement for God, to nature as the *manifestation* of God. When Rameses I revisited earth, his house had been completed in his name, justice was done in its halls, religious and political assemblies met in its courts, and his grandson honored his memory. This was Florence's favorite temple:

> Upon the steps of that colonnade I have sat for hours, moving with the shadow of the columns, as it turned with the sun, and looking out upon that matchless view under the different lights.[29]

While she told her family she personally *loved* the place, she did not tell them why, which we find later in her diary.

Sethos I (Seti, 1318—1304 B.C.E.), warrior, artist, and philosopher, built his house to the concealed God, the great Unknown, the Infinite that treats small and great, minutes and a thousand years, darkness and light, good and evil, the same.[30] Sethos' temple at Karnack was designed around the hours and minutes of a day so that when the column shadows moved, people remembered that each minute, though small, cast a shadow on *all* the future. Sethos named his Unknown God "Come," because this Unknown, although hidden, *comes* to us, revealing the divine Self. Like everyone else, Florence was overwhelmed with Karnack's size and labyrinth of columns. Nineteenth-century travel writer John Stoddard wrote:

> Soulless indeed must be the traveler who can walk among the ruins of Karnack without emotions too profound for words. In the whole world there is no temple that can be even remotely compared to it.[31]

In one hall alone stood at least one hundred and thirty columns, thirty-six feet in circumference and sixty-six feet high, each covered with sacred characters engraved several inches into the stone, polished their entire depth, and colored like mosaics. Its enormous size, mazelike layout, and intricate hieroglyphics forced worshipers to stop and meditate, in contrast, Florence said, to the long, wide aisle from door to altar in St. Peter's, where

> the feeling, unthinking, ardent heart has rushed at once to its Creator, careless of all problems which it has regarded as temptations to its faith, and has left to a devil to solve. The Egyptian loved his God with all his mind; the Roman Catholic, with all his heart.[32]

Karnack was also a comprehensive history of a race, because many additions had been made to the temple from 3000 B.C.E. to 300 B.C.E., and the hieroglyphics depicted not only the evolution of images of God but also information about everyday life. Egyptians believed that *knowledge* was sacred, making *any* possessors of knowledge of *any* sort also sacred, rather than just an ordained few—the rulers and high priests. The Spirit was incarnate in everyone:

> To the Egyptians Sir Isaac Newton would have been as holy as St. Augustine; the one kind of knowledge was as much inspiration as the other. It was a part of religion as much to take care of your health as to go and sacrifice in the temple...The priest was not the doctor or the lawyer, but the doctor or the lawyer was a priest...You find the priestly caste in every office, disdaining none, extending from the king, who was often a high priest, down to the porters of the palaces...The women, too, had offices and vocations in the church—as in every church except ours.[33]

In Florence's story, Sethos originally imagined a God containing only the good, but decided that, even with God, impossibilities are impossible, thus God must encompass both evil and good:

> Can man have the good of patience without suffering?…Can he be taught without evil?…without consequences there would be no law. Let us have evil, he cried, O my God. And he caused himself to be represented gifted with life by the two spirits of God, Good and Evil, that all the people might see that their king accepted suffering.[34]

In the Karnack temple, Florence found Sethos I kneeling in front of both the Good *and* Evil Spirit pouring life over him "as if to say, Give me thyself, my son, and thou shalt learn to draw life out of evil as well as good—out of all experience—'all things work together for good to them that love God.'"[35] In all the temples, Florence had been overwhelmed by the different ideas about God, searching as she was for some answers of her own. The ideas she found all foreshadowed the arguments of her day—is God known through nature, or through special revelations such as miracles, or can we only talk about nature since we cannot even know about God? Sethos and Karnack were now offering her a *new* vision that addressed the old question—how to reconcile a good, just, and loving Creator with the problem of evil (theodicy[36]). What if, as Sethos' carvings suggested, good and evil were *both* part of God? What if God gave *both* good and evil, the evil necessary to know and experience good and to progress through mistakes? Perhaps Florence had already toyed with this idea herself, but now found affirmation?[37] She had observed that Egyptian faces wore "the most wonderful ideal of sublime serenity and childlike trust and confidence I ever saw," and decided this serenity came from "the first fruits of a spirit soaring to God" rather than a spirit returning to God in repentance, as Christians believed:

> There is that absence of the doctrine of repentance which has struck me so much in these records of a nation's religion. The Christian ideal has sinned and suffered—there has been struggle, asceticism, the cheek is pale with vigils, the eye stained with tears—it is resignation, not serenity—meekness, not trust,—composure rather than happiness—the spirit has weaned itself after long effort and weary suffering from the love of sin and earth, and placed its joy alone in the beyond, in the far away, in the future.[38]

The Egyptian, on the other hand,

> is a sinless soul which has never left God's bosom which finds him, the Omnipresent, as near in one Spot of his creation as in

another, which does not wait for another world to enjoy His
presence. The Christian looks for *comfort* in His society hereafter—
the Egyptian for *happiness* in it *here*. There is no asceticism in the
Egyptian ideal,—all the gifts of its Father it will accept from the
Father's hand—there is no struggle, the soul has never loved
anything better than its God—there is no hope, it is all trust, trust
that the present is as much its Father's blessing, its Father's gift, as
the future can be—there is no resignation, for where evil is to give
life as well as good, it is absurd to talk of resigning oneself to a
benefit. Then it is love, not resignation.[39]

In Florence's allegory, God decreed Sethos' temple should last forever
so that the idea of both good and evil as part of God would be
remembered. When Sethos returned to Earth, the people had forgotten
his name, but his message about good and evil remained in the temple
hieroglyphics—for Florence to see. And she took good notice—the idea
of God containing both good and evil shaped her later theology as well.

She found the idea repeated at the Ipsambul temple of Athor, with
Rameses being crowned by the good and evil principle on each side.

What a deep philosophy!—what theory of the world has ever gone
farther than this? The evil is not the opposer of good, but its
collaborator—the left hand of God, as the good is His right…the
king at his entrance into life is initiated into the belief that what *we*
call the evil was the giver of life and power as well as the good…The
old Egyptians believed that out of good came forth evil, and out of
evil came forth good; or as I should translate it, out of the well-
ordered comes forth the inharmonious, the passionate; and out of
disorder again order; and both are a benefit. The Romans, who
were a more literal people, and we their descendents, never
understood this, and have set our faces against evil, like the later
Egyptians, and scratched his nose.[40]

Florence recounts in her allegory that Sethos, returning after his
purification, met a "silent, melancholy northern race" visiting his temple
(Christians, no doubt) who told him:

We have suffered much Evil, yet a thought *comforts* us—it will pass
away; this is but a world of trial, therefore we can endure.

Sethos replied to them—and also to Florence via the symbols on his
temple wall:

I have suffered much Evil, but a thought *inspires* me—it will not
pass away, it bestoweth life; this world is eternal, and giveth eternal

life, therefore we need no *comfort*, for evil is but another name for good.[41]

The next ruler, the great Rameses (Rameses II, 1304—1237 B.C.E.), warrior and philosopher, taught that God was known only by God's works—the *effects* of the Great First Cause. Since the first effect was harmony, Rameses built his temple to Harmony "for wherever the Lord is, there is Harmony, which is grace or strength."[42] In his temple, he built sanctuaries for Intellect, Religion, Justice, and Nature, because God's grace was in *all* his works. He also built a library for the learned, a temple for the devout, a hall for justice, and a tower to survey the worlds so *all* human faculties could be cultivated:

> The Complete, the Perfect, shall be the Genius of my temple, and the spirit of my mind, because Perfection, or the harmony of all things, is the characteristic of God, who doeth no exaggerated nor imperfect thing. My temple shall not be awful in size nor stupendous in art, but it shall be finished in all its parts.[43]

When Rameses returned to Earth, God had decreed the temple remain so that Rameses' devotion to Perfect Goodness would continue to influence the Earth. Later we will see that Perfect Goodness becomes Florence's metaphor of choice for God, known through all our faculties, as depicted by Rameses' four sanctuaries and libraries. Rameses the Great was Florence's favorite, and she sat for hours in the Ramesseum struck by the continuities of religious thought. On the walls were sacred boats or shrines, which Moses, growing up in an Egyptian court, likely copied for the Ark of the Covenant and the tabernacle. Those in the boats did homage to *Amun* ("Come"), the Unknown or Concealed God, whose real name was too sacred to say:

> How many hours I have sat in that small hall of the eight columns [library]…and felt as much reverence as ever [an] Egyptian did before those treasures, which trained the men who trained Moses, who trained the world; those books, which taught us—us whom the Egyptians had never heard of—the name of God.[44]

After Egypt's power declined, Rameses the Third (1198—1163 B.C.E.) extended Egypt's might, calling his God the Most High God since only the greatest God was worthy to be *his* guardian deity. Rameses III emblazoned his victories on monuments and history, but Egypt's prosperity ceased, and its religion ceased to be inspired. Rameses III had not yet returned after his purification when Florence wrote, but would find his temple destroyed to serve another religion—a church was built over it. Nothing but a record of his power and low ambition had remained. Obviously, Florence did not like Medina Tabou, Rameses III's building, with its celebration of power and dominion, yet she found its hieroglyphics informative for her research:

> One seems to be positively reading the Old and some parts of the New Testament—viz., the Book of Revelations. There is the tabernacle of the Jews carried by the priests…there are the cherubim of Ezekiel, with two wings stretched upward, and two covering their bodies, sitting upon the sacred ark…and as to the four Evangelists, the Egyptian would find himself as much at home under the dome of St. Peter's, or in the Book of the Revelations…. There is the ox of St. Luke, the lion of St. Mark, the eagle—no, not the eagle, it is a vulture or a hawk, and the Egyptian might as well march into St. Peter's, and seeing the gigantic Evangelists under the dome, pronounce the Christians guilty of the most idolatry, deifying four biographers under the symbols of beasts! As we utter the same accusations against the worshippers of Medina Tabou.[45]

I have spent much time on Florence's "Vision of Temples" because it reflects emerging ideas that, though not obvious to the reader at this stage, will appear later, shaping her theology. Like contemporary thinkers, she challenged the static metaphors of God from previous cultures, and shows in this allegory how ideas of God have evolved as culture progresses, and that these images determine the way we act toward God, and vice versa.[46] Thothmes worshiped a God of military power; Amunoph saw Nature and Law as objects of worship in *themselves*; Rameses I saw nature, not *as* God, but the manifestation of the unknown God; Sethos envisaged a God of both Good and Evil, evil instructing the good; Rameses the Great saw God as the Perfect, Harmonious Being, discovered through the cultivation of all our faculties—knowledge, worship, experience, and justice. Rameses III saw *himself* as God's deputy, enjoying the rewards and pleasures of power, but proving that enlightenment is not always progressive—it can degenerate, in individuals and nations, just as Egypt went into decline. Using this argument, Florence will challenge, in *Suggestions for Thought*, the images and descriptions of God's character in vogue in *her* day, and declare a moratorium on the word *God* until it was unloaded of unhelpful, theological baggage.

Florence also highlighted the fact that many Egyptian rulers had not known, or had not tried to decipher, the reason they were put in the world as leaders; thus their work was in vain. In the same way, too few in her day understood either:

The words "the vanity of human greatness" press into my mind with a force a sermon never gave them…Divine greatness always endures; but what is human greatness, when you look at this desolation of the finest country in the world?[47]

Florence, on the other hand, was *fully* absorbed in discovering the purpose for which *she* had been set on Earth. Learning from the Egyptians, she believed that duty was not concentrated in appointed leaders, but that each person had a task by virtue of God's spirit or gifts within. She knew she had been called to a task but was frustrated that, as yet, she had not identified it.

Egypt also consolidated Florence's thinking on reincarnation (as will be discussed later). Many Christians in her day believed in reincarnation, as did the Egyptians. She wrote home, "The spirits of the old Egyptians are such good company, and preach such nice cheerful sermons upon death and the hereafter."[48] "Vision of Temples" was built around the Egyptian idea of the dead returning to activity in this world or another, a focus Florence found enthralling, and which would also enter her theology:

Death was to them more interesting than life, or rather death, as they put it, did not differ from life; life was so small a fragment of the whole to them, that the whole became a course of immeasurably more consequence, not as being different from the part, but…of the whole being greater than its part…The Egyptians seem…to have said, we will consider this life as interesting only in its connection with the whole of which it is a part. I have often thought how dull we were not to see that Christ's life showed us this more advanced stage of existence which we call heaven; how we have persisted in calling him the "man of sorrows," instead of calling him the man who is already in the state of blessedness, the man who has progressed and succeeded.[49]

The *Hermetica*, a collection of Latin and Greek texts from the second and third Centuries C.E., mixed with Egyptian theology, taught that following death, the senses go back into their own sources, becoming parts of the universe. There they enter into fresh combinations to do other work, while the spirit ascends through the heavenly spheres to the presence of God, entering into God. Florence would argue that the soul goes through *many* stages of trial and tribulation before reaching perfection, and she was constantly amazed with the continuity of this idea in different religions.

Theories of reincarnation—of the stages by which a soul arrived in the presence of God—seemed to appreciate "how this life is only a little piece of an eternal education." And if this is so, the things we mourn—sudden death, loss of opportunities—are insignificant in the scope of such "eternal" life of proceeding to God.[50]

Perhaps her greatest enlightenment, also experienced in Rome, was the *continuity* of religion from the beginning and the futility of sectarian exclusivity. Whatever the era, people stood in places of worship

who felt and thought like us, who cared for their brothers, and mourned over their dead with an everlasting love and a preserving memory like us…and while the sound of their names has died away into a hieroglyph, the sound of the beating of their hearts still echoes.[51]

In the great temple in Ipsambul, gradually being reclaimed by sand, Florence thought of the spiritual rather than chronological pulse of time:

I thought of the worshippers of 3000 years ago; how they by this time have reached the goal of spiritual ambition, have brought all their thoughts to serve God or the ideal of goodness; how we stand there with the same goal before us, only as distant as the star…how to them all other thoughts are now as nothing, and the ideal we all pursue of happiness is won; not because they have not probably sufferings, like ours, but because they no longer suggest any other thought but of doing God's will, which is happiness. I thought how, 3000 years hence, we might perhaps have attained—and others would stand here, and still those old gods would be sitting in the eternal twilight.[52]

Florence was especially listening for the beating of *women's* hearts in Egypt, always looking for lessons from other cultures as to the role and status of women. In the Egyptian goddess Eilethyria, the mother protectress of humanity, she found a feminine image of God, spreading her overshadowing wings on temple ceilings, hovering over kings going to battle or folding her wings about them for protection when meeting the gods. Florence wrote:

I never understood the Bible till I came to Egypt…"He shall cover thee with his feathers, and under the shadow of his wings shalt thou trust." "The Almighty shall overshadow thee"; and, "as a mother will I nurture thee."[53]

Eilethyria's image continued in the head-dress of Rameses the Great's queen who was always with him in temple drawings, occupying "the place which the most advanced Christian civilization gives to woman—always the one wife, nowhere the face veiled, often the regent, the sovereign, or the co-ruler with a brother. Woman may be quite satisfied with her *Christian* position in old Egypt."[54] In the temple Beit el Welee, the beautiful goddess Anouke (or Vesta, and goddess of domestic purity) whispered advice to Rameses the Great:

> And the child-like attitude of the great hero, as the goddess breathes her admonitions into his ear; the simplicity and humility of the conqueror; the youthful dignity of the virgin goddess—a more beautiful ideal never entered the mind of man. And a fond and a faithful husband it is evident he was; and in the next compartment, to show how he attended to the words of the goddess, his wife appears with him at sacrifice. They were happy women, those Egyptians of olden times, to be under the protection of such an admonitrix.[55]

The Muslim hareem, on the other hand, presented a stark contrast. In the hareem of the future Viceroy of Cairo, Florence passed through successive curtain-draped chambers of marble and fountains, led by beautiful young wives, to the inner room of the number one wife, a most beautiful woman in an ornate place "the closet thing to hell," with nothing to do but sit in splendid clothes:

> There we sat, without even the weather to talk of; coffee came, of course, and pipes covered with diamonds; and the Circassians, the most graceful, and the most sensual-looking creatures I ever saw (like dancers) stood in a semicircle, or knelt round us. The very windows into the garden were wood-worked, so that you could not see out. The cold, the melancholy of that place! I felt inclined to cry.[56]

When she visited the poor boat cook's hareem, the principal wife was *also* adorned like an oriental queen, but seated on a mud floor with no furniture, the window holes stuffed with mats. The second wife stood at the door, the mother baked downstairs, and two slave wives silently stared at them. In Philae, the women of a Nubian family entertained her in the hut for both people and animals. The women and animals listened with great attention through an interpreter to accounts of Victorian marriage:

> That one man should keep faithful to one woman his whole life, and not send her back to her parents, and marry another, is more unheard of among the poor than among the rich, because the rich man maintains all his wives by etiquette—the poor man just sends

them back...The women never pray; no Mahometan poor woman does, excepting the haggs or pilgrims...The belief among the women in a future state seems to be very small; if they express any feeling about it at all, it is that they shall be servants there to the men.[57]

Florence was appalled at what polygamy did to women. She always thought Sarah and Rachel of the Hebrew Bible had behaved badly toward the other wives, but, confronted with the reality of the situation, she was amazed they had not behaved worse!

Polygamy strikes at the root of everything in woman—she is not a wife—she is not a mother;—and in these Oriental countries, what is a woman, if she is not that? In all other countries she has something else to fall back upon. The Roman Catholic woman has a religion—the Protestant has an intellect; in the early Christian, in the old Egyptian time, women had a vocation, a profession, provided for them in their religion, independent of their wifedom; here, she is nothing but the servant of a man. No, I do assure you, the female elephant, the female eagle, has a higher idea of what she was put into the world to do, than the human female has here.[58]

Florence was also frustrated that Egyptian Muslim women were excluded from the mosque. However, the beauty of the *Arabian* Muslim mosques in Cairo stunned her, as did the devotion that the praying Muslim had for his God, a concentration in prayer nothing could distract:

The Mahometan religion takes man on the side of his passions; it gratifies all these; it offers him enjoyment as his reward. The Christian religion takes him on the side of penitence and self-denial. This seems the fundamental difference: otherwise there is much good in the Mahometan religion. Charity is unbounded; and it is not the charity of patronage, but the charity of fellowship. If any man says to another "Inshallah," in the name of God, he may sit down at his table and partake of anything that he has, and no man will refuse. The beggar will do this with the greatest dignity.[59]

She was also struck by Islam's "strict Unitarianism" (the idea of one God without incarnations or other manifestations), with no images or deeds of saints to "speak to my eye, to excite my thoughts," nothing to alter the purity of one God. Yet nothing was spared in design, stonework, calligraphy, and marble to offer to this one Name. God was to have *all*, resulting in a perfect harmony of the whole that helped the Muslim man find God within his own solitary heart. How Florence longed for Muslim women to be able to make equal use of this sacred space and inspiration.

The Christianity Florence encountered in Egypt was an eclectic mix. Fourth-century Egypt had been Christian, its harsh deserts covered with religious orders and Alexandria the refuge for European heretics. Egypt was now de-Christianized, and what remained was not always "the leaven in the lump." In the desert of Skeikh Hassan, the monks who swam out from hermit clifftop retreats to her boat to beg made her ashamed. Elsewhere, Christian scribes made a living preying on the disadvantaged. Even the Anglican Church in Cairo, while struggling to do its best, seemed somewhat irrelevant.

> One's feelings towards the Anglican Church are very different when she is hiding in corners, struggling with the devil, and still adhering to her own beloved ritual, to when she is stretched out in fatness, with the millstone of the richest hierarchy in the world about her neck, and the lust of the world tempting people to make her a profession and not a vocation. I feel a very warm attachment to her here, though I suspect the good she is doing, with her translations of the prayer book into Arabic, is next to nothing.[60]

All in all, she joined the general Muslim disdain for the Christian presence, concluding that the only ones doing good were the Roman Catholic sisters. In Alexandria, she visited the Sisters of St. Vincent de Paul, noting their religious structures:

> The St. Vincent sisters take no vows, and are not engaged for more than a year, when they may marry, or do anything else, *sans blesser leur conscience*. They support the establishment by taking *pensionnaires*, and reckon that, for every *pensionnaire*, they can take two *orphelines*. So that these labourers not only bring in the harvest, but work for their bread;—not only work without hire, but pay for their own work. I think St. Paul would have been pleased.[61]

Their teaching methods impressed her, compared with England's "machine" turning out "children wholesale, like pins, with patent heads." The older ones cared for the younger ones, as Florence had seen in Rome. Even those from what Victorian culture would call the least civilized cultures took seriously their responsibility of caring for others.

> I have seen the idea of the "age" system in the Ragged Schools, where the dirtiest boy is made to look after the cleanliness of the

others, and a large thief to superintend the morals of a smaller, and where it acts excellently too, but never so well carried out as here.[62]

This further confirmed her conviction that the English theological argument that attributed intelligence and morals to certain higher classes was wrong. These nuns were "writing another law" in their scholars' hearts.

At the beginning of this chapter, I indicated that Florence's diaries told a different story from her letters and stories. The devastated heart that left for Egypt did not mend instantly before its glorious sights. Day after day, cryptic words and sentences recorded an ongoing conversation with God in her diary, on which we can eavesdrop. In the Osiris Hall of Rameses' temple in Ipsambul, Florence was transported back into a world where ancient hearts had also reached out to the Unknown God. In her letter home, she mentioned the impression the temple had made on her—"I never thought I should have made a friend and a home for life of an Egyptian temple, nor been so sorry to look for the last time on that holiest place."[63] In her *diary* however, for January 16, 1850, she says, as the sun entered the temple lighting up the figures along the walls, "I made a vow in the sacred place."[64] The next day, she "dreamed in the very face of God."[65] Three days later, in Gerf Hossayn's cave of Phthah, the god of fire, she joined a ceremony where "serpents" made from twisted lit palm fibers were carried into the dark cave to this god who welcomes back "tired spirits" to their accustomed home, refining away all but the pure ore. Florence described the "wildness" of the scene in her letters, but in her diary, *she* was the "tired spirit" praying, "Oh heavenly fire, purify me—free me from this slavery," her constant dreaming of what she might do.[66]

In Philae, she loved the temple to Isis, who resurrected husband Osiris after his murder by brother Seth. This resurrection symbolized spring's regeneration of all life after the annual Nile flood. The similarity to Christ's passion played on Florence's mind, making Philae her "Passion Week" in her diary. In her letters, she wrote (January 28, 1850):

> Oh Philae, whom I shall never see again, may she be to many others what she has been to us during the happy, happy week which we have spent there...I never *loved* a place so much...Every moment of that precious week, from before sunrise to long after moonlight had begun, I spent upon the Sacred Island, most of it in Osiris' chamber...I cannot describe to you the feeling...The myths of Osiris are so typical of our Saviour that it seemed to me as if I were coming to a place where He had lived—like going to Jerusalem; and when

I saw a shadow in the moonlight in the temple court [temple of Isis], I thought, "perhaps I shall see him: now he is there." The chamber of Osiris was like the place where *He* was buried; and after our little service on the Sunday morning, I went and sat there, and I thought I had never sat in any place so sacred, nor ever could, except in Syria.[67]

The temple was not beautiful, but she told her family "It is like a friend of whose face one does not think whether it is ugly or beautiful—one does not *know*."[68] She loved it for the "truths" it had taught.

In her diary, Philae's "Passion Week" had a deeper meaning. Like Jacob wrestling the angel, she encountered Christ through Osiris and his willingness to fulfill his mission even to death. On the first night by Isis' temple, she noted, "I thought I should see Him (Christ). His shadow in the moonlight in the Propylaeum."[69] The next day she "discovered the Chamber of Osiris" at sunrise, like the chamber where Christ was buried. She did not elaborate—*she* knew the meaning of her cryptic entry. Later in the day, she visited the chamber and "stayed there till 3 o'clock." The next day of "Our Passion Week," she spent almost all day in the "Sacred Chamber," not even deterred by noisy tourists from Northampton. On Friday, January 25—her "Good Friday," she went to other sites, including Bidji, but added two words—Osiris Chamber— prior to dinner. Saturday the twenty-sixth was spent at Bidji, Florence noting how much better it looked because "Yesterday I spoiled it all with dreaming. Disappointed with myself & the effect of Egypt on me— Rome was better."[70] In Rome, her struggles had been supported by Madre Santa Columba, but Egypt was awakening so many ideas, and her dreaming about how she could fulfill them had returned to haunt her. The final encounter with Christ came on her "Easter Sunday," January 27—"took my crucifix up before breakfast to lay it in the sacred dust of the Chamber of Osiris. Prayers."[71] After a day of touring, she noted, "Farewell moonlight walk. All night with my head out of the window learning every line of the temples under the palms by heart."[72] She had identified her life and mission with Christ's.

After Philae, the three weeks in Thebes spawned "Vision of Temples" and her own question—if she could choose, like the returning Pharaohs, what would she choose to do? Since she calculated that Rameses V was currently choosing his next mission in his afterlife, she wrote:

If I were a Pharaoh now, I would choose the Arab form, and come back to help these poor people; and I am going tomorrow to a tomb of a Rameses, 1150 BC. to meet him and tell him so.[73]

She had observed the disasters of Pharaohs who had not understood their divinely assigned task, or who failed to do it, but what about herself? Guilt and frustration surged and ebbed in her "spiritual and intellectual whirlwind" at Thebes. Her diary mentioned days that she did not go out because "the demon of dreaming had possession of my weakened head all the morning."[74] Biographers who lightly dismiss Florence's absorption with God have not read her diaries from Egypt.

Although she wrote home enthusiastically of Septhos' mortuary temple at Koorna, her favorite spot in Thebes, she did not tell them what happened there. Her diary says (February 22): "Sat on steps of Portico, moving with the shadow of the sun and looking at that (to me) priceless view. God spoke to me once again."[75]

During the ten-day boat trip between Thebes and Oysoot, Florence began writing up the notes, her ideas that would become *Suggestions for Thought*. On Thursday, February 28, "hard at work" on "Vision of Temples," she wrote, "God called me with my Madre's (Mother Santa Columba from Rome) words."[76] Madre's emphasis was always on doing God's will within her present circumstances—*writing* was the one thing she could do at that moment, frustratingly limited though it might be. Florence did not write home during these ten days, blaming the bad weather, yet her diary tells the real reason:

> Did not get up in the morning but God gave me the time afterwards,
> which I ought to have made in the morning—a solitary 2 hours in
> my own cabin, to "meditate" on my Madre's words.[77]

After a gale all day and night, she noted, "God called me in the morning & asked me, 'Would I do good for Him, for Him alone without the reputation.'"[78] Florence's reputation was something Madre had also mentioned, and she recalled this the next day: "Thought much upon this question. My Madre said to me, Can you hesitate between the God of the whole Earth & your little reputation?"[79] The following day, Florence came to some resolution about her reputation, writing, "During half an hour I had by myself in the cabin…settled the question with God."[80] *Reputation* could mean more than one thing. Fanny had expressed concern about what people would think if Florence *worked*— the upper class did *not* work for pay, and *not* working distinguished them from the *working* class. The type of work Florence wanted to do in hospitals and other places was that of a scullery maid with little "reputation"—meaning moral reputation. On the other hand, Florence was obsessed by the "sin" of shining in society, what her mother called her "European reputation" among learned men. In Paris, she had been distressed lest society's praise divert her from her call. Was her reputation in society blocking her willingness to do anything God wanted of her?

The struggle continued. One day Florence was at peace, only to lose it again the following day.

Sunday 10 read some of my Madre's words—Can you give up the reputation of suffering much & saying little, they cried to me.

Monday 11 Thought how our leaving Thebes which was quite useless owing to this contrary wind (we might have had another fortnight there) but without it I might not have had this call from God.

Tuesday 12 Stood at the door of the boat looking out upon the stars & the tall mast in the still night against the sky (we were at anchor—they were all asleep & I could not go to bed) & tried to think only of God's will—& that every thing is desirable only as He is in it or not in it—only as it brings us nearer or farther from Him. He is speaking to us often just when something we think untoward happens.[81]

Something untoward *did* happen. God spoke to her again at Memphis in a beautiful oasis where the statue of Rameses the Great lay fallen in the grass. Here Moses grew up as a Pharaoh's grandson, and

derived his ideas of a pure worship, and (sifting the chaff from the wheat) thought how he could retain the spirit of the religion, while getting rid of the worship of animals....I have often thought he may have tried the Egyptians first, and failing, gone to the Hebrews...How grieved he must have been to leave Memphis,— guilty of ingratitude, as he must have seemed, towards his princess-mother, who had so tenderly and wisely reared him, and given him the means of learning all he valued so much, as the way of raising his brethren—that great, that single instance in history as far as I know, of a learned man, a philosopher, and a gentleman, forming the plan of himself educating savages, and devoting himself to it...We should have said, what a waste! to squander such talents among miserable slaves, who won't understand you; keep in your own sphere; you will do much more good among educated men like yourself. I do not know any man in all history with whom I sympathize so much as with Moses—his romantic devotion—his disappointments—his aspirations, so much higher than anything he was able to accomplish, always striving to give the Hebrews a religion they could not understand.[82]

Florence's March 15 entry reads, "God has delivered me from the great offense—& the constant murderer of my thoughts (dreaming not doing)."[83] Obviously, Moses had provided a model for her own call, having discovered a religion among the Egyptians that he wished to teach to the Hebrews. Moses was like her—an upper-class, educated man reaching out to the disadvantaged as a "savior" or "deliverer," just as Florence felt of herself. Florence identifies with Moses' grief at leaving the woman who raised him—would she think him ungrateful, the charge Florence had always heard from her mother? Florence also knew the resistance Moses experienced of peers who did not understand—why squander talent on slaves? Keep in your own sphere and do good there. The reassurance from Moses delivered her temporarily from her dreaming. Like him, she must leave family and class to answer God's call to give the common people a religion and free them from bondage. Just as the exodus would inspire liberation theologians of the twentieth century, Florence found the same inspiration in her call to be a liberator. She wrote home:

> Memphis has wound itself round my heart—made itself a place in my imagination. I have walked there with Moses and Rameses, and with them I shall always return there.[84]

In using "savage" for Hebrew slaves, Florence is reflecting Victorian assumptions about "civilized" and "uncivilized" nations. Moses was raised in a highly developed ancient Egypt compared with the tribal culture of the Hebrew slaves. This new resolution brought a new question—*where* should she serve God?

> Can I not serve God as well in Malta as in Smyrna, in England as at Athens? Perhaps better—perhaps it is between Athens & Kaiserswerth—perhaps this is the opportunity my 30th year was to bring me. Then…God told me what a privilege he had reserved for me, what a preparation for Kaiserswerth in choosing me to be with Mr. B. [Bracebridge] during his time of ill health & how I had neglected it—& had been blind to it. If I were never thinking of the reputation, how I should be better able to see what God intends for me.[85]

On Thursday, March 21, 1850, Florence's party disembarked in Cairo, and Florence's diary records a "delicious" hour in the gardens of Heliopolis "undisturbed by my great enemy." To the family, she said:

> I had always made a sort of saint's day to myself of the day I should spend at Heliopolis, where Plato walked and Moses prayed, where

Pythagoras and Solon, and Thales learnt all their wisdom; the nurse of Athens, the Alma Mater of Egypt, and, through her, of the world...It shall be my Sunday, I thought; not even Thebes is so sacred as this.[86]

The model of Moses was actively shaping her mind as someone who did not just think, but acted, even replacing her beloved Plato:

For whereas Plato only formed a school, which formed the world, Moses went straight to work upon the world...the chisel as it were to the block, his delicate perceptions acting upon those miserable savages. He was not only the sculptor, but the workman of the statue, the scholar, the gentleman, and the hard-working man, all in one.[87]

Florence had been reading Harriet Martineau's *Eastern Life,* and Harriet had compared Moses and Plato in the same way: "Moses redeemed a race of slaves, made men of them, organized them into a society, and constituted them a nation while Plato did only theoretical work of that kind."[88] Moses was God's sign to Florence that she *also* must act, not think and wait. God called, and Moses acted, despite his feelings of inadequacy—did not God promise to be with him and give him the words to say? In this flush of inspiration, Florence wrote home about a sermon she heard in Cairo:

How could a man preach such a sermon in the land of Moses! Oh, go out, good people, to Heliopolis, and see what your race can do; you will not learn it in that church.[89]

Cryptic notes continued—"Spent much time at home reading my Madre's words"—"Looked out upon the silent city in the moonlight— & thought what He would have done here."

I thought how Christ, if he had been there, would have felt; how he would have yearned over Cairo, and how he would have been straitened till his task was accomplished. Behold that great city— how would he have set about her deliverance?[90]

It was now the *real* Easter weekend, a time to reevaluate Christ's life. On Good Friday, she stayed home, reading her Madre's writings, wondering, "Did Christ thank God this day when it dawned upon him?" By the end of the weekend, she wrote: "Not able to go out, but wished God to have it all his own way. I like Him to do exactly as He likes, without even telling me the reason why."[91] With this confidence, Florence left Cairo for Alexandria and then Greece, telling her diary:

Oh God, thou puttest into my heart this great desire to devote myself to the sick and sorrowful. I offer it to thee. Do with it what is for thy service.[92]

CHAPTER FOUR

From Dreaming to Action: 1850–1851

Today I am 30—the age at which Christ began his mission.
Now no more childish things. No more love, no more
marriage. Now Lord let me think only of Thy Will,
what Thou willest me to do. Oh Lord Thy Will, Thy Will.[1]

In early April 1850, Florence and the Bracebridges sailed for Greece, a change of countries for Florence, but not of resolve. Her diary of April 21 noted, "Let me serve thee & thee alone with the strength thou hast given me."[2] She had found a role model in Moses as a deliverer of the poor and oppressed, and she was determined to turn it into action. In Athens, she met Anglican missionaries Frances and John Henry Hill. Florence cross-examined Frances about Frances' call. Like the Madre. Frances claimed never to have moved a finger on her own, always allowing Providence to open the way. Once again, Florence tried to conform to this passivity, as she had done with Aunt Hannah:

> I have felt here like the suspension of all my faculties. I could not write a letter, could not read. Could not exert myself in any way. But I am thankful for it—it teaches me to wait upon the will & laws of God—that I may do every thing only for the sake of doing His will. Lord, let me give everything to thee.[3]

On her thirtieth birthday, May 12, 1850, Florence made her final spiritual vows, the vow that heads this chapter, not to a religious order of any church but, like many mystics, to her God.

Her "cloud of witnesses" came not just from the people she met in life, but also from the kindred souls she met through her reading as she jotted down relevant quotes to fuel her own journey. St. Catherine of Genoa cried in anguish, "Oh Lord, no more world, no more sins."[4] Jesus had said, "Not what I will, but what thou wilt" (Mark 14:36, KJV). Henry Martyn's *Memoirs* reverberated with Florence's experiences, and she copied copious quotes from his writings:

> "This day I finished the thirtieth year of my unprofitable life...I am now at the age at which the Saviour of men began his ministry."

> "I look back with pity & shame upon my former self, when I attached importance to my life & labours."

> "It is because I am one with Christ that I am so wounded."

> "I wish for no created good or for men to know my experience: but to be one with thee & live for thee."

> "To have a will of my own, not agreeable to God's is a most tremendous folly: let me never dare to think of being dissatisfied."

> "I see no business before me in life but the work of Christ, neither do I desire any employment to all eternity but his service."

> "I pass so many hours as if there were no God at all."

> "I like to find myself employed usefully, in a way I did not expect or foresee, especially if my own will is in any degree crossed by the work unexpectedly assigned me: as there is then reason to believe that God is acting."[5]

Florence also spent time with Mary Baldwin, a woman working with the Hills, and again Florence questioned her about the circumstances of her call:

> She had no strong belief in her mission, no presentiment, no conviction that this was her vocation—but to take what was presented to her, to follow the indications of the will of God & prepare herself for them, that was her mission, that [was] her way.[6]

Florence's battle lay with the conflict between her own experience of longing to act, and the type of counsel she was receiving. To Martyn's thoughts, she added her own note, "Now they all think only of God's will, of finding out what is His will for them to do, this man, my Madre, Mrs. Hill."[7]

Florence also had with her some account of her spiritual journey thus far, which she was constantly rereading, "a history of miserable woe, mistake & blinding vanity, of seeking great things for myself."[8] This "breathing space" away from family allowed her to think and talk with others who had acted out their calling, and also remind God that she was open to further direction:

> I place myself in thy hands. Thy will is all my desire—if it be thy will that I shall go on suffering hell, let it be so—but let me only learn only to desire what Thou desirest...Lord, thou askest me to do thy will, & I am to ask of thee life, life to do it for I am dead.[9]

This reflection simply prolonged the inaction, and did not quench the dreaming or ease her striving against it, her trying to mold herself into the passive theology of the Madre and Frances Hill:

> Now I am 30—the year when I thot [thought] I should have accomplished my Kaiserswerth mission—but let me only accomplish the will of God. Let me not desire great things for myself.[10]

William Cowper joined the ranks of her spiritual mentors as she identified with his roller-coaster faith journey of great piety alternating with great despair.[11] Cowper wrote the wonderful hymns "O for a Closer Walk with Thee" and "How Sweet the Name of Jesus Sounds to a Believer's Ear," yet he sunk to the depths of mental illness, believing he had committed the unforgivable sin. After trying to commit suicide several times, he dreamed that God said to him, "It is all over with thee. Thou hast perished."[12] While Florence never seemed to despair of God's presence, she did despair at her own sinfulness and unworthiness, often wishing simply to die.

> Friday I sat before breakfast &. thought of my despair—this day twelve months [ago], June 7, 1849 I made that desperate effort, that Crucifixion of the sin [dreaming], in faith that it would cure me. Oh what is Crucifixion—would I not joyfully submit to Crucifixion, Father to be rid of this? But this long moral death, this failure of all attempts at cure. I am just in the same state as I was last June 7. I think I have never been so bad as this last week...when living intercourse with these dear Hills could not recall my attention to actual things. And I thought when I was 30, I should be cured. 8 months since the last incentive to sin, & not a day has passed

without my committing it. I went & sate [sat] in the cave of the Eumenides alone, &. thought how they [the evil spirits] pursued me—&. how would it end? A wretched [*sic*] that I am. Who shall deliver me from the body of this death?...I shall be in just the same state June 7, 1851 according to human calculation as I am now.[13]

Sometimes, only the depths of despair offer a view in a new direction. Florence's spiritual advisers thus far—the Madre, Aunt Hannah and Frances Hill—all believed she should be *nothing* but passive in awaiting a sign from God, and that any thought of cocreating with God was "sin"—a lack of love, trust, and worthiness. Florence had tried so hard to accept her present state as God's will, but in vain, given the nature of her person. She continued to drift into dreaming—imagining what she might do for God—but was forced to see this as sin, making her even more unworthy. This cycle of struggle against her own nature and inevitable defeat became pathological as she blamed herself for failing but, at the same time, was also tempted to question the logic.

June 10. The Lord spoke to me: he said, Give five minutes every hour to the thought of me. Couldst thou but love me as Lizzie [Herbert] loves her husband, how happy thou wouldst be—in all situations. But Lizzie does not give five minutes every hour to the thought of her husband. She thinks of him spontaneously every minute. So also in time shalt thou do.[14]

Sightseeing in Greece was as nothing to her, "sold" as she was to the enemy of dreaming. All she wanted was respite from the thoughts that plagued her:

June 13. Half an hour of dark solitary silence—it was a moment of repose in the series of struggles, in which I am always worsted, of defeats under which I am sinking and dying.

June 17. After a sleepless night, physically & morally ill & broken down, a slave...I had wish on earth but to sleep, an unbroken sleep in my little bed at Lea Hurst. There it seemed to me as if forgetfulness opened her mother's arms to me. There I wished to be, but only to sleep.

June 18. I let all the glorious sunrises, the gorgeous sunsets, the lovely moon lights pass by. I had no wish, no energy. I longed but for sleep. My enemy is too strong for me—every thing has been tried. Mrs. Hill's teaching, the beauty of the East—all, all is in vain.[15]

Florence was reading Charlotte Brontë's novel *Shirley*. In it, the dutiful Caroline, without family or income, depends on her uncle. Caroline longs for an occupation like a man, to earn her own money rather than sitting in her uncle's drawing room. Her uncle does not understand, thinking "everything but sewing and cooking above women's comprehension, and out of their line."[16] Caroline resorts to dreaming like Florence, envisaging another fifty years stretching before her and wondering, "How am I to occupy it? What am I to do to fill the interval of time which spreads between me and the grave?"[17] Like Florence, *Shirley*'s author Charlotte Brontë refused marriage to pursue an independent life, and spoke her ideas through Caroline's voice and character. Realizing she may never marry, Caroline bemoans the "very convenient doctrine for the people who hold it" that the place of single women is to "do good to others, to be helpful whenever help is wanted."

> I perceive that certain sets of human beings are very apt to maintain that other sets should give up their lives to them and their service, and then they requite them by praise; they call them devoted and virtuous. Is this enough? Is it to live? Is there not a terrible hollowness, mockery, want, craving, in that existence which is given away to others, for want of something of your own to bestow it on?…Does virtue lie in abnegation of self? I do not believe it. Undue humility makes tyranny; weak concession creates selfishness…Each human being has his share of rights. I suspect it would be conducive to the happiness and welfare of all if each knew his allotment, and held to it as tenaciously as the martyr to his creed.[18]

In Florence's *Suggestions for Thought,* first drafted at this time, Florence launches a similar critique on Victorian family life and the use and abuse of single women, no doubt fueled by *Shirley:*

> Daughters are their mothers' slaves…they are considered their parents' property; they are to have no other pursuit, nor power, nor independent life, unless they marry; they are to be entirely dependent on their parents—slaves in the family, from which marriage alone can emancipate them. Mothers acknowledge this, even while feeling they are their daughters' slaves too.[19]

As the Bracebridges and Florence made their way across Europe, Florence's diary recorded alternate bouts of freedom and entrapment from her "enemy." She could not believe she was in amazing places so dear to her heart yet was ignoring them in her despair.

July 3. How little I thought that I should have been at Prague & so despairing, so helpless as I was to night—as I lay in bed meditating [on] my utter hopelessness of relief, how lost I was & past redemption, a slave that could not be set free.[20]

In Dresden, she stood before the painting *Ecco Homo* (Behold the Man) of Jesus being handed over by Pilate to the people—"It reflected my feelings —it spoke despair—no hope—all had failed." She had never felt so bad:

The habit of living not in the present but in the future of dreams is gradually spreading over my whole existence. It is rapidly approaching the state of madness when dreams become realities.[21]

By the time they arrived in Berlin, she did not even want to get up in the morning: "What could I do but offend God? I never prayed. All plans, all wishes seemed extinguished."[22]

Florence was obviously suffering from depression. Although by this time, Selena Bracebridge had arranged for Florence to visit her beloved Kaiserswerth, Florence shrank from the idea, perhaps afraid that the possibility of fulfilling her longtime dream would disappear again, or that she would not be able to follow it through, or maybe that it would force her finally to make the break from family and commit to this way of life. She could also have known they were to meet the unmarried Monckton Milnes in Hamburg, and was wondering whether marriage to him was a simpler alternative. Her diary reveals her ambivalence:

On the brink of accomplishing my greatest wish [Kaiserswerth], with [Selena] positively planning for me, I seemed to be unfit, unmanned for it —it seemed not to be the calling for *me*. I had 3 paths among which to choose—I might have been a married woman, a literary woman, or a Hospital Sister. Now it seemed to me, as if quiet, with somebody to look for my coming back, was all I wanted. I did not feel the spirit, the energy for doing anything at Kaiserswerth. To search out the will of God for me seemed so far from me. I could not do it.[23]

But Berlin wove its magic charm with its life "so full & free & rich." Florence's energy and enthusiasm surfaced again as she visited hospitals, deaf facilities, a Ragged School, and libraries. She also met a woman who had trained at Kaiserswerth and who advised her as to what training to pursue there. Florence noted that her "hopes revived."[24] When she met up with Monckton Milnes, she said he was himself again. He married a year later, but they stayed good friends.

On July 31, 1850, Florence finally arrived at Kaiserswerth, her parents completely unaware of the visit. "I could hardly believe I was there—with the feeling with which a pilgrim first looks on the Kedron, I saw the Rhine—dearer to me than the Nile."[25] On her first night, she wrote, "I felt queer, but the courage which falls into my shoes in a London drawing room rises on an occasion like this. I felt so sure it was God's work."[26] Florence stayed two weeks, observing all she could and helping with the children. There were one hundred and sixteen deaconesses there then, those with nurse training being sent to hospitals all over Europe. With Florence's desire to establish a similar sisterhood in England, she was anxious to see if the system could accommodate educated women as well as working-class women. While she was there, she wrote a pamphlet in English about the institution for Pastor Fliedner, the director, presenting basic information to attract English women "going mad for want of something to do" to consider Kaiserswerth.[27] The pamphlet was also aimed at overcoming English reticence, showing that such institutions were not all proselytizing arms of Roman Catholicism. Florence argued that deaconesses like these, free from vows or cloistered cells, existed in the early church, and that it was an appropriate nonsectarian vocation for unmarried women and widows to follow a life call free of church wrangling and to respond to Christ's words "I was sick and you visited me," without vows of obedience. The pamphlet, *The Institution of Kaiserswerth on the Rhine for the Practical Training of Deaconesses, under the direction of the Rev. Pastor Fliedner, embracing the support and care of a hospital; Infant and Industrial Schools, and a Female Penitentiary,* was published in England in 1851 but without Florence's name because of the family's opposition to her interest in Kaiserswerth. Florence was impressed with the institution's tone, and its spiritual training and discipline:

> Never have I met with a higher love, a purer devotion, than there. There was no neglect. It was the more remarkable because many of the deaconesses had been only peasants: none were gentlewomen when I was there.[28]

She wrote in her diary, "Left Kaiserswerth feeling so brave as if nothing could ever vex me again."[29] When she reached London a week later, her furious family, who had heard of her visit to Kaiserswerth, confronted her. Florence later wrote to Rev. Henry Manning:

> I was in disgrace with them for a twelvemonth for going to Kaiserswerth. My sister has never spoken the word to me since…I think the persecution of the Emperor Domitian must be easy to

bear, but there is a persecution from those we love…which grinds one's very heart out, especially if one is not quite sure one is right.[30]

Florence's "bravery" after Kaiserswerth dissipated under the months of family punishment. Parthe's hysterics were blamed on Florence's desertion of her, and the fear that Florence might leave them for good, now that she had discovered a Protestant order without long-term vows, filled the already explosive atmosphere. The family believed that Florence must be *forced* to accept her duty at home. Florence wrote:

> There are Private Martyrs as well as burnt or drowned ones. Society of course does not know them; and Family cannot, because our position to one another in our families is, and must be, like that of the Moon to the Earth. The Moon revolves round her, moves with her, never leaves her. Yet the Earth never sees but one side of her; the other side remains for ever unknown.[31]

Both WEN and Fanny insisted that Florence devote herself entirely to the thirty-one-year-old Parthe for six months. Later calling it "insanity," Florence agreed, and was trapped until the spring of 1851. She was permitted to teach at a school for factory girls near her home until Parthe became hysterical over that as well. In December 1850, four months after her return, she wrote a long, sad soliloquy of her life:

> My present life is suicide. Slowly I have opened my eyes to the fact that I cannot now deliver myself from the habit of dreaming which, like gin drinking, is eating out my vital strength. Now I have let myself go entirely…I have no desire but to die. There is not a night that I do not lie down on my bed, wishing that I may leave it no more. Unconsciousness is all I desire. I remain in bed as long as I can, for what have I to wake for? I am perishing for want of food— & what prospect have I of better? While I am in this position, I can expect nothing else. Therefore I spend my days in dreams of other situations which will afford me food. Alas! Now I do little else. For many years, such is the principle of hope. I always trusted that "this day month" I should be free from it. God, thou knowest the efforts I have made. Now I do not hope. I *know*. I know that I, my nature and my position remaining the same, same nature can generate but same thoughts. Dec. 30, 1851, I shall be but so much more unable to resist these dreams, being so much the more enfeebled. Starvation does not lead a man to exertion—it only weakens him. O weary days. On evenings that seem never to end— for how many long years have I watched that drawing room clock & thought it never would reach the ten & for 20 or so more years to

do this. It is not the misery, the unhappiness that I feel so insupportable, but to feel this habit, this disease gaining power upon me—& no hope, no help. This is the sting of death. Why do I wish to leave this world? God knows I do not expect a heaven beyond—but that He will set me down in St. Giles' at a Kaiserswerth, there to find my work and my salvation in my work, that I think will be the way, if I could but die.[32]

Like many of her day, Florence believed in a succession of further states and tasks after death rather than a permanent heaven, a belief that comforted those caught in a disastrous life in the present. In another note to herself, she despaired of her effect on the family, and wished God had made her as she was now in a *later* world, not this one:

What is to become of me? I can hardly open my mouth without giving my dear Parthe vexation—everything I say or do is a subject of annoyance to her...My God, I love thee, I do in deed. I do not say it in open rebellion, but in anguish and utter hopelessness— why didst thou make me what I am? A little later, oh my God, a little later, when I should have been alone in the world or in the next stage—not now, not yet, not here.[33]

At no point did Florence reprimand Parthe or the family for their behavior, always heaping blame on herself as the problem, since the rest of her family seemed to accept their lot. She penned another long soliloquy to help sort out in her mind the causes of tension in her family, revealing much about upper-class life:

What makes me so unlike them?...My father is a man who has never known what struggle is. Good impulses from his childhood up—& always remaining perfectly in a natural state, acting always from impulse—& having never by circumstances been forced to look into a thing, to carry it out. *Effleurez, n'appuyez pas* [Touch lightly, do not dwell on them] has been not the rule but the habit of his life. Liberal by instinct not by reflection. But not happy, why not? He has not enough to do—he has not enough to fill his faculties—when I see him eating his breakfast as if the destinies of a nation depended upon his getting done, carrying his plate about the room, delighting in being in a hurry, pretending to himself week after week that he is going to Buxton or else where in order to be in legitimate haste. I say to myself how happy that man would be with a factory under his superintendence—with the interests of 2 or 300 men to look after. My mother is a genius. She has the Genius of Order, to make a place, to organize a parish, to form Society. She has obtained by her own exertions, the best society in England—she goes into a school & can put this little thing right which is wrong—she has a genius for doing all she wants to do & has never felt the absence of power. She is not happy. She has too much fatigue & too much anxiety—anxiety about Papa, about Parthe's health, my duties, about the Servants, the parish. Oh, dear good woman, when I feel her disappointment in me, it is as if I was becoming insane. When she has organized the nicest Society in England for us, & I cannot take it as she wishes.

Parthe—she is in her Element if she had but health—& if she had but not me she is in her Element. It is her vocation to make holiday to hardworking men out of London, to all manners of people who come to enjoy this beautiful place. And a very good vocation it is—no one less than I wants her to do one single thing different from what she does. She wants no other religion, no other occupation, no other training than what she has—she is in unison with her age, her position, her country. She has never had a difficulty, except with me—she is a child playing in God's garden & delighting in the happiness of all His works, knowing nothing of human life but the English drawing room, nothing of struggle in her own unselfish nature—nothing of want of power in her own Element. And I, what a murderer I am to disturb this happiness...

I, what am I, that I am not in harmony with all this, that their life is not good enough for me? oh God, what am I? The thought & feelings that I have now I can remember since I was 6 years old. It was not that I made them. O God, how did they come? Are they the natural cross of my father & mother? What are they? A profession, a trade, a necessary occupation, something to fill & employ all my faculties, I have always felt essential to me, I have always longed for, consciously or not. During a middle portion of my life, college education, acquirement I longed for—but that was temporary—the first thought I can remember & the last was nursing work & in the absence of this, education work, but more the education of the bad than of the young.

But for this I had had no education myself—& when I began to try, I was disgusted with my utter impotence. I made no improvement, I learned no ways. I obtained no influence. This nobody could understand. You teach better than other people, was the desperate answer always made me—they had never wanted instruction, why should I? The only help I ever got was a week with my Madre at Rome, which I made use of directly & taught my girls at Holloway [Village near Lea Hurst] always on that foundation & my fortnight at Kaiserswerth. Still education I know is not my genius—tho' I cd do it if I was taught, because it is my duty here.

But why, oh my God, cannot I be satisfied with the life which satisfies so many people? I am told that the conversation of all these good clever men ought to be enough for me—why am I starving, desperate, diseased upon it? Why has it all run to vanity in me, to—what impression I am making on them?…Is it enough to say that rice disagrees with one man & agrees with another? that…the ground of sincerity lies in talking of what you are interested about— so none of the subjects of society interest me enough to draw me out of vanity…death, why it's a happiness—oh how I have longed for a trial to give me food—to be something real. A nourishing life—that is the happiness—whatever it be—a starving life, that is the real trial. My God, what am I to do? Teach me, tell me. I cannot go on any longer waiting till my situation should change. Dreaming what the change shall be to give me better food. Thou hast been teaching me all these 31 years what I am to do in this? Where is the lesson? Let me read it—oh where, where is it?[34]

To crown her despair at this time, she met Monckton Milnes again and found him offhand—he became engaged a few weeks later. Florence cried into her diary: "I wanted to find him longing to talk to me, willing to give me another opportunity, to keep open another decision."[35]

When Florence's sentence to care for Parthe ended in April 1851, Dr. Elizabeth Blackwell, the first woman doctor in the United States, visited Embley, and these two women close in age became friends, staying in touch until death. Despite different backgrounds, their dreams for social reform and women's freedom coalesced, even to the hope they would work together one day. Elizabeth had mystical experiences as well, but she introduced Florence to a different version of them than that of the Madre, Aunt Hannah, and Frances Hill. With a supportive family, Elizabeth had *fought* her way into medicine despite great opposition, so determined that this was her *vocation*. For the first time, Florence realized that *her* call might also include the struggle to free herself rather than passive waiting. This astounding revelation, previously veiled by admonitions from well-meaning spiritual mentors, swept Florence along a different path of thinking about her relationship with the family and her dependence on their approval—"There are knots which are Gordian and can only be *cut*."[36] She resolved to her diary:

> Let me honestly & with sympathy of purpose set to work, not to complain, but to find the means to live. I must *take* some things, as few as I can to enable me to live. I must *take* them, they will not be given me—take them in a true spirit of doing thy will—not of snatching them for my own will. I must do without some things—as many as I can—which I could not have without causing more suffering than I am obliged to cause anyway.[37]

First, she would spend at least an hour each day teaching at the local school, which would put her in a better frame of mind to do the family's wishes the rest of the day. Second, she would protect her hour and a half of "steady thinking" before breakfast, to keep her sane. Third, she would place her relationship with them on a different footing by accepting that they would never understand her, and cooperating with their plans only when it did not compromise her own call. This way, she would not be constantly "at the bottom" and treated as a child.

> I must expect no sympathy or help from them...I have so long *struggled* to make myself understood, been sore, cast down, insupportably fretted by not being understood (at this moment I even feel it when I retrace these conversations in thought) that I must not even try to be understood. I know they can not. I know that to try for it and fail irritates me...Parthe says that I blow a trumpet—that it gives her indigestion—that is also true. Struggle must make a noise—and everything that I have to do that concerns my real being must be done with struggle.[38]

Florence now had some new spectacles to train on her difficulties, seeing them, not as occasions for more submission to God, but as obstacles to overcome. She was a *victim*, not a criminal, and her "sin" was not the *succumbing* to dreaming, but in not *challenging* the obstacles in her way, and changing her dreaming into reality.[39] Now seeing with new eyes and taking some control over her life, Florence found an opportunity almost immediately. Parthe needed three months' treatment at a spa in Carlsbad, Germany, and Florence agreed to accompany them on condition she could spend the time at Kaiserswerth. Since the Bracebridges, Herberts, and von Bunsens were all supporting Florence, Fanny had to concede, but on *her* condition that Florence travel both ways with them to Carlsbad, going to Kaiserswerth from there and not telling anyone at home.

She arrived for her three months' stay at Kaiserswerth on July 6, 1851, leaving again October 7, 1851. Despite the hard work and spartan conditions, it was heaven for Florence, donning the uniform of the other deaconesses, most of whom were ten years her junior, and following their strict regimen, basic peasant food, and evening Bible study. Kaiserswerth entrants were required to write a curriculum vitae of their spiritual path to Kaiserswerth. In hers, Florence revealed her dislike of upper-class life, her concern for the poor, and her lifelong conviction that God had a special plan for her.

> God has led me by ways which I have not known. He has never cast me off for all I have done against Him. What I owe Him I can never tell in these few minutes, but I can bless Him now for bringing me here.[40]

She made more than one hundred pages of notes while she was there, observing surgical procedures, the use of the new chloroform, and diverse symptoms and treatment. Everything fascinated her. She made copious analyses of Kaiserswerth's administrative structures, especially its hospital, centralized under one woman superintendent who reported only to the pastor's wife and who was responsible for both the spiritual and physical needs of the nurses under her. Intrigued at the possibilities of such an establishment in England, Florence later wrote to Dr. Howe:

> I wish the system could be introduced in England where thousands of women have nothing to do and where hospitals are ill nursed by a class of women not fit to be household servants.[41]

Much later, Florence would deny she learned her nursing at Kaiserswerth, as nurse training was the weakest part of the institution, but the experience was something she could not then get in England, and it gave Florence a starting point from which to organize her own ideas. European and English nursing would follow different models because of Florence's influence on English nursing. She insisted that the control of the nursing staff should be in the hands of a trained nurse, not doctors; that nurses train nurses; and that the profession be structured as a secular one. This model was adopted in England and America, while Germany stayed with the system where nurses were instructed by doctors and lived in a motherhouse under a woman superior. Although Florence may not have learned nursing at Kaiserswerth, she experienced at last the satisfaction of living out her vocation. When the Herberts visited her there, Pastor Fliedner told them "no one had ever passed so brilliant an examination or shown herself so thoroughly mistress of all she had to learn."[42] On Florence's request as she left Kaiserswerth, Fliedner consecrated her to her vocation, even though its specific nature was still uncertain. When

Fliedner died, Florence wrote of her spiritual mentor, "For me it is as though I have lost a father."[43]

Her own family did not share the same enthusiasm for Florence's actions. Early in her stay at Kaiserswerth, Florence wrote to her mother:

> I find the deepest interest in everything here, and am so well in body and mind. This is Life. Now I know what it is to live and to love life, and really I should be sorry now to leave life. I know you will be glad to hear this, dearest Mum. God has indeed made life rich in interests and blessings, and I wish for no other earth, no other world but this.[44]

When her mother continued to ignore what Florence was doing, Florence pleaded:

> Give me time, give me faith. Trust me, help me. I feel within me that I could gladden your loving hearts which now I wound. Say to me, "Follow the dictates of that spirit within thee." Oh my beloved people, that spirit shall never lead me to anything unworthy of one who is yours in love. My beloved people I cannot bear to grieve you. Give me your blessing.[45]

Neither Fanny nor Parthe responded to Florence from Carlsbad about her work, though Florence wrote again for their blessing:

> I wish I could hope that I had your smile, your blessing, your sympathy upon it, without which I cannot be quite happy. Very beloved people, I cannot bear to grieve you…Speed me on my way to walk in the path which the sense of right in me has been pointing to for years.[46]

When they met up again to return to England, Fanny and Parthe punished her with silence. Parthe's cure was declared a failure because of her constant anxiety over Florence at Kaiserswerth.

Nothing changed at home. Fanny was in total revolt against Florence's vocation. In frustration, Florence penned an imaginary letter to her, demonstrating some newfound strength on Florence's part to resist:

> You don't think that with my "talents" and my "European reputation" & my "beautiful letters and all that," I'm going to stay dangling about my mother's drawing room all my life—I shall go and look out for work, to be sure. You must look upon me as your son, your vagabond son, without his money. I shan't cost you near so much as a son would have done. I haven't cost you much yet—

except my visits to Egypt and Rome. Remember I should have cost you a great deal more if I had married or been a son—Well, you must now consider me married or a son—You were willing to part with me to be married.[47]

WEN, however, was about to make a move. Florence had accompanied him to his health spa at Umberslade near Birmingham in early 1852, allowing the long-time duo time together. WEN's appreciation of Florence's uniqueness and difficulties grew. From the spa, she went to stay with some relatives, including her favorite, Aunt Mai, and WEN suggested Florence write to him at his London club so they could continue their conversations without interference from Fanny and Parthe—he had become increasingly disturbed about their behavior. A few years before WEN's death, Florence wrote to him to report her conversations with the ailing and mellowing Fanny:

> I hope to remember throughout eternity things she has said to me this year & last, such as: ("Your father has never had a cross?") *"I have been his Cross."* "He has been a better husband to me than I deserved"…My mother's memory & appreciation of *life*— especially of *her life with you*—is in fact better & truer now than it has been during the whole of her half-century with you.[48]

Florence stayed with Aunt Mai and Uncle Sam until spring, reveling in their shared spiritual and social interests. In the company of those who understood and supported her, Florence found time and energy to work further on her *Suggestions for Thought*.

While still with Aunt Mai, Florence received another "call" from God on May 7, 1852, this time to be a "savior" to the poor. Such a savior was not the Christian concept so exclusively bound to ideas of Christ's atonement, but the concept that she found in Plato's "guardians." In *The Republic*, Plato argued that everyone was born with an aptitude for a task, which gave him or her a particular role in society. Women and men could have the same roles of action and responsibility because Plato believed that the argument for women's inferiority was a perversion of nature and a waste of resources. There were three societal groupings based on natural ability—artisans (craftsmen and merchants), auxiliaries (soldiers), and rulers or elders. In addition, there were the guardians from the ruling group, usually men but sometimes women, who had special gifts of knowledge and skills to be used for the whole, and who should not be diverted by everyday cares and chores. Dugald Stewart (1753–1828), whom Florence also read, shared this idea, calling people with the gift of distinguishing truth from error "enlightened conductors." Such people should be educated in order to be available to the world.[49] Florence also saw Jesus' task as savior in this light, a leading from error, as explained in John's gospel.

With no further hint as to how she would be a savior, Florence, claiming her newfound inner permission to actively pursue her call rather than sit impatiently and dream, toyed seriously with converting to Roman Catholicism. This was not something unique to Florence at this time. Many in the Church were pursuing the same thoughts after the Oxford Movement's influence. This movement emerged within High Church Anglicanism in the early 1800s as a movement of the heart, preaching a return to the orthodoxy, tradition, ritual, and order of the ancient Church and Creeds. Since the beginnings of Anglicanism, "High" had described those within the Church who advocated the rigid observation of church rules, prayer, fasting, church privilege, and the English Establishment and Tory politics. Theologically, the High Church deferred to the ancient church fathers as the authoritative interpreters of scripture, orientated themselves around the sacraments, and strongly supported ecclesiastical authority based on its continuity from the early apostles through apostolic succession. In the early 1800s, some Anglican clergy previously of "Low" church persuasion (an emphasis on inner feeling and conviction rather than ritual and sacrament) entered the High Church camp, taking with them their piety, with its feelings and emotions, which then became expressed as awe, mystery, and reverence through the sacraments, symbols, and vestments. This High Church "holiness" movement, rooted firmly in the orthodox tradition from the fourth-century credal church, became known as the Oxford Movement.

As with many religious movements, politics brought the Oxford Movement to the fore. Ireland, England, and Scotland had been united under one crown since 1800, but Roman Catholics had not been given enfranchisement. In the early 1800s, Prime Minister William Pitt became convinced that Irish stability would be achieved only if Irish Catholics, and all Catholics, could vote and be elected to the United Parliament, a privilege restricted to some members of the Church of England. Pitt's proposal met fierce cries of popery, the fear that Catholics would be loyal to an Italian pope before the English crown, but when it became obvious that emancipation must happen, Catholics were admitted to the franchise and to Parliament in 1829. The popery fear continued to simmer, boiling over when Parliament, now including Roman Catholics and nonconformists, voted to reduce the number of Anglican Bishoprics in Ireland. Could Parliament do this? What if Parliament tried to reform the Church as well? It was time that Britain was reminded that Church authority resided not only in the crown but also with its bishops in apostolic succession from the primitive church. The Church of England was not some national or parliamentary possession, but the agent in England of catholic truth.

John Keble, a parish priest and professor at Oxford, preached at Oxford's University Church in 1833 on "National Apostasy," urging England to repent and return to its religious roots in the Church Fathers, creeds, and rites of the primitive church, thus reclaiming its commission as Christ's church in England. John Henry Newman heard the sermon, and he and Keble met with fellow Oxford dons Hurrell Froude and E. B. Pusey to work for the Church's return. This "Oxford Movement" published a series of *Tracts for the Times* with Newman as guiding light and major author. As Lytton Strachey said:

> The waters of the true Faith had dived underground at the Reformation, and they were waiting for the wand of Newman to strike the rock before they should burst forth once more into the light of day.[50]

John Henry Newman, born a Low Church evangelical, had moved toward the High Church in his Oxford years. His early tracts emphasized apostolic succession as the guarantor of the Church of England's authority and succession, arguing that the Roman Catholic Church had wandered from the primitive church. Later Newman decided the primitive church did not have the whole truth, and that, under the Spirit's guidance, Rome had led to a more complete truth. His famous Tract 90, *Remarks on Certain Passages in the Thirty-Nine Articles* (1841), argued that the Church of England's *Thirty-Nine Articles* were basically the same as the assertions of the Roman Catholic Church at the Council of Trent in the 1550s, and that the Church of England was simply a modification of Rome. There was nothing in the *Thirty-Nine Articles* that prevented a Roman Catholic from signing.[51]

While the Oxford Movement initially promised a disheveled Church a road back to stability, Newman's drift in favor of a return to Rome was incendiary, especially in exclusively Anglican Oxford, whose ecclesiastical homogeneity was preserved by the *Thirty-Nine Articles*. No one could receive a degree from Oxford, Cambridge, or Durham, England's institutions of higher education, without signing these Articles, which successfully kept the leadership of Church and government strictly in Anglican hands through its graduates. What if Roman Catholics began to flock into Oxford, happily signing the same Articles? Newman's tract was condemned, and he was forbidden to publish further. He resigned his benefice in 1843 to become a Roman Catholic, declaring in his *Essay on Development* that Rome was the only successor to the primitive church. Rome did not receive Newman with open arms, however, and he was isolated in Birmingham, misrepresented and alienated as a Catholic and a theologian. His writings were read more after his death, especially around Vatican II, when the Catholic Church was ready to consider contemporary ideas. Newman had written in 1839:

> We cannot, if we would, move ourselves back into the times of the Fathers; we must, in spite of ourselves, be Churchmen of our own era, not of any other, were it only for this reason, that we are born in the nineteenth century, not the fourth.[52]

Newman's colleague in the Oxford Movement, Edward Pusey, stayed within the Church of England and became an influential High Church figure, continuing Newman's ideas and hoping, in vain, that the Vatican Council of 1870 would reunite the church of England with Rome. Pusey opposed the revision of the *King James Bible*, the entry of German biblical scholarship into England, and the more moderate Broad Church Movement, which Florence's Oxford friend Benjamin Jowett supported, and which we shall consider more closely later in this book.[53]

The Oxford Movement *did* bring a renewal of sacramental life and worship, new schools, women's religious orders, and a new sense of the continuity of the Church from its early days as a rock in a sea of uncertainty at a time when the Bible was under attack. As its leaders said:

> Surely the sacred volume was never intended and is not adapted to teach us our creed...From the very first, the rule has been, as a matter of fact, for the Church to teach the truth, and then appeal to Scripture in vindication of its own teaching.[54]

As the center of English Catholicism, the Catholic See of Westminster grew in numbers, including influential converts from the Church of England. Prime Minister Gladstone published a pamphlet, *Vaticanism*,[55] that outlined dire consequences to England if Catholic civil obedience was subordinated to papal infallibility. The people Florence had met in Rome, which included Anglican priest Henry Manning and the Herberts, were some such influential people attracted to Newman's writings and his defection to Rome. While Sir Sidney Herbert would remain in the Church of England until his early death, his wife Liz would convert to Rome, as did Manning. Manning was, like Newman, born into Low Church Anglicanism, and he had stayed on the fringes of the Oxford Movement at Oxford, becoming Archdeacon of Chichester. His inward doubts and the early death of his wife pushed him to depression.

Drawn to Newman's ideas, he recuperated in Rome (where Florence met him) and spent time talking with nuns, priests, and even the pope. In 1847, when a Low Church clergyman was accused by the Church courts of having opinions contrary to the *Thirty-Nine Articles,* and was then exonerated by the secular Privy Council, Manning was devastated. A committee of *laymen* and an act of Parliament had decided whether an Anglican clergyman had violated his ordination. Since Parliament now included Roman Catholics and nonconformists, Manning was in agreement with Newman and Keble that the Anglican Church had lost its way. He resigned his office in 1851 and joined the Roman Catholic Church, becoming Archbishop of Westminster and then a Cardinal, and he played a significant role in Florence's life, as we shall see.

Florence first met Manning in Rome with the Herberts, but they met again when Florence wanted to place in a safe home a young prostitute she had found. After finding no place in Church of England institutions, Manning had placed the child in a Roman Catholic convent, and, given Florence's leanings toward Catholic orders at the time as a way to pursue her call, she confided in Manning her family difficulties and her desire to serve God and the poor:

> If you knew what a home the Catholic Church would be to me! All that I want I should find in her. All my difficulties would be removed. I have laboriously to pick up, here and there, crumbs by which to live. She would give me daily bread. The daughters of St. Vincent would open their arms to me. They have already done so, and what should I find there. My work already laid out for me instead of seeking it to and fro and finding none; my home, sympathy, human and divine…Why cannot I enter the Catholic Church at once as the best form of truth I have known, and as cutting the Gordian knot I cannot untie [the family].[56]

Despite the conflict Florence had experienced in Rome with what she perceived as lack of freedom of thought within Catholicism, she was desperate enough to follow her call that she was willing to overlook the dogmas she couldn't believe or the submission of obedience she would have to follow within an order. All this was preferable to her own church, which was too careless and indifferent to ask whether she believed or not and unable to offer her a task to do. She wrote to Manning:

> You would have me snatch at the blessing the Catholic Church has to give, without having given her my unconditional allegiance— & make my own conditions (tacitly) instead of receiving hers. So

have I done all my life with the Anglican Church. I have snatched her Sacraments (a faithless child—but she never asked me why) tacitly making my own conditions to myself. I stand now trembling where I stood firm before. Those I have known left the arms of one church but to go to those of another—a more faithful mother. I have a precipice behind me...if I do not reach the Church.[57]

In Manning's wisdom, he did not encourage her toward a Catholic order, having read her writings and having realized that her Unitarian-influenced theology was far from Catholicism. His reference to her "eclectic" beliefs brought a reaction from her:

The Eclectic has been at least as strong an element as any other in filling the stream towards Catholicism. Why cannot I join it?...You will not perhaps believe it, but the search after truth has been to me a martyrdom, tearing up everything I love, forcing me upon conclusions I recoil from, shutting the door upon what looks to me Paradise.[58]

Manning also recognized Florence's independent drive and creative brilliance and realized it was incompatible with submission in an Order under a Mother Superior in a church that Florence had already described as an "over-busy mother":

She [the Roman Catholic Church] imprisoned us; she read our letters; she penetrated our thought; she regulated what we were to do every hour; she asked us what we had been doing and thinking; she burns us if we had been thinking wrong. We found her an over-active mother, and we made the Church of England, which does not "interfere" with her children at all.[59]

Submission was certainly a central concept in Florence's vocabulary, but to *God*, not an intermediary. As Mary Clarke (Clarkey) said of her:

Florence Nightingales like to carry out their own systems and not other people's...It is scarcely natural that a person of energy sufficient to leave a quiet home will turn quiet enough to carry out other people's ideas.[60]

Manning *did* arrange, however, for Florence to visit the Sister of Mercy Hospital in Dublin and the Sisters of Charity in Paris to further her research in the care of the poor.

With a new call and the possibility of Dublin and Paris ahead of her, Florence's renewed focus shone through a letter written at Aunt Mai's house to her father on her thirty-second birthday:

I have come into possession of myself…I am glad to think that my youth is past and rejoice that it never, never can return—that time of follies and bondage, of unfulfilled hopes and disappointed inexperience when a man possesses nothing, not even himself. I am glad to have lived; though it has been a life which, except as the necessary preparation for another, few would accept…I hope now that I have escaped from that bondage which knows not how to distinguish between "bad habits" and "duties"—terms often used synonymously by all the world…I hope that I may live, a thing which I have not often been able to say, because I think I have learned something which I think it would be a pity to waste…When I speak of the disappointed inexperience of youth, of course I accept that, not only as inevitable, but as the beautiful arrangement of Infinite Wisdom, which cannot create us gods, but which will not create us animals, and therefore wills mankind to create mankind by their own experience—a disposition of Perfect Goodness which no one can quarrel with.[61]

Anxious to share more of her thoughts "which would be a pity to waste" with him, the one who trained her to think in the first place, she added, "I shall be very ready to read you, when I come home, any of my 'Works,' in your own room before breakfast, if you have any desire to hear them."[62] The "works" were the drafts of *Suggestions for Thought*, the new religion she wanted to offer the working class, along with her poor reform.

The possibility of Florence's visits to Dublin and Paris precipitated a breakdown in Parthe, who was packed off to the family doctor, Sir James Clark, in Scotland.[63] Florence accompanied Dr. Fowler to the British Scientific Association meeting in Dublin, but her more important plan to spend time with a Catholic order was foiled. The Hospital of the Sisters of Charity was closed for repair, and she also learned some unexplained "terrible lesson" that diverted her from Roman Catholicism. As for the Paris visit, Clarkey was recruited to ensure that those plans were not aborted as well. Clarkey wrote to Florence's cousin Hilary:

Tell Flo and yourself that the thing I like best is that she [Florence] should be perfectly free to do her own foolishness, let alone wickedness, if she likes…Mrs. Nightingale knows I am very discreet, so if after a time Flo tells of a fancy to go to some wicked (Kaiserswerth or some convent) place the folk in England will fancy she is still with me, and I will keep it snug.[64]

Since a "good person for her to go with" was needed before Florence could be allowed to leave for Paris, Clarkey tried to persuade Hilary to accompany Florence, since Hilary also needed to escape and pursue her artistic career:

> Will you come NOW, or not at all!...*Don't* undertake a hundred small things in England, which you *must* do...Thus and thus life slips through your fingers, and as all these are perfect whims, when you have administered to them, nobody recollects them, except that Hilary is a very useful person to have in the house.[65]

On the way home from Dublin, Florence stopped to collect Parthe in Scotland. Dr. Clark, who knew of Florence's entrapment in the family, told Florence that her presence only aggravated Parthe's "fixation" on her, and, since no one else in the family would do anything, Florence should leave home. Of this wonderful, unexpected release, Florence wrote to Manning:

> Under these circumstances, I have but one course to pursue. No one will act but me...I shall go...to the duty nearest at hand—to nurse a sick aunt—& wait to see what I can find out to be God's work for me.[66]

Florence took Parthe home and prepared to go to the Sisters of Mercy in Paris. A few weeks before her departure, Fanny rescinded her permission for Florence to go, and elicited WEN's tired acquiescence since "company" was expected for Christmas and Parthe would be uncontrollable without Florence. How could Florence leave her mother with such burdens, and why must Florence go to Roman Catholic sisters in a foreign country anyway? What about helping sick Great-aunt Evans instead? Florence yielded to the last plea and, over Christmas, endured increased family pressure to accept WEN's offer to buy an estate near the family home and start her *own* sisterhood close to them. Parthe wrote a scathing letter to Clarkey, telling her that Florence spent most of the year away, leaving Parthe and her mother, both "very unwell," to care for "those eternal poor," delivering the "talkey-talkey broth and pudding," which Florence held in such contempt—Florence felt her mother and sister should do much more than offer token gifts of soup and advice. Parthe's angry verdict on Florence was:

> I believe she has little or none of what is called charity or philanthropy, she is ambitious—very, and would like well enough to regenerate the world with a grand *coup de main* or some fine institution, which is a very different thing...I wish she could be

brought to see that it is the intellectual part that interests her, not the manual...her influence upon people's minds and her curiosity in getting into the varieties of mind is insatiable. After she has got inside, they generally cease to have any interest for her.[67]

Despite the numerous times Florence had been forced to care for her, Parthe did not think Florence was much of a *practical* nurse, perhaps because Florence was *also* aware of the manipulative nature of Parthe's "illnesses."

This time Florence was resolute. In February 1853, she left for Paris to visit various hospitals and institutions. She also planned to enter the convent of the Sisters of Charity at Maison de la Providence as a postulate in training. This institution encompassed an orphanage, nursery, and hospital for sick women. She would don the nun's habit, but eat and sleep in a separate cell from the sisters. Only a few days before her entry, Florence was recalled to England. WEN's mother was dying. Florence nursed her in her last days, earning WEN's undying gratitude but Fanny's criticism for leaving the sick Parthe—"for seeking duty away from the sphere in which it has pleased God to place me."[68] Before returning to Paris, Liz Herbert found Florence a London position as superintendent of the Institution for the Care of Sick Gentlewomen in Distressed Circumstances. When the family heard this, Fanny and Parthe collapsed and WEN retreated to his club, after first agreeing to give Florence a yearly allowance to enable her to leave and take on this assignment. Florence returned to Paris, hiding the purpose of her visit from her new Anglican employers, who were "quite as much afraid of the Roman Catholics as my people are," a reflection of the bitter sectarian feelings of that day which Florence detested.[69] Unbelievably, she was again thwarted in Paris, contracting measles after the first few days and having to return to London. Florence did not go home, however, staying in London to make arrangements to begin her job. Parthe had obviously complained to Clarkey, who wrote to Florence suggesting she talk her actions over with Parthe. This time Florence was adamant and wrote to Clarkey:

> I have not taken this step without years of anxious consideration. I mean the step of leaving them. I *have* talked matters over with Parthe...*not once but thousands of times*. Years and years have been spent in doing so...it is a fait accompli.[70]

Throughout these long, harrowing eighteen months since Kaiserswerth, Florence's call had not lain idle, despite the constant obstacles put in her path. She had spent the time honing her theological ideas scribbled in note form over many years. In London she had visited the working men's institution with Mrs. Truelove, who, along with her husband, was a publisher and retailer of radical freethinking literature, to see what type of theology already appealed to working-class people. She discovered that even "the most thinking and conscientious" of the artisans had no religion at all, a concern she also expressed to Dr. Howe and Henry Manning. On New Year's Eve in 1852, the moment when her dreaming might finally turn into practical reality, she wrote:

> I am so glad this year is over; nevertheless it has not been wasted I trust—I have remodeled my whole religious beliefs from beginning to end. I have learned to know God. I have recast my social belief. Have them both ready written for use when my hour is come. I have learnt to know Manning…Have been disappointed in my Dublin Hospital plan. Formed my Paris one…Lastly, all my admirers are married…and I stand with all the world before me…It has been a baptism of fire this year.[71]

CHAPTER FIVE

A Scream of Pain—"*Cassandra*": 1852

"For joy that a man is born into the world," Christ says.
And that is a subject for joy. But a woman must be born into a family.
If she were born into the world, it would be a joy too. But what joy is there
in her being born into the smallest of all possible spheres,
which will exercise perhaps no single one of her faculties?
Everyone will say this is preaching doctrine subversive of all morality.
But what right have a man and woman to absorb all the powers
of four or five daughters?[1]

In Greek mythology, Cassandra, daughter of King Priam and Queen Hecuba of Troy, was granted the gift of prophecy by the god Apollo, whose ulterior motive was to become her lover. When Cassandra rejected his advances, Apollo altered his gift. Cassandra's prophecies would be correct, but no one would believe her. She warned of Paris' escapades, his liaison with Helen, and against bringing the wooden horse into the city. She was ignored, Troy fell, and Cassandra was taken prisoner and murdered. A *Cassandra*, therefore, is one whose predictions, although accurate, are not heeded.[2]

Among the remodeled beliefs Florence was editing in 1852 into her draft of a new religion, *Suggestions for Thought*, was "Cassandra," an autobiographical writing of despair and anger attacking Victorian upper-class family life and its use and abuse of women.[3] Florence included it in her theological arguments as an example from her experience of how religion, with its culturally based support of the British class system, kept the less powerful—including women—in their proper place. When Benjamin Jowett first read Florence's draft in his single, male academic environment of Oxford, he was stunned, suggesting Florence's ideas about women's experience must surely represent that of only a few women. He therefore thought that her personal tirade on how such theology affected middle-class women "weakened" or lessened the weight of the other things she said, suggesting to her that any reflections on families should be less volatile and prominent, and more general, taking "less the form of individual experience."[4] From his own prison of "correct" theological method, Jowett could not see the groundbreaking theological moves Florence was making on at least three fronts, moves that would be taken up a century later by feminist theologian sisters: first, to validate experience as an important category in theology; second, to challenge religious rules about women based on cultural assumptions and held in place by arguments borrowed from selective biblical texts; and third, to challenge current ideas of christology, the person and work of Christ, with a feminist christology.[5]

In "Cassandra," Florence spoke for many women like her. As she wrote, her single cousin, Hilary Bonham Carter, spent a year with Mary Clarke (Clarkey) in Paris developing her exceptional artistic talent only to be summoned home because her mother, surrounded by husband and servants, "could not be left alone." Florence, as we have seen, had been exploring the possibility of a convent to escape her destiny and fulfill her call. No doubt the family had been very vocal against this idea, as Florence writes in frustration:

> Women don't consider themselves as human beings at all. There is absolutely no God, no country, no duty to them at all, except family…I have known a good deal of convents. And of course everyone has talked of the petty grinding tyrannies supposed to be exercised there. But I know nothing like the petty grinding tyranny of a good English family. And the only alleviation is that the tyrannized submits with a heart full of affection.[6]

Those biographers of Florence who embellished her great "sacrifice" in leaving home to go to Crimea had no concept of the much greater sacrifice she endured for so many years—*staying at home* in an idle, affluent environment. Monckton Milnes knew better than anyone. When her sacrifice was praised at the launch of the Nightingale Fund, he spoke from his heart: "God knows that the luxury of one good action must to a mind such as hers be more than the equivalent for all the loss of all the pomp and vanities of life."[7]

In Victorian England, women were worshiped only as "angels of the home," and valued only as wives and mothers or potential wives and mothers.[8] Single "redundant" women, a major problem in Victorian England, became family slaves in upper-class families, shunted from house to house to care for the sick. In middle-class families, they were forced to work as poorly paid governesses for rich families, and working-class single women were employed in factories and mills in dreadful conditions for half the male wage—the alternative was prostitution. For married women of any class, rich or poor, the husband legally owned all property, including the wife's money, body, and children. Women sold themselves, Florence argued, whether in upper-class marriage or as women "we may not name." "Cassandra" concentrates on the powerlessness and subordination of a *privileged* Victorian daughter, not just under fathers or husbands but also to the whims of sons, relatives, and guests. "Cassandra" decries a daughter's loss of identity except in relation to a man; the triviality and boredom of her life and the consequent demeaning of her because of this; her lack of education and thus her insubstantial conversation; and the utter waste of her talents and mind. It is no wonder young women dream "thoughts which alone are free" all day, and think they are going mad at night because of "the accumulation of nervous energy, which has nothing to do during the day."[9]

Florence saw herself as a Cassandra, the voice of one crying in the crowd, "Prepare ye the way of the Lord."

> One alone, awake and prematurely alive to it, must wander out in silence and solitude—such an one has awakened too early, has risen up too soon, has rejected the companionship of the race, unlinked to any human being. Such an one sees the evil they do not see, and yet has no power to discover the remedy for it.[10]

Like Cassandra, Florence had no guarantee she would be heeded, but her arguments, though from a different context and social milieu, reverberate today in feminist challenges to a male-favoring society and religion. The *scandal* for women, Florence wrote, is that they have passion, intellect, and moral activity, yet their place in society allows none of these to be exercised. Men say God punishes those who complain, and they become irritated when women are not happy with their "ordained" lot. Women can only complain to God, yet are afraid to say "Thy will be *not* done," thus claiming an order of society different from what God has made. They teach their daughters to conform as well.

Young women are taught that passions or desires and hopes are disgraceful, or don't exist, and that women must be content with their drawing-room role. Thus they seek a phantom companion or adventure through dreaming, struggling all the while against this "temptation":

> What are the thoughts of these young girls while one is singing Schubert, another is reading the *Review*, and a third is busy embroidering? Is not one fancying herself the nurse of some new friend in sickness; another engaging in romantic dangers with him, such as call out the character and afford more food for sympathy than the monotonous events of domestic society; another undergoing unheard-of trials under the observation of someone whom she has chosen as the companion of her dream?[11]

Romance novels were so popular because they offered women idyllic situations where the heroine had no family ties and no controlling mother, but instead the independence to have the deep feelings scolded in real life as "going too far." Florence knew only too well:

> We fast mentally, scourge ourselves morally, use the intellectual hair shirt, in order to subdue the perpetual daydreaming, which is so dangerous!...Never, with the slightest success. By mortifying vanity we do ourselves no good. It is the want of interest in our life which produces it; by filling up that want of interest in our life we can alone remedy it.[12]

Part of the "want of interest" in an upper-class family came from a woman's lack of time or encouragement to *think* or do something of her own, so filled was her time with reading aloud, trifling conversation, driving in carriages, writing letters, and going to endless formal meals and teas: "How are you to think? When are you to think?...the best way is to give up all subjects of thought, and that is what people do."[13] If a woman had imagination and talent to write or paint, she couldn't because she had no time to follow anything consistently to completion, Florence bemoaned. If she was at dinner for three hours a day, she could not be painting. If she was writing little notes for another three hours, she could not be drawing, and so on ad infinitum through life:

> It is impossible to follow up anything systematically. Women often long to enter some man's profession where they would find direction, competition (or rather opportunity of measuring the intellect with others), and, above all, time.[14]

While many might not understand such creative discontent, Florence pleads that all women be given back their rightful access to adventure, passion, and suffering, rather than forced into a life of "indifference."

> Better have pain than paralysis! A hundred struggle and drown in the breakers. One discovers the new world. But rather, ten times rather, die in the surf, heralding the way to that new world, than stand idly on the shore![15]

Monasteries have provided such creative space for women by setting apart time each day for thought, training, and opportunity, but in society if time were set aside, women would feel they should be doing something for somebody else. There are such different rules, Florence argued, for men and women. If a young *man* was idling in his mother's drawing room looking at prints, doing embroidery, and reading little books, everyone would laugh, but if a daughter refused to appear for her mother's friends as a son does, she would be chided:

> Is man's time more valuable than woman's? Or is the difference between man and woman this, that woman has confessedly nothing to do? Women are never supposed to have any occupation of sufficient importance *not* to be interrupted...and women themselves have accepted this, have written books to support it, and have trained themselves so as to consider whatever they do as not of such value to the world or to others, but that they can throw it up at the first "claim of social life." They have accustomed themselves to consider intellectual occupation as a merely selfish amusement, which it is their "duty" to give up for every trifler more selfish than themselves.[16]

Florence identified only three circumstances in which it was suitable for a Victorian gentlewoman to work—widowhood, a husband's ill health, or extreme poverty. Most intellectual women were therefore forced to fritter life away in idle conversation, never too long-winded, too deep or too absorbing. If a woman yearned for more intellectual activity, she could only gain solitary moments by rising early or staying up late—what Florence did. In the drawing room, everyone read aloud out of different books, making comments every few minutes, or listened to someone reading aloud, the "most miserable exercise of the human intellect."

> It is like lying on one's back, with one's hands tied and having liquid poured down one's throat. Worse than that, because suffocation would immediately ensue and put a stop to this operation. But no suffocation would stop the other.[17]

Since it is accepted that women have nothing important to do, anyone can visit them, literally robbing them of their time in a way never done to men. A businessman can complain if someone overstays an appointment because it costs him his earnings, but a woman cannot, as it is "only her time."

> They [women] are taught from their infancy upwards that it is wrong, ill tempered, and a misunderstanding of "a woman's mission" (with a great M) if they do not allow themselves willingly to be interrupted at all hours.[18]

It is no wonder that Florence, on returning from the Crimea to work on army reform, set up her home as an office, working from her bedroom through a secretary who screened visitors and made appointments. She knew that in order to do a "man's work" as a woman, she must claim the lifestyle of a professional man, valuing her privacy and time despite criticism. The idea of doing things at "odd moments" was most dangerous.

> Would not a painter spoil his picture by working at it "at odd moments"? If it be a picture worth painting at all, and if he be a man of genius, he must have the whole of his picture in his head every time he touches it, and this requires great concentration, and this concentration cannot be obtained at "odd moments"…Can we fancy Michael Angelo running up and putting on a touch to his Sistine ceiling at "odd moments"?[19]

Virginia Woolf quoted Florence's argument about odd moments in *A Room of One's Own* (1929), talking about Victorian women novelists who had to write amidst drawing room chatter: "As Miss Nightingale was so vehemently to complain—'Women never have an half hour…that they can call their own'—she was always interrupted."[20] Virginia also noted that Victorian women's writings were often touched by bitterness and frustration—a need to protest their confinement. Florence, Virginia wrote, "shrieked aloud in her agony" at women, trying to live by their intellect, but finally giving up in despair when conventional frivolities called duties forbade it—the constant letter writing, being amusing at breakfast, and driving with company in the carriage. Young women's noble ambitions and heroic dreams withered before age thirty because of the poverty of their idle lives.

The family was too narrow a space, Florence argued, to develop a person's immortal spirit, whether male or female. The *variety* of tasks for which people are destined by God's gifts placed within them cannot be experienced or developed in such a closed setting. The family therefore uses those within its clutches for its own purposes, "even though that member may be destined for science, or for education, or for active superintendence by God, i.e. by the gifts within. This system dooms some minds to incurable infancy, others to silent misery."[21] The family considers itself *successful* if it has created individuals, especially women, with "no personal desires or plans," happy to abandon anything at a moment's notice: "Women's life is spent in pastime, men's in business. Women's business is supposed to be finding something to *'pass'* the *'time.'*"[22] No wonder women embrace marriage eagerly and ignorantly, "throwing the gifts of God aside as worthless, and substituting for them those of the world."[23] Most women would prefer an option of some "steady moral activity" for which they were suited or trained, rather than their piecemeal life, dabbling only in charity: "Were the physician to set to work at *his* trade, as the philanthropist does at his, how many bodies would he not spoil before he cured one!"[24]

Women long for a chance to learn the laws of the human mind and how to analyze their experiences, yet they cannot abandon the breakfast table or some other duty—so they dream:

> Dreaming always—never accomplishing; thus women live—too much ashamed of their dreams, which they think "romantic," to tell them where they will be laughed at, even if not considered wrong. With greater strength of purpose they might accomplish something. But if they were strong, all of them, they would not need to have their story told, for all the world would read it in the mission they have fulfilled.[25]

Florence's "mission" in "Cassandra" was to tell the story of ordinary women, unable to fight society, who give up their destiny as not worth the struggle to accomplish it. Some entered the convent, but most simply wore out, sapped of the energy to withstand continual argument, discouragement, and self-doubt. Self-doubt was very real, since women had long been told they were inferior in every occupation to men—but how could they feel otherwise if they could only pursue an occupation at "odd times"? Would a man become skilled in his profession by working only at odd moments? Other women abandon their dreams of an intellectual, artistic, or active life because they know they must sacrifice such a life in marriage:

> A man gains everything by marriage: he gains a "helpmate," but a woman does not…Behind *his* destiny woman must annihilate herself, must be only his complement. A woman dedicates herself to the vocation of her husband; she fills up and performs the

subordinate parts in it. The fact is that woman has so seldom any vocation of her own, that it does not much signify; she has none to renounce.[26]

A married woman who tries to develop a vocation must do it in a "sketchy" fashion, rarely finishing anything, like a painter working on five pictures at once with constant interruptions. If a woman makes a deep study of anything, her husband thinks she is neglecting his dinner or destroying their domestic life. Florence was not *against* marriage—she thought it the highest, truest love where two people worked together for God's purpose, throwing themselves "fearlessly into the universe…[to] do its work, secure of companionship and sympathy in one instance" and "not shrinking from any temporary absence from it."[27] But such unions, in her experience of Victorian elite life, were rare. Couples seemed so little part of each other with so little to say to each other. How *could* they, if they were together only to be idle, doing nothing to form a real tie? If a husband has deep thoughts, Florence says, he hides them from his wife, afraid of "unsettling her opinions." She agreed that many women would be shocked at a husband's unorthodox religious ideas, disinterested if he shared political thoughts, and suspicious if he raised socialist ideas.

Despite all this, young women were eager to marry because, with nothing else to do, there was no reason *not* to. They were seldom in love—how could they be the way they chose partners? Some were acquainted since childhood, often cousins. Most formed slight acquaintances by accident, and, as if in a lottery, the woman accepted if the man fell in love with her. Less socially acceptable was when two sufficiently independent people, not concerned with public opinion, worked on a friendship with the option to break it should it not work out. Rarely in real life, but always in novels, some circumstance emerged in which the usual restraints were removed enough to give food and space for the development of mutual sympathies. In any case, how could a deep relationship flourish under the ever-present maternal eyes, fed only on gossip and trivia? From her own experience, Florence blamed mothers for pushing daughters into marriage, although Clarkey disagreed, seeing mothers caught between the relative merits of an arranged marriage and a single daughter's fate dependent on pocket money from a father who might spend "more every year on his dog-kennels than he will give to her."

> They [daughters] are his playthings, but as to thinking of their future well being, he never does. You always see mama sneered at because she wants to marry them well; the papa is never ridiculous.

He thinks they are there to make his tea and amuse him when he is old and gouty, and that is what they were born for.[28]

Later Florence relented somewhat about mothers, realizing Fanny herself had been a victim of the same system.

Women were starved, Florence said, of food for their heads, hearts, and bodies. A newspaper report of a death from starvation would bring an outcry, but "death of thought from starvation" or "death of moral activity from starvation" would simply make people laugh. Women have been so long starved that they have lost all individual and independent life, Florence said. Realizing too late they have already killed themselves, they hate their idleness but are powerless to do anything but live with regret:

> Those dreams against which they so struggle, so honestly, vigorously, and conscientiously, and so in vain, yet which are their life, without which they could not have lived; those dreams go at last. All their plans and visions seem vanished, and they know not where; gone and they cannot recall them...And they are left without the food either of reality or of hope. Later in life, they neither desire nor dream, neither of activity, nor of love, nor of intellect.[29]

The intellectual dreams went last, Florence thought, since women always hoped their experience might benefit someone else, yet never had time to write their thoughts down.

It seemed as if the female spirit of the world were mourning everlastingly over "blessings *not* lost, but which she has never had, and which, in her discouragement, she feels that she never will have, they are so far off."[30] Florence believed that her era was the furthest from hope because women's education in Victorian England was so completely severed from any *vocational* training, leaving her only with dreaming.

> She is like the Archangel Michael as he stands upon Saint Angelo at Rome. She has an immense provision of wings, which seem as if they would bear her over earth and heaven; but when she tries to use them, she is petrified into stone, her feet are grown into the earth, chained to the bronze pedestal. Nothing can well be imagined more painful than the present position of woman...when the young imagination is so high and so developed, and reality is so narrow and conventional—there is no more parallelism between life in the thought and life in the actual than between the corpse, which lies motionless in its narrow bed, and the spirit, which, in our imagination, is at large among the stars.[31]

Despite all this, if a woman complained of the dualism between her dreams and action, other women would also blame her for not being content with "small things" and for trying to abolish domestic life (is there nothing new under the sun?). Men were afraid their homes would not be as comfortable if wives made themselves "remarkable." Women worried they would be unattractive to men, and so wrote books persuading themselves that the "sacred hearth" was their only true sphere.

> Sacred it is indeed. Sacred from the touch of their sons almost as soon as they are out of childhood—from its dullness and its tyrannous trifling *these* recoil. Sacred from the grasp of their daughters' affections, upon which it has so light a hold that they seize the first opportunity of marriage, *their* only chance of emancipation. The "sacred hearth"; sacred to their husband's sleep, their sons' absence in the body and their daughters' in mind. Awake, ye women, all ye that sleep, awake! If this domestic life were so very good, would your young men wander away from it, your maidens think of something else?[32]

Or women were told that "since we live in this world, we must walk in its ways," yet history's *male* reformers, such as Christ and Socrates, were not so advised. *Their* gnawing concern over the world's miseries led them to act, yet women could only complain or protest.

> The great reformers of the world turn into the great misanthropists, if circumstances or organisation do not permit them to act. Christ, if He had been a woman, might have been nothing but a great complainer. Peace be with the misanthropists! They have made a step in progress; the next will make them great philanthropists; they are divided but by a line.[33]

In a very modern turn of thought, Florence longed for a *woman* savior who would resume in her soul all the sufferings of her gender. She calls for a women's rebellion.

> Jesus Christ raised women above the condition of mere slaves, mere ministers to the passions of the man, raised them by this sympathy, to be ministers of God. He gave them moral activity. But the Age, the World, Humanity, must give them the means to exercise this moral activity, must give them intellectual cultivation, spheres of action.[34]

No such female Christ was on the horizon, however, or even one to "go before her face" preparing hearts and minds. Society was not yet ready, even for a male savior:

> People talk about imitating Christ, and imitate Him in the little trifling formal things, such as washing the feet, saying his prayer, and so on; but if anyone attempts the real imitation of Him, there are no bounds to the outcry with which the presumption of that person is condemned.[35]

Should a *woman* do this, the outcry would be quadrupled since a *female* Christ would, like a male one, claim the priority of her ministry over domestic demands. When Jesus was talking with his followers and his mother and brothers interrupted Him "to take Him home to dinner, very likely," He would *not* interrupt his work even for them, saying, "Who is my mother? and who are my brethren?" (Matthew 12:46–50). If a woman savior did the same, Florence said, she would be accused of "destroying the family tie" or diminishing the obligation of the home duties. A female Christ could not emerge until major changes have been made in the way society values *all* individuals, including the *"female* spirit of the world."

Florence's "female Christ" metaphor must be imaged beyond traditional atonement ideas. Florence did not believe in a *single* incarnation of God only in Jesus. Using John's gospel as her source, she took seriously Jesus' promise that the Spirit that was in him would *also* be in the community after his death, leading them to more truth. The "divinity" of Jesus was the divine Spirit in him, the Spirit promised also to all those who continue Jesus' saving work, his followers. While everyone had this Spirit within, "saviors" were especially gifted people commissioned by God to lead people from error at different moments of history, whether Rameses the Great or Florence's good friend Sir Sidney Herbert. Humanity's goal was to discover God's laws in the universe and act in accordance with them to bring the reign of God into the here and now, but people made mistakes, so God sent "saviors" to save people from repeating their errors. Florence believed she was *also* called to be a "savior"—to lead people out of the "error" of the bad theology that justified their imprisonment, and also to help them change their situation:

> God's plan is that we should make mistakes, that the consequences should be definite and invariable; then comes some Saviour, Christ

or another, not one Saviour, but many an one, who learns for all the world *by* the consequences of those errors, and "saves" us from them…There must be Saviours from social, from moral, error. Most people have not learnt any lesson from life at all—suffering as they may, they learn nothing, they would alter nothing…We sometimes hear of men "having given colour to their age." Now, if the colour is the right colour, those men are saviours.[36]

We need to remember that, as Florence was writing "Cassandra," she had just received her call to be a "savior." Her comments are highly significant. She images a future woman savior (the Greek word for a Jewish messiah or messenger that had no connotation of divinity) farewelling her friends before she dies. They weep over her wasted talents, her work still to be done. She assures them that though the world might be set back a little by her death, it has already been set back by a "death which has taken place some years ago in me," Florence's present wasted life and talent. Remember, Florence believed in reincarnation, a series of lives where our talents will be used—she is a female savior in a future life, if not this one:

> My people were like children playing on the shore of the eighteenth century. I was their hobby-horse, their plaything; and they drove me to and fro, dear souls! never weary of the play themselves, till I, who had grown to woman's estate and to the ideas of the nineteenth century, lay down exhausted, my mind closed to hope, my heart to strength…And so is the world put back by the death of everyone who has to sacrifice the development of his or her peculiar gifts (which were meant, not for selfish gratification, but for the improvement of that world) to conventionality.[37]

Florence's ideas in *Cassandra*, this passionate piece of writing penned at "white heat" in a most traumatic moment of her life, are further developed in her expanded *Suggestions for Thought* completed in 1860. Here, some seven years later, and after her experiences in the Crimea, Florence moved beyond the frustrations of family life to offer a broader vision for family and relationships—the idea of *God's* family as the basic unit of food and nourishment. Biological families assumed parents and children were naturally alike, and should have the same work, tastes, and thoughts, yet this was not so in reality—the laws of God in the universe seem to be *against* repetition:

> If one of the family, as often happens, is superior to the rest, the rest, and especially the heads of the family, seem to want this one to be one with them, as we try to become one with God; he is to

devote all his talent and genius to forward their ideas, not to have any new ones; to put their opinions, their thoughts, and feelings into a better dress, a more striking light, not to discover any new light; and above all, he is not to find out any untruth in their ideas, or think he has any new truth, "for there is no such thing!"[38]

The meaning of life in God's family, on the other hand, is to live and be ourselves, not afraid of saying things or shocking others, not knocking against one another's prejudices and suspicions "chained together for life, so close in the same cage."

As long as the iron chain is drawn tight round the family, fettering those together who are not joined to one another by any sympathy or common pursuit, it must be so...those who like it [are those] who can say aloud the things which they would think to themselves, if they were alone. But how few can do this at home! There is no tyranny like that of the family, for it extends over the thoughts.[39]

Florence dreamed of a community where people of *like mind* became an extended family, accommodating both individuality and relationships of affection and sympathy, not a group dictated only by blood.

We want to make a family where there shall be companionship in work, mutual attraction, love and tenderness, we want to make *God's* family. We would not take away *anything*, we would enlarge and multiply.[40]

She had found this in some Catholic orders and in Kaiserswerth, and envisaged it for Harley Street and the secular order she toyed with forming but never created during her lifetime. The closest she got was her sympathetic "little War Office" family—the men, including Sir Sidney, with whom she worked on Army reform. In God's family, however, all are included in the command "go forth and conquer the earth and possess it," not just men. This was so different from the biological family that promises sympathy, love, fellow feeling, and tenderness, but does not deliver nor allow its daughters to follow God's command.

Exodus should always follow the Genesis. Generated by the parents, they should, when they are supposed to be *re*-generated, go forth,—but unfortunately then comes the Leviticus, a number of rules and laws must be laid down, because they always misbehave when they have gone forth.[41]

Florence was not advocating that all women be forced out of the home, but that they be given the choice and opportunity to be where their God-given gifts were best exercised, an issue for feminist theology still. She too had identified the patriarchal family model as the problem:

> It is vaguely taken for granted by women that it is to be their first object to please and obey their parents till they are married. But the times are totally changed since those particular days. Man [and woman too] has a soul to unfold, a part to play in God's great world…There is a higher object than this [pleasing the parents] for the being which is to be one with God.[42]

Daughters were trapped with no practical means of independence. Men legally came of age at twenty-one and were expected to leave to work, travel, or marry. Women had no financial means outside of marriage or familial dependency, so they could not choose to leave. From her own experience, Florence described how intelligent daughters suffered more, since their parents did not understand them and considered them "geniuses unfit to judge for themselves in the common affairs of life." The family erected obstacles against letting such daughters leave, since they were "quite incapable of doing anything reasonable," reasonable meaning what the family did.[43] Brought into the world without being consulted, adult daughters were "robbed and murdered" by a family who demanded lifelong servitude out of gratitude to "the mother that bore you." Instead, Florence advocated that unmarried daughters receive their inheritance at twenty-one, or an allowance from which their maintenance was deducted should they continue at home, rather than waiting until their parents' death to carry out any personal plan that required money.

While "Cassandra" described "murder in an upper-class drawing room," Florence's concerns for *any* women unable to develop her own character, so important to an English gentleman, went further in her other writings. She had been disturbed from childhood by the predicament of poor women. With the Industrial Revolution, many women had been displaced, especially widows and surplus single women, going "into service" as nannies or governesses to survive, or into factories and prostitution. In *all* cases, they were dependent on others. Florence felt that no woman, whether prostitute, servant, society wife, or aristocratic daughter should be the captive of another, but have power to "create herself" in God's image according to her God-given gifts and God's command to bring about the reign of God. Her theology rejected a "natural order of creation" predestining people into unchangeable classes. Just as she would prove that the common soldier, given proper facilities and opportunities, was as noble as anyone, women of all classes were not to accept dependency as God's plan, but live "a life full of steady enthusiasm walking straight to its aim, flying home, as the bird is now, against the wind—with the calmness and the confidence of one who knows the laws of God and can apply them."[44]

The sense that *all* had been called by God to a life of purpose offered strength to women to cast off restricting claims of home and family and rediscover the emancipation proclaimed in the New Testament—that "Jesus Christ raised women above the conditions of mere slaves, mere ministers to the passions of men, raised them by His sympathy, to be Ministers of God."[45]

Thus, Florence taught factory girls in the village, wrote guidelines for home health care for uneducated cottage women, challenged upper-class charity instead of systemic change, and developed a paid hospital profession for women of all classes to work toward independence. This is why Queen Victoria wrote to her in Crimea of her wish to "make the acquaintance of one who has set so bright an example to our sex."[46] This is why Lord Stanley said of her work:

> Mark what, by breaking through customs and prejudices, Miss Nightingale has effected for her sex. She has opened for them a new profession, a new sphere of usefulness. I do not suppose that in undertaking her mission, she thought much of the effect which it might have on the social position of women. Yet probably no one of those who made this question a special study has done half as much as she towards its settlement. A claim for more extended freedom of action, based on proved public usefulness in the highest sense of the word, with the whole nation to look on and bear witness, is one which must be listened to, and cannot easily be refused.[47]

Stanley's words hint at other challenges being made about women at this time. England was in the early stages of agitation for women's being allowed to vote. Even the most aristocratic woman's status was derived from and dependent on a male, whether father or husband. As Florence was writing "Cassandra," women had no rights to their children and, until the Marriage and Divorce Bill of 1857, a husband, even one who had deserted his wife, could claim her earnings or inheritance. A man could divorce his wife for adultery, but a woman could not do likewise until 1896. When Florence was fifty, married women were finally allowed to own property, make a will, and bring a lawsuit—unmarried women were still financially dependent on their fathers. Florence did not have the option to leave home, except for a convent or marriage, until WEN agreed to an allowance for her at thirty-three. No wonder she saw the need for education and training in a paid profession for women of all classes. This is why she did not become actively involved in the emerging women's suffrage movement, which was gathering force after the exclusion of women from the franchise reform of 1832. A few votes for upper-class women would not solve the more pressing needs for *all* women for which Florence worked.

The women who initiated the fight for the women's vote found support in John Stuart Mill, who, after reading "Cassandra," addressed Parliament on the rights of women. In his 1869 book *The Subjection of Women*, Mill used Florence's argument about "odd moments."

> If he [a man] has a pursuit, he offends nobody by devoting his time to it; occupation is received as a valid excuse for his not answering to every casual demand which may be made on him. Are a woman's occupations, especially her chosen and voluntary ones, ever regarded as excusing her from any of what are termed the calls of society?...She must always be at the beck and call of somebody; generally of everybody. If she has a study or a pursuit, she must snatch any short interval which accidentally occurs to be employed at it. A *celebrated woman*, in a work which I hope will some day be published, remarks truly that everything a woman does is at odd times. Is it wonderful, then, if she does not attain the highest eminence in things which require consecutive attention, and the concentration on them of the chief interest of life?[48]

Mill argued that women's subjugation throughout history had no *innate* authority, but was maintained by political, religious, and psychological assumptions to keep women from power, independence, and creative fulfillment. Just as other dominations were being rejected in modernity, this also must go, upholding instead the complete equality of men and women in all legal, political, social, and domestic relations.

In 1867, when Mill wrote to Florence asking her to serve on the board of the new National Society for Women's Suffrage, she refused. Those who claim Florence did not support the women's movement read her out of context. She had valid reasons not to commit time and energy to this particular cause at this time, with more than enough reform work to do in areas in which she alone could make a unique contribution, given her Crimea experience. She also had to preserve her energy against illness. Florence told Mill she would not give her name to something without also working for it, and she thought she could work better for women "offstage." Second, like fellow reformers Octavia Hill and Josephine Butler, Florence thought the early suffrage movement self-centered, a movement of elite women seeking power and prestige for a few, long on personal complaint and low on social *action*. She wrote to her friend Lady Canning:

> One is sick of the cant about Women's Rights. If women will but shew what their duties are first, public opinion will acknowledge these fast enough. I dislike almost all that has been written on the subject...Let the "real lady" as you call her, be as much professional, as little dilettante as possible—let her shew that charity must be done, like everything else, in a business-like manner, to be of any use...and all that is good will follow provided, of course, that the real love of God & mankind is there.[49]

Florence did not *personally* see an urgency for a vote, never short of economic security or political power herself. When reprimanded for her upper-class myopia, she did admit her reactions were too clouded by the "noisy elite" to see the plight of ordinary women, and conceded that they might need the vote. When she told journalist Harriet Martineau that she was "brutally indifferent to the wrongs or rights of my sex," Florence was referring to this vote for a few elite in comparison with the quite substantial wrongs inflicted unchallenged on *poor* women. She was also concerned that the noisy elite might claim her work for *their* cause after her death should she become actively involved. Biographers Wintle and Witts quote Women's Suffrage writer Mrs. Jameson, whose writings Florence did *not* like:

> Many people thought it an improper thing that young English ladies should undertake the work of nursing wounded soldiers. Mrs. Jameson, who was somewhat in advance of the ideas of her own day, wrote this: "It is an undertaking wholly new to our English customs, much at variance with the usual education given to women in this country. If it succeeds, it will be the true, the lasting glory of Florence Nightingale, and her band of devoted assistants, that they have broken down a 'Chinese wall' of prejudices, religious, social, professional, and have established a precedent which will indeed multiply the good to all time."[50]

Another "woman missionary" acknowledged Florence's reticence about involvement in their cause, but appropriated her anyway:

> Miss Nightingale is very zealous for all that can uplift and improve the lives of women, and give them a higher conception of their duties and responsibilities. She supports the extension of Parliamentary representation to women, generally, however

putting in a word in what she writes on the subject, to remind people that representatives will never be better than the people they represent. Therefore the most important thing for men, as well as women, is to improve the education and morality of the elector, and then Parliament will improve itself.[51]

Florence did in fact support other women's reform work and belonged to the National Association for the Promotion of Social Science, a platform for social reformers working outside of Parliament. Their meetings allowed women to speak, although not serve on the council, and, by 1858, one third of the members were women. Florence was not always comfortable with the motives and methods of other women, showing an ambivalence to those who did not make personal sacrifices such as abandoning family and marriage for their causes as she had done. Her dream had been to form an order of women dedicated to the poor, but none had been prepared to alter their whole lives to work with her—no women had followed her lead; no nurse continued with her in army reform after the Crimea. Yet Florence's personal action paid off in many women's hearts and minds. A friend wrote to Parthe of her awe of Florence's silent revolution for women, stirring their hearts by example, not words:

> Florence has explained to many, the cause of the sense of unsatisfied existence they have had—& in what direction to look for satisfaction—viz. in the fulfillment of some service; some real, active service of love to their fellow beings. And men's hearts & eyes are preparing to recognize something more in the nature of woman than has hitherto been supposed to belong to it. A movement has been begun which *will* henceforth work…I believe the movement is of God—& that the true & the good in it will prevail. What a veiled & silent wonder she has always been—manifesting her womanhood in deeds, not words, by the fulfillment of duties, not the assertion of rights.[52]

Florence had a further reason not to be involved. She knew the vote would not be given to *all* women for many years, and did not see a few votes for upper-class women curing society's ills from economic injustice. Writing to Mill in 1867, she said:

> No one can be more deeply concerned than I am that women should have suffrage. It is so important for a woman to be a "person" but it will be years before you obtain suffrage for women. In the meantime there are evils that press more hardly on women than the want of suffrage. Could not the existing disabilities as to

property and influence be swept away by the legislature as it stands at the present?—and equal rights and equal responsibilities be given as they ought to be, to both men and women? I do not like to take up your time with giving instances, *redressible* by legislation, in which women, especially married, poor women with children, are most hardly pressed upon now. I have been a matron on a large scale the greater part of my life, and no matron with the smallest care for her nurses can be unaware of what I mean, e.g., till a married woman can be in possession of her own property there can be no love or justice.[53]

She was concerned that the time and energy absorbed in hearing the debate on the women's vote would absorb Parliamentary time and energy needed for reform that would help the poor. Despite her desire for women's independence, she chose her battles well, knowing the wisdom in Christ's words "I am sending you out like sheep into the midst of wolves; so be wise as serpents and innocent as doves" (Matthew 10:16). The vote for women flew in the face of ingrained social and religious prejudices about women's ordained place, which would take years to attack, and Florence did not want it to delay straightforward legislation to greatly benefit *all* women, such as education and financial independence. She was right. Reforms guaranteeing a woman's right to her children, property, and a divorce were in place long before England would grant women the vote.[54]

As the women's movement discovered, the biblical story of Adam and Eve, which theologized the headship of men, was tightly bound into the social structures of England's class and family systems.[55] While one might assume Queen Victoria supported the women's vote, Sir Theodore Martin tells of how she responded "in royal rage" to a meeting on women's suffrage in 1870 because the whole idea challenged the biblical order of things:

> The Queen is most anxious to enlist everyone who can speak or write to join in checking this mad, wicked folly of "Women's Rights," with all its attendant horrors, on which her poor feeble sex is bent, forgetting every sense of womanly feeling and propriety. Lady —— ought to get a *good whipping*. It is a subject which makes the Queen so furious that she cannot contain herself. God created men and women differently—then let them remain each in their own position…Woman would become the most hateful, heartless, and disgusting of human beings were she allowed to unsex herself; and where would be the protection which man was intended to give the weaker sex?[56]

In old age, Florence warned probationary nurses in her annual written address not to let the slow gains made for women in nursing slip away unnecessarily by choosing unwinnable battles: "Let her not forfeit it by being the Arrogant—the 'Equal with Men.' She does not forfeit it by being the help 'meet.'"[57] While this grates on feminist ears today, Florence knew better than anyone that a woman must negotiate her causes carefully in the contextual minefield of life.

The education of women was the key to all Florence's work for women. Education at the time was considered a waste, except for upper- and middle-class women needing "accomplishments" for the marriage market. Unmarried or widowed "genteel" women could aspire to governessing, and poor women exhibiting a touch of gentility might obtain a millinery or dressmaking apprenticeship or a domestic position. The rest were consigned to exhausting labor in factories and mines, charwomen ("nurses") in public institutions and hospitals, or prostitution. During her life, Florence never ceased to search for new ways to employ and empower women, and her enthusiasm convinced others. Her friend Benjamin Jowett wrote to her after employing a private nurse in his failing years:

> They have a dignified position, and are made ladies of by force of circumstances. I wish there were more opportunities for persons to pass from one rank of society to another, it would be a great good. At present, the dead level of the middle class appears to me to be one of the most oppressive evils of society, there is no way out of it. No distinction can be attained but by literature and art, or by the way of making a fortune.[58]

Florence recruited poor young girls and trained them in health care to work in the poorhouse, where they received better pay and respect than in domestic service. She trained women health missioners to bring general education to cottage women. Even in her final years, she was always asking about the poor. "Are the people improving in their habits?" or "Tell me about these model dwellings which they are putting up everywhere. Have they had a good effect on the personal habits of the people?"[59] At seventy-two, leading a health crusade among Buckinghamshire villages, she wrote to the village mothers:

> Dear Hard-working Friends, I am a hard-working woman too. May I speak to you? And will you excuse me, though not a mother? You feel with me, that every mother who brings a child into the world has a duty laid upon her of bringing up the child in such health as will enable him to do the work of his life. But though you toil all

day for your children, and are so devoted to them, this is not at all an easy task. We should not attempt to practice dressmaking, or any other trade, without any training for it; but it is generally impossible for a woman to get any teaching about the management of health; yet health is to be learnt...The cottage homes of England are, after all, the most important of the homes of any class: they should be pure in every sense, pure in body and mind. Boys and girls must grow up healthy, with clean minds, and clean bodies, and clean skins.[60]

After emphasizing the home as the first and most influential teacher of children, Florence stated the core of her theology—that God intended people to help themselves by discovering God's laws for improvement and acting on them:

When a child has lost its health, how often the mother says, "Oh, if I had only known! But there was no one to tell me." And, after all, it is health and not sickness that is our natural state—the state that God intends for us. There are more people to pick us up when we fall than to enable us to stand on our feet.[61]

For the same reason, Florence supported Josephine Butler's work among prostitutes, a complex phenomenon of Victorian times.[62] Venereal disease was increasing; birth control was primitive and unreliable; illegitimate children were not accepted by the middle class; marriage was delayed for financial security; masturbation was declared harmful by doctors and perverted by clergy; and *nice* Victorian women only "tolerated" the sexual act. Respectable Victorian males therefore quietly frequented brothels with little public remonstrance. Josephine Butler argued that prostitution was not only exploitation of women but of the poor, since the men who argued the *necessity* of prostitution never offered their own daughters for the job. A skewed Calvinist theology also declared "degradation" a sign of sin, so prostitutes, forced into this by poverty, were doubly damned, rejected by humanity and God. When the Contagious Disease Act was introduced into England in 1864, demanding regular medical examination of the prostitutes associated with the army, Florence opposed the law, mainly because she did not accept the emerging germ theory of disease, and she objected to the assumption that the common soldier was an "unmanageable animal" who *needed* prostitutes, something she had proved wrong at Crimea. Later, she attacked the act for its most brutal discrimination against the *woman*, leaving the man unchallenged, and turned her attention to these women as well, believing they could be rescued by education and training and given an alternate, respectable career.

Florence always launched her battles through *action*, finding concrete injustices to fix. Out of this action, Florence the theologian reflected, realizing that the debilitating rules of a patriarchal theology kept her and other women in place by claims of authority and fear of reprisal—throwing oneself "under the wheels of the divinity's car" as Florence called such blind obedience:

> So long as *power*, not to be questioned or criticized, was acknowledged in Heaven and at the head of the family, these doctrines remained in force...These two questions of religion and family are so intimately connected that to ask concerning the higher power or powers acknowledged in heaven and on earth are one.[63]

A feminist theologian before her time, Florence challenged such power over others, whether from church or government, justifying her challenge by showing that in the past, men worshiped deities and yielded to the master of the family, whatever his character, purely because of some arbitrary power, assigned by class or gender to the author over the one authored—God over humans; man over the family. Such authority was considered innately good and any rebellion bad. However, people now realized that both the divine and human parent "must excite in us the consciousness of love, goodness, wisdom, righteousness; then we shall love and revere, trust and sympathize."

> If the human as well as the divine parent is not in the state of being to *call forth* these sentiments, and if the child is not in the state to *admit* of them, there will be no relations between the divine or the human parent, and the child except the latter yielding when he cannot help it.[64]

Previous claims of male power over women reflected *physical* differences at a time when physical strength was needed to dig fields, hunt, and protect the family from wild beasts or one's enemies, but this has been superseded (we are past the Stone Age!). The male no longer needs to be in power as the personal defender of women, and Florence emphasized that society should not let an ancient, gendered belief imprison the daughters of her day, stifling their ability to exercise their faculties as God called them to do.[65]

Florence advocated a new model of power and authority that moved away from the patriarchal model—one where the "Author," whether parent or God, made the existence created for the "authored" a blessing, seeking their improvement through love, trust, and sympathy.[66] Just as this mutual model of power is preferable for the deity, parents would also have an immense power for good if they saw power this way—as wisdom, goodness, righteousness, developing a strong bond with their children that also called forth such qualities from the child. The parents should "make worth having" the existence into which they brought the child. Such a change in the understanding of power and authority offers a tremendous challenge to society, and will cause much uneasiness in family life, Florence rightly predicts; thus she calls for "'saviors" for the daughters of England to "offer these means of instruction for living a true life." We know Florence well enough to realize this call is directed to her.[67]

> A few of peculiar nature, or peculiar circumstances, mothers or daughters, are urged, either by suffering from the trammels of conventional life, or by feeling the want of opportunity to learn what they would do, if they could, to wish for something springing from a truer foundation than conventional life. It is for these sufferers to lead the way, if they can. It is not necessary for *all* to suffer. Some through suffering must find out truth; but when found, its loveliness will attract others.[68]

Florence, in this last volume of *Suggestions for Thought*, suggested that *mothers* could be saviors, having previously blamed them for much of the problem. No doubt Florence had reflected on her upbringing and realized that Fanny was as much a victim of her times as she was. Florence admitted that mothers were given no resources, no education or training, and no support from husbands in their "natural" role of being everything for everyone, empathizing with all their children even when they were so different. Like daughters, they also trod a desperate "desert," supposed to organize the governess, society, and servants without any preparation:

> Naturally, she presides so imperfectly over some, if not all of these duties, that the daughters soon begin to criticize. In youthful spirits, knowing little of difficulties—in the "irresponsibility of opposition," they do this. The more in her maternal affection or conscientiousness or in her ambition that they should excel she has striven for them, the more capable they will be to criticize.[69]

Florence insisted that women be given an allowance at twenty-one and be able to choose a mate, even if he did not have "means." Beautiful and intelligent Fanny had fallen in love, but, when her parents disapproved of the suitor's lack of means, Fanny had married WEN on the rebound.

What can be done? Florence gives another nod in the direction of feminist theology by arguing that we find the rules, not from the authority of a person or a book, but by "observation and experience" of human nature, including family, the criterion being happiness—the "natural flow of sympathy, affection, gratitude, respect, appreciation"— which allows for the right exercise of parental guardianship only as long as is necessary. This theology of family comes not from a sacred book or a church, but from praxis leading to reflection, the method of feminist liberation theology. From her own experience and that observed in others, Florence challenged the loss of dignity and worth experienced by women and children, especially daughters, in patriarchal systems, whether nuclear family or religion. Instead, she saw hope in the model of the Spirit within *all*, urging the full use of faculties of knowledge and experience to bring a revolution in relationships to family, religion, and society, so that "sympathy, affection, gratitude, respect and appreciation" would become the norm, rather than power and control.

Some one hundred and fifty years later, feminist theologian Nancy Victorin-Vangerud offers the same challenge.

> We live today within a diverse and interdependent world household. Yet as beautiful and profound as our world can be, from within this house emerge the groans of fear, unrecognized loss, and suffering. Dignity, as the blessing of God the Spirit, provides a pneumatological concept with connections to social movements within and beyond the Christian churches that struggle for justice in our shared household. Through the blessing of the Spirit, persons experience the retrieval of their humanity and intrinsic value as part of God's creation, and are sustained in their struggle for the mutual recognition of their dignity. The struggle entails hopeful conflict and transformation toward the We of a shared humanity without neutralizing differences, but respecting and encouraging the many gifts of all God's people...In the past lies a brokenhearted, patriarchal model of family life—an economy of domination—that advances the will of the One while subordinating and twisting the wills of others in conformity to the One. In the brave future lies the model of mutual recognition based on values of shared authority, equal regard, proper trust, and diversity-in-dignity...God the Spirit's multifaceted, emergent struggle for liberated life brings new energy for our interdependent projects of social transformation.[70]

CHAPTER SIX

Harley Street and the Crimea: 1853–1856

Lord Raglan...asked me "if my father liked me coming out to the East."
I said with pride that my father is not as other men are. He thinks that daughters
should serve their country as well as sons. He brought me up to think so;
he has no sons, and therefore he has sacrificed me to my country,
and told me to come home with my shield or upon it. He thinks God sent women,
as well as men, into the world to be something more than "happy," "attentive,"
and "amusing." "Happy and dull," religion is said to make us—"happy and
amusing" social life is supposed to make us—but my father's religious and social
ethics make us strive to be the pioneers of the human race, and let "happiness"
and "amusement" take care of themselves.[1]

Florence's glorious moment finally arrived in early 1853 when she accepted an offer to become the unpaid superintendent of the Anglican Institution for the Care of Sick Gentlewomen in Distressed Circumstances, supervising both its move to upper Harley Street and its total reorganization. She was not a nursing superintendent, but the C.E.O. of the institution. As she explained to Mary Clarke (Clarkey):

> I am to have the choosing of the house, the appointment of the Chaplain, and the management of the Friends, as the Committee

121

are at present minded. But Isaiah himself could not prophesy how they will be minded at eight o'clock this evening.[2]

"Distressed Gentlewomen" were mostly governesses who had outlived their usefulness in a family and were abandoned in old age. While Harley Street is forgotten now in the shadow of the Crimea, it was, for Florence, her longed-for release from the family to her vocation. While she had her father's moral and financial blessing, Fanny again withheld hers on such an "impossible undertaking." Florence reminded herself in private of Jesus' words, "He that loveth father or mother more than me is not worthy of me" (Matthew 10:37, KJV).[3] Her new allegiance was now to God's family, with a calling she had nurtured through sixteen years of constant note-taking, reading government blue books, visiting institutions for the poor, and dreaming of an order for women. At last, all would be put to use in reorganizing this institution of twenty-seven beds, and she was ready. The Crimea might have "made" Florence, but she was established in her course long before that. Harley Street and the Crimea were the *outcome* of what had been decided between her and God long before.

Harley Street was also not when Florence became a *nurse,* but rather, her first full-time assignment in her call to serve the poor. She was an institutional manager responsible for tasks as diverse as creating a facility efficient in design and operation, staffing, providing patient care, hanging curtains, supervising builders, rerouting plumbing, reorganizing the kitchen, and streamlining the delivery and payment of goods—not unlike Lea Hurst on a crowded weekend! She accompanied doctors and chaplains to patients, instigated many schemes to care for the whole patient, and was answerable to a committee as well as visiting doctors. Within weeks, she faced the first of sectarian battles that would plague her work for years. The committee refused to admit Catholic patients or allow clergy of other faiths to visit, but, under her threat of resignation, committee members finally agreed to Florence's demands that all faiths be admitted and all clergy allowed to visit. Florence assured them:

> I will receive (in any case whatsoever that is not of the Church of England) the obnoxious animal at the door, take him upstairs myself, remain while he is conferring with his patient, make myself responsible that he does not speak to, or look at, any one else, and bring him downstairs again in a noose, and out onto the street...from Committees, charities, and Schism—from the Church of England, and all other deadly sin—from Philanthropy, and all the deceits of the Devil, Good Lord, deliver us.[4]

Despite such frustrations, her religious calling was the clearest it had ever been. At the end of the year, she wrote, "I have never repented or looked back, not for one moment. And I begin the New Year with more true feeling of a Happy New Year than ever I had in my life."[5]

Florence did, however, see no possibility at Harley Street of developing her idea to train women into a profession, her primary aim in hospital work. In discussion with Sir Sidney Herbert, who was also passionate about hospital and nursing reform, both were convinced that a new type of well-trained, reliable hospital nurse was needed. Florence confided her dream of a training school to Dr. Bowman, a surgeon who had patients at both her institution and King's College Hospital. In August 1854, after advising her committee that she would seek another opportunity to fulfill her goals, Florence began negotiating with King's College Hospital to be their superintendent of nursing. She hoped to enroll farmers' daughters into a training program based on Kaiserswerth. The same month, however, London's worst cholera epidemic broke out close to Harley Street, and Florence went to help at Middlesex Hospital. Many of the sick were prostitutes, and Florence recounted one experience of holding a young girl in her arms as she was dying. The girl whispered to her, "Pray God that you will never be in the despair I am in at this time," to which Florence, realizing the girl feared meeting a God who condemned and rejected her, replied, "Oh my girl, are you not now more merciful than the God you *think* you are going to? Yet the real God is far more merciful than any human creature ever was, or ever can imagine."[6]

After the epidemic, Florence took two weeks' rest at Lea Hurst, where the popular author Elizabeth Gaskell was staying.[7] Gaskell was impressed with Florence, comparing her determination to follow her call against family opposition with St. Elizabeth of Hungary:

> She must be a creature of another race, so high and mighty, and angelic, doing things by impulse or some divine inspiration—not by effort and struggle of will. But she seems almost too holy to be talked about as a mere wonder…She seems so completely led by God as Joan of Arc…It makes me feel the livingness of God more than ever to think how straight He is sending His Spirit down into her as into the prophets and saints of all.[8]

Empathetic Aunt Mai also wrote to her at this time of change with a premonition about Florence's future. Even as British troops were gearing up for the Crimea, Aunt Mai said, "If you will but be ready for *it*, something is getting ready for you, and you will be sure to turn up in time."[9]

The rest is history. As Florence considered her move from Harley Street, the *Times* newspaper called for English nurses to match the French Sisters of Charity in the Crimea.

> Are there no devoted women amongst us, able and willing to go forth to minister to the sick and suffering soldiers of the East in the hospitals of Scutari?...France has sent forth her Sisters of Mercy unsparingly, and they are even now by the bedsides of the wounded and the dying, giving what women's hand alone can give of comfort and relief in such awful scenes of suffering...Must we fall below the French in self-sacrifice and devotedness, in a work which Christ so signally blesses as done unto Himself?—"I was sick and ye visited Me"?[10]

There was no hesitation as Christ's words spoke directly to Florence. Urged by friends to lead a private party of women, Florence contacted a Kaiserswerth establishment in Constantinople, planning to take some Harley Street nurses with her. She wrote to Liz Herbert, asking leave of the Harley Street committee of which Liz was a member, and also to gauge Sir Sidney's opinion, as Secretary at War, on the matter. Her letter crossed with one from Sir Sidney, asking her to go as the official Superintendent of the Female Nursing Establishment in the English General Military Hospitals in Turkey. Five days after meeting with Sir Sidney, Florence was on her way with thirty-eight assorted nurses.

Florence and the Crimean War have been well described over the decades—this will *not* be another book on that. My focus is on Florence's vocation and theology. Those traveling with her to the war wrote of her quiet calm and determination. Within weeks of arrival, she wrote home:

> In the midst of this appalling Horror (we are steeped up to our necks in blood) there is good, and I can truly say, like St. Peter, "It is good for us to be here"—though I doubt whether if St. Peter had been here, he would have said so.[11]

Like much that Florence did in her life, this was a first. The British Army never sent female nurses to battlefield hospitals, providing doctors and male orderlies for the wounded and sick. The appeal, therefore, was not for *medically* trained people, but for a group of women who, like the Sisters of Charity, would do whatever was needed for the soldiers—cooking, washing, cleaning, and comforting under directions from the medical and military staff. Sir Sidney, who shared Florence's interest in developing training for such women, chose Florence for this experiment to demonstrate the usefulness of well-trained hospital nurses, asking her to "superintend the whole thing," with plenary authority over all the nurses and full assistance and cooperation from the medical staff. Florence would have unlimited access to the government for whatever she wanted for the mission's success. Sir Sidney wrote to her:

> I think upon your decision will depend the ultimate success or failure of the plan. Your own personal qualities, your knowledge and your power of administration, and among greater things your rank and position in society give you advantages in such a work which no other person possesses. If this succeeds, an enormous amount of good will be done now, and to persons deserving everything at our hands; and a prejudice will have been broken through, and a precedence established, which will multiply the good to all times.[12]

In the early days at Crimea, Florence did only what was asked of her by medical and army staff, sensing their resistance to the group of women foisted on them. However, when everything at the Scutari Hospital became paralyzed under huge numbers of wounded and there were no supplies, most of her colleagues were happy for whatever help they could get. Florence assigned her women to various areas and used her own funds when army supplies were tied up. She refitted wounded soldiers coming in without packs, reformed the kitchen and cooking, reorganized the wards, restored a derelict barrack, organized teachers for the recuperating illiterate soldiers, established games and coffee rooms, and initiated a medical school on site to train doctors in surgery and pathology and to gather statistics for research. This was hardly meddling, as some biographers suggest. Florence was an *expert* on hospital organization. Few of her colleagues had visited and studied as many as she had, read as many hospital reports, or reorganized a place like Harley Street. While some resented her influence with Sir Sidney, her letters to him were not to sabotage others or establish her power, but to inform him of their successes and problems, and suggest improvements, in line with their mutual interest in hospital reform.[13] Florence said of herself in the Crimea:

> My strength here lay in coming to Hospitals miserably disorganized or rather unorganized, & in organizing them. Had I come to an Institution cut & dry—what would I have done to alter it?[14]

Florence encountered constant resistance, however, from Chief Medical Officer Sir John Hall, who had a long and distinguished career behind him. Their clash, according to Florence, was a difference of approach:

> Dr. Hall is indefatigable in detailed work, & wants only a governing system to work under. But he is wholly incapable of originating one. And we have no system for General Hospitals, in time of war.[15]

Hall could have pulled rank on anyone else, but he knew of Florence's political connections and her immunity to career censure, as she explained:

> The real grievance against us is that we are independent of promotion & therefore of the displeasure of our chiefs—that we have no prospects to injure—& that, although subordinate to these Medical Chiefs in office, we were superior to them in influence & in the chance of being heard at home. It is an anomalous position. But so is War, to us English, anomalous.[16]

While Crimea created Florence the nurse, nursing was her least important function there. Central to her focus was the common soldier, whom she had been sent to serve—officers had their own medical attention and comforts. She did not glory in war, but hated it for what it did to ordinary people. As the Franco-Prussian War began in 1870, she bemoaned, "After the fighting come the miseries of the poor people, and a victory is only less dreadful than a defeat."[17] Her famous lamp-lit night rounds were *not* medical calls—the doctors and orderlies did that—but concern for her "children," as she called them. Florence described her duties:

> do the needful for the sick, give them all the Extras (& cook them), all the medicines, & the wine and brandy—& see to the cleanliness of the Patients. These four things, the Extras, medicine, stimulants & cleanliness were the chief points.[18]

Soldiers wrote home, not of Florence's nursing skills, but of her nightly assurance and long vigils with those in need. They adored her for her dedication to their welfare and her acceptance of them as human beings. Florence's theology rejected the prevailing opinion that the common soldier was irredeemable, showing that with coffeehouses, libraries, education, and an opportunity to save their money, soldiers responded. Florence said:

> I have never been able to join in the popular cry about the recklessness, sensuality, and helplessness of the soldiers. Give them suffering and they will bear it…Give them work and they will do it. I would rather have to do with the army than with any other class I have ever attempted to serve.[19]

Of the many songs that helped spread her fame in England, the following one shows her theology:

> Her heart it meant good, for no bounty she'll take
> She'd lay down her life for the poor soldier's sake.
> She prays for the dying, she gives peace to the brave
> She feels that the soldier has a soul to be saved.[20]

Florence's concern for the soldier as a person with dignity inspired England's working class in general. Novelist Elizabeth Gaskell, who wrote about life in the factories and mills of Manchester, wrote to Parthe:

> Babies *ad libitum* are being christened Florence here; poor little factory babies, whose grimed stunted parents brighten up at the name, although you'd think their lives and thoughts were bound up in fluffy mills. But it's the old story "for we have all of us one human heart," and these poor unromantic fellows are made, somehow, of the same stuff as *her* heroes in the East, who turned their faces to the wall and cried at her illness.[21]

The soldiers and the working class judged rightly that Florence was a woman working out God's purposes as a "handmaid of the Lord"— her preferred phrase. Praise was not the reason for her mission nor did she ask to be spared the work's horrors. She had dreamed of this vocation in the stifling comforts of her home for so long:

> Praise, Good God! He knows what a situation He had put upon me. For His sake I bear it willingly, but not for the sake of Praise. The cup which my Father hath given me shall I not drink? But how few can sympathize with such a position![22]

Her friends at Kaiserswerth understood, regarding her as one of their family of deaconesses sent out into the world. Florence wrote to Mrs. Fliedner:

> The whole army is coming into the hospitals. The task will be gigantic. Alas, how will it end? We are in the hands of God. Pray for us. We have at the moment five thousand sick and wounded. My only comfort is, God sees it, God knows it, God loves us. Remember me to my Sisters.[23]

But what of her own family? When Sir Sidney first approached Florence to go to the Crimea, he asked whether her parents would consent, suggesting that the public honor Florence would receive from her official rank might persuade them. He knew them well. Ironically, after their resistance to every other project, Fanny and Parthe took personal pride in and credit for Florence's fame. Despite the previous hysterics that had trapped Florence for years, Parthe wrote to her cousin:

> It is a great and noble work. One cannot but believe she was intended for it. None of her previous life has been wasted, her experience all tells, all the gathered stores of so many years, her Kaiserswerth, her sympathy with the Roman Catholic system of work, her travels, her search into the hospital question, her knowledge of so many different minds and classes.[24]

Fanny, having refused her blessing on less sordid endeavors, wrote to Florence in Scutari after the triumphant London launching of the Nightingale Fund:

> I cannot go to bed without telling you that your meeting has been a glorious one. I believe that you will be more indifferent than any of us to fame, but be glad that we feel that this is a proud day for us.[25]

Florence replied with the agony of a daughter, loved by so many others, yet grasping at the crumbs of affirmation from her mother's table:

> If my name and my having done what I could for God and mankind has given you pleasure, that is real pleasure to me. My reputation has not been a boon to me in my work; but if you have been pleased, that is enough. I shall love my name now, and I shall feel that it is the greatest return that you can find satisfaction in hearing your child named, and in feeling that her work draws sympathies together some return for what you have done for me. Life is sweet after all.[26]

Despite the daily horrors, Florence wrote after six months:

> I am in sympathy with God, fulfilling the promise I came into the world for. What the disappointments of the conclusion of these six months are no one can tell. But I am not dead, but alive.[27]

Sectarian infighting, steering "between the Protestant howl and the Roman Catholic storm," was exported with the army from England and caused Florence endless pain and frustration.[28] The Church of England's power and privilege had been challenged by many in the first quarter of the nineteenth century. Within its ranks, many frustrated by its elitist complacency and vague theology were swept up in the evangelical awakening of clergyman John Wesley, who abandoned the Calvinist doctrine of election in favor of Arminius' teaching that Christ died to save *everyone*, poor and rich, inside and outside the Church, not just a preordained few.[29] The movement emphasized inward experience, an awareness of sin, a personal commitment to Jesus Christ, the scriptures, active membership, social responsibility, and religious "enthusiasm." Wesley and his followers crossed England on horseback spreading this inclusive message, preaching in fields when there was no church. His practical message to common people included moral admonitions, rules of hygiene, and basic literacy, communicated through simple commentaries on the Bible, politics, medicine, and general civility. Wesley established small covenant groups everywhere to strengthen people's faith and give the working class, ignored by the Church, a religious home. Wesley never separated from the Church of England, encouraging his followers to attend the parish church. He saw his message as a fresh wind blowing through its arid halls. After his death, some followers stayed within the Church of England and some left to become Wesleyans or Methodists. Splinter groups formed within Methodism, but the 1851 census listed two million people attending Methodist chapels. Those remaining within Anglicanism became known as Evangelicals (Low Church), advocating a heart-rather-than-head religion, a literal approach to the Bible, personal salvation, holy living, and a focus on eternity. This theology sent them into the world to transform it, as well as save souls.

Nonconformists (or Dissenters), anyone not Anglican or Roman Catholic, came in different shapes and sizes—Unitarians, Methodists, Evangelicals, Calvinists, Quakers. Initially powerless, they accepted their limitations or left, as did the Pilgrim Fathers. After the Industrial Revolution, many became wealthy merchants and landowners, determined to follow their religious beliefs without interference from the Church. Needless to say, the Church did not want to surrender its ecclesiastical or fiscal power, especially its bishops in the House of Lords. While the Church considered Roman Catholics disloyal to England because of their allegiance to Rome, Nonconformists were seen as disloyal to the King because they challenged his headship of the Church. In Florence's day, Nonconformists had at least five major grievances:

1. Except for Quakers and Jews, legal marriages could only take place in an Anglican Church.
2. Births were *officially* registered only in these parish churches.
3. Outside big cities, the parish church owned the cemeteries, and burial included a Church of England service.
4. Every citizen of any means had to pay taxes to the parish church.
5. The *Thirty-Nine Articles* had to be signed for a degree from Oxford, Cambridge, or Durham.[30]

In 1811 a proposal surfaced in the House of Lords that magistrates regulate who could preach in England's churches and chapels. Nonconformists of *all* breeds came together to fight this, and in 1828 the Test and Corporation Acts were repealed, removing Nonconformist worship restrictions and allowing them to hold public office. The Catholic Emancipation Act opened Parliament to Catholics in 1829 (but not to Jews until 1858). In 1831, the House of Lords bishops rejected a reform bill extending the franchise and defining more equitable electoral distribution, reducing the Church's power in some areas. The government was ousted, and the incoming Whig government passed the bill in 1832, giving the vote to one fifth of adult males (but no women), and agreeing to restructured electoral boundaries. In 1836 University College, London, was opened to Nonconformists, breaking the Anglican Oxford-Cambridge monopoly on education. Nonconformists (men only) were admitted to Oxford in 1854 and to Cambridge in 1856, changing each, according to Benjamin Jowett, from a "sham monastery" and breeding ground for Anglican clergy and politicians into a center of nondenominational education.[31] Change moved slowly and, when only one Nonconformist was in Parliament by 1837, many joined a new Liberal Party of Whigs and Radicals with middle-class leadership.

The Church had been a reluctant reformer in all this, and sectarian feeling still ran high, whether against popery or enthusiasm. On the other side of the fence, Catholics, Unitarians, and Calvinists defended their positions with equal zeal against re-encroachment by the Church. Having experienced her Anglican committee's reticence to admit non-Anglican patients to Harley Street, Florence had taken great care to include all religious flavors in the women she took to the Crimea. She did not need her mission sabotaged by sectarian accusations, and she also wanted to respect the soldiers' religious diversity—one third were Irish. Her nurses comprised eight Anglican Sellonite sisters, six nurses from the Anglican St. John's House, five Roman Catholic nuns from Bermondsey under Mother Mary Clare Moore; five Catholic nuns from Norwood, and fourteen assorted nurses from London hospitals, all answerable to Florence ahead of mother superiors. Other Protestant groups refused to send nurses unless they could answer to their denominational home committees.

In such a sectarian climate, Florence's "religious" suitability also came under the microscope. Her denominational allegiance was hard to categorize at a time when this information was vitally important. Born with Unitarian roots, raised a dissatisfied Anglican, educated and influenced by a classical scholar father, and flirting with Catholicism, she *was* difficult to "box." Some accused her of "popish" tendencies while others labeled her Unitarian because of her laxity in checking the religious convictions of those who worked with her. An Irish priest in the Crimea reportedly said, "Miss Nightingale belongs to a sect that is unfortunately very rare in these days, the sect of the Good Samaritan."[32] At the height of a controversy with one of the Mother Superiors, Florence wrote:

> I am so glad that my God is not the God of the High Church or of the Low—that He is not a Romanist or an Anglican—or an Unitarian. I don't believe He is even a Russian—tho' His events go strangely against us. A Greek once said to me in Salamis, "I do believe God Almighty is an Englishman."[33]

Florence had few problems with the original sisters who went with her, as they had been carefully instructed to obey Florence, to care for any soldier regardless of religious affiliation and to do no proselytizing, even to patients of their own faith—that was the job of chaplains. Rev. Mother Mary Clare Moore, mother superior of the Bermondsey sisters and Florence's lifelong friend and spiritual mentor, graciously acceded to this and helped build bridges with other Catholic workers in the Crimea.[34] The Vatican, however, and the newly converted Henry Manning, wanted more Catholic sisters for the Irish soldiers and were not pleased with the restrictions. Sir Sidney was therefore pressured to send off a second group of mostly Irish Sisters of Mercy under a "neutral" leader, Florence's Anglican friend Mary Stanley, who, it turned out, was in the process of converting to Rome. Through a series of misunderstandings, accidental and deliberate, their mother superior, Rev. Mother Bridgeman, believed her nuns would live in a separate community, wear habits instead of nursing uniforms, have their own chaplain, and do religious duties as well as nursing.[35]

The arrival of the Kinsale nuns, as they were called, was a disaster. They were not expected, and there was no room for them at Scutari Hospital. When they would not divide up, Florence was accused of being "like Herod sending the Blessed Virgin across the desert."[36] Furious with Sir Sidney, who had promised not to send more nurses without her permission, Florence would not accept them and resigned. After much negotiation, she was forced to renege, sending some of her original nurses to other hospitals or home to England to accommodate this new group. Mother Bridgeman refused to assign any of her sisters to Mother Mary Clare of the same order, even though the Kinsale sisters had been gathered from different convents across Ireland. When a special chaplain arrived for the Kinsale sisters against government orders and tried to assume duties for the Bermondsey sisters as well, Mother Mary Clare refused, creating a breach between her and Mother Bridgeman. Mary Stanley and Mother Bridgeman, encouraged by those military officers hostile to Florence, became Florence's opposition for the rest of her time in Crimea. The Kinsale sisters eventually went to Koulali hospital, then to Balaclava on the battlefront, but they continued their opposition, as one sister's poem indicates:

> This bird of note so passing sweet —
> In this eastern land, how strange to say —
> To all but nestlers at her feet
> Has almost proved a bird of prey.[37]

Complex reasons fueled this standoff. Unfortunately, the Kinsale sisters had somehow been assigned to the medical officer at Scutari rather than to Florence, weakening her ability to organize a large group of women as one in a difficult situation. Florence and Mother Bridgeman were both strong characters—Manning described Mother Bridgeman as "an ardent, high-tempered, and, at first, somewhat difficult person—but truly good, devoted and trustworthy."[38] The Kinsale sisters saw their independence from the rest of the nurses as a Catholic triumph at a time when their church had recently been recognized officially in England, and they wanted to prove themselves, as Irish Catholics, patriotic members of the British Empire:

> They were going to the war as nurses in the service of the Queen of England; that, in itself, was something. But as Sisters of Mercy they were long since enlisted in the service of the Queen of Heaven, and that, indeed, was everything. This distinction, and the religious dress they wore, marked them off from all the other nurses in the Crimea. Their independence of Miss Nightingale in all matters not pertaining to hospital regulations was another point of discrimination peculiar to them alone.[39]

The tragedy was that the Kinsale sisters could not see in Florence a woman *also* enlisted in God's service, with her *own* call and undying commitment to those she served. While she did not have a habit or an order, she was marching as surely as they were to the divine drumbeat. Her passion for the health and spiritual welfare of the soldiers in *this* life was as strong and focused as their passion for the soldiers' souls in death.

Florence's stance stemmed from her wide experience of Catholic orders and their primary focus on souls rather than bodies. In any other situation, this might not have been such a problem, but when soldiers were dying even as they were being carried into the hospital, their urgent medical needs might be sidestepped in favor of their souls. Florence set rules against proselytizing from the beginning, and to be able to enforce this when necessary, she had insisted on her authority over any mother superiors. Mother Mary Clare had no problem with this, but Mother Bridgeman had spent her life working with the poor and sick and was not about to answer to an upper-class English, nonreligious woman who, in Bridgeman's eyes, had little hands-on experience and was demanding that she surrender her religious responsibilities. Florence's concern was proved right when Kinsale sisters were finally allowed on the wards in a cholera epidemic (Florence had previously assigned them to work in the kitchens and away from patient care). Their biographer notes that this gave them their opportunity for the "higher functions of religious nursing"—to speak words "which brought back recollections of saving truths perhaps long since forgotten," and ensure

> that no Catholic was allowed pass through the valley of the shadow without receiving the consolation of the Last Sacrament and the benefit of every comfort provided by Mother Church for the journey to eternity.[40]

Administering the Sacrament was the priest's task, and sisters diligently searched for him for confession before tending the physical needs of a dying patient. The Kinsale biographer reports that the sting was now gone from death and "a holy and calm resignation" reigned, "quite at variance with the vaguely-hopeful longings of the less fortunate non-Catholic patients" accustomed to a "more attenuated form of Christianity, and neglected in great measure by their own ministers."[41] The journals of the Kinsale sisters record their "help" to non-Catholics as well, despite the rules:

> If we knelt to whisper a prayer or instruction to a poor Catholic the almost breathless silence in the ward (where the majority were always Protestants) was quite thrilling. This was the more remarkable as the same respect was seldom shown to the officiating Protestant clergyman. Under such circumstances, the instruction on religious subjects given to the Catholics reached all in the vicinity of the one being spoken to, and on many occasions wrought miracles of grace.[42]

No one could say that Florence was anti-Catholic, anti–Catholic orders, or anti-Irish. She had sought out many Catholic orders over her years of preparation. Of Mother Mary Clare Moore, both Catholic and Irish, she wrote after the war:

> You were far above me in fitness for the General Superintendency, both in worldly talent of administration, and far more in the spiritual qualifications which God values in a Superior.[43]

And of the Catholic Bermondsey sisters:

> It is impossible to estimate too highly the unwearied devotion, patience & cheerfulness, the judgment and activity, & the single-heartedness with which these sisters (who are from Bermondsey) have laboured in the Service of the Sick.[44]

Florence *did* see a problem, however, with the *Irishness* of the Kinsale sisters, not as a racial defect as did Sir Sidney, who said, perhaps excusing his mistake in sending them, "You cannot make their lax minds understand the weight of an obligation," but from a political stance, as Florence explained:

> It is the old story. Ever since the days of Queen Elizabeth, the chafing against secular supremacy, especially English, on the part of the R. Catholic Irish. I am very sorry for it. For I think it is fraught with mischief. For these Irish nuns are dead against us—I mean England—the way their priests talk is odious. The proportion of R. Catholics & of Irish has increased inconceivably in the army since the late Recruits. Had we more nuns, it would be very desirable, to diminish disaffection. But *just not* the Irish ones. The wisest thing the W[ar] Office could now do would be to send out a few more Bermondsey Nuns…to join those already at Scutari & counterbalance the influence of the *Irish* nuns, who hate their soberer sisters with the mortal hatred which, I believe, only Nuns & Household Servants *can* feel towards each other.[45]

Florence also did not hold with Henry Manning's adoration of religious sisters regardless of their performance. Manning's analysis of the "problem" blamed Florence's ignorance of Catholicism:

> I doubt if Florence Nightingale, and certainly not the Herberts, knows how sensitive the Catholic Church is—from the Holy Father to the wounded Catholic soldier—as to the respect due, not to the person so much as to the character of a Religious.[46]

Florence believed that *all* nurses, sisters, seculars, or ladies were to be judged and respected on what they did for the good of the soldier. When tensions reached a new high over Florence's authority over the Balaclava Hospital, and Sir Sidney asked Florence to compromise, she responded to *his* letter "from Belgrave Square," an elite London address: "I wrote from a Crimean hut. The point of sight is different."[47] She told Sir Sidney that her resistance was *not* a popish plot, but a split among the Catholics themselves:

> The seculars are divided against the regulars. This we have often seen before but never so much now…in order to be "in" both ways, so the R. Catholics have one set of priests & nuns *with* the Gov't & one *against* it. Mrs. Bridgeman & her 11 Irish nuns are against, the secular priests & Bermondsey nuns for…The Rev'd Mr. Duffy, Jesuit, has been instructed to refuse confession & therefore Holy Communion to, or even to visit those Bermondsey Nuns…& he calls them, among other epithets in a note to themselves, a "disgrace to their Church"…On the other hand, the secular priests repudiate the Irish Nuns…even Father Cuffe, who used to call me "Herod," now licks my hand.[48]

Florence's concern about the proselytizing was not only a respect for the rights of dying soldiers who might not wish to be pressured back into the "true" church at that moment but also involved the *theological* assumption that a dying soldier's most pressing need was absolution. Common soldiers were thought low on the righteousness scale, and a sister's primary duty was to find a priest, thus denying the patient the "real love of God & mankind" at that moment. Florence was also concerned with Catholic theology's "incapacitation" to do the best good for a patient, consoling the suffering produced by an evil rather than removing the causes of the evil. She cites a sister who refused to join her in protest against the canteen's serving alcohol to patients— "I never could persuade her that it was any use to take Preventive Measures against drunkenness or anything else."[49] This theology was not only Catholic but also fairly universal in England at that time. Since God was assumed to be in control of everything, one simply smoothed the pillow and allowed the inevitable to happen. Florence's theology was the opposite. Life was not about accepting one's pathetic lot on Earth and ensuring a place in heaven by constant absolution from sin. It was about discovering the laws of God in the universe in order to *change* the world and bring about God's reign on *Earth*.

Mother Bridgeman's opposition took its toll on Florence. Even when Florence was granted General Orders over all hospitals in the Crimea because of Colonel Lefoy's fear that army nursing might be taken over by Catholic orders, Mother Bridgeman continued to resist, assuming Florence's attacks would be seen as anti–Irish Catholic, something the English government would not touch. Some argued that Florence should have wielded her General Orders more graciously, but, as she repeatedly reminded Sir Sidney, the stress and horror of the Crimea and the official ambivalence over women nurses demanded a discipline and control that did not always allow for "graciousness." In the end, only one thing was important to her—that she had served well the noble common soldiers who had fought a horrendous war, folded their mantles about their faces, "and died in silence without complaining." Florence wrote:

> As for myself, I have done my duty. I have identified my fate with those of the heroic dead, & whatever lies these sordid exploiteurs of human misery spread about us these officials, there is a right & a God to fight for & our fight has been worth fighting. I do not despair—nor complain. It has been a great cause.[50]

The sectarian battles did not end as the Crimean shores grew dim on the horizon. Given the public focus on Florence after the war (not of her own doing or wishing), a few books emerged describing the work of other women in the Crimea, often laying blame on Florence, directly or indirectly, for monopolizing the glory. In *The Sisters of Mercy in the Crimean War*, written from Mother Bridgeman's journals by another Sister of Mercy, Evelyn Bolster, Florence is painted as racist, unjust, and threatened by a superior woman with a long experience of serving the "poor, sick and ignorant" as a Religious. Evelyn Bolster claimed that Florence's ideas on health and nursing were learned from Mother Bridgeman and other sisters whose institutions she visited, and, while the Nightingale School may have created a nursing model for English *civil* hospitals "where nurses were till then recruited from the flotsam and jetsam of the Sairy Gamp (character) category," she was not the first:

> Side by side with, and antecedent to, the Nightingale Reform, stood the Catholic Church with her eternal message of faith and hope and healing; and within the framework of this universal Church the Sisters of Mercy, while their Congregation was still in its infancy, attained proficiency as nurses.[51]

The author also argues that Florence was an *administrator* at Scutari, not doing actual nursing, an assessment Florence would no doubt support, and says that Florence "drew back" from her desires to become a nun, hinting at a lack of true commitment. This idea is repeated when the author describes Mary Stanley's conversation:

> [Manning] had led her as he had previously led Florence Nightingale, to the door of the Church, and now she [Mary] passed over the threshold to find at last that peace of soul which she sought

and to add another illustrious Victorian name to the list of nineteenth-century converts from Anglicanism.[52]

In rightly bringing to public attention the great work in the Crimea of the Sisters of Mercy, it is sad that Evelyn Bolster chose to do it by condemning Florence for plagiarism and lust for power. Florence rejected many opportunities to promote her fame after the war, and at no point hid her indebtedness to various Catholic sisters. When Manning secured her a visit to those in Paris, she wrote:

> For what training is there compared with that of a Catholic Nun? Those ladies who are not Sisters have not the chastened temper, the Christian grace, the accomplished loveliness and energy of a regular nun. I have seen something of different kinds of nuns, and am no longer young, and do not speak from enthusiasm but experience.[53]

Evelyn Bolster's promotion of the Sisters of Mercy at the expense of Florence fails through its unrealistic attack on everything Florence achieved. Dismissing Mother Mary Clare, also a Sister of Mercy, as a "tool" manipulated by Florence is ludicrous given Mother Mary Clare's strength of character and leadership both in the Crimea and beyond and her continued friendship and correspondence with Florence until her death. Mother Mary Clare realized what Mother Bridgeman and Evelyn Bolster never saw—that despite Florence's lack of an order, her calling was the same. Florence wrote to Mother Mary Clare after the war:

> I never can express what I feel of all you have been to me & to the work in which we were both engaged…I always felt with you that you understood without my telling you…a great many of my trials which none of my other ladies did & which I never told to you or any one. And I cannot tell you what a support your silent sympathy & trust became altho' I never acknowledged them.[54]

Bolster claimed that the only difference between Florence's ideas and what the Sisters of Mercy were already doing was the absence of vows, which meant the ability to leave one's work at any time. Yet this is a major difference, a substantial innovation. Catholic sisters received training in their orders, but there was no training for nurses at secular hospitals, no general oversight, no reporting to a board. Individual, poor women simply lived on wards as caretakers, cleaners, cooks, and general helpers without supervision. Some Anglican sisterhoods had emerged since the Oxford Movement, but Florence was not tempted to put her efforts and ideas into them, given her distaste for the Church of England at the time:

> The Church of England has for men bishoprics, archbishoprics, and a little work…For women she has—what?…I would have given my head, my heart, my hand. She would not have them. She did not know what to do with them. She told me to go back and do crochet in my mother's drawing room; or, if I were tired of that, to marry and look well at the head of my husband's table…She gave me neither work to do for her, nor education for it.[55]

Florence's litmus test for religion was that faith resulted in action, and Catholicism allowed that to happen in its orders. This opportunity came, however, with dogmas to be believed and a vow of obedience, something Florence thought unnecessary for the pursuit of God's call to service. She had discussed with Sir Sidney the need for well-trained nurses in army hospitals and at home, and went to the Crimea harboring a plan not possible at Harley Street—to train a secular order of women for hospitals and the care of the sick poor, by combining the best of what she had learned at Catholic and Protestant institutions with the absence of permanent vows of obedience. Her experience in the Crimea, so nearly destroyed by sectarian squabbling, convinced her of two things—the need for a profession of intelligent, well-trained nurses, and the need for that profession to be separate from religious proselytizing and control under *any* creed. Florence was not rejecting a religious motivation for service—that was central to her understanding. She said of the St. John's House Anglican sisterhood:

> St. John's House possesses great advantages…Not because it includes a Sisterhood, a system in which I for one humbly but entirely disbelieve, but because the laborious, servile, anxious, trying drudgery of real hospital work requires like every duty, if it is to be done right, the fear and the love of God.[56]

In her report on female nursing in military hospitals to the Secretary of State for War in 1858, Florence outlined her ideas of a nursing profession for the army:

> This I propose doing not by founding a Religious Order but by training, systematizing and morally improving as far as it may be permitted, that section of the large class of women supporting themselves by labour who take to hospital nursing as a livelihood, by inducing, in the long run, some such women to contemplate usefulness and the service of God in the relief of man…and by

incorporating with both these classes a certain proportion of gentlewomen who may think it fit to adopt this occupation. The main object I conceive to be, to improve hospitals, by improving hospital nursing, or by contributing towards the improvement of the class of hospital nurses whether nurses or head nurses.[57]

It is hard to imagine today the innovative nature of Florence's plan. There was *no* structure in secular hospitals for the women who worked there, not even an overarching administration of the women workers. Such nursing had earned a bad press through Charles Dickens's caricatures, but a physician's letter to the *Times* of April 15, 1857, was more charitable:

> Hospital nurses have for the last year or two been the victims of much unmerited abuse. They have their faults, but most of these may be laid to the want of proper treatment. Lectured by committees, preached at by chaplains, scowled on by treasurers and stewards, scolded by matrons, sworn at by surgeons, bullied by dressers, grumbled at and abused by patients; insulted if old and ill-favoured; talked flippantly to, if middle-aged and good-humored; tempted and seduced, if young and well-looking,—they are just what any woman might be, exposed to the same influences,—meek, pious, saucy, careless, drunken, or unchaste, according to circumstances or temperament; but most attentive, rarely unkind.[58]

Florence's idea was a structured profession coordinating this work and inspiring its workers in their efforts as in a religious order. In this secular order, poor working-class women would be paid while in training, then go on to work in hospitals. Gentlewomen who wished to train would pay their *own* way, avoiding the stigma of work for money, and the sick poor would have better care. All would be well trained and monitored, with gentlewomen having no special status over lower ranks, and head nurses emerging from the working class with no difference in status to upper-class leaders.

> I would rather than establish a religious order open a career highly paid. My principle has always been that we should give the best training we could to any woman of any class, of any sect, paid or unpaid, who has the requisite qualifications moral, intellectual and physical for the vocation of Nurse. Unquestionably the educated will be more likely to rise to the post of Superintendent, but *not* because they are ladies but because they are educated.[59]

Although she sounded harsh toward women at times, Florence insisted that women train conscientiously and always be *worthy* of their calling. She had spent her life fighting their cause, and became frustrated when women, given this hard-won opportunity, did not take it seriously, reinforcing all the stereotypes about women Florence had worked to dispel:

> I would say to all young ladies who are called to any particular vocation, qualify yourselves for it as a man does for his work. No one should attempt to teach the Greek language until he is master of the language: and this he can only become by hard study. If you are called to a man's work, do not exact a woman's privileges— the privilege of inaccuracy, of weakness, ye muddleheads. Submit yourselves to the rules of business as men do, by which alone you can make God's business succeed; for He has never said that He will give His success and His blessing to inefficiency, to sketchy and unfinished work.[60]

In Florence's secular order of nursing, there would be no religious test for admission, but all recruits would pray together twice a day, eat together, and collectively attend the established Church on Sundays. Most importantly, there would be no vows, since vows defeated the purpose. When asked her opinion about the Geneva Convention's requiring countries to *promise* to care for all those wounded in war, she likened it to vows, "People who keep a vow would do the same without a vow. And if people will not do it without a vow, they will not do it *with*."[61] When advising on nursing in Canada, Florence emphasized the *vocational* nature of nursing that did not need a vow to authenticate it. "By encouraging an obedience of intelligence, not the obedience of slavery," secular nurses made better nurses than those in religious orders that sought to prevent abuses by "enforcing blind, unconditional obedience through the fears and promises of a Church."[62]

> It is true we make "no vows." But is a "vow" necessary to convince us that the true spirit for learning any art, most especially an art of charity, aright, is not a disgust to everything or something else? Do we really place the love of our kind (and of nursing, as one branch of it) so low as this?[63]

All along, Florence struggled with a word to describe the vocation she envisaged, finally choosing *nursing* for want of a better one, but always concerned at its limited connotation of "little more than the administration of medicines and the application of poultices." Hers was a broader meaning:

It ought to signify the proper use of fresh air, light, warmth, cleanliness, quiet, and the proper selection and administration of diet—all at the least expense of vital power to the patient.[64]

She did not see nurses as doctors' assistants trained by doctors as in the European system, but as having an autonomous role, attending to *sanitary* practices not addressed by doctors at this stage prior to the germ theory—the distinction between sanitary and medical. Florence's opposition to women doctors reflects this distinction as well. With the existence of a profession for women by women in the ancient and honored female tradition of midwifery and health care, why would women prefer to be "third-rate men" in a low-profile male profession (Florence thought medicine as bad as it could be at the time, with few geniuses rising above it).

> I would earnestly ask my sisters to keep clear of both the jargons now current everywhere...of the jargon, namely, about the "rights" of women, which urges women to do all that men do, including the medical and other professions, merely because men do it, and without regard to whether this is the best that women can do: and of the jargon which urges women to do nothing that men do, merely because they are women, and should be "recalled to a sense of their duty as women," and because "this is women's work," and "that is men's"...Surely woman should bring the best she has, whatever that is, to the work of God's world, without attending to either of these cries...You do not want the effect of your good things to be, "How wonderful for a *woman*!" nor would you be deterred from good things by hearing it said, "Yes, but she ought not to have done this, because it is not suitable for a woman." But you want to do the thing that is good, whether it is "suitable for a woman" or not.[65]

In later years, as both medicine and nursing improved, Florence agreed that women should have both options, but be admitted on *equal* qualifications, leaving the public to decide their skills (Florence herself had a female doctor in her later years).

Doctors were, not surprisingly, wary of such an organization of intelligent women with their own code rather than women employed as their assistants. While religious sisters also had a code of obedience to superiors, they worked with doctors as women committed to *service*, not autonomy. In Florence's new order, a nurse obeyed the doctor on *medical* treatments but her head nurse on patient care and sanitation. When the germ theory was established around 1870, doctors *also* became interested in sanitation and asepsis, collaborating with nurses and changing the face of both professions. Nursing moved away from many of Florence's ideas, but her legacy remained in the changed image of secular care for the sick and those who did it, no longer simply women at home, women disappointed in love, or women incapable of anything else. "We are often told that a nurse needs only to be 'devoted and obedient.' This definition would do just as well for a porter. It might even do for a horse."[66] Her famous *Notes on Nursing*, published in 1859, gave dignity to the caring role of the women in the family responsible for the sick. Journalist Harriet Martineau called it a "work of genius" that will no doubt "create an Order of Nurses before it has finished its work."[67]

Although she had little to do with establishing the Nightingale School, Florence turned her attention to it in the 1870s, writing an annual address to be read to probationers both at St. Thomas's and in Edinburgh. Here, her ideas of nursing as a vocation of service to God and humanity come through strongly. In an 1873 address, she warned against trying to influence patients in matters of religion, saying that religion was expressed through one's life and actions:

> A real deep religious feeling and strong personal motherly interest for each one of our patients; a strong practical (intellectual if you will) interest in the *case*; the pleasures of administration, which though a fine word, means only learning to manage a ward well.[68]

In another address that year, she reminded the nurses that it was not what one believed or felt, but the work done for God that counted in the long run and that "anyone can make the short run."

> It is by the silent influence of a consistent Christ-like life that a Nurse in charge of Wards makes her Ward say: *Go and sin no more*...It takes long, long years of patient, steady persevering endeavour to bring any work to perfection. And when it is grown, still, O still must it be watered every day with constant care and with heaven's own dew.[69]

In an 1874 address, she quoted David Livingstone:

> People often make the mistake of thinking that the great, the heroic spirit, was an indifference to trifles; but Christ came to teach us that real greatness is in doing every detail and every thing we have to do so well as to make a perfect whole; doing it for God.[70]

Of the necessity of a "hidden life with Christ in God," and the religious nature of all we do in service, Florence mentioned Wilberforce's slave trade protest (her maternal grandfather was also involved) in an 1875 address as an example of the lonely path of those "whom God is forming for himself," and, in 1878, she reminded them of what had been and still was the motto of her life:

> Be heroic in your *every day's* work, your *every day's* resolutions, even if you don't work up to them quite, you can do better every day.[71]

CHAPTER SEVEN

Loving God and the World: 1856–1910

We can do no more for those who have suffered and died
in their country's service; they need our help no longer;
their spirits are with God who gave them. It remains for us
to strive that their sufferings may not have been endured in vain—
to endeavour so to learn from experience as to lessen such sufferings
in the future by forethought and wise management.[1]

Crimea gave Florence to the public; it gave Florence a new mission. In January 1855, at the height of the war, more soldiers were in Crimean hospitals than were on the battlefield. The peak mortality rate that month was 1,000 per 1,174 men, "a calamity unparalleled in the history of calamity."[2] Had the War Office been prepared, this tragedy was avoidable. When a motion was passed in Parliament to investigate the situation, the government fell, and Sir Sidney Herbert resigned as Secretary at War.[3] He remained a member of Parliament, even more resolved to fight for Army reform since his name was linked to the tragedy. Lord Palmerston became Prime Minister and appointed Lord Panmure to the newly named position of Secretary of State for War. When Lord Palmerston's investigatory Sanitary Commission reached Scutari in March of 1855, they found that the hospital was sitting on a cesspool. Once it was cleared, the hospital mortality rate fell from 42.7

deaths per thousand to two per thousand. Sir John McNeill and Colonel Tulloch were then sent to do a more general investigation.[4] From these visits, Florence gained two lifelong friends and supporters—Dr. Sutherland from the Sanitary Commission, and Sir John McNeill.[5] The damning McNeill-Tulloch report against Army mismanagement was smothered in Parliament for all sorts of political reasons, much to the dismay of Florence, who had hoped some changes would result from it. When a confidential report went to London from Scutari's chief purveyor, an opponent of Florence, charging her and her nurses with all sorts of things, Florence's determination to expose the complete shambles was set. While still in the Crimea, she addressed the charges against her step-by-step, warning her friend Colonel Lefroy of the fight she intended to make for a public inquiry into *all* aspects of organization and management of army hospitals and supporting services once she got back to London.[6] She would not complain "in feeble driblets" against individuals, but against the problematic *system*. Her post-Crimea call was taking shape: "Let me modify and alleviate by my presence the evils of that system, live thro' & know them by experience, & then a time may come when I may represent them as they are."[7]

Those who call Florence power hungry and ambitious and accuse her of wanting to build a post-war empire or public image by pursuing Army medical reform overlook her anonymous return from the Crimea, her endless reports submitted by others without her signature for which they received the credit, and the note in her much-read copy of *Imitation of Christ*. Thomas à Kempis wrote, "Put not off thy soul's welfare to the future, for men will forget thee sooner than thou thinkest," and Florence added in her own script, "I only wish to be forgotten."[8] As Michael Calabria says, "If she had been a man, would she have been called overzealous and ambitious?"[9] She was, instead, following God's call to the poor and disadvantaged, in this case her soldiers. She had developed an undying devotion to them and to their unrecognized bravery and saw them as victims needing a savior to ensure they would never again be subjected to such horror and neglect, either at war or at home. After the traumatic winter in the Crimea, she wrote to war officials in London:

> No one can feel for the Army as I do. These people who talk to us have all fed their children on the fat of the land and dressed them in velvet and silk while we have been away. I have had to see my children dressed in a dirty blanket and an old pair of regimental trousers, and to see them feed on raw salt meat, and nine thousand of my children are lying from causes, which might have been prevented, in their forgotten graves. But I can never forget. People must have seen that long, dreadful winter to know what it was.[10]

Her work had also proved what she set out to prove—that women were capable of doing many things and that there was room for them as nurses in the Army, yet this would have to wait, since God had shown her a more desperate need that she alone had the knowledge and experience to address, and that had to be remedied before war broke out again and repeated the tragedy.

> If we are permitted to finish the work He gave us to do, it matters little how much we suffer in doing it. In fact, the suffering is part of the work...But surely it is also part of that work to tell the world what we have suffered and how we have been hindered, in order that the world may be able to spare others.[11]

If Florence's only goal was to be a nurse and train nurses, her behavior toward the Nightingale Fund is puzzling. Headed by influential men, approved by the nation, and poised to fund the nursing school she wanted to establish, it should have won Florence's happy espousal. However, while nursing might have been her early vision within the confines of Lea Hurst and Embley, she had now found a wider vocation. She wrote to Aunt Mai:

> I have not the least expectation of returning home. I am quite determined, *Deo volente* & the War Office, to remain with our Army as long as that Army is carrying on war, & as long consequently as it has General Hospitals....What better can I do in England? There I might have many hundred patients as here I shall have thousands, UNDER WHATEVER circumstances. Every where we have to organize kitchens, baths, linen, stores, washing.[12]

When Sir Sidney asked her in January 1856 about the proposal to start an institute for the training of nurses with the Fund, she wrote back:

> My present work is such as I would never desert it for another, so long as I see room to believe that what I may do here is unfinished. May I then, beg you to express to the Committee that I accept their proposal, provided I may do so on their understanding of this great uncertainty as to when it will be possible for me to carry it out.[13]

The Fund organizers requested from her a prospectus of her plans for the training institution, but Florence, puzzled as to why this could not wait until her return, said she could not provide one:

> To furnish a cut & dried Prospectus of my Plans, when I cannot look forward a month, much less a year, is what I would not if I could, & I could not if I would! I would not if I could, because everything which succeeds is not the production of a Scheme, of

Rules & Regulations made beforehand, but of a mind observing & adapting itself to wants & events. I could not if I would, because it is simply impossible to find time in the midst of one overpowering work to digest & concoct another—& if it could be done, it would be simply bad & to be hereafter altered or destroyed.[14]

Mr. Bracebridge was then recruited to approach her, but again Florence reiterated that she did not want something launched with great show by prominent people with little preparation and thought. Florence knew how long good things took to evolve, and she also knew the type of person to jump on board a hasty bandwagon.

These are not theories, but experience. And if I have a plan in me…it would be simply this—to take the poorest & least organized Hospital in London & putting myself in there—see what I could do, no touching the Fund perhaps for years, not till experience had shown how the Fund might be best available.[15]

When she later refuted the vicious charges made against her and her nurses in the chief purveyor's report, Florence again hinted at her next move: "If I have served my country well, this is the reward I should wish—the power of continuing that service—of continuing it in Asia, should the war take us there—or of resuming it in any future war."[16]

As she wound up her affairs in the Crimea before returning to England at the end of the war, Florence, discouraged by the chief purveyor's report and its aftermath, outlined her thoughts, frustrations, and future plans to her dear friends the Bracebridges, who had shared her experiences at Scutari. She had no intention of seeking fame, power, or the Nightingale School, but every intention of continuing on in her vocation:

As for me I have no plans. If I live to return, what I should like to do, after a short visit at home, would be to go to some foreign Hospital where my name has never been heard of & discharging myself of all responsibility, anxiety, writing & administration, work there as a nurse for a year. Every other position seems to me impossible. At home I should go distraught with admiring friends & detracting enemies, with answering attacks like poor Col. Tulloch—at a foreign watering place I should go mad with inaction. My health is too much broken for a position of responsibility & power. With the story I have to tell I never would enter the world again, not on account of the sickness & suffering, but of the corruption & incapacity I have to tell of. My last two months (most dreadful of all) experience would make me wish to live to fight the battle of the Medical Officers against their Inspector General, disgusting and disgraceful as it is, but the fate of Sir J. McNeill's report, which report I could never equal in its completeness, makes me feel such work hopeless. Were my Grandmother or Aunt alive I would go to them. But how deep the meaning of those words "Foxes have holes & birds of the air have nests, but the Son of man hath not where to lay his head."...I shall buy a revolver & shoot the first person who asks me questions in private, (excepting the Queen, Lord Panmure & Sir B. Hawes). In public I shall decline answering all questions excepting in a report as to what I have done with Private Fund & Free Gifts, i.e. as to accounts. Depend upon it the "tug of war" is to come.[17]

Florence's mission was to be an ongoing savior of the common soldier. The Crimea gave her an independence from family that she had to protect, public recognition of her skills in organization and reform, a unique knowledge of the soldiers' needs, and close links with Parliamentarians, through whom she could effect reform. She suspected, and her hunches proved correct, that British soldiers at home in England were also neglected, impoverished, and disdained (their death rate would prove to be twice that of the working classes in civil life). There was no time to lose. She had shown in the Crimea that, contrary to public opinion, soldiers were responsible human beings:

Give them opportunity promptly and securely to send money home—and they will use it.

Give them a school and a lecture and they will come to it. Give them a book and a game and a Magic Lanthorn and they will leave off drinking. Give them suffering and they will bear it. Give them work and they will do it. I would rather have to do with the Army generally than with any other class I have ever attempted to serve.[18]

In keeping with her sense of vocation, Florence arrived incognito into London and went straight to Mother Mary Clare and the sisters at Bermondsey, her larger "family." Mother Mary Clare was the only Catholic whom Florence said never tried to convert her. When she died, Florence wrote to the sisters, "It is we who are left motherless when she is gone."[19] While Florence never joined them in body, she did in spirit, and Mother Mary Clare recognized her faith as theirs:

Though apparently you are not a member of the Church, your most upright will & heart makes you such, for if you knew of any thing more you could do to please our Heavenly Father, you would do it unhesitatingly…it is very clear that our Lord loves you very much & that you love Him with your whole heart & mind & strength.[20]

The next day she arrived, unannounced, at her biological family's home. They could not understand her avoidance of publicity. Parthe wrote to a friend:

As for her perfect indifference to praise it is something almost incredible, I cannot get her to hear the things in the papers…God must prosper work in such hands, which are so truly striving to do all for Him and through Him—nothing else could have held her up under the superhuman fatigues of the last 22 months, night and day.[21]

Florence needed time to recuperate from her horrific experience, weep for the soldiers she had lost, and plan her next move on their behalf. She was suffering from extreme physical and mental exhaustion, chronic insomnia, anorexia, nausea, and the after-effects of Crimea fever, and could only concentrate for short intervals, pacing endlessly in her room at night. There was only one thing on her mind, a royal commission to look into the organization and sanitary conditions of the Army.

Oh my poor men who endured so patiently. I feel I have been such a bad mother to you to come home & leave you lying in your Crimean grave, 73% in eight regiments during six months from disease alone—who thinks of that now? But if I could carry any one point which would prevent any part of the recurrence of this our colossal calamity…then I should have been true to the cause of those brave dead.[22]

Of the 97,800 British soldiers who went to Crimea, 2,700 were killed, 1,800 died from wounds, and 17,600 died from disease. Florence wanted to focus public attention on this *avoidable* carnage and initiate necessary reforms, something she was uniquely positioned to do. Otherwise, she said, "You might as well take 1100 men every year out into Salisbury Plain and shoot them."[23]

Despite her fame, Florence had two disadvantages—she was a woman, and she did not want to play on her public persona. She therefore approached Colonel Lefroy as to the best way to proceed, not for her own glory, but for her mission on behalf of her "dead children," the soldiers—a wrong approach could ruin her chances of being effective. As she told Colonel Lefroy: "It will be hard, no doubt to compel the Doctors to consider [her reform suggestions] & still harder to accept improvements proceeding from a woman."[24] Should she simply ask the Queen for a Female Nursing Department in Army hospitals "without making myself more obnoxious than I am,—or should I state boldly the whole case at first?" With the "buzz-fuzz" about her name, she did not wish to do the Nightingale School at present because it would simply attract "much of the vain & needy & frivolous elements of England" rather than people prepared to work on the problem.[25] Perhaps she should take a small, remote hospital and "indirectly but *not nominally* pursue my object of training women"? The crux of her inquiry was, however:

> If I could find a mouth-piece, not obnoxious to the same hostility which the Army Surgeons naturally feel towards me...I would gladly give every suggestion that has occurred to me to be worked up & promulgated for the benefit of the Service.[26]

Her suggestion found fertile ground, and Lefroy assured her that the War Office needed "an account of the trials you have gone through, the difficulties you have encountered, and the evils you have observed—not only because no other person ever was or can be in such a position to give it, but because...no one else is so gifted."[27] Lefroy suggested she press the Queen for an inquiry. This was all Florence needed. The family's doctor Sir James Clark arranged an interview with Queen Victoria and Prince Albert, and they were impressed. The Queen spoke with Lord Panmure, who agreed to Florence's request for a royal commission to look into "the whole Medical Department of the Army, and everything regarding the health of the Army." Panmure asked Florence to write a formal report on her experiences and reform suggestions, giving her the sanction to inform her family she would not be returning home: "For the next three or four months I shall have business (imposed upon me by Panmure) which will require hard work & time spent in London & elsewhere to see men & Institutions whom & which I must see to get up my Precis."[28]

Anticipating a speedy process, Florence wrote to Lady Canning, "Lord Panmure has given me six months' work (but no wages or *character*). After that, I go to the nursing business again."[29]

Florence moved to the Burlington Hotel in London, close to the government offices, and set up her "office." Despite his poor health, Sir Sidney agreed to chair Panmure's commission, having hoped Florence would choose the lesser task of nurse training. Despite the Crimea disaster, Sir Sidney was a respected Parliamentarian with long experience at the War Office, and was as passionate as Florence to make changes. Florence's "cabinet," as her colleagues were called, met almost daily in her apartment, the "little War Office," or at the Herbert home, and mail was delivered between them all two or three times daily. Florence and Sir Sidney were close friends and excellent collaborators. He provided the public voice in Parliament, and she worked in the background, producing facts, arguments, and strategies, a talent she recognized in herself—"I believe it the rarest, tho' by no means the highest talent, to be able to gather all the threads of a *new* subject and put the knot on."[30] Sir Sidney and the others had Parliamentary and family ties, but Florence, funded by her father's allowance, had her full-time vocation. As Cook said:

> She was not a politician. She had no party to defend, no officials to shield, no susceptibilities to consider. She had nothing to gain, nothing to lose, nothing to fear. She stood only for a cause; and, come what might, she was resolved to fling every power of mind and body into it. Among her private notes of 1856 I find this: "I stand at the altar of the murdered men, and while I live I fight their cause."[31]

From 1856 to 1861, Florence virtually lived the life of a tireless hermit, somewhat like Queen Victoria after Albert died. She worked reclining on a sofa because of her ill health and was entirely free from dependence on, or affection for, "things," simplifying her life to the bare necessities of a nun. When her father wanted to send things for her drawing room, she told him she had none, since it was "the destruction of women's lives."[32]

Florence drew up the plans for a royal commission to investigate health issues in the Army and suggested its membership. Dr. Sutherland, who had led the Sanitary Commission inquiry of Scutari, agreed to serve and remained closely involved in all of Florence's reform; Dr. William Farr, founder of medical statistics, was not on the commission but worked behind the scenes.[33] Farr had been impressed with Florence's figures and diagrams from the Crimea, calling her memorandum to the Royal Commission Report "the best that was ever written on statistical 'Diagrams' or on the Army." He also helped Florence discover the tragic increase of deaths at Scutari after she arrived—the result of overcrowding, they thought, until the germ theory revealed the full horror. Farr also remained in contact with Florence's later projects, recommending her as the first woman member of the Statistical Society of London. Despite Florence's planning however, the commission's inauguration was delayed. Impatiently biding her time, Florence visited civil and military hospitals and wrote on military hospital nursing. In only six months, she produced an 830-page report for Lord Panmure on the Crimea, which became the cornerstone of the final Royal Commission Report. However, when nothing official had happened by February 1857, Florence threatened to publish *her* report with suggestions for Army improvement, a move that hurried the approval of a commission to "investigate the sanitary conditions of the army, the organization of military hospitals, and the treatment of the sick." As a woman, Florence could not sit on the commission, but she provided the facts, figures, and questions to be asked of witnesses. She also stayed in the background because she had stirred up enough Army personnel with her reform efforts in the Crimea, and she thought the commission had more chance of success if it was seen to be independent of her. Strachey's caricature, whether accurate or not, of Florence's tenacity toward "the Bison," Lord Panmure, best summarizes the political tensions of the situation.

> The Bison was no match for the lady. It was in vain that he put his head down and planted his feet in the earth; he could not withstand her. The white hand forced him back. But the process was an extraordinarily gradual one. Dr. Andrew Smith and all his War Office phalanx stood behind, blocking the way; the poor Bison groaned inwardly, and cast a wistful eye towards the happy pastures of the Free Church of Scotland; then slowly, with infinite reluctance, step by step, he retreated, disputing every inch of the ground.[34]

There has been much speculation surrounding government and crown intrigue over this Commission of Inquiry. Our interest, however, is Florence, working some twenty hours a day on her divine mission, eating and sleeping badly, but responsible for the bulk of the work. The report, showing Army health sadly lacking both in war and peacetime, became public in February 1858 and received excellent reviews. Many recognized Florence's contribution. The *Edinburgh Medical Journal* wrote:

> [Miss Nightingale] possesses, not only the gift of acute perception, but that, on all the points submitted to her, she reasons with a strong, accurate, most logical, and, if we may say so, masculine intellect, that may well shame some of the other witnesses…When you have to encounter uncouth, hydra-headed monsters of officialism and ineptitude, straight hitting is the best mode of attack. Miss Nightingale shows that she not only knows her subject, but feels it thoroughly. There is, in all she says, a clearness, a logical coherence, a pungency and abruptness, a ring of true metal, that is altogether admirable.[35]

Florence's own report requested by Lord Panmure, *Notes Affecting the Health, Efficiency, and Hospital Administration of the British Army,* was used by the commission but never published, though Florence had some privately printed. Sir John McNeill called this report a body of information such as never before brought to bear on a similar topic—"a gift to the Army and to the country altogether priceless."[36] Dr. Henry Hurd from Johns Hopkins Hospital in Baltimore, U.S.A., called it, in retrospect,

> one of the most valuable contributions ever made to hospital organization and administration in time of war. Had the conclusions she reached been heeded in the Civil War in America, or in the Boer War in South Africa, or in the Spanish-American War, hundreds of thousands of lives might have been saved.[37]

Four subcommissions were appointed to implement the report, with Sir Sidney chairing each of them. Their tasks were: (a) put Barracks in sanitary order, (b) organize a Statistical Department, (c) institute a medical school, and (d) reconstruct the Army Medical Department, revise hospital regulations, and write a warrant for promotion of medical officers.

The month the commission ended its inquiry, Florence collapsed and was ordered to Malvern spa for a water cure. While the doctors called it exhaustion from overwork, Florence said she needed to be alone, quite alone—she had pursued her incredible commission work with Fanny and Parthe "lolling" in her apartment, warning each other not to exhaust themselves arranging flowers! She refused to follow their request that she go to Embley, and recruited Aunt Mai to stay with her to keep the family at bay, though Sir Sidney and other members of her war cabinet were allowed to see her. Parthe wrote to a friend:

> Others will have all the credit of the very things she [Florence] suggested and introduced, at the cost one may say of life and comfort of all kinds, for it is an intolerable life she is leading—lying down between whiles to enable her just to go on, not seeing her nearest and dearest, because, with her breath so hurried, all talking must be spared except when it is necessary, and all excitement, that she may devote every energy to the work.[38]

Florence seemed frantic and impatient, wanting everything removed from life but work. She chided Sir Sidney and Dr. Sutherland for going fishing when there was so much to do, wishing for a man who would suggest, "at risk of being shot," an organization to save the Army:

One who will find the truth & tell it, in a way that it used to be told, in the way which colours a century, which rouses a generation, which spreads till it becomes an organization of minds. And, if no one is found, will not the decline of this nation begin?[39]

Florence had not forgotten her disquiet at witnessing through its ruins the fall of Egypt, and her fear that the same could happen to England if it did not learn from its mistakes. She sought a *male* savior, realizing her own public limitations as a woman. In planning what she would say to the Royal Commission if they questioned her authority, she had written:

You will say, who is this woman who thinks she can do what other great men don't do? But, if I could leave one man behind me, if I fall out on the march, who would work the question of Reform, I should be more than satisfied, because he would do it better than I.[40]

Having been so near death at Malvern, Florence no doubt worried that all the unfinished work would die with her. She had already drawn up a will and written a letter to Sir Sidney to be sent on her death:

I am sorry not to stay alive to do the "Nurses." But I can't help it. "Lord, here I am, send me" had always been religion to me. I must be willing to go now as I was to go to the East…Perhaps He wants a "sanitary officer" now for my Crimeans in some other world where they are gone.[41]

She also dedicated herself again to God's purpose, whatever it might be:

Thou wilt send us where most work is wanted to be done. Lord, here am I, send me. Perhaps when I was sent into this world, it was for this, Crimea & all.[42]

Florence's "collapse" began her retirement from the world. Although she refused public appearances when she first returned, she did see friends and family and visited medical and army institutions for her research. Now she had strength only for work, declaring herself an invalid at thirty-seven. By December 1857, she had recovered enough to resume an intense workload for the four subcommissions. Her disgust at Fanny and Parthe's abuse of her space while she was working so hard led to Aunt Mai's installment as permanent guardian of her privacy, issuing reports to the family but refusing to let them move to London to "look after" Florence. Aunt Mai's son-in-law, Arthur Clough, became her secretary.[43] Operating from an invalid's chair, bed, or couch, Florence saw one person at a time and no more than three or four a day. Each person had to have a written invitation and was scheduled a time slot, canceled if Florence was busy or sick. She ate all meals alone and hated any personal publicity, although she ensured that her reform projects remained solidly in the public eye. A change of government in 1858 removed some of her allies, but her "little War Office" continued its work, with Florence as their "commander-in-chief." Cousin Hilary Bonham Carter joined Aunt Mai and Arthur Clough as Florence's personal assistants, and Parthe's new husband, Sir Harry Verney, a widowed member of Parliament, also lent political and intellectual support.[44] When Lord Palmerston returned as Prime Minister and appointed Sir Sidney as Secretary of State for War in June 1859, the subcommissions moved along and the Reports were presented to Parliament without delay in 1861. Three years after their implementation, the fatality rate of soldiers stationed in England fell to less than half the previous number, and many innovative reforms for soldiers' health were in place.

Florence, her office and privacy secured by her "illness" and Aunt Mai, turned to other needs she identified in the Crimea. Having seen the statistical usefulness of patient record-keeping, she proposed a scientific, standardized approach to gathering hospital data on admissions and diseases, designing a series of forms, including surgical ones, to be used by *all* hospitals. While not all successful, at least they drew attention to a need. She also tried to get health questions included on government census forms. From her association with Belgian statistician Adolphe Quetelet, she realized that Statistics was the most important science, able to glean information and predict probabilities that could be used in preventive or proactive ways.[45] When Quetelet died, Florence wrote to Dr. Farr:

> I cannot say how the death of our old friend touches me; the founder of the most important science in the whole world: for upon it depends the practical application of every other and of every art; the one science essential to all political and social administration, all education, and organization based on experience, for it only gives exact results of our experience.[46]

Encouraged by Edwin Chadwick, a leader of sanitary reform, Florence wrote some books on sanitation.[47] The first, *Notes on Hospitals*, focused on sanitary requirements in hospital construction, design, and management and was so popular Florence received requests for advice from hospitals all over the world. Her second book, *Notes on Nursing*, became the best known of her writings, the first edition of 15,000 selling out in a month. Not about hospital nursing, it was an encyclopedia of hygiene for ordinary people to help them care for themselves and their families, the first theoretical book on this ever published. As well as practical advice, it included Florence's theology—that the healing process was regulated by God's natural laws and that the caregiver cooperated with God by putting the patient in a position where nature could heal.

Florence was convinced that most problems surrounding the poor could be solved by changing the *system,* something that makes sense today, but that went against Victorian assumptions. She had shown that disease and death could be reversed with sanitation in the Crimea and had seen health "missionaries" turn a village around, not just by curing the sick but by keeping people well through better living standards and education. She opposed Poor Law amendments that wanted to bring all the poor and sick into large workhouses, mixing together the mentally incapacitated, old, and sick. In an article, "A Note on Pauperism," she advocated that the poor should *not* be punished for being old or sick, but cared for according to their specific needs, as one would do with other classes.[48] They also deserved well-trained nurses and doctors, hence Florence's scheme to train nurses for the workhouse. Many Victorians believed the poor should simply save more money and help themselves, with philanthropy or "poor-peopling" available to assist the *worthy* poor, rather than trying to change God-given systems. Florence called such Band-Aid philanthropy "humbug," arguing that a government effort was needed to employ the unemployed and give the sick poor good care, regardless of whether they were "worthy" by Victorian standards of morality:

> So long as a sick man, woman or child is considered administratively to be a pauper to be *repressed* and not a fellow creature to be nursed into health, so long will these shameful disclosures have to be made…They are not paupers, they are poor in affliction. Society owes them every care for recovery…Sickness is not parochial, it is general and human and should be borne by all.[49]

Florence was against hospitals for the same reason that she was against poorhouses. In her article "A Subnote of Interrogation — what will our religion be in 1999?" in the July 1873 edition of *Fraser's* Magazine, Florence prophesied what 1999 might look like. She predicted that humanity would have learned God's universal laws and followed them, solving all the problems of the poor and of education, and "making religion and God a real personal presence among us, not a belief in a creed, a going to a room or church for what we call our prayers."[50] Hospitals would be obsolete because everyone would pursue a healthy lifestyle and being adequately cared for at home. In 1862, she wrote, "I wish my life were beginning. I think I could do something to inoculate the country with the view of preventing instead of 'cure.'"[51]

Florence's invalidism and seclusion after the Crimea spawned a plethora of books and papers. Brucellosis (Crimea fever), lupus, chronic sciatica or some other chronically debilitating illness, post-traumatic stress, opium (the common pain treatment) addiction, or a psychological, psychiatric, or psychosomatic illness were all suggested as the cause. Florence gave different diagnoses at different times—overpressure of the brain telling on the spine, rheumatism of spine and elbow, shortage of breath, spasm of the lungs, chest attacks, weakness, feeling as if the top of her head was blown off, too ill to move, uncountable pulse, a threatened return of diabetes, nervous fever, and pleurisy.[52] The doctor's diagnosis was "tension of the nerves," and Aunt Mai talked of her "failing health and general weakness." The illnesses were thought life threatening several times, but in each case, the "cure" was solitude and rest. Even at the spa, Aunt Mai reported to the family that Florence took few water treatments, but "the comparative quiet makes it very suitable for her."[53] Whatever the medical problem, it did not seem to interfere with the incredible volume of writing and research she could produce in a short time, working all through the night. When Mary Clarke (Clarkey) Mohl's husband visited Florence in 1861, he wrote:

> She is always in bed and very weak, but not more so than I saw her three years ago, only she is fat, which I believe is no good sign, in so abstemious a person. It is wonderful to see this poor, bedridden lady working to organize the sanitary condition of India…The India Board furnishes her with every paper she asks for.[54]

Such reclusiveness was not out of character for Florence. In her curriculum vitae written at Kaiserswerth in 1851, she wrote:

> I had a sickly childhood…I could never like the plays of other children. But the happiest time of my life was during a year's illness, which I had when I was 6 years old…And I was shy to misery.[55]

As a young child, she agonized over the prospect of encountering a new face or attracting unnecessary attention at dinner. In her youth, she chided herself constantly for being too fond of society and its praise. While awaiting the chance to pursue her call as a young woman, she followed a pattern of structured seclusion to prepare herself, as a note from this period shows:

> I desire for a considerable time only to lead a life of obscurity and toil, for the purpose of allowing whatever I may have received of God to ripen, and turning it some day to the glory of His Name. Nowadays people are too much in a hurry both to produce and consume themselves. It is only in retirement, in silence, in meditation, that are formed the men who are called to exercise an influence on society.[56]

In a biographical collection of Victorian men and women published while Florence was still alive, the author said of the Crimean commission, "Miss Nightingale, *who endeavored to shun notice and fame*, was induced to take on herself the onerous duty of superintendence."[57] While some of this reticence had to do with the belief that public acclaim substituted for *God's* praise (Matthew 6:1–4), Florence was obviously a loner by nature. Biographers Wintle and Witts interviewed people who knew her, and of this "now white haired lady who lives so quiet a life in a house near Hyde Park, varied by visits to Buckinghamshire," they could find little information, except that "from her couch she is continually organizing, making plans, and writing letters. In her own words, she has hardly 'ten minutes of idle time in a day.'"[58]

Because of this reclusiveness, most people, after her initial return, forgot she was still in their midst:

> Her actions in returning incognito from Scutari are indicative of her whole character. She is so retiring a disposition that it is next to impossible to get correct information about anything concerning her, except in so far as her public career is concerned. She once wrote in a letter: "Being naturally a very shy person, most of my life has been distasteful to me"; and again, "Wait till I am no more, before you write my life."[59]

Biographer Barbara Dossey has analyzed Florence's letters according to the Myers-Briggs Type Indicator(MBTI©), and showed her to be the epitome of the INTJ (Introversion, Intuition, Thinking, and Judging) personality type—visionary, independent, private, individualistic, and single-minded. *Introversion* describes those who prefer to focus on their inner world of ideas, emotions, or impressions.[60] Florence's spiritual mysticism also supports this analysis, as does her desire to reject the demands of people and family in favor of the solitude in which to pursue her goals, admitting only people and things that forwarded those goals.

Some biographers build a psychological or psychiatric conclusion on Florence's reclusive "illness," interpreting her Victorian theatrical turns of phrase as erratic, dramatic, melodramatic, or psychologically unstable. Although there are elements of exaggeration in Florence, we have to evaluate this alongside the general emotional overstatement of her day. Others diagnose post-Crimea trauma—stress-induced anxiety neurosis, stress burnout, and post-traumatic stress disorder.[61] Given the appalling near-death conditions in which the wounded arrived in Scutari, the inability to save so many of them, the inadequate experience in trauma medicine among nurses and medical staff, overwork and sleepless nights, the awful truth that this disaster was caused by the War Office's lack of preparedness, and the resultant cover-ups by officials, Florence had more than enough reason to suffer a post-Crimean stress breakdown. Sidney Osborne, a chaplain at Scutari, wrote of his own pain and outrage at the Crimean fiasco:

> Are we to forget, or lightly forgive the treatment to which these and others as brave as our soldiers were so wantonly exposed? In my opinion, neither in triumph of victory...or in the shame of degradation of defeat...should this nation forget, that it is its bounden duty to trace out how, by whose negligence, by whose ignorance it happened, that men whose deeds of heroism we were swift to acknowledge in the field, when wounded and sick, were subjected to such want of the commonest care and humanity...It would be to me a betrayal of justice, treason to every Christian feeling, if I did not state what I believe to be the truth.[62]

Hugh Small's biography *Florence Nightingale: Avenging Angel* took the psychological diagnosis in a new direction. Small argues that Florence's health broke down when she discovered, on analyzing her records, that hospital deaths in Scutari had *increased* after her arrival, that 14,000 soldiers died because she and the medical staff neglected elementary sanitary precautions. Having come home satisfied with her achievements, Florence began the Army reform, hoping her fame would help the common soldier where others had failed. She planned to return to nursing after Army reform. However, she was innocently drawn into a cover-up between the Government and the Crown over who was responsible for the Army, and then discovered it was *her* extension of the hospital's capacity and her centralizing of medical care at Scutari that caused the huge death rates through overcrowding and poor sanitation (later shown to be infection). This caused her mental and physical breakdown, changing the direction of her life. She became obsessed with hygiene and sanitary conditions to compensate for the deaths. Sir Sidney's devotion was a shared guilt since he had chosen the hospital site, built over a sewer, and had sent the people who approved it. Florence's persistent efforts to expose the tragedy, rather than allow her sacred image to survive untarnished, revealed her strength of character, according to Small. She sent her findings to journalist Harriet Martineau, offering to pay her to write *England and her Soldiers*, which reported thousands of soldiers dead in army hospitals because of bad ventilation, with Florence's barracks the worst ventilated. Florence bought fifty copies to donate to lending libraries. Shamed, she spent the rest of her life working frenetically in seclusion to rectify the tragedy she had been unable to realize or prevent. At great personal cost, she pursued the facts, publishing them herself when hindered by government reticence, in order to preserve the evidence for history so that such a disaster would not happen again.[63]

Yet there was much more to Florence's seclusion than illness, shyness, guilt, and introversion. Given her lifelong struggle to extract herself from her family and Victorian expectations, Florence needed to protect her freedom once back in England. Already, Fanny and Parthe had moved into the Burlington Hotel to "help" her, no doubt seeing a whole new world for them with Florence's fame. They threw themselves into London's social whirl, oblivious of the magnitude of Florence's work, and frustrating her with their idleness and frivolous pursuits. Florence wrote:

> I have seen scenes among [the idle rich] quite worthy of Moliere, where two people, in tolerable and perfect health, lying on the sofa all day long and doing absolutely nothing, have persuaded themselves and others that they are the victims of their self-devotion for an other [person] who perhaps is really dying from overwork.[64]

Beyond their intrusion, Florence was rightly bitter about their change of face with her fame and their eagerness to benefit from it:

> What have my mother & sister ever done for me? They like my glory—they like my pretty things. Is there anything else they like in me? I was the same person who went to Harley St. & who went to the Crimea. There was nothing different except my popularity. Yet the person who went to Harley St. was to be cursed & the other was to be blessed.[65]

Both the public and her family knew little of what Florence had actually done in the Crimea or since her return, yet they had changed their attitudes because of the "accident" of her acquaintance with Sir Sidney. Florence was deeply hurt by this, having experienced so little support from her mother growing up:

> In reality, for everyone of my 18,000 children [soldiers], for every one of those poor, tiresome Harley St. creatures, I have expended

more motherly feeling and action in a week than my mother has expended for me in 37 years.[66]

Their proximity, in addition to being impossible for her work, also dragged up countless past hurts as they praised her now for what they had forbidden her to do with Dr. Fowler:

Since I was 24 (probably long before, but certainly since then) there was never any vagueness in my plans and ideas as to what God's work was for me. I could have taken different kinds of work—education, Hospitals etc. But each was definitely mapped out in my mind after a plan. I cannot, after having had the largest hospital experience man or woman has ever had, perceive that the plan I formed, at 24, for learning in Hospitals was imprudent or ill advised.[67]

Not only were they praising her actions, but they were also taking credit for having "promoted that which they called me unprincipled for proposing."[68] As recently as Harley Street, Parthe had treated Florence "like a criminal" for taking the position. "And I felt like one, *then & all my life* till within the last four years."[69] What was such praise worth?

Because her own family had "worn out half her life" by hindrances, Florence now felt justified in choosing her "true family"—Aunt Mai, her "spiritual mother"; Mrs. Bracebridge, a "mother to me too in another way"; Arthur Clough; and the Herberts. However, excluding those who felt they had rights to her was not easy, but Victorian society had the perfect ploy—the cult of the invalid. While Florence's isolation and illness might seem strange to us today, there were many "invalids" around London doing the same thing in her day. Bram Dijkstra, in his book analyzing attitudes toward Victorian women, talks of the romanticized notion of a woman as "a permanent, a necessary, even a 'natural' invalid."[70] Physical weakness was a sign of delicacy, breeding, and idle leisure; activity and energy were a social faux pas. The languishing, fading female exuded a sensitivity and delicacy of class that required fastidious protection:

More fragile than a child, woman absolutely requires that we love her for herself alone, that we guard her carefully, that we be every moment sensible that in urging her too far we are sure of nothing. Our angel, though smiling, and blooming with life, often touches the earth with but the tip of one wing; the other would already waft her elsewhere.[71]

There is no doubt Florence did have physical ailments, perhaps serious and chronic ones, but it is hard to correlate her "near death" maladies with the tremendous volume of work she generated at the same time. One thing Fanny and Parthe did understand and respect were the rights of the "invalid" and the importance that others sacrifice everything for the sick one—had not they used this strategy on Florence for years? In an ironic twist, Florence appropriated their weapon against them, demanding *they* stay away now because of *her* illness when, for many years, she had to stay *close* because of *their* illnesses. Florence always had little sympathy for feigned illness (which indicates she most likely *did* have some severe problems), being quite strict in Harley Street with governesses who used the institution simply as somewhere to stay. Yet she saw her own salvation through this same means of control, talking constantly of her "sickness near death" in letters to signal to all and sundry to keep away unless they contributed to her work. Aunt Mai was the perfect protectress, knowing the family's history with Florence better than anyone did and, having been in the Crimea, knowing the importance of Florence's work. She acted as the go-between, reporting that Florence was too weak even to write when they tried to persuade her to come back home, still not understanding her call. No doubt Florence's feelings of "betrayal" when Aunt Mai finally returned to her own family in March 1860 after a number of years spent protecting Florence had much to do with her feelings of vulnerability—would the family move in to care for her?

In "Cassandra," Florence bewailed the fact that a man could go into his study or city office and demand not to be disturbed. If someone wanted to see him, he had the right to refuse an audience or to make appointments at his convenience. Women never had that option, since no one took their time or work seriously. When Florence returned from the Crimea and was asked to write the report for Lord Panmure and advise on the commission, she had an assignment as important as any man's. She therefore set herself up in an office, as any important man would do given the same task, the only difference being that the office was her home—which was why she needed to thwart family visits. Operating out of her bed-sitting room, her companion-secretary, whether Aunt Mai, Hilary, Arthur Clough, or Dr. Sutherland, intercepted visitors downstairs and made appointments. Florence wrote notes to them, even when no other guests were in the house, the way any man would communicate with a secretary. Coworkers came to "the little War Office" each day, the nickname indicating how *they* viewed her work. Other women in Victorian and other times have gone to great lengths to be accepted in a male world, even dressing as men or adopting male names. Florence's tactic was to present herself and her work to the world, as any respectable man would do.

This was not the first time Florence had structured her life as a professional man would. At Harley Street, she worked at the institute but had her own rooms outside. At Scutari, a cubicle was known as her office where she wrote and recorded patient statistics and interviewed people. In both those places, she had a "place of work." Now that place was her home, and her "illness" allowed her to be unavailable— very un-Victorian for a woman—in her own home. This not only excluded the family but also put Florence in a position of strength—people came to *her* by appointment, and prominent people seemed happy to do so. She could control the situation by seeing only one person at a time and could focus on whatever absorbed her interest, quite impossible in the drawing room. Her illness caused people to treat her with deference— no one wanted to be responsible for a "turn." It also made her a "martyr" in the eyes of her loyal fans. While she had no seat in Parliament, she had the affection and support of the Queen and a claim on the hearts of the people. Many of Florence's biographers recognized this strategic advantage of her "illness." Strachey saw her "convenient" illness and seclusion as the mainspring of her life, while others called it a power game, ruling through "invisibility." Others agreed it was a strategy to further her work, keep a tight rein on her time, and allow herself to focus. Cook said:

> She framed a regimen which shut her off from many of the common enjoyments of life which to some degree impaired the flow of her domestic affection but which enabled her, through nearly fifty years of recurrent weakness, to follow her highest ideals and to devote herself to work of public beneficence.[72]

Sabatini is one of the few biographers who saw Florence's seclusion and illness as reminiscent of a vocational lifestyle: "She had emancipated herself from home-ties, much in the spirit of a priest who, taking the whole world for his family, lays claim to no personal one."[73] This is the argument I would make for her seclusion, given the centrality of her call to service. Had she been in a Catholic order, no one would have questioned her breaking family ties and confining herself to a solitary cell and a life of austerity and religious focus. She may not have had a motherhouse, but she had a Reverend Mother in Mary Clare Moore, and the discipline she learned from Mother Colomba in Paris. She did not have a mother church, but her mystical experiences assured her that union with God did not need the mediation of church or priest. She did not have an order, but she made her own vows in Egypt when she was thirty, and renewed them with regularity, living them intensely. She wrote to Liz Herbert in 1869:

There have been those who wished for nothing, neither to die nor to live, except as they fulfilled God's will—who had so strong a feeling of their own lives being one with the will of God as to exclude every other feeling, every care, every hope or fear of living or dying. How far am I from this—True, it is easier in a contemplative life than in an active strife in God's service, such as you and I have to live—but may we not hope that each year of strife may bring us nearer to this absolute oneness with God's will, making our active life a "spiritual exercise"?[74]

Florence rejected marriage and children as those in orders did, yet took on mothering the whole world—her soldiers, her poor, the Indian continent, women of all classes—calling them her "children" and bringing "many to perfection—out of darkness into light."[75]

As with the mystics she loved to read, her solitary existence helped her live a life toward absolute oneness with God's will, not distracted by the world yet *very* distracted by the world's misery, enough to enter the thick of it as a savior. She had, metaphorically and physically, formed an order of one with her secluded, disciplined life, yet because "unofficial" orders have no cloister walls to keep out the prying, interrupting world, Florence made use of the only cloistering option she had as a Victorian woman—invalidism. When Florence refused to see Clarkey during a busy time, Clarkey was convinced she could talk Florence out of this sober cloistered life she had adopted, telling Aunt Mai:

I can't help thinking a little talk and fun would do her more good than the solitary-confinement system you have established, seeing no one but the clergyman and the business people about the Barracks. I believe the constant tension on one subject is bad for her.[76]

Clarkey told Florence of her disappointment with Florence's "stoicism," and Florence replied:

If you think that my living the Robinson Crusoe life that I do is the effect of Stoicism, there never was a greater mistake. It is entirely the effect of calculation. I cannot live to work unless I give up all that makes life pleasant...I never said it *was* "best for me." All I said was, it was best for the work—or rather that it is the only way in which the work could be done, with the present habits of people of my class.[77]

PART II

The Evolution
of a
Theologian

CHAPTER EIGHT

Liberation Theologian and Mystic

Unless you make a life which shall be the manifestation
of your religion, it does not much signify what you believe.[1]

These old Mystics whom we call superstitious, were far before us in their ideas
of God & of prayer—that is, of our communion with God—in their knowledge
of who God is—in their understanding of His character, in short.
Where they failed was supposing the world not to be what God has given us
to work upon. There will be no heaven unless we make it. And it is a very poor
Theodike [theodicy] which teaches that we are not to "prepare" this world—
but only to "prepare for" another. Must we not "possess" God here, if we wish to
"possess" Him hereafter?[2]

Florence's biographers often just call her a *mystic*—she used that word—as a nod in the direction of her spiritual bent, and then move on quickly. Mysticism is notoriously hard to define, since it goes beyond any ordinary language and defies what we can think or describe by analogy. "Union with God," "experiencing God," "knowing the Divine," have all been used for this awareness beyond the consciousness of ordinary life, of being one with or in direct communion with what is beyond normal experience. Florence explained it this way:

For what is Mysticism? Is it not the attempt to draw near to God, not by rites or ceremonies, but by inward disposition? Is it not

169

merely a hard word for "The Kingdom of Heaven is within"?
Heaven is neither a place nor a time…That the soul herself should
be heaven, that our Father which is in heaven should dwell in her,
that there is something within us infinitely more estimable than
often comes out, that God enlarges this "palace of our soul" by
degrees so as to enable her to receive Himself, that thus he gives
her liberty but that the soul must freely give herself up absolutely
to Him for Him to do this, the incalculable benefit of this occasional
but frequent intercourse with the Perfect; this is the conclusion and
sum of the whole matter, put into beautiful language by the
Mystics.[3]

For Florence, everyone can experience within themselves God's presence
without clergy, religious rites, or institutions. Such a union with God is
achieved by detaching oneself from personal desires, giving everything
to God and working toward perfection.

Is it not feeling, as distinct both from intellect and from the affection
of one human being to another?…feelings called forth by the
consciousness of a presence of higher nature than human,
unconnected with the material, these we call spiritual influences;
and this we are conscious is the highest capability of our nature.
Whenever we love, admire, reverence, trust this higher presence—
whenever we sympathize with, partake in the purpose, thought,
feeling, of this highest presence—these are our best moments.[4]

Florence demonstrated her mystical orientation even before she
knew such an experience could have a name. As a child, she was deeply
aware of God in a family that eschewed religious enthusiasm. She once
wrote to Hilary:

How one feels that the more real presence in the room is the invisible
presence which hovers around the death-bed and that we are only
ghosts, who have put on form for a moment, and shall put it off,
almost before we have time to wind up our watch.[5]

Finding relief from her stifling world by moving into the different level
of consciousness she called dreaming, Florence was torn between the
freedom she found there and the condemnation she encountered from
those who declared her escape a rebellion against God's will. When she
shared her mystical thoughts with others, she was accused of
"imagining" things, yet *this* plane of her life was more genuine than
her physical reality. Like many other Victorians, Florence believed in
an ongoing life of the soul through repeated worlds, making the

immortal soul one's *permanent* existence rather than our temporary bodies. This did not diminish the importance of bodily existence, however, as it was the building of God's heaven on earth, which fueled progression toward perfection.

> We believe, from experience, that man is capable of living always, as it were, in a state of reference to that higher Being…Deep souls who wanted it fled to wilderness, to monasteries…although it is hard to understand what it means, since the world is what we have to mould, not fly from.[6]

Florence loved reading the mystics. As a young woman she imbibed Plato's metaphysical ideas of the material world as the imperfect expression of transcendent reality: "If we can trace as existing in man, limited only in degree, all that we know or can know of God, is it not evident that man is God 'manifest in the flesh'?"[7]

Before going to Egypt, she read the *Hermetica,* and also Gnostic writings that talk of mystical knowledge.[8] She sought inspiration in eastern mysticism through the writings of Friedrich Max Müller and Rowland Williams.[9] Although she disliked much about the institutional church and its claim to mediate God, Florence thought the eucharist was a helpful mystical symbol of the divine received into the human, and the human becoming one with the divine.

> Is it possible to deny that we have this invitation? He is ready to manifest himself to us, as He did in Christ, to make us also Saviours, to partake Himself with us. We may be one with Him and with each other.[10]

Florence loved the gospel of John, finding the mystical union with God described there—abiding in God and God in us *now,* but also being called to build God's reign in the world: "For myself the mystical or spiritual religion as laid down by St. John's Gospel, however imperfectly I have lived up to it, was and is enough."[11] This mystical religion in John's gospel was not about passivity or withdrawal, but about a shared *task.* While John's gospel is stereotyped as most representing a divine Jesus, Florence *rightly* saw Jesus' claims in this gospel as sharing God's *task* rather than *being* God.[12] Jesus' *task* was "to do the will of him that sent me, and to finish his work" (John 4:34, KJV):

> What is this but putting in fervent and the most striking words the foundation of all real Mystical Religion?—which is that for all our actions, all our words, all our thoughts, the food upon which they are to live and have their being is to be the indwelling Presence of

God, the union with God, that is, with the Spirit of Goodness and Wisdom. Where shall I find God? In myself. That is the true Mystical Doctrine. But then I myself must be in a state for Him to come and dwell in me. This is the whole aim of the Mystical Life, and all Mystical Rules in all times and countries have been laid down for putting the soul into such a state.[13]

Florence meant this shared *task* when referring to herself and others as saviors. The ongoing task of God was to lead out of error and was not limited to one person and time, as atonement theories argued, but assigned to many in history through the ongoing presence of the Spirit, as Jesus had promised. Frustrated in 1874 both with her friends' deaths and her own limits, Florence wrote of the continuity of this task:

We have a higher & a better hope than from anything we can do or not do: namely, whether we live to see it or not, He who is Perfect Wisdom will complete His work, even thro' our failures and disappointments.[14]

Her major spiritual mentors were the medieval mystics. Mysticism had found a new height in the twelfth to sixteenth centuries, particularly among women as a way to approach God when the church denied their spiritual validity. Seeking to become one with God, these mystics described their visions and heightened awareness in often erotic metaphors of surrender to a loving God as divine light, Lord of the Dance, divine bridge, interior room, divine love, intoxication of the soul, and more. They devoted their lives to God through reclusive contemplation or active service, claiming as their authority an unmediated experience of God. While they might function in a church and be loyal to its teachings, it was not their primary guide. They were "not for Church but for God," throwing overboard "all that mechanism" and "living for God alone."[15] Florence was fascinated by these men *and* women—St. Angela of Foligno, Jane Frances de Chantal, St. Francis of Assisi, St. Teresa of Avila, St. Francis Xavier, St. John of the Cross, Peter of Alcantara, and Thomas à Kempis—and was writing a book, never finished, entitled *Notes from Devotional Authors of the Middle Ages, Collected, Chosen and Freely Translated by Florence Nightingale,* in which she translated many of them for the first time.

Florence also recorded the anniversaries of her *own* mystical calls in a notebook by her bed:

This is the word of the Lord unto thee, London, May 7, 1867. It is thirty years since I called thee unto my service. Embley, February

7, 1837. It is fifteen years today since I called thee to the perfection of my service (to be a saviour). Tapton, May 7, 1852. How hast thou answered? What opportunities have I not given thee since then? I entered thee at Harley Street August 12, 1853—Scutari, November 4, 1854—with Sidney Herbert, July 28, 1867. I have seen his face—the crown of glory inseparably united with the crown of thorns giving forth the same light. Three times he has called me. Once to His service, February 7th, 1837; once to be a deliverer, May 7th, 1852; once to the Cross, June 8th, 1865.[16]

Despite such experiences, she was somewhat wary of mystical ecstatic states, their having as much to do, she thought, with one's strong will or a strong cup of coffee. Mystical experiences had no use *alone,* but had to be confirmed in other ways. In her notes on the medieval mystics, she wrote:

It is very plain how "ecstasies" were bred in people half-starved by long fastings & long watchings. So far from wondering that these half-starved people believed in their Visions, we wonder that they had not more. The "mystical" state—by which we understand the drawing near to God by means of—not Church or Ceremony but—the state in which we keep, through God's Laws, our own soul—is real & should be permanent. The "ecstatic" state is unreal, & should not be at all.[17]

Asceticism had similar problems. Florence thought this was *not* Jesus' way, but the "trifling of an enthusiast with his power, a puerile coquetting with his selfishness or his vanity, in the absence of any sufficiently great object to employ the first or to overcome the last."[18] The basic premise of asceticism, renouncing worldly enjoyment and cultivating self-contempt, implied that the world was a mistake:

The three things which prevent us from thinking of ourselves are, interest in the work we are doing, devotion to God, or devotion to our neighbour. And anyone of these three things would prevent us from taking pleasure in praise. This would be a healthier and more real state of mind than "loving contempt," as the Catholic has it. And this is more in accordance with the thought of God than to "love contempt."[19]

Some biographers have analyzed Florence under Evelyn Underhill's "mystical stages."[20] Michael Calabria suggests the following stages:

1. Awakening, the conversion or shift of consciousness after a period of restlessness—Florence's youth and first call

2. Purgation, the subsequent realization of imperfection and alienation from God, resulting in removing obstacles—Florence's struggles in Egypt leading to her vow

3. Illumination, a state of peace and joy, and a change from self-centered to God-centered living, often with oscillation between illumination and purgation—Florence's roller-coaster experience in Egypt, Greece, and much of her life, one day in despair and the next in joy

4. Dark night of the soul, the time when God seems absent—a frequent experience for Florence throughout life[21]

5. Union with God, Florence's constant theme in *Suggestions for Thought*—"True religion is to have no other will but God's."[22]

Calabria thinks that Florence never made the final leap of becoming one with God because her reform work constantly thrust her into harsh political and personal battles that angered her, for which she chided herself afterward.[23] However, I question whether such a leap into union with God *must* involve the eradication of worldly stress and conflict in order to be consummated once and for all. The union with God Florence spoke of was an ongoing *process*, a lifelong dialogue with God and the world, as reflected in her diaries. Nancy Boyd's collection of entries from Florence's diaries, made between 1876 and 1877, when Florence was working on Indian reform, speaks to this ongoing, changing journey:

> November 8–9. Take, oh take from me ever the wish to impress—cause of my unrest.

> December 12–13. Oh God, I do not know at 57 whether I am thy servant or even whether I wish to be thy servant. I wish to be allowed to do this irrigation [in her Indian project], to work for myself. Oh God, how canst thou take on as Thy servant one who is bedridden and unable—oh take me as thy hired servant.

> August 9–10. If it is possible take this cup from me [Indian irrigation] God—it is all *imagination* and *self love* (your agony).

> December 7, '77. 7 a.m. The Voice: If I do what you want about the Indian irrigation, would you give up all your name in it? Yes, Lord, I think I would; answer before 7:30. Or: Yes, Lord, I am sure I would.

> December 7,'77. Perhaps when all things go wrong for me and my name it is a sign that God is fulfilling his promise that things are going right with the Indian ryot [peasant].

December 8. Oh God, how couldst thou put such a creature as me in this place? Oh God take my place and cast me out, act instead of me.

August 16. Oh God, who makest the stars, sun and moon to obey thee, makest the beautiful sunrises, can nothing be done for these poor people in the India family?

"I want to help God"; how preposterous...It is He who has set my work.[24]

Florence was adamant that the mystical experience was *not* obtained by, nor did it lead to, withdrawal from the world, but to action *in* it. In her annotated copy of à Kempis' *Imitation of Christ*, she added the following note after à Kempis' sigh, "Oh when shall I be with thee in the Kingdom?":

Thy Kingdom—Thy laws—This world is Thy Kingdom, as well as any other. Here are the Laws. Let me see their glory—their perfectness. I may be with Thee in Thy Kingdom now. I shall be with Thee in Thy Kingdom here, if Thou art "all in all to me."[25]

Underhill agreed: "True mysticism is active and practical, not passive and theoretical."[26] While the *initial* motive for uniting with God might be devotion to God, that devotion is the "spring" or source of a love for humanity. Not surprisingly, the mystics Florence most admired were not off in some mountain cave, but working actively in the world—St. Catherine of Siena as a politician; St. Catherine of Genoa as a medical missionary; St. Teresa of Avila as an administrator.[27] Although Florence did not like Teresa's *capricious* God or her excessive reliance on divine intervention, she found inspiration in Teresa's idea that perfection comes through works of love. This affirmed Florence's own desire to immerse herself completely in God and God's work with the poor, not just to do so in her spare time or as her "duty." Florence's family conflicts had not been about her wanting to do *good*—she could do that in the village— but about giving her life completely to God and this cause.

Florence's active emphasis mirrors not only Unitarianism's "deeds not creeds" theology but also her own idea that we improve the world and move to perfection by finding God's laws and acting on them. This is why the mysticism of Aunt Hannah, the Madre, Mary Baldwin, and Frances Hill, which accepted a passive inactivity as God's plan, never fitted Florence's personality or experience. Rather than whipping herself for wanting to serve God with her gifts, Florence needed a theology that *affirmed* her gifts as God's nudge toward her life direction, and that described God not in conflict with her personality but working with her. Florence later made this "conversion" of thought:

> The "mystical" state is the essence of common sense if it be real; that is, if God be a reality. For, we *can* only, act and speak and think of Him; and what we need is to discover such laws of His as will enable us to be always acting and thinking in conscious concert of cooperation with Him. We cannot conceive that this, the very best gift we can have, can be the gift of arbitrary caprice on the part of our Almighty Father. But if we find out that He gives us "grace," i.e. the "mystical" state in accordance with certain laws which we can discover and use—is not that a truth and common sense?[28]

This distinction between thought and action raised questions in Florence about Plato's world. In 1868, overwhelmed with Army reform, she wrote to Benjamin Jowett, absorbed in "mind" work at Oxford with his translations of Plato:

> I entirely repudiate the distinction usually drawn between the man of thought & the man of action, between the seeker of the ideal (philosopher) & the political man...I too should be a much happier & better woman, if I were to be *thinking* only of the *Ideal,* if I were to be writing about an ideal moral Army—instead of struggling daily, hourly, with the selfishness, indifference, willful resistance, which are all that surround me now—while you...are in the calm regions of the Ideal. It is the difference between swimming against a strong current, with the waves closing over your head, (which is my state) & standing on the bank, looking at the blue sky. But where would the army be, if I did not think of incarnating the Ideal in political life—which *ought* to be the "mission" of *every political* man. No: let the Ideal go, if you are not trying to incorporate it in daily life: if you seek it only for your own calmness sake.[29]

One mentor who *did* help Florence's spiritual growth was Mother Mary Clare Moore, superior of the Bermondsey sisters in the Crimea. Mother Mary Clare shared with Florence a mystical but practical working faith despite their differences—upper-class Protestant laywoman and Catholic mother superior. She once wrote to Florence:

> I have never felt restraint in speaking with you, or rather, you are almost the only one, dearest Miss Nightingale, to whom I can speak freely on religious subjects—I mean my feelings on them.[30]

While Mother Mary Clare wished Florence had the joy of partaking in the sacrament as they did in their order, she also believed quite certainly that the Blessed Lord would give Florence "that union with Himself which your heart seeks for so sincerely":[31]

> It is very clear that our Lord loves you very much & that you love Him with your whole heart & mind & strength—I wish I could say I did, & I am trying with His grace to do better.[32]

Florence, in turn, told her struggles to Mother Mary Clare. On the anniversary of the Reverend Mother's vows in 1865, Florence wrote:

> The greatest blessing is to know & feel, as you say, that one is doing his will. I never am in full possession of this feeling tho' I have nothing left at all in this world, except to do His will. But I have not deserved that He should give me this feeling which is the greatest strength of all.[33]

These two women kept in touch throughout their lifetimes. Mother Mary Clare offered to nurse Florence in the 1860s when she was sick and lent Florence many books on the medieval mystics, which they then discussed by letter. With no other except Jowett would Florence share her spiritual struggles so deeply. However, Jowett was always wary of mysticism, seeing it as a "spiritual ideal" to be experienced occasionally, a taste of heaven in daily life, but not a permanent feeling. "Do you think," Jowett asked Florence, "it would be possible to write a mystical book, which would also be the essence of common sense?"[34] While Jowett was Florence's "kindred spirit," sharing a passion for social and religious reform, theology, and all aspects of life—classics, poetry, reading, music, politics, even gossip—Florence shared her mysticism with her "Mother Superior." In a letter to Mother Mary Clare in 1868, Florence poured out her heart:

> I feel as if I was only quite in the infancy of serving God. I am so careful & troubled and have such a want of calmness about His work & His poor—as if they were *my* work & *my* poor instead of His...I feel, you know, that if I really believed what I say I believe, I should be in a "rapture" (as St. Teresa calls it) instead of being so disquieted. And therefore I suppose I don't believe what I say I believe. I *think* I seek first the Kingdom of God & His righteousness. But I am sure I don't succeed in being filled with His righteousness. And so I suppose that I regard too little Himself & too much myself. I should like to try to listen *only* to His voice as to what He wishes me to do, among all His poor...But it does me good, I assure you it does (tho' I can't bear myself) if I think that your dear Reverence is offering me to God, that whatever He wills may be carried out in me. I have so little of the only true patience.[35]

While Jowett despaired at times of "sorting" Florence's theology into the formal categories he learned at Oxford, James R. Price III, in a contemporary analysis of mysticism, highlights a recent trend in Liberation Theology that gives place to Florence's combination of mysticism and activism:

> The relationship of spirituality with social justice is receiving serious attention from political and liberation theologians. In discussions of praxis, it is increasingly recognized that in order to do what is right and just, one must be right and just. This way of being requires spiritual discipline. Mysticism involves a spiritual discipline that leads to the conformity of one's consciousness with the mind of God. If, as Christians hold, the mind of God is incarnate in Jesus of Nazareth and definitively revealed by him as committed to love and justice, then some interesting questions emerge. For example, What is the relationship of mysticism to social action? Can love and justice be fully attained without the cultivation of mystical consciousness?[36]

Florence had *always* found her model of union with God and outward active service in Jesus. When Jesus returned after his baptism and temptations to his hometown synagogue, he chose a passage from Isaiah to read. The Israelites, having experienced economic repression on returning from exile, had reinstated the pagan rituals simmering always below the surface. In Isaiah 61, the prophet announces God's judgment on both the oppressors of the poor and those turning to other gods, promising delivery to the faithful (v. 8). Prior to this assurance, the prophet had stated his prophetic credentials, and it was *this* that Jesus read aloud:

> "The Spirit of the Lord is upon me, because he has anointed me to bring good news to the poor. He has set me to proclaim release to the captives and recovery of sight to the blind, to let the oppressed go free, to proclaim the year of the Lord's favor." (Luke 4:16–19)

When Jesus had finished, everyone's eyes fixed on him and he said, "Today this scripture has been fulfilled in your hearing" (v. 21). Like Isaiah, Jesus *also* had been sent as a savior to the poor to liberate them— this was Florence's call as well.

Poverty, or the state of being poor, was spoken of two ways in scripture. There are a few practical warnings of the consequences of laziness or ineptitude—"Do not love sleep, or else you will come to poverty; open your eyes and you will have plenty of bread" (Proverbs

20:13). However, the majority of references name poverty as the product of social injustice—"The field of the poor may yield much food, but it is swept away through injustice" (Proverbs 13:23). "The poor" are not individuals down on their luck, but a whole class whose situation had *nothing* to do with personal deficiency, laziness, or failure, but with social inequities, injustice, and oppression, held in place by oppressors. The Hebrew word for the poor meant the needy, without power or access to life's essentials and abused by those with power through the power structures of society (Leviticus 14:21; 25:35).[37] In Hebrew history, the poor were those who had lost land in economic battles and had become slaves to those who robbed them of their livelihood, the commercial and landed aristocracy. This feudal system of land in a few hands worsened at the time of eighth-century prophets Micah, Isaiah, and Amos, and against these powerful landowners who exploited the poor the prophets railed:

> The LORD enters into judgment with the elders and princes of his people:
>
> It is you who have devoured the vineyard;
> the spoil of the poor is in your houses.
> What do you mean by crushing my people,
> by grinding the face of the poor? says the Lord GOD of hosts.
>   (Isaiah 3:14–15)

Amos, in predicting the annihilation of this whole class of people through oppression, promised a day of salvation when Israel would be restored—"when the one who plows shall overtake the one who reaps, and the treader of grapes the one who sows the seed" (Amos 9:13). The suffering servant in Isaiah 52—53 wounded for our iniquities (an individual or the nation) has been so overlaid with christological interpretation that we have lost the *Hebrew* meaning of savior and the type of salvation or liberation promised to this poor, oppressed *group*. Salvation as liberation was not about a life after death as a recompense for suffering on Earth, but liberation in *this* world from political and economic domination. This hope was repeated by the Hebrew woman Mary for *her* oppressed and dominated people—that through her son, God would bring down the powerful from their thrones, lift up the lowly, fill the hungry with good things, and send the rich away, according to the promises made to Abraham and his descendants (Luke 1:52–55).

The plight of the poor, therefore, was *central* to the biblical message and faith—"'Because the poor are despoiled, because the needy groan,

I will now rise up,' says the LORD" (Psalm 12:5). God's faithful *action* on behalf of the poor should be feared by those who oppress:

> You who make iniquitous decrees,
>> who write oppressive statutes,
> to turn aside the needy from justice
>> and to rob the poor of my people of their right,
> that widows may be your spoil,
>> and that you may make the orphan your prey!
> What will you do on the day of punishment,
>> in the calamity that will come from far away?
> To whom will you flee for help,
>> and where will you leave your wealth,
> so as not to crouch among the prisoners
>> or fall among the slain?
> For all this [God's] anger has not turned away;
>> [God's] hand is stretched out still. (Isaiah 10:1–4)

God's demand for the poor was empowerment—to "strengthen the power [hand] of the poor and needy" (Ezekiel 16:49, KJV). Because of this, the Hebrew poor were entitled to glean some of the harvest; enjoy loans without interest or economic hardship; and receive from the portion of the rich, which was their duty to share. Every seventh year, the debts of the poor were to be canceled and the land distributed equally. Jesus grew to adulthood within this ethos. His words, "You always have the poor with you" (Mark 14:7), in response to the disciples' indignation at an expensive ointment poured on his feet, was not an acceptance or trivialization of the poor, but a statement about *duty*— giving to the poor was their ongoing and permanent obligation *regardless* of this special tribute paid to Jesus.

A messiah or savior would deliver the poor and oppressed Hebrews and crush their oppressors. Jesus, at the beginning of his ministry, announced *he* was the fulfillment of this hope. In the same way, Florence was called to be a savior in *her* time, sent by God for a particular task for her generation of poor. Unfortunately, over centuries of church history, the *task* of Jesus to proclaim a new reign of God with liberation for the poor was lost as the *man* Jesus became the *message*. Subsequent generations concentrated on Jesus as the pawn in some cosmic transaction between God, humanity, and Satan, an atonement that did not necessarily release the poor from systemic distress, but saved individual souls for a hoped-for *heavenly* reward through belief in a doctrine or eating the mass. This individualized, otherworldly salvation obliterated the *this*-worldly promise of a liberating reign that Mary had hoped her child would bring. By Florence's day, the few scriptural references to poverty's stemming from laziness or inadequacy (sin) had become the normative spectacles through which the majority of biblical references about the poor were read. In Calvinistic theology, hard work was rewarded by God (the Calvinist work ethic) and poverty became linked with personal sin, deficiency, or the sins of the fathers. Thus, the poor, in a theological climate where the class system was God's designation, were permanently condemned to their fate, and any resistance was named as sin. Christian duty to the poor was no more than philanthropy, and the oppression that Jesus had challenged was legitimized by the religion claiming to teach his message. The Jesus who hung on the cross because his radical demands for the poor disturbed the privileged ruling class had become the Jesus who hung on the cross to ensure *continuation* of the ruling class's power and privilege, offering the poor no liberation in this life and little guarantee of reward in the next.

Florence realized the devastation of such theology for the poor among whom she worked. They needed not only help for physical betterment but also a theology that liberated rather than condemned them, a Jesus who came to loose their bonds, not tighten them and promise a better deal in another world. Once again, Florence was ahead of her time. Her approach would be called liberation theology one hundred years later, and she a theologian of liberation. These terms were first used in Latin America in the 1960s for the ideas that emerged from dialogue between Roman Catholic priests and their poor congregations as they reflected together on their social-political-economic struggles. Here, life experiences came *first*, the reality of struggle and oppression. Theology, the attempt to understand that life experience in relation to God's purported love and care, came *second*, out of that situation of struggle:

> First, life experience; then the social analysis of that experience (seeing); thereafter, a theological reflection on that experience under the light of the Scriptures (judging); and afterward, planning a praxis directed towards the transformation of the shared experience (acting), which leads to a new experience worthy of further analysis.[38]

Liberation theology is a *response* to a particular context by a Spirit-filled community. In the case of Latin America's poor, Liberation theology came from a struggle for freedom from multiple oppressions by claiming God's activity in their midst, even though the struggle was often against the dominant church and its political power groups.

Central to this theology was not some bundle of handed-down, outdated doctrines or "truths" to be believed regardless of the circumstances, but the conviction that God's *priority* was the liberation of the oppressed—the message Jesus taught and put into action. Jesus was killed, as were so many people in Latin America, because of his efforts and convictions on behalf of the marginalized:

> What liberation theology brings to the theological conversation is not so much new themes as a new way of looking at all the ancient themes of Christian theology—God, the Christ, the Spirit, the Trinity, the reign of God, the church, sin, salvation, and the sacraments. In addition, liberation theology makes the clear claim that this new approach is, in actuality, the oldest one in Christian history; that of the first Christian communities.[39]

Liberation theology argues that by starting from the perspective of the oppressed, the "underside" of history, God becomes the God of the poor, moved by the suffering of innocent victims. The teachings of Jesus showed God's preferential option for the poor, and to be like Christ is to hear the cries of the poor and live in solidarity with them, bringing about the "reign of God."

> For liberation theology, this utopian reign of God is both "already among us"—in each one of our Spirit-filled acts and relationships of love, solidarity, justice—and "not quite here yet," insofar as it is always possible and necessary to go further, collectively and individually, in the incarnation of God's loving call. It is both to be pursued, built, deepened, and consolidated in the here-and-now of our concrete lives—pursued spiritually, ecclesially, culturally, politically, and economically—and to be fulfilled in the hereafter, in the plenitude of our communion with God.[40]

Sin is the tendency to work *against* this reign of God, against those who work for God, and against one's own being or essence. Sin is seeking idols, such as greed, honor, and fulfillment rather than *God's* aims for the poor. Sin is the ongoing sacrifice of the poor on altars of corporate profit and the thirst for power and affluent privilege, made more grotesque when *God* is evoked as their justification.[41] The gathering together as "church" exists not for itself as an institution but to enable the coming of the reign of God. The *reign* is the ultimate criterion, and the church must be critiqued as to its usefulness in bringing this about. This is what Florence did. Although the Roman Catholic Church provided her a way to work for the poor, its theology did not, nor did she find such enabling in any other church, seeing them as stumbling blocks rather than the means of bringing in God's reign. To the end of her days she insisted to Jowett that she did not need "outward forms of religion" to do her work for God, seeing *her* church as her struggles shared with Jowett, Mother Mary Clare Moore, and others—"where two or three are gathered in my name, I am there among them" (Matthew 18:20).

Liberation theology emerges from a particular context; therefore, its conclusions may not apply in another context where the oppression and players are different; nor does any emergent theology become an unchanging monolith, even for the community that gave it birth. The particular context that birthed Latin American liberation theology was a loss of hope in American support after John F. Kennedy's death; the overthrow of many democratic experiments by military coups endorsed by the United States government; Protestant and Marxist ideas loosening Roman Catholicism's monopoly on thought; the growing support of religious leaders, encouraged by Vatican II and the World Council of Churches, advocating social and economic reform; an emerging radical theology of the poor imported from Europe and America; neighborhood ecclesiastical communities of poor people confronting their problems; and Paulo Freire's education theories, which affirmed a grassroots responsibility for formulating "truth."[42] A small number of clergy and other religious people were prepared to stand with the poor and act as catalysts for a theology to emerge that would empower people to seek their own liberation. This combination of events produced a particular description of God's activity in their midst. In Florence's time, the circumstances and events that confirmed *her* resolve to stand with the poor were different. While Florence penned *Suggestions for Thought* herself, it developed out of her experience of struggle with the disadvantaged—daughters in Victorian families, the village poor, and the Crimean soldiers, to name a few. Unique circumstances in her context included the crisis of faith in the Church of England and its consequent openness to theological exploration; the advent of biblical criticism; science's (including Darwin's) challenge to the "natural order of creation," which had imprisoned the poor; the worsening of conditions for the working class after the Industrial Revolution; reformers willing to address these problems; the philosophy and social theory of Jeremy Bentham, August Comte, and John Stuart Mill; the Crimean war and its exposure of Army inadequacies; and Florence's rare combination of upper-class influence, social passion, intelligence, and religious fervor, and her propulsion into the limelight, which enabled her to be the catalyst for change.[43]

Just as Latin American liberation theology was attacked as a thinly disguised pseudo-Christian argument for legitimizing Marxist socialism and violent revolt, Florence's commitment to the poor was attacked by those whose security and status were threatened—her family, her Crimean colleagues, the church, and those who profited from the gendered social hierarchies of class. Like her Latin American counterparts, Florence's liberation theology enlisted not just religion but sociology, anthropology, economics, history, psychology, and philosophy in its analysis. Her writing, thinking, analyzing, and acting from her youth up had been almost completely occupied with her concern for the poor and oppressed, whether in villages around her family estates, in Egypt, in the Crimea, or in hospital wards. Her reflection on *all* aspects of these situations produced a theology that, in turn, provided the tool for the poor to act.[44] She gave them, in Jesus, not some uncertain hope after death, but a God suffering *with* them:

> He [God] shows himself in the persons of our suffering fellow creatures—not, as in those legends, where Christ appears as a beggar and then flies away, but because He is really there. It is really Himself descending into hell. For all those prisoners, those criminals, those sick, those infirm, are there by His laws. It is Himself we see, His word, His work, in them.[45]

This is why Florence never ceased throughout her life to get her ideas into print for the common people. Unfortunately, she lived at a time when the rules of theology could not accommodate her style, approach, or gender, and so she was constantly thwarted.

Florence wrote her first draft of *Suggestions for Thought* and "Cassandra" that frustrating winter after returning from Kaiserswerth in October 1851. At the spa with WEN and then at Aunt Mai's, she gathered random thoughts from diaries and letters and organized them into sixty-five pages and three chapters—the first being "On Law," and the others clarifying and illustrating the first. The extended version flowed from her pen in her solitary "cell" around 1859–1860, covering 829 pages and three volumes, addressing a wider audience than artisans. The first volume described her theology—"Law as the basis of a New Theology." The second was devoted to "practical implications," including "Cassandra" and another long section on women. The third volume, more a collection of various ideas, summarized and expanded her argument once again. Florence would have preferred to teach her ideas directly to the working class, afraid they might remain theoretical if captured only in print. However, at this stage she was worried she might not have long to live, and later told Jowett:

I think I could teach it [*Suggestions for Thought*] *viva voce* to a few working men. What I am so afraid of is that even if anybody would listen to it, it would lead to nothing but a philosophical school, not a religion. I should like to say to them—now it does not signify in the least whether you believe this or the reverse, unless you put it into practical truth in your lives...I have such a strong feeling that he who founds a Soldiers' Club (to keep them out of vice) is doing more than he who teaches abstract *religious truth*, that I would not teach "the Stuff" if I could do anything else practical—but I can't now...I don't want the Stuff to enter anyone's mind without improving his life.[46]

Arthur Clough (1819–1861) must take credit for *Suggestions for Thought's* ever seeing the light of day. Clough, an Oxford graduate disillusioned by the Oxford Movement, had become a voice for Victorian religious skepticism through his poetry, lecturing also with transcendentalist Ralph Waldo Emerson in America. Clough married Aunt Mai's daughter Blanche and became secretary of the Nightingale Fund, doing double duty as Florence's reform assistant. While deeply interested in her reform, he was fascinated by Florence's theological ideas, encouraging her to publish them. Florence was conscious of their disorganization, repetition, and need of editing, done as they were in "odd moments." Clough suggested she print a few draft copies for critique, which she did in 1860, anxious to get feedback. They went to her father; Aunt Mai's husband, Sam Smith; Richard Monckton Milnes; and Sir John McNeill. Since Florence had recently read John Stuart Mill's *History of Logic* (on free will and necessity), a copy went to him as well, and the final one to Clough's friend Benjamin Jowett, a well-known classical scholar whom Florence had not yet met. To introduce her work, Florence wrote:

Many years ago, I had a large and very curious acquaintance among the artisans of the North of England and of London. I learned that they were without any religion whatever—though diligently seeking after one, principally in Comte and his school. Any return to what is called Christianity appeared impossible. It is for them this book was written.[47]

Artisans, Florence explained in another context, were not *ignorant* people—"tailors and shoemakers are generally reckoned among the most intelligent part of the community"—yet they had no reasonable religion to appeal to their minds.[48]

To put the names of Comte and Mill into perspective, the Church of England, ever since Henry VIII established himself as its head in place of the pope, had been indistinguishable from English society and government. Lytton Strachey described the Church in Florence's day:

> For many generations the Church of England had slept the sleep of the…comfortable. The sullen murmurings of dissent, the loud battle-cry of Revolution, had hardly disturbed her slumbers…To be in the Church was in fact simply to pursue one of those professions which Nature and Society had decided were proper to gentlemen and gentlemen alone. The fervors of piety, the zeal of Apostolic charity, the enthusiasm of self-renunciation—these things were all very well in their way—and in their place; but their place was certainly not the Church of England…The great bulk of clergy walked calmly along the smooth road of ordinary duty. They kept an eye on the poor of the parish, and they conducted the Sunday Services in a becoming manner; for the rest, they differed neither outwardly nor inwardly from the great bulk of laity, to whom the Church was a useful organization for the maintenance of Religion, as by law established.[49]

This complacent Christianity had survived the Enlightenment challenge but was now facing challenges from a scientific world. While many theologians scurried to redefine God and creation in ways that accorded with new scientific discoveries, other challenges were emerging from the societal dynamics produced by the Industrial Revolution. Philosophical, religious, legal, and cultural rules had long been grounded on the "social contract"— the idea that society, as surely as the universe, was created by God, with people divinely placed in the classes in which they were born. This idea sat well with Church and Crown, since a divine order of creation helped secure their own authority. Jeremy Bentham (1748–1832), however, in 1776, exposed the dire consequences for the poor of this long-held belief in *Fragment on Government*.[50] While allowing for an order in society, he argued that leadership and power should not be based on class, but on moral behavior, and that morality was not something inherited, but legislated—that which provided the greatest good for the greatest number of people. Bentham's ideas freed his followers, including Florence's father, from the prison of outmoded medieval and Greco-Roman laws sanctioned by the Church—which Bentham *also* critiqued in *Church of Englandism.* This heavily endowed but socially deficient institution, despite glaring class and economic problems, was absorbed with ecclesiastical and political power struggles that left little time to address the problems of the masses. Long after the Industrial

Revolution's population redistribution, new churches had still not been built and priests did not live in their parishes. The Church had simply relegated its social responsibility to independent, committed laity such as Joshua Watson, who personally revolutionized poor education in the Church's name.[51] While Unitarian and Nonconformist theologies appealed to the middle class, many working-class people simply stopped attending church.

Others looked elsewhere for a satisfactory religion, finding it in French philosopher Auguste Comte's "positivism," a secular religion that was suspicious of theology or metaphysics and that limited its claims to rational, empirical answers only.[52] Comte's "religion" advocated Humanity—past, present, and future—as its Great Being, and organized a rigidly ordered society of rituals, holy days, and worship. "Clergy" included sociologists who counseled and preached this positivist gospel, encouraging people simply to live for others. Love for God became love for humanity, and immortality resided in one's example being handed down for posterity. Florence's frustration with Comte's religion was that, though she agreed with his assessment of the demise of traditional religion, she believed there were still ways to find a place for God, albeit a new image of God.

John Stuart Mill (1806–1873), philosopher, political economist, and reformer, also struggled with traditional religion and sought a secular compromise.[53] He and his wife wrote *A System of Logic* (1859), which emphasized empiricism, what one can observe, as the ultimate source of knowledge. *Principles of Political Economy* (1848) targeted capitalism as the cause of the wretched conditions of the working class, and *On Liberty* (1859) defended personal freedom and the limits of government. In *Utilitarianism* (1863) Mill named and expanded the system developed by Jeremy Bentham and Mill's father. Following from Comte's secular religion, Mill argued for a social morality that sought not the largest *quantity* of happiness for the most people, but the largest *quality* or depth of happiness for the greatest number. Acting on his theory, Mill sponsored many reforms during his three years in Parliament, including Irish land reform and women's rights. Consequently, Mill was very impressed when he read Florence's critique of Victorian society in "Cassandra," and suggested, after some editorial and format changes, that she publish it. In his book *The Subjection of Women* (1869), Mill alluded to "a celebrated woman" whose work he hoped would soon be published, quoting Florence's argument that men's pursuits were valid excuses for refusing demands made on them by others, yet women's occupations, especially voluntary ones, were never excuses for being unavailable to everyone's whims. No wonder women never developed anything of their own or attained eminence in things that needed dedicated time.[54]

Jowett, on reading Florence's work, told Clough, "It seems to me as if I had received the impress of a new mind."[55] He assured Florence of its quality and her genius:

> I should be very sorry if the greater part of this book did not in some form see the light. I have been greatly struck by reading it, and I am sure it would similarly affect others. Many sparks will blaze up in people's minds from it.[56]

He suggested she address it, not to artisans, but to *all* classes since they shared one intellectual world with common ideas and since Florence's social criticism condemned the upper class as much as it encouraged the working class (the second and third volumes were called *Suggestions for Thought for Searchers after Religious Truth*). Along with Monckton Milnes and Sir John McNeill, Jowett urged publication, but only after considerable work was done on style, focus of the arguments, and elimination of repetition:

> No one can get the form in which it is necessary to put forth new ideas without great Labour and thought and tact. It takes years after ideas are clear in your mind to mould them into a shape intelligible to others...I should not care if only a comparatively small part of your work is finished. Its greatest value will be that it comes from you who worked in the Crimea.[57]

Jowett was a cautious and fastidious scholar who saw only a fraction of his own work published because of constant rewriting and editing. He transferred his caution to Florence's work, thinking her ideas valuable, but urging conciliation and moderation. New ideas, as far as possible, should be grafted onto old ones, rather than promote a total upheaval. Believing her combative and revolutionary passion would offend, Jowett urged her "not to find fault with the times or with anybody, but to endeavour out of the elements that exist to reconstruct religion."[58] Theology was an ever-changing discipline, each age adding something to the idea of God; therefore, Florence must lead *gently*, not by knocking people over the head. Jowett knew Florence's published work would receive great attention because of her fame, and he wanted to be sure her important message was not lost because of the tone of the writing:

> You have a great advantage in writing on these subjects as a Woman. Do not throw it away, but use the advantage to the utmost. In

writing against the World...every feeling, every sympathy should be made an ally, so that with the clearest statement of the meaning there is the least friction and drawback possible.[59]

Jowett was also concerned about her systematic perspective and theological "school," but Florence, an original feminist theologian, was not trying to fit her work into some "correct" or recognized theological system, but arguing passionately from her experience.

Sir John McNeill, Florence's friend from the Crimea, was concerned with the work's readability for the class to whom it was addressed, but was sure it was "a mine which will one day be worked by many hands and that much precious metal will be drawn from it."[60] He critiqued her "lack of artistic style" and her repetition, as he had also done with her *Notes on the Army*, but thought this added the "unmistakable stamp of earnestness and truth—such as no reader or ordinary perception can doubt."[61] Biographer Edward Cook agreed with McNeill on Florence's style, accepting its loose structure for her discussion of the randomly organized War Department, but thought it lacked "sustained coherence" for a *philosophical* treatise, with its repetition and variation in chapters written at different times. Wondering why she did not correct this before publishing, Cook said:

> The explanation is to be found, I think, partly in a view which she had come to hold of the literary art, and partly in a certain impetuosity of temper. She had put literary pursuits away from her as a vain temptation. She cared for writing only as a means to action, and she could not see that literary form is of the essence of the matter if writing is to influence current thoughts on difficult subjects. Infinitely laborious, again, when action was in sight, and capable of infinite patience when she saw the need, she was content to throw out her thoughts careless of the form. There was a complete and consistent theme underlying her *Suggestions;* it was ever present in her own mind; and she could not be troubled to pare and prune, to revise and recast, in the interests of what she described as mere artistry...Those who are capable of completion in one field are often impatient of it in another.[62]

Florence acknowledged the "patchiness" of her writing in comparison with standard theological treatises of her day. However, her *style* would be acceptable in feminist theology today. The first volume flows logically through different themes, introducing them generally to the reader. The second volume revisits the themes, providing entertaining and practical stories as examples. The third section *is* disjointed—little jottings that repeat ideas in the first and second volumes. Florence may have pulled together this last volume from random notes in order to include all her ideas in the draft. In sending the first volume to Mill, she wrote:

> I am sure you will not suspect me of false modesty when I say the "want of arrangement" & of "condensation" I feel to be such, that nothing but my circumstances can excuse my submitting it to you in such a state.[63]

The purpose of publishing a few copies, as Clough had suggested, was to receive feedback on her ideas, but reader reaction to her style confirmed what she bewailed in "Cassandra." To produce *anything* during her life had entailed rising early to write, wrapped in a shawl against the winter, before "society" became the order of the day. Even at the spa with her father or at Aunt Mai's, Florence had to grab unclaimed "odd moments." Although glad of the positive response to her *content*, she put the work aside, perhaps hoping Clough would shape it into an acceptable form at a later date. She asked Jowett to do this years later, still anxious to get the message to her working class, but he did not do it. A few years after her death, Cook wrote:

> Unpublished therefore, it is likely, I suppose, to remain. But as it stands it is a remarkable book. No one, indeed, could read it without being impressed by the powerful mind, the spiritual force and (with some qualifications) the literary ability of the writer. If she had not during her more active years been absorbed in practical affairs, or if at a later time her energy or inclinations had not been impaired by ill health, Miss Nightingale might have attained a place among the philosophical writers of the nineteenth century.[64]

Feminist theologians were subjected to the same sort of criticism in the 1970s—lack of cohesion and system in their arguments. While this discouraged them at first, they went on to argue that to measure the validity of an argument by its conformity to artificially imposed *male* rules of systematization was *part* of a male-favoring system. Did a contrived system make it *right*? Lytton Strachey, who gleaned his information from Cook without reading *Suggestions for Thought*, carried on Cook's critique of her layout, calling it theology interspersed with "bitter railing against the life of a Victorian woman":

> Her mind was, indeed, better qualified to dissect the concrete and distasteful fruits of actual life than to construct a coherent system of abstract philosophy. In spite of her respect for Law, she was never at home with a generalization. Thus, though the great achievement

of her life lay in the immense impetus which she gave to the scientific treatment of sickness, a true comprehension of the scientific method itself was alien to her spirit. Like most great men of action—perhaps like all—she was simply an empiricist. She believed in what she saw, and she acted accordingly; beyond that she would not go.[65]

Strachey exposed his own enslavement to the male rules of coherency and generalization, both of which have been challenged by feminist theology as sacrificing diversity to uniformity. Feminist theology, like Florence's writings, values experience, diversity, and story, none of which are conducive to systematization unless one excludes experiences that do not fit the norm. Feminist theology's challenge has allowed experience and emotion to become acceptable theological categories today, and other areas of theology are adopting them as well. Did Florence *really* not have time to tailor her writing, given the volumes she produced on everything else, or did she realize she would have to conform to the accepted criteria for theological and philosophical arguments, taught at universities that denied her entrance? Did she despair of compressing her passion into sterile categories, or did she see more immediate practical causes around her than the vanities of "tailoring"?

Suggestions for Thought was destined to remain unedited and unpublished. At the height of Florence's work on Army reform, Aunt Mai heeded her family's request to return home, having taken care of Florence both in the Crimea and in London. Florence took this as a betrayal, causing a twenty-year rift between the women. Cousin Hilary took Aunt Mai's place, but Florence never forgave Aunt Mai's choice of family over Florence's work—or was it Florence's concern that Aunt Mai might betray the true nature of her "illness" to the family, leaving her vulnerable to them? Mary Clarke Mohl (Clarkey) wrote:

> Flo's...imagination is so great a part of her life that if a crack is come to some of the images she has stood up there, all fine china, she sees the crack for ever and can't look at anything else. I am convinced it is partly this malady, partly her solitude—Flo said to me, "Do what I will, my mind is always hanging on my Aunt and all those grievances. I do what I can to chase them away, but it *will* come back. [She] has an intensity of feeling verging on madness."[66]

Aunt Mai was not the only one to "desert" Florence at this time. Sir Sidney's diagnosis of advanced kidney disease was devastating for her, and some biographers blame her for badgering him to his death to finish their reform. However, he was as determined to finish as she was, having been held responsible for Crimea's chaos, and he appreciated Florence's unyielding focus in achieving what they both sought. Like Florence, in his deeply religious heart he saw reform as more than a political move: "I am more and more convinced every day that in politics, as in everything else, nothing can be right which is not in accordance with the spirit of the Gospel."[67]

Florence, also ill and able to work only half-hours at a time, chided the failing Sir Sidney for dooming the Army—"No man in my day has thrown away so noble a game with all the winning cards in his hands."[68] When Sir Sidney finally died in August 1861 at fifty-one, his last words were "Poor Florence! Poor Florence! Our joint work is unfinished! God bless you."[69] Florence felt both her work and her life die with him:

> Now not one man remains (that I can call a man) of all whom I began work with, five years ago. And I alone, of all men "most deject and wretched," survive them all. I am sure I meant to have died.[70]

She admitted later she had pushed Sir Sidney to keep going, but this work had been his life as well. They had labored and sacrificed their health "exactly like two men" for a cause to which they *both* were passionately committed. Florence called him a savior:

> He with every possession which God could bestow to make him idly enjoy life, yet ran like a race-horse his noble course, till he fell—and up to the very day fortnight of his death struggled on doing good, not for the love of power or place (he did not care for it) but for the love of mankind and of God.[71]

If this was not enough, her faithful secretary and mentor Arthur Clough died three months later at age forty-three. The distraught Florence wrote:

> He was a man of rare mind and temper. The more so because he would gladly do "plain work." To me, seeing the inanities & the blundering harasses which were the uses to which we put him, he seemed like a race horse harnessed to a coal truck…He helped me immensely, tho' not officially, by his sound judgment, and constant sympathy. "Oh, Jonathan, my brother Jonathan, my love to thee was very great—passing the love of women."[72]

With Clough died Florence's hope that he would edit her theological writings. In the midst of her grief, she received Clarkey's new book claiming women were more sympathetic than men. Florence reacted violently. She had found sympathy—that quality of shared feeling and commitment to do a work—most perfectly in Sir Sidney, Clough, and a few other men, a sympathy that gave you "thought for thought, receive yours, digest it, and give it back with the impression of their own character upon it, then give you one for you to do likewise."[73] Sir Sidney's sympathy had kept him writing dry regulations, which he hated, over long hours when it needed to be done. Clough, the sensitive poet, had learned nursing administration in order to work with Florence on the Nightingale Fund. In comparison, *not one* of the women who worked with Florence in the Crimea "gave herself for one moment after she came home to carry out the lesson of the war or of those hospitals," and even Aunt Mai deserted her.[74]

At this tragic moment in Florence's life, Sir John McNeill stood by her. Of all doctors, Florence admired him the most. He had been a surgeon in India and Teheran, and was sent, at sixty, to the Crimea to check on mismanagement in army hospitals. Florence met him there, and they remained friends. McNeill received one of Florence's theology drafts, and now he wrote to her, encouraging her to continue, and expressing his confidence in her great spirit and influence for good in the world:

> His [Clough's] death leaves you dreadfully alone in the midst of your work but that work is your life and you can do it alone. There is no feeling more sustaining than that of being alone—at least I have found it so...So I doubt not it will be to you, for you have a strength and a power for good to which I never could pretend. It is a small manner to die a few days sooner than usual. It is a great matter to work while it is still day and so to husband one's powers as to make the most of the days that are given us. This you will do. Herbert and Clough and many more may fall around you, but you are determined to do a great work and you cannot die till it is substantially if not apparently done. You are leaving your impress on the age in which you live and the print of your foot will be traced by generations yet unborn. Go on—to you the accidents of mortality ought to be as the falling of the leaves in autumn.[75]

CHAPTER NINE

A Religion for the Working Class

What is faith? Is it belief that God will break his own laws,
that he will vary from the nature whence they spring?
No, it is belief that his nature, and consequently his laws, are invariable.
He had given us the means to recognize what goodness and benevolence,
and righteousness, and wisdom are. Men have varied, indeed, and do vary,
as to their consequences of what these are. So they have done, and do,
concerning other truths, which are yet within human ken.
But on every subject there is a truth; and unity of opinion will come
just in proportion as mankind gain knowledge of truth,
and improvement of being.[1]

Florence's theological ideas could be categorized by a number of technical theological terms—liberationist, revisionist, feminist, process, deconstructionist, constructive, contextual, or liberal—because they exhibit features of all these approaches now honored with titles. I choose *radical,* not as a specific method or political stance, but in its common meaning. *Webster's Dictionary* defines radical as "going to the center, foundation, or source of something; fundamental; basic." The second meaning is "favoring fundamental or extreme change; specifically favoring such change of the social structure."[2] Both fit Florence's life and work. She *did* go back to basics, wanting to organize a new religion for a new age, to reimagine a Perfect Being free from cultural overlay.

Her new religion was prompted by the need for fundamental change in the social structures legitimized by traditional religious beliefs. As a *radical* theologian, Florence challenged the stagnation of organized religion in the Church of England, not by "warming its heart" as John Wesley did or returning it to its earliest roots as John Henry Newman did, but by denouncing its self-satisfaction and indolence as the official truth-bearer, and relegating its doctrines and forms to the archives of superseded beliefs. Truth had moved beyond the Church's vision, and a new religion, not a repair job, was needed.

> Many know that they are in a state of "twilight faith." But what can they do? If they step out of it, they step into a state of darkness. They have not admitted the principle, "Search," and it is like stepping out of a rickety house into the blank cold darkness of unbelief.[3]

Florence's formal theology is contained in the three volumes of *Suggestions for Thought,* two 1873 articles in *Fraser's* Magazine summarizing her larger manuscript, and her notes on the mystics for an unfinished book. Informally, her theology pervades almost every one of her thousands of letters. In the introduction to *Suggestions for Thought,* she outlines its purpose as not to declare the Truth, but to ask readers to join her in a search for truth, exercising all their faculties—spiritual, intellectual, physical, moral, and experiential. This search was not out of reach for the "poor and ignorant" as many claimed. With the help of "saviors," everyone could discover for themselves "the nature of God, the nature and destination of man, and how practically to pursue that destination."[4] Their authority on the search was not something external, but the Spirit of truth abiding within (John 14:16–17)—"Man is to discover from the means within and without his nature, all the truth to find which that nature is competent."[5]

Florence's intended audience was England's artisans, but, as John Stuart Mill and Benjamin Jowett pointed out, the needy audience was far broader in this time of religious uncertainty. Many in England were surrendering their own authority to the "certainties" of the Oxford Movement or Rome—through skepticism, not belief, Florence said.

> They required their sense of a truth to be stronger and more complete than it was. The more they urged themselves to believe, the less real was their feeling of belief, till, at last, they took refuge in the belief of others to supply that which they did not have in themselves.[6]

Others trod the roads to atheism, indifference, or theism, while still others simply concentrated on avoiding religious error rather than discovering truth. People no longer knew *what* to teach their children— even atheists who could not bear to teach *no* God didn't know *which* God to teach. Florence summarized the situation thusly:

> What is this age?…is it not a time of indifference and unbelief? We do not believe in a type of perfection into which each man is to be developed, we do not believe in social progress, we do not believe in religious progress, we do not believe in God. Our political progress is the only thing which we do believe in; but as to any development of our Church, any improvement in society which shall mollify the two great extremes of luxury and poverty, we do not so much as imagine it. In the last 300 years much has been gained politically, but what has been done for religion? We have retrenched a good deal, but we have put nothing in place of it. It has been all denying and no constructing.[7]

In any era, poets and writers become barometers of public sensitivity, and Victorian England was no exception. Poet Robert Southey voiced his religious confusion in 1814:

> I am neither enthusiast nor hypocrite, but a man deeply and habitually religious in all my feelings, according to my own view of religion, which views differ from those of the Church which I defend…*Not* believing in the inspiration of the Bible, but believing in the faith which is founded upon it, I hold its general circulation as one of the greatest benefits which can be conferred on mankind. *Not* believing that men are damned for not being Christians, I believe that Christianity is a divine religion, and that it is our duty to diffuse it.[8]

William Wordsworth (1770–1850) questioned the morality of a Cause and Ruler of things when his brother drowned, and Wordsworth wondered if there were not more signs of love in *human* nature than in God's nature. When Church dogma could not convince him, he turned elsewhere:

> I look upon Nature, I think of the best part of our species, I lean upon my friends, and I meditate upon the Scriptures, especially the Gospel of St. John; and my creed rises up of itself with the ease of an exhalation yet a fabric of adamant.[9]

Samuel Taylor Coleridge (1772–1834) also explored the theological options of his day and settled on a practical religion: "Christianity is not a Theory, or a Speculation, but a *Life:*—not a *Philosophy* of Life, but a Living Process...TRY IT."[10] Poet Christina Rossetti (1830–1894) no doubt *had* tried it, but was reduced to crying into the void:

> My faith burns low, my hope burns low,
> Only my heart's desire cries out in me
> By the deep thunder of its want and woe
> Cries out to thee.[11]

Lord Alfred Tennyson (1809–1902) struggled with conflicting doctrines and reduced his faith statement to "There's a something that watches over us; and our individuality endures: that's my faith, and that's all my faith."[12] Robert Browning's (1812–1889) world was so full of beauty that it could not ultimately be pointless, yet he admitted, "How very hard it is to be a Christian! Hard for you and me."[13] The less hopeful Matthew Arnold (1822–1888) simply bemoaned the bleakness of it all:

> And we are here as on a darkling plain
> Swept with confused alarms of struggle and flight,
> Where ignorant armies clash by night.[14]

Victorian life was best exposed by Charles Dickens, who wove a critique of the religious bankruptcy of his day into his characters. He abhorred the exploitation of bodies in factories and offices, and of minds by "Puseyisms and daily outrages on common sense and humanity." His novels satirized Evangelicals and derided Italian Catholics. Although he attended a Unitarian chapel in the 1840s and subscribed to his local parish in later life, he resisted all dogmas, teaching his children "humbly to try to guide themselves by the teaching of the New Testament in its broad spirit, and to put no faith in any man's narrow construction of its letter here and there."[15]

How had the Church of England got into such a state? At the turn of the century, William Paley's *A View of the Evidences of Christianity* (1794) neatly summed up the Church's theology—obedience to the Crown and the doctrines of the Church on the grounds that both increased human happiness.[16] As the order of God's creation bore witness, God was benevolent and observable through nature, and Jesus preached a civilized religion and morality, encouraging humans toward a virtue that reflected God's benevolence. *Not* addressed was the fact that while all this resonated with wealth and privilege, it had little to say to England's working class, whose existence was far from happy and delightful. They were not in a position to "work out their salvation" by doing good to humanity, since *they* were the eternally designated recipients of the good from others, allocated that place by God.

Paley's "happy world" would be shaken. Just as the eighteenth-century Enlightenment challenged the church's claims for divine revelations over against what could be known by human reason alone, the challenge reappeared with the rise of science in the nineteenth century. The big questions were: How do we know God? In what way is God revealed—through supernatural occurrences such as miracles and the resurrection, or through our reason and observation of God's activity in the universe? Is there a benevolent order detectable in the universe, or is science showing something different? For Evangelicals, it was straightforward. The Bible with its prophecy, miracles, and resurrection was to be taken literally, and God's self-revelation in Jesus Christ to be believed by faith. Nature existed in order to show God's creation and providence, and science, as the servant of scripture, was to demonstrate this. On the other end of the spectrum, the successors to the eighteenth-century Deists rejected supernatural claims altogether, declaring the "book" of Nature sufficient proof of God. Between these poles, theologians struggled to hold on to a Moral Design active in the universe while remaining open to new ideas of science to explain the universe.

Two other ingredients should be thrown into this bubbling pot before we examine the theological solutions offered. While Comte, Mill, and others had solved their questions by transferring the crown from God to a secular religion of science and reason, science's most famous son-to-be was quietly gathering *his* "evidences" on a world trip on the HMS *Beagle*. During this voyage from 1831–36, Charles Darwin threw overboard Paley's benevolent order in nature (which looked exactly like the Anglican God), having now experienced *many* religions.[17] Darwin decided that the Old Testament was to be no more trusted than other sacred texts; that there was not clear enough evidence to believe in miracles; and that God had never given one single, authoritative self-revelation. How could a good and loving creator ordain the bloodbath of nature exhibited by the survival of the fittest? Darwin published *The Origin of Species by Means of Natural Selection* (1859) on his return, and the sensational public reaction was not so much to his theory of human evolution as to the consequences for biblical authority. If the biblical creation account was not *literally* true, was the Bible true in *any* sense—where was the "stopping place"? And if humanity had simply evolved from the lower animals, how could human dignity and authority over all creation be argued? Without a divinely created order that set humanity above the animals, and some humanity above others in the English class system, would not all humankind simply sink into the lowest grades of degradation? Darwin had not set out to address *these* questions. He was basically a conventional man, believing, as Comte did, that humanity and society needed a moral rule of life independent of Christianity, which Darwin thought offered an *immoral* thesis— condemning people to hell who did not believe its teachings. A *moral* thesis for society would urge a person "only to follow those impulses and instincts which are strongest or which seem to him (or her) the best ones."[18] Darwin's challenge was the most public one, but science was crumbling Christianity's traditional foundations in other areas as well. Geological and archeological discoveries had cast doubt on previously held ideas of the age of the universe drawn from interpretations of the biblical story of creation. Paley's neatly packaged theology was coming apart at the seams, even as theologians struggled to hold on to an observable benevolent Moral Design in the universe as a proof of God.

While Darwin's challenge to biblical authority came from the new science, the Bible was also under scrutiny from French and German scholarship. British minds traveling abroad brought these "foreign" ideas back into England, seriously disturbing the Church of England's monopoly on religious thought. German biblical criticism, as it was called, owed its origins to David Strauss (1808–1874), who described supernatural elements in the gospels as hagiographic legend, not historical fact, built up around Jesus' life between his death and the emergence of the gospels. Rather than interpret these events as extraordinary occurrences that no longer happen, biblical scholars should move behind the texts and reconstruct the events, people, and religious and social practices from which these stories came, discerning how they were used at that time. This was done by comparing New Testament documents with other literature from that time, contrasting different copies of an ancient text to see the changes, and evaluating a text for stylistic changes that might indicate additions or compilations. Strauss was not doing something new by challenging the literal reading of the text. The early church fathers believed in a multilayered reading of the Bible, with the literal interpretation ranked below an allegorical or spiritual meaning. When Strauss's *Leben Jesu* (1835–36) was published, however, he was dismissed from the University of Tübingen, but his ideas flourished in the fertile soil of German intellectual life and became attractive in England as well.[19]

How then did the Anglican divines open to negotiation between scientific and religious beliefs try to resolve this complex mix? Divinity professor Renn Hampden argued that humanity had two texts that had to be read together.[20] Nature (science) was one type of literature about God, and the Bible with its miracles was another. Hampden noted that there were events in nature, such as electricity, that were no more provable than the biblical miracles, and so we could live with both texts as God's revelation. Henry Mansel argued from the human mind.[21] The mind can intuit certain things, such as a feeling of dependence, moral obligation, and its own limitations, all of which point to the *possibility* of an Absolute Being. The step of faith is to believe that this intuited Being is the Bible's God, the Bible then giving us a language to talk about that intuited God. F. D. Maurice argued that God the Spirit (Word/ Son) was incarnated in the universe (nature and science), revealing God's intent; thus everything—science, Greek philosophers, the Bible, and miracles—demonstrate God's activity, and we recognize this through the instruction of the Spirit within.[22] Hampden avoided the challenges from biblical criticism by reading both texts, Bible and nature, as different types of information, and Mansel and Maurice avoided it by transferring the authority for "truth" from the biblical text to the activity of the Spirit within each of us. In each case, the idea of a benevolent Moral Design (God) acting in the universe could be incorporated with scientific discoveries.

The challenge of Darwin and others, however, to a benevolent Being behind the "bloodbath" of nature, together with biblical criticism's questioning of the miracles and supernatural events in the Bible, forced Benjamin Jowett to abandon arguments for a Moral Design in the universe as proof of God. Jowett argued that the mid-nineteenth century, with its burgeoning scientific knowledge, was far too complex to argue for a Benevolent Design that

> fixes our minds on those parts of the world which exhibit marks of design, and withdraws us from those in which marks of design seem to fail. We collect, in short, what suits our argument, and leave out what does not.[23]

Rejecting the arguments of his three colleagues as flawed, Jowett argued instead for a *"roughness"* in all experiences of the divine, including those recorded in scripture. We had to move beyond our credulous awe of carefully constructed doctrines and unifying belief systems based on supernatural events. The sheer complexity within a *person*, let alone human variety over time and culture, defied this. While the Spirit or the Giver of a revelation might stay consistent, the gift or revelation was always mediated by humans, resulting in a variety of beliefs, speculations, and doctrines, even within the New Testament.

As an expert on Greek thought, Jowett pointed out how different readers through the centuries had brought their own cultural limitations to the original biblical texts:

> The interpreter is apt to read into an inscription more than is ready to be found in it. The record of the contemporary history is necessarily imperfect, and he exercises his ingenuity in making anything which he knows fit in with the fragmentary document which he has to decipher.[24]

The inconsistency of the New Testament is proof of this, not as error, but as the struggle of the various writers to put exceptional experiences into words and concepts, often across cultures. Paul searched for adequate metaphors and symbols to explain a Jewish Jesus as a Greek Christ, and the church fathers, anxious to determine orthodoxy against heresy, turned his metaphors and symbols into fact. "What was shadow to St. Paul was becoming a reality to the Nicene, and had actually become one to the Medieval Church."[25]

To this point, theology had been more concerned about establishing a belief *system* than in preserving truth, and the *new* task, according to Jowett, was to separate out the figurative language, historical influences, and doctrinal developments from what Paul and the gospel writers originally intended. Rather than scurrying for more watertight "supernatural proofs" as science shattered the old beliefs, Jowett insisted that the science and religion dialogue be taken seriously, allowing new ideas of God to evolve from this conversation.

> Any true doctrine of inspiration must conform to all well-ascertained facts of history and science. The same fact cannot be true in religion when seen by the light of faith, and untrue in science when looked at through the medium of evidence or experiment.[26]

Jowett identified with what was loosely called in the Church of England the "Broad Church," an eclectic group of intellectual, disenchanted Anglicans huddled between the Low Church Evangelicals and the High Church Anglo-Catholics. Its ranks included Christian von Bunsen, Thomas Arnold, Arthur Stanley, Rowland Williams, Richard Monckton Milnes, F. D. Maurice, and Arthur Clough, all names we encounter in Florence's circles.[27] Von Bunsen (1791–1860), a scholar and leader in the movement and Prussian Ambassador to the Court of St. James's (1842–54) had helped introduce German biblical critical scholarship to England. This group advocated an open approach to doctrine and scripture and freedom of inquiry in their scientific age. Like Unitarians, their emphasis was on ethical applications of

Christianity rather than allegiance to the *Thirty-Nine Articles* and *The Book of Common Prayer*. They critiqued doctrines such as original sin, eternal punishment, and the atonement, and rejected a literal reading of the Bible. They also argued that God had revealed the divine Self to humankind over the course of human history, not exclusively in Christianity.

In 1860, frustrated at the "terrorism" in the Church against those who took seriously the challenges being made to the Church's *Thirty-Nine Articles* and *The Book of Common Prayer*, the Broad Church published the highly controversial book *Essays and Reviews*, which demanded an intellectual approach to both theology and biblical study as rigorous as in other academic disciplines, and that other disciplines be admitted into theological inquiry. According to one essayist, "There are more things in heaven and earth than were dreamt of in patristic theology."[28] The book caused an outcry among Anglican clergy and bishops. The fact that Darwin's *Origin of Species* had been published three months earlier added to the public frenzy. Although many in the laity found the *Essays* an authentic expression of their own concerns, those affronted by them demanded ecclesiastical censure, even though many bishops and church academics supported the essayists' position. Some of the essayists were condemned before the Church Court then later exonerated by the Privy Council, losing their Church careers or having them truncated. F. D. Maurice was dismissed from King's College, London, for denying the doctrine of eternal punishment, and Jowett's appointment as Master of Balliol College, Oxford, was delayed because his opinions were seen as a "dangerous tendency, and likely to unsettle the minds of the theological students."[29] Frederick Temple withdrew his essay from subsequent editions following his appointment as Bishop of Exeter, and Thomas Arnold and Arthur Stanley never received bishoprics.[30]

Florence was well connected with this Broad Church movement, and it is no accident that the draft of *Suggestions for Thought* was privately printed within months of *Essays and Reviews*, dealing with the same topics. Von Bunsen had introduced her to Egyptology and the German theologians, including his friend, the famous German theologian Friedrich Schleiermacher.[31] Stanley's sister Mary served with Florence in the Crimea. Clough, Florence's secretary, had urged her to publish her writings at the same time as the *Essays*. Jowett read her manuscript, beginning their thirty-year correspondence and intimate friendship. F. D. Maurice's sister had served on the Harley Street Institution's board when Florence was its superintendent, and Florence quoted many Broad Church theologians in her writings. Despite these links, nowhere in the literature on nineteenth-century Anglicanism is Florence mentioned in this context. Historian Basil Wiley identified three explosions that shocked Christendom at this time and sent believers scuttling for shelter—Darwin's *Origin of Species;* the Broad Church's *Essays and Reviews,* and John Colenso's 1862 *Pentateuch and Book of Joshua Critically Examined.* Had Florence's work been published, it might have been the fourth.[32]

As in any other theologically explosive period of church history, the majority of people simply plodded on their way, accepting the *Thirty-Nine Articles'* supernatural claims and *The Book of Common Prayer's* passive theology without question. Providence, that "wisdom and power which God continually exercises in the preservation and government of the world, for the ends which he proposes to accomplish," was not just in the background in Anglican theology, winding up the world and letting it work according to fixed laws like the Deist's God. Providence was *intrusively* active in the universe and its laws, "upholding all things by a *direct* exercise of his potency":

> The uniformities of nature as his *ordinary* method of working; its *irregularities* his method upon occasional conditions; its *interferences,* his method under the pressure of a higher law, which law is the necessary manifestation of his own nature.[33]

"Special" Providence was a particular exhibition of God's power in *emergencies,* changing and manipulating natural laws and performing miracles "to awaken the conviction of his interest in and guardianship over his creatures."[34] Floods, pestilence, violence, hunger, and war were products of this divine maneuvering—rewards and punishments that could be negotiated with prayer and penance. "Although we for our iniquities have worthily deserved a plague of rain and waters," *The Book of Common Prayer* said, and though "we do now most justly suffer for our iniquity" this famine in the land, God may be persuaded, through prayer, to desist from such activity. As one historian said of a corporal dying of cholera after surviving the River Alma battle in the Crimean War:

> Seeing one man interred who died of pestilence was more depressing than seeing all the hundreds that surrounded us, that had fallen in fair fight—one was the work of man, the other a visitation of the Almighty.[35]

The Book of Common Prayer litany, "Good Lord, deliver us," covered fornication, deceit, the flesh, famine, lightning, tempest, and false doctrine, while the "We beseech thee to hear us, O Lord" litany covered travel mercies, health, childbirth, and industry. As pawns in a cosmic drama, people could do little but pray, worship, and wait. If things went wrong, they prayed for pardon and peace; in "trials" they endured, waiting for a change or a better world afterward; and if they made "well-meaning" mistakes, they hoped God would weigh their good intent.

While the *medieval* world had few other resources to explain natural catastrophes, the idea of Providence as the explanation for natural and humanly instigated disasters was open to question and ridicule in a *scientific* world. The nineteenth-century *Encyclopedia of Bible, Theological and Ecclesiastical Literature* listed several serious challenges to such theology being made in Florence's time:

1. If Providence is the care exercised by a God of infinite goodness and purity, God cannot be implicated in the wicked actions of humanity.
2. God's majesty is degraded by assuming divine interest and involvement in all nature's minutiae.
3. The prosperity of the wicked and the afflictions of the righteous are inconsistent with the idea of a just and holy Providence.
4. The laws of nature sufficiently account for the order of nature; Providence is not necessary.[36]

From as early as she could remember, Florence similarly rebelled against Church teachings, no doubt encouraged by her father's Unitarian ideas. She had abandoned the asking petitions of *The Book of Common Prayer* long ago. As a child, she could not understand why people's minds wandered in prayer because hers was so busy—the litany was never long enough to ask for everything. When the ship *Amazon* burned, the passengers' blood was on her head because she had missed the litany for "all that travel by land or by water." In private, she recorded the prayers she prayed, the "request by" date, and whether it was answered—"It never was," or if it was, it would have happened anyway.[37] *She* prayed for definite things, but noted others took refuge in indefinite prayers with indefinite answers, always not sure if they were answered and not disappointed if they weren't. Florence rebelled against such passive platitudes and resignation to one's fate—or to God:

> Resignation—I never understood that word. It does not occur once in the Bible. And I believe it is impossible. The Stoics tried it and failed. Our Saviour never resigned himself. And in all the great sufferings I have seen, I never felt inclined to say, "Resign yourself," but "Overcome." [38]

In 1831, King William IV (Queen Victoria's predecessor) ordered a special prayer against cholera, calling it God's judgment on a sinful nation. The following year when he declared a day of fasting and humiliation as the epidemic continued to spread, some people demanded the closing of the theaters and better Sabbath observance. This was not how Florence read the scriptures. "It is a religious act to clean out a gutter and to prevent cholera...it is not a religious act to pray (in the sense of simply asking to take cholera away)."[39] She had witnessed the dreadful cholera outbreaks in the mining towns around Lea Hurst, claimed to be God's doing until John Snow, a young doctor, ignored Church teaching and investigated the link between contaminated water, diarrhea, and shared food in the "huge privy" of a coal pit. Subsequent mapping of the disease showed the worst cases emerged with poor sanitation in crowded towns where excrement was thrown on the streets and rivers were open sewers. Florence wrote to her father soon after the Crimea:

> Do you believe that He (God) stops the fever, in answer not to "From plague, pestilence and famine, Good Lord, deliver us" but to His word and thought being carried out in a drain, a pipe-tile, a washhouse? Do you believe that mortality, morality, health and education are a result of certain conditions which he has imposed?[40]

Florence was appalled at the Church's insensibility to such discrepancies between an ancient worldview and contemporary thought. Congregations hypnotically chanted Hebrew Psalms praising God for murdering the Egyptians, as if God similarly favored the English over her enemies:

> That such things should be "sung and said" by educated men in every church in England through the year! Two hundred years hence, what will be thought of us?...people in lunatic asylums are more sensible. Is it as extraordinary that a man should think himself a teapot as that we should think God like this?[41]

Those who protested against this irrelevance were accused of threatening England's faith, usually by men without belief themselves who attended church only because their wives and England depended on it. The House of Commons started the day with prayer, but what did it mean?

> You say your prayers and you don't know whether God has heard you or not, whether He will answer you or not, nor *why* He has heard you, nor how to bring Him to answer you. Some few feel,

from the sensation of comfort and satisfaction in themselves, that He has answered them; other few are miserable because no such feeling in themselves gives them a conviction that He has heard them. The greater part go their way, having "done their duty" in "saying their prayers," and never look for any result at all.[42]

According to Florence, Church attendance in England had become a farce—"doing one's duty," but to whom? Was *God* to be flattered, she asked, or was it for the neighbors and the reputation? While women dressed for church, men joked about whether to go—"and this is called a Church, and this religion!"[43] The poor had no such dilemma, since few had a nearby church to attend—which was why John Wesley mounted his horse and took his ministry into the fields and marketplaces so that the poor could hear that God's salvation was for them as well, not just a predestined few. Florence was not critical of the disillusioned *not* attending—she did not attend a church either, nor align herself with one, seeing them all as "more or less unsuccessful attempts to represent the unseen to the mind."[44] Rather, she was appalled at such an inadequate religion being propagated through ancient liturgies and worldviews, ignoring scientific conclusions of a universe governed by verifiable and unchanging laws, and continuing to preach an arbitrary God who changed nature on a whim and a prayer. As for the *social* crisis overwhelming England that had forced Comte, Mill, and Bentham to question long-held moral codes, the Church was equally impotent, preserving the status quo morality of being "careful of the poor" and doing "little kind things by everybody," when the more pressing question was whether it was *right* to keep people dependent on benevolent "crumbs" from the master's table (Matthew 15:27).

Protestant reformer John Calvin had argued that God chose and saved a sinner through unmerited grace, but later Calvinists emphasized a deterministic view that denied *all* human freedom to respond to God, declaring God's unfathomable election or predestining of some and not others. Added to the Roman Catholic idea of the necessity for absolution before death, a horrifying image of God had emerged:

> The scheme of God is the creation of a vast number of beings, called into existence without any will of their own, the fate of the greater number of which is to be everlasting misery, of the lesser number eternal happiness, and this after a period of "trial."[45]

Recounting a dying pauper telling his nurse, "It does seem hard to have suffered so much here, only to go to everlasting torment hereafter," Florence called a God who initiated and sanctioned a scheme where only some would be saved and the rest tortured forever, a monster and *worse* than human. Her indignation came, not from a theologian's armchair, but from watching the daily terror of those dying in the Crimea and the frantic, often futile attempts made by sisters and priests to "catch a soul before death," often at the expense of their palliative care.[46] At the other end of the life cycle, the Church was debating Baptismal Regeneration in infants—whether unbaptized babies were condemned if they died. Florence believed babies were born neither righteous nor unrighteous, developing according to circumstances acting on them. A God who would condemn infants to endless suffering was "abominable," and equally abominable was a Church who decided, after a long debate, that this was an open question:

> People might believe one thing or the other, as they liked, which is equivalent to saying, it did not signify. Did not signify whether God was the worst of tyrants and murderers or not![47]

The doctrine of the Atonement did not escape Florence's critical gaze either. She thought the quid pro quo ethic of the Church's Atonement theory "barbarous" and "morally offensive," needing "a church to keep (it) up."[48] That an innocent Son should suffer and die because his Father was offended was a "curious sort of compensation," an argument her feminist theologian sisters would take up again some one hundred years later. If God was loving, forgiveness should be freely given.

> People have dogmatized about religion, building upon a few words in a book (and a book the evidence of whose authenticity it is necessary to master) immense schemes.[49]

Not surprisingly, Florence thought a new *religion* was necessary, not just a few nips and tucks in the old. Ideas of Special Providence, a "satisfaction" Atonement theory, the Trinity, miracles, sin and forgiveness, no longer sat well in an age of science and reform.

> The most moral and the most intellectual of the English artisans are now learning to live satisfied without Him, and really seem to think it does not signify His not being there. And they are not likely to feel any want. They live in a state of triumph. And they have morality; they have sympathy; they have benevolence; they will not feel these wants. If a man were alone, he might come to feel the want of God. But these say, "I don't know whether there is a God or not; but if there is, I cannot understand Him, and it is, therefore, no use to seek Him."[50]

Since not everyone could go to the "fountainhead" and work out her or his new religion, Florence felt called to do this for others—"to proclaim the character of the Lord." A new religion however, had to come *out* of the social context and then *improve* that context with its conclusions— we can't comprehend the nature and purpose of God properly when we "live poorly."

Florence believed the first need to be a "reasonable" image of God.[51] Prefiguring this contemporary argument, she recognized that any language about God limited God and made "the same sort of mistakes as the man who fashions an idol with his own hand."

> Let us remember that our conception, our comprehension, our feeling of God must be ever imperfect, yet should be ever advancing…In proportion as we partake the attributes of God, we shall know Him better.[52]

Images of God depended on the conceptual possibilities within a culture, and, as civilizations evolved, so did their concepts of God. Given the layers of baggage contained in the word *God* over the centuries:

> It would be the greatest gain religion has ever made, if, for a time, the word God, which suggests such various and irreverent associations (irreverent, that is, to a spirit seeking right,) could be dropped,—and the conception substituted of a perfect being, the Spirit of Right.[53]

Therefore, when someone asks, "Why do you believe in God?" the response should be, "Which idea of God do you mean?"

> Whether the God of the Old Testament, who commanded the extirpation of the Canaanites? Or the God of the New Testament, who commanded submission to the yoke in many things in which, as we worship Him now, we believe that He commands the struggle for freedom? We could not believe Him a perfect God, if He did not.[54]

To argue her point, Florence outlined what she saw as the development of the concept of God. Like all of us, she was a person of her time, and thus she was limited by the cultural and anthropological assumptions of Victorian England. Victorian anthropology assumed that being "civilized" included a belief in a High God, the feature that separated a religion from a superstition. Florence said that the "lowest" civilizations were incapable of conceiving a God at all. She called the Australian aboriginal child she met in Alexandra with the Sisters of

Charity the "lowest conceivable state of animal existence," but described how, in England, it had advanced "by the most rapid strides from an animal into a human being. *It now believes in God*"[55] (my italics). While these assumptions about Australian aboriginal beliefs were quite wrong and are offensive today, Florence's paralleling of culture with God concepts foreshadows the contemporary discussion of how divine images and metaphors are shaped by context and are *metaphorical*, thus open to change.

Earlier civilized nations, Florence argued, saw power as God's major characteristic—an engine that was greater than human beings to account for Creation, and a Providence with power to effect what they could not. Such a power did not have to act within any rules—in fact, the more rules it could break, the more powerful it was. To take advantage of such power, humankind had to propitiate this God by offerings, worship, prayer, or simply by being good. But was this true religion? Florence asked. Is *fear* a religion? Because God is *powerful,* does a moral God have a right to use that power on a whim? From these questions, "perfection" then overtook "power" as the most desired characteristic in God, but the *meaning* of perfection also evolved through the centuries. Earlier nations thought revenge was a virtue, thus revenge became a characteristic of their perfect God. The Hebrews initially worshiped the God of Abraham, Isaac, and Jacob, not of the whole Earth, but this idea evolved into God as the one and only God (monotheism) because God was not perfect if there were more than one. Other attributes were applied to a perfect God at different times—love of glory, anger, indecision. Yet these were not qualities considered part of perfection in Florence's day. Florence argued that goodness characterized a perfect God in her context, even more than did perfect knowledge:

> Is not goodness for this purpose higher than intellect? Has not the innocent child probably an idea of God nearer the truth than that of Voltaire or Gibbon? "Unless you become as little children, you shall not enter into the kingdom of Heaven." We believe the carpenter's son, who humanly did not know that the earth moved around the sun, to have had a truer conception of deity than the philosopher, who had fathomed the laws of creation...the more highly man's *moral, intellectual* and *spiritual* faculties are cultivated, the more nearly will he approach a true conception of God.[56]

The all-powerful, all-knowing God still being preached was from an ancient and outdated worldview, Florence argued. Religion could not continue to be organized on miraculous, revelatory, and supernatural ideas of God or the literal truth of the Bible stories when these were being challenged by science and culture, nor should it wait until such beliefs were totally bankrupt before searching out new ways of talking about the character of God.

Where did Florence place herself on the "reason versus revelation" continuum for knowledge of God? While she agreed with Jowett's theological honesty and the bankruptcy of supernatural claims, she did wonder whether his deconstruction offered *any* religion in its place:

> [Jowett] has stripped religion of many superstitions and has killed innumerable parasites which choked her vigour, truth and beauty but it has not led to the knowledge of God. May it rather have killed religion with the cure of superstition?[57]

While Florence rejected a God who interrupted the laws of nature with miracles and other supernatural activity, she also challenged Comte's "no God" conclusion. Other people's experiences of God could not be dismissed by simply asserting *his* position as correct—this was a *metaphysical* judgment, something he, as a positivist, had ruled out of order! All he could do was place *his* experience of no God against *her* and others' experiences of God. (In the same way, later feminist theologians would challenge male theologians who described the *male* experience as universal and normative).[58]

Jowett always worried about how Florence could mix medieval mysticism with Enlightenment rationalism in her theology, but she did what feminist theologians would later do, influencing others to follow suit. She took her experience seriously, then let the theology develop out of this experience, or at least in full recognition of its validity, whether it fitted accepted theological norms and philosophical categories or not. Thus, she could begin with her experiences as a mystic and describe that which she experienced in accommodation with Enlightenment rationalism and a new age of science. The gospel of John provided Florence with the framework for her argument. The writer talks about the reign of God within—mysticism—but also about establishing the reign of God in the world—a rational explanation of how God acts in the universe through laws, and of how the understanding and discovery of these laws lead to the perfection of this reign.

Florence began with her experience of the reign of God within or the "indwelling of the Spirit," an inner consciousness of the existence of a Perfect Being. This inner "sense of truth," developed and nurtured, was as "strong and complete" as the sense of truth that asserts a tree is not a house.[59] Florence is distinguishing here between *faith* and *belief* (a distinction I develop in my book *In Defense of Doubt: An Invitation to Adventure)*.[60] Faith is an inner *response* to something experienced; beliefs are formalized ideas, concepts, or propositions to be *believed*. It is the difference between "What do you believe?" and "On what or whom do you set your heart?" For her, the seat of religion was the human heart, religion being the connection between the perfect and imperfect, the eternal and temporal, the universal and individual, the "omnipotent spirit of love and wisdom" and the human heart. This is why she rejected Comte's teachings' being considered a religion—there was no transcendent with which humans bonded. From her inner consciousness, Florence defined the "omnipotent spirit of love and wisdom" thus:

> By *omnipotence* we understand a power which effects whatever would not contradict its own nature and will. By *spirit* we understand a living thought, feeling, and purpose, residing in a conscious being. By *love* we understand the feeling which seeks for its satisfaction the greatest degree and the best kind of well being in other than itself. By *wisdom* we understand the thought by which this satisfaction is obtained.[61]

It is the Spirit "within" that encourages this intuition of the Divine presence and character. Florence would agree that this is a mystical conclusion, which is why she insisted that such experiences do not stand *alone* as arguments for God, but must be substantiated by evidence from all the disciplines through the employment of all our faculties. Experience is valid, but it must be confirmed by science, social theory, and so forth.

> He who feels and comprehends, by his feeling God's love, will know God better and better as he penetrates into His wisdom, as revealed and revealing itself in the everlasting tale of the universe...Love, without knowledge, will form a poor conception of God; knowledge without love will form none at all.[62]

For those who challenge the validity of experience to describe God's character, Florence answered:

> If it be said that this is reducing the wise and good God to the measure of my own understanding and heart, I answer, not to mine, but to the accumulated and accumulating experience of all mankind...Our Perfect Being *is* goodness, *is* wisdom, *is* power, not a good, wise, and powerful God.[63]

This inner consciousness of a Perfect Being was not *her* experience alone, but that of many through the centuries. No one can argue that there is no God simply because his or her experience and consciousness tells nothing of one—that is like saying there is no tree because a blind man cannot see it. By searching the experiences of the saints through history, which Florence was doing with her writings on the mystics, we see evidences in their experiences of some degree of wisdom, power, and goodness above the human's as the *spring* of that existence:

> A spirit of the same nature as that of which I, at times, am conscious in others of mankind, and in myself. Thus much we can say without any straining after mysticism. When we seek truth, if we are not seeking it from man, it is from this spirit that we seek it.[64]

Having posited the idea of God from her *inner* consciousness (the reign of God within), Florence then searched other human faculties for knowledge of God (the reign of God without). What can we know of this Being from the universe? Like Plato, Florence believed there was an objective Truth that transcended and was independent of the human mind—"a thought, a sentiment, a purpose which comprehends all existence."[65] There were three ways to learn any truth: to believe conscientiously in something, whatever it is; to *make* people believe something through fear of damnation; and to believe that there is a Truth, and we will find it out in time. Florence opted for the third alternative. There *is* but one truth even if we don't yet know it, and it is possible to discover this truth over time through the evolution of human understanding of God's laws, which eventually will lead to our union with this Truth, to perfection with the Perfect Being. Although we cannot "know" this Being from the beginning of our search (God in God's Absolute self), we know the *Spirit* promised in John's gospel: "Let us distinguish God the Father as the spirit of perfection, incomprehensible to us; God the Holy Spirit, as what is comprehensible to each man of the perfect spirit."[66]

In drawing near to this Being, not by rites or ceremonies, but by inward disposition, the Spirit within enables us, by exercising our capabilities, to discover the divine laws of the universe—God's "thoughts"—and become one with God. This Spirit is incarnate, not just in Jesus, but in *everyone*, according to John's gospel, making the Trinity not three—God, Christ, and Spirit—but Infinity, God as Spirit in *all* humanity.

Discovering God's laws and progressing toward the Perfect through the Spirit's guidance are not part of an individual journey but are experienced by everyone over successive generations, each person hearing the Spirit and exercising his or her faculties to advance everyone from present corporate ignorance, causing suffering, to a better understanding of God's laws. The Spirit speaks through us to others, since no two people are alike.

> Each therefore, will be able to give and receive, to give to others some light from God which others have not, to receive from others some light from God which he has not. We are to have the voice of the One Perfect, ever the same; the varied voices of all mankind; but for both we are to work. Both will be heard, only in proportion as man works; and, in proportion, as man works aright, one and the same God will be recognized by all; for truth is one.[67]

Two other things help this process. The right organization of society puts people in a state that calls forth their natures into right exercise, and special saviors are sent to help lead us out of error and ignorance. This moving toward the Perfect, the "Kingdom of Heaven," is therefore the task of all *humankind* guided by the Spirit within, not just something God does to us or for us, the traditional idea of Providence and human passivity:

> Hence we must be careful not to dogmatize, remembering that the light by which we work is imperfect, though more and more is attainable, whenever we work for it in the right direction. How great is Thy wisdom who keepest silence, excepting in the never-silent voice of law, and excepting in those voices, those human voices, inspired by Thee, in accordance with law! [saviours][68]

How does this process work out in practice? Florence believed that the new science's demonstration of universal and invariable laws had provided a path for humankind beyond superstition. Instead of believing the religious hearsay of a few, the verifiable universal laws are available to all. Nitpicky doctrines and supernatural claims as truth can be left behind, and God's character recognized instead in the world through God's laws. Besides, it is an insult to claim God's revelation only arrived four thousand years after the world began (the Hebrew Bible). What sort of a God would wait so long? Revelation comes, not through a book or church, but to everyone, the *constant* revelation of the divine Self from the beginning of time through laws, and through people exercising their human faculties. Florence distinguished between God's unknowable *essence,* and God's *character knowable* through the "laws" of the universe—God's "thoughts." The universe is the incarnation or embodiment of this transcendent Being whose thoughts are manifest as laws. Everything down to the minutest particular is governed by laws seen in their effects—nothing is left to chance. This was not determinism because, though the *laws* never vary since they spring from the Omnipotent Spirit of Truth, their *manifestations* are spectacularly diverse. By discovering the laws, humans become cocreators with the Spirit to work out their particular ramifications in their particular context. These laws are also not the mechanistic laws of an absent Watchmaker, but God's *thoughts,* the active and ongoing manifestation of God's presence in the world, where God is always thinking.

> This spirit wills the same coexistences, the same succession through eternity. This we call law. Hence springs infinite variety. Hence springs development, evolution. There is nothing dull in the operation of invariable law. The universe varies throughout, in every part, in each person from every past. The Almighty never repeats Himself in His wonderful work. Yet His law, whence it springs, never varies. The thought, the feeling whence all springs are ever the same; the activity, His manifestation, ever varying…what nature shall inspire such certainty as the one whose wisdom is such that in Him "is no variableness or shadow of turning"?[69]

The *character* from which these "thoughts" emerge can be discerned through applying all our faculties—physical, spiritual, intellectual, and experiential—to discovering and understanding the laws. As expressions of their cause, they point to their Cause, an intelligent Will, and manifest its character:

> Granted we see signs of universal law all over this world, i.e. law or plan or constant sequences in the moral & intellectual as well as physical phenomena of the world—granted this, we must, in this universal law, find the trace of *a* Being who made it, and what is more of the *character* of the Being who made it.[70]

To those who object to her extrapolation from universal laws to a Will behind the laws, Florence argues that, if there are laws, there must be a purpose or will behind them, and so it is not unreasonable to inquire after the "Willer." She sees signs and hints in the universe suggesting a Will different from the human—"possessing more wisdom and power to effect those same purposes which human will tried for"—and argues that the *character* of that Will is a *Perfect* Being, of whose thought the universe in eternity is the incarnation. "All we can say is, that we recognize a power superior to our own; that we recognize this power as exercised by a wise and good will."[71]

That this Being is perfect and benevolent, whose character is goodness, wisdom, and power (not force but empowerment) is basic to Florence's theology. How can she make this argument for benevolence and perfection? She says that while we can't *dogmatize* this Will as perfect and good, we recognize in past *tendencies* plenty of indication for a benevolent Will, and not the same amount of evidence for an evil or malevolent Will. Even when this Will causes suffering, it is wise and benevolent, because suffering and mistakes lead to a better understanding of God's laws. "Signs of benevolence" might not *prove* God, but suggest an explanation for "those uniformities which observation or experiment have shown to exist, but upon which we hesitate to rely, for want of seeing *why* such a law should exist."[72]

Florence realized the problems with her argument for a perfect, benevolent God—Mill pointed them out when he read her work. While the universe *did* show signs of an intelligent power wishing the human well, there were *also* indications to the contrary. Florence, however, thought these superficial, believing that a wider view not available to us would show the less happy present leading to a more happy future. The divine purpose may not be clear to us "running around on the anthill," but it *is* clear and organized from God's viewpoint.

> If we stop at the superficial signs, the Being is something so bad as no human character can be found to equal in badness...But go deeper & see wider, & it appears as if this plan of *universal* law were the only one by which a good Being could teach his creatures to teach themselves & one another what the road is to universal perfection.[73]

Suffering urges people to further exercise their human faculties to understand the cause and to bring about happiness by removing that suffering.

> The Great Will made the happiness of mankind to depend on the exercise of the capability of mankind, thus calling forth a greater degree of exercise, and with it the greatest happiness, in truth, possible.[74]

Florence's theodicy— the role of a loving God in evil and suffering —most intrigued Jowett.[75] In Christian history, evil has been traditionally catalogued as moral evil (the actions of human agents) and natural evil (harmful natural occurrences). Theodicy tries to reconcile three ideas—God as omnipotent or all-powerful creator; God as benevolent or all good; and the presence of evil. If God (omnipotent) can prevent evil and doesn't, God is not benevolent. If God (good) desires to prevent evil and doesn't, God is not omnipotent. If God can and does prevent evil, evil should not exist. Solutions to these questions vary. Some modify God's omnipotence, arguing that God is limited by other beings, or self-limited to give humans free will. Some retain God's omnipotence by giving creatures free will but claiming that God determines that they only choose good. Contemporary theologians reimagine God's *power*, not as domination or coercion, but as persuasive or empowering—God *attempts* to influence rather than forces behavior. Some reject an all-good God after events such as the Holocaust (theodicies of protest), refusing to profane the dead by justifying God. Some preserve God's goodness by claiming it is acceptable to allow evil as punishment for sin or necessary for growth. Some resist defining evil's origins, focusing instead on God's choice to suffer *with* us. Some question the *reality* of evil, arguing its positive nature in a bigger picture we cannot see. Others see present evil and suffering as earning rewards "an hundredfold" in heaven. Others simply work to combat evil, lament it in liturgy and community, then reflect later on how to talk of it theologically.

The theodicy question had no doubt percolated through Florence's brilliant brain before Egypt, but the hieroglyphic of her beloved Rameses the Great receiving his divine commission from Good *and* Evil convinced her that evil was a *necessary* part of God's plan for human evolution to perfection—"evil is not the opposer of the good, but its collaborator—the left hand of God, as the good is His right."[76]

> We cannot conceive of *perfect* wisdom, perfect happiness, except having *attained*…perfection throu' work…it is rather that we cannot explain or conceive of Perfection except as having worked throu' Imperfection or sin than we cannot conceive or explain how there can be sin if there is a Perfect Being. The Eternal Perfect almost presupposes the Eternal Imperfect.[77]

This idea was not unique. St. Augustine named two types of evil—corruption or perversion of the good, and a necessary element in God's universe that appeared as evil in humanity's limited perspective. German mystic Meister Eckhart thought that evil, as the privation of good, was necessary for the divine plan, driving humans toward greater goodness. Italian philosopher Giordano Bruno saw evil as necessary for a soul to realize perfection:

> On the one hand evil is necessary for good, for were the imperfec-
> tions not felt, there would be no striving after perfection...It would
> not be well were evil non-existent, for it makes for the necessity of
> good, since if evil were removed the desire of good would also
> cease.[78]

Friedrich Schleiermacher agreed that God *allowed* sin to exist because
otherwise, God would destroy it—the reality of evil assisted the
evolution of our full consciousness. Rowland Williams, Florence's
contemporary, placed the root of evil in God's mind: "Since that which
we call evil, comes of eternal possibilities, or of necessities conditioned
to creation, so it has, in one sense, its root nowhere else than in the
mind of the Creator."[79]

Florence believed that humanity was "divine" (one with God), but
temporarily modified through ignorance of God's laws. God's plan was
that humanity move toward actualizing its divine nature, and God
created circumstances so that this evolution through knowledge of God's
laws could happen. Knowledge was gained through trial and error, so
mistakes would be made. What were called sin, evil, and suffering came
from ignorance, both of God's law and ultimate plans. Evil therefore,
was *within* God's plan, to alert humanity to its mistakes on the road to
perfection.

> There will always be evil because there will always be ignorance.
> But there will not be always masses of evil, lying untouched,
> unpenetrated by light and wisdom...Why are we standing
> wondering that God permits evil? Do we want Him to give us no
> work? Or do our work for us? Would that be wisdom, benevolence,
> love in Him?[80]

As for the question of *why* people suffer for that which they did not
cause, Florence turned the argument around. People are outfitted with
God's *power* to deal with life and work toward perfection. Since this
work takes many lifetimes (our reincarnation through many worlds),
the fear of death, lost opportunity, or eternal punishment is diffused,
and humanity can focus on seeking the good rather than resisting the
evil. Although suffering *helps* God's plan for our education, we do not
ignore suffering, or the sufferer, but try to alleviate it by learning from
the mistake that caused it. There is no contradiction between recognizing
poverty as a teacher of social and economic reform and the passion to
help the pauper. Using herself as an example, she said that from the
"evil" of the family drawing room, she learned that such a life did *not*
exercise her human nature to its highest capacity, and so she strove to
change her situation and eventually, that of all other women:

You feel very uncomfortable, therefore change it as soon as you can, pick up everything you can from it while you are in it; but find out the life, as soon as you can, which *does* call out all the goodness and wisdom of which human nature is capable. Can He speak plainer than He does? Could it, if He spoke in words, be more clearly His voice to me?[81]

This is poles apart from the Victorian theology that *justified* the evil perpetuated on the poor as God's will—to endure but not change—where God's *love* was demonstrated by the "charity" of the rich:

It is a radical mistake fatal to all progress to say that we are to remain in the position "in which God has placed us." The very object of all the teaching which we have from God is that we may *find out* the "calling" to which we are called. He leaves *us* to find out. If He were to rub out the wrong figure in the sum and put in the right one Himself, would that be exercising our faculties at all as it does to make us do it ourselves?[82]

Florence changed the theological focus from what we do *wrong* to what we do *right*, from our "desperate wickedness" in need of God's pardon to learning from our mistakes as part of working toward perfection.

We are told to forgive because God forgives us. Although we have been affronted by the other person, we are made to feel the bad guy—we must have done something if God has forgiven us, and we become doubly bad if we don't now forgive. Perhaps God will not forgive us the next time. God's *wrath* becomes the central issue, not the original act done. What a God, who says we must forgive when something bad is done to us, because if we don't he will punish us more! No wonder we love Christ for having come to save us from Him![83]

The idea of *God* forgiving is a stranger doctrine. God cannot forgive. His laws have defined consequences. We may have done something or made a mistake, and this is part of God's teaching of us through cause and consequence of laws. What then has God to forgive us for? God was *in* it.[84]

Instead of one Fall damning humanity forever, there are *many* "falls"—mistakes made. Each event is positioned to aid progress, all connected so intimately that the smallest difference in any part alters the whole. The consequence of these falls "*will* be on the human race till the Savior comes," not as original sin needing the sacrificial death of *one* Savior, but as an error of ignorance repeated until successive saviors come along to help us learn from our mistakes.

> Would not the practical effect of such a belief be to inspire vigorous effort, where effort can be made,—calm patience where it cannot be made, no doubting but that the time will come when effort can be made?[85]

Progress comes step-by-step. The first person cannot know, but when he or she finds out, it becomes, like advances in science, knowledge for everyone. This search for "salvation" together brings in our salvation, the reign of God. The eternal, omnipotent Spirit of righteousness is the inducement that lures the active, individual will to attain righteousness and knowledge, and, when we fail, we are *still* one with God, not condemned, a oneness that gives comfort now and encouragement in the future:

> All the suffering, all the privations of human existence, is because it is the education of mankind which is going on, so that his will shall attain to be right; not that he shall be driven at the will of another, his own being passive.[86]

Florence's theology made sense of the many mistakes at Scutari. The tragic mistake of overcrowding sick soldiers was done in ignorance prior to the germ theory, causing the soaring death rate from infection. Florence learned the mistake from her statistics after the war. Devastated, she punished herself emotionally at first, but then turned what she learned from the mistake into a lifelong passion to teach others what to avoid—her sanitation reform.

> God's laws *are* the origin of moral, as of physical evil—that it is so is part of His righteous rule. Through them, by our mistakes, we find truth; by our errors, knowledge; by our sufferings, happiness; by our evil, good.[87]

Florence's efforts to publish her mistakes baffled those less willing to expose their failures, but she saw this as her "savior role"—leading others from error by explaining yet another of God's laws. *This* is why God called her, the right person at the right time:

> Our belief amounts to this: that I may look back on any particular moment of the past, and truly feel that it was impossible at that moment (God's laws being what they are, and having operated on all proceedings that moment as they did) that I should have willed other than I did. It is therefore untrue and useless that I should cry

out "Oh, how worthy of blame, how deserving of punishment I was." My good friend, I should rather say to myself, "Don't be afraid, you will have suffering enough in what you have done. You exhaust the powers which you have in you for finding out the laws to alter nature or circumstance, by these exclamations." "Come back," I would kindly say to myself, "I know you could not help it. Let us have patience with ourself, and see what we can do."[88]

In a much later article, Florence wondered whether "organized blunders" were *always* beneficial—she decided that foresight was better than trial and error if possible, but was never hesitant about revealing her mistakes for the sake of future knowledge.

In Florence's theology, the "divine goal" is always that humans, individually and collectively, become one with the Perfect One—building "heaven," the place of God's abode, here on earth. *"Time is all that intervenes between man as he is, and man made one with God."*[89] Like many of her time, Florence abandoned traditional teachings on heaven and hell as distant places, in favor of the kingdom of heaven in John's gospel as a *state* of being in the presence of God.

> "Thy kingdom come." If we seek Christ's most abiding, his uppermost thought, it was this. And what did Christ understand by "Thy kingdom"? He explains in those memorable words, "the kingdom of God is within you." There are no more satisfactory words of His…Earth may (can) be heaven.[90]

Since the laws of the universe are God's thoughts, the thinking God is *in* the universe, not external to it. The universe is the "incarnation" of God—"heaven" or where God is. "Heavenly things" are the things pertaining to God. Florence's analysis was in keeping with the Hebrew understanding with which Jesus was raised. In Hebrew Scriptures, *heavenly* had two meanings—the firmament or physical dome that covered the sky, and an adjective for God's presence and activity (1 Kings 8:27–30). God's activity was never restricted to the physical blue dome, but anywhere—didn't Solomon say of the first temple, "But will God indeed dwell on the earth? Even heaven and the highest heaven cannot contain you, much less this house that I have built" (1 Kings 8:27). If God's "house" is where God is, "In my Father's house are many mansions" (John 14:2, KJV) does not mean an otherworldly resting place, but being "with God," even after death. The "heavenly household" is the state of being with God *in* the universe, the continuation of our present state, the "Kingdom of Heaven within," but without a body. If the universe is God present, the "Kingdom of Heaven" is not just within, but also without. Our work as cocreators with God is to make this an ongoing reality by discovering God's thoughts and acting on them. Human ignorance and apathy are all that stop us, not original sin. Since this is a corporate effort to create a corporate "Kingdom" or reign of God, everyone must be "on the job." Florence's call was to teach this reality, not just to the rich, but to the poor:

> It was to the poor the Gospel was preached. And, if another Christ came to draw fresh supplies from the well of truth which fails not, he would still speak to the poor. Truth is a speculation among the rich. Among the poor, there might be a few who would listen and care to find more truth in life than it now manifests. We must be patient, but never failing in fervour for God's work, ready to work and, which is much harder, ready to wait. Then may some seed be sown in this world, and we may be learning for other spheres, when we cannot learn for this.[91]

Since heaven is wherever God dwells, not a far-off place of pearly gates and golden streets, then our immortal soul continues with the ever-present God after death. Like others of her day—William Blake, P. B. Shelley, William Wordsworth, Samuel Taylor Coleridge, Robert Browning, Alfred Lord Tennyson, Richard Monckton Milnes, and Arthur Clough to name a few—Florence saw the soul continuing to be active, not relaxing after a job well done. This activity happened through successive reincarnations in this world and other spheres not necessarily comprehended by the Victorian mind—"In my Father's house are many mansions" (John 14:2, KJV). The task of discovering God's laws is not accomplished in one lifetime.

> The more, in ages to come, mankind shall become convinced, by the evil actually remedied by man, of human possibility to remedy all evil—of human possibility to progress in righteousness and knowledge by progress actually made—the more the experience how each existing character can help the human family as no other can—the stronger will become the conviction that each individuality is intended to help God's family in the universe after, as well as during, his present phase of being. Hence, without increased means of conceiving the mode of existence after death, human belief in it may be strengthened. The ceaseless change which goes on through all existence except One, whose will directs it, is all development—all the fulfilling of purpose. Time, in one sense, is as nothing to the eternal One. He will realize the full, the perfect

development which is His thought, though it require ages beyond the grasp of our minds to conceive.[92]

Plato taught that the soul existed before birth; thus children were closer to God because they could still remember. Florence had noted that the Egyptians seemed more interested in the ongoing whole than one short life, and she also explained Jesus from this idea:

> I have often thought how dull we were not to see that Christ's life showed us this more advanced stage of existence which we call heaven; how we have persisted in calling him the "man of sorrows" instead of calling him the man who is already in a state of blessedness, the man who has progressed and succeeded.[93]

This idea, of course, was not orthodox! F. D. Maurice was dismissed from King's College for calling hell the state of being "without the knowledge of God who is love, and of Jesus who had manifested it" and heaven as "having the knowledge of God and of Jesus Christ."[94] In 1860, ten thousand clergy signed a petition upholding eternal damnation and hell as a central tenet of the Church against alternate views expressed in *Essays and Reviews*. However, Florence found the idea of ongoing work for and with God after death, rather than a permanent hell or heaven somewhere, much more reasonable. Since each human being's nature was uniquely developed by God with much experience to communicate, it was inconsistent to obliterate a being still working toward perfection.

> Without the belief in a continued identity, there is really no belief in [God's] wise and good superintendence...What would we say of a Being who could cause such sufferings for no future benefit to the sufferer, but for future temporary benefit to some future being?[95]

When she could not activate her call in her early years, the idea that it *would* happen, even if not in this life, assured her—she could die "trusting and remembering that there is eternity for God's work."

> The longer I live the more I feel as if all my being was gradually drawing to one point, and if I could be permitted to return and accomplish this in another being, if I may not in this, I should need no other heaven, I could give up the hope of meeting and living with those I loved (and nobody knows how I love) and been separated from here, if it would please God to give me, with a nearer consciousness of his presence, the task of doing this in the next life.[96]

Death held no morbid horrors for her—it simply freed her to work in a different mode of existence. While *physical* laws showed death as the end of human existence, thought, like God's thoughts, continue:

> Is it asked, what beings will live after this life ceases? Every mode of being which admits of thought and feeling; for such modes of being require eternity for their development. No thought, no feeling, can have attained perfection, can have acted and lived perfection, in any limited period. Each individual thinking, feeling being, by the law of the Perfect, works upward, directly or indirectly—attains to the perfect thought and feeling which comprehends all, which feels and wills all truth,—and then again sets forth to work and live, and manifest, and realize fresh phases of being, guided by the law of the all-comprehensive spirit.[97]

This was God's work, and this was the work to which she also was called, now and in many futures.

CHAPTER TEN

Creating Heaven Here and Now

There will be no heaven for me, nor for anyone else, unless we make it—
with wisdom carrying out our thoughts into realities.
Good thoughts don't make a heaven, any more than they make a garden.
But we say, God is to do it for us; not we. We?—what are we to do?—
we are to pray, and to mean well, to take care that our hearts be right.
"God will reward a sincere wish to do right." God will do no such thing:
it is not His plan. He does not treat men like children;
mankind is to create mankind. We are to learn, first, what is heaven,
and secondly, how to make it. We are to ascertain what is right,
and then how to perform it.[1]

In contrast to a passive resignation before God's Providence, as promoted in *The Book of Common Prayer,* Florence's new religion was a call to action—humankind creating humankind as cocreators with God. What might this mean in practice for the artisans of England?

First, the task was one involving the whole of humankind and penetrating every aspect of life—physical, intellectual, emotional, and spiritual—and every part of the universe. Knowledge of God through God's laws or "thoughts" was found not *only* in the Bible or the Church, as traditionally taught, but "in the history of material phenomenon and of consciousness."[2] Since individuals cannot listen for God's voice in everything all the time, we all listen within our particular "departments" of life and communicate what we hear to others:

225

This is not rendering up the *whole* being to anyone. It is each man hearing the voice of God as well as he can in one thing for the rest. Each is the Superior in one thing. We cannot be supposed to listen to the voice of God in astronomy, in chemistry, in theology, in natural history. In all these things, there must be leaders for each.[3]

Florence demonstrated this in her own life, meticulously observing and recording facts across many disciplines and analyzing them to find general laws. In her day, most disciplines were still in their infancy, in need of much work to develop them further, and Florence applied her fine analytical brain to them all. The patterns and symmetry she found, especially from her statistical analysis, she attributed to God's laws, the "thoughts" of the Lawgiver. This is why she called statistics a "sacred" science—it was the language God used to tell us what to do through laws.

Second, the task did not allow for a few to claim authority of knowledge for everyone, the problem with the Church's self-styled authority to interpret religion for the masses. Florence had been inspired by the idea of "priesthood" in the Egyptian hieroglyphics—this idea that everyone had responsibility for seeking knowledge through universal laws within their own experience or profession—science, sociology, politics, motherhood. Everyone therefore was a *priest* by virtue of the sacred knowledge they had acquired. The Egyptians did not appoint general officers that ruled over *everything* and claimed a universal knowledge because of their office. Rather,

All knowledge and science being holy, the profession of any science made the priest...It was not as if a great and ambitious body had by degrees worked itself into all the power and influence in the country; it was as if the power and influence of knowledge, being sacred, made their possessors sacred. It was a part of religion as much to take care of your health as to go and sacrifice in the temple, therefore the doctor was as much a priest, or a sacred character, as the Hierophant or the Sacrificer. The priest was not the doctor or the lawyer, but the doctor or the lawyer was a priest...you find the priestly caste in every office, disdaining none, extending from the king, who was often a high priest, down to the porters of the palaces...The women, too, had offices and vocations in the church— as in every church except ours...how can we conceive a nation...to whom religion was what politics, what railroads are to us? There is something very beautiful in all knowledge being so religious that the very professing of it consecrated a man. To the Egyptians

Sir Isaac Newton would have been as holy as St. Augustine; the one kind of knowledge was as much inspiration as the other.[4]

Florence was critical of church orders, Protestant or Catholic, for this reason. The authority for "truth" was given to *one* powerful mind set over many obedient, childish minds so that, if another powerful mind caused trouble, it had to be silenced, stunting progress. This hierarchical pattern promoted a narrow, exclusive belief that God's laws were as the *Church* saw them from its limited perspective, and that the world consisted only of its obedient community. True "papacy," the real doctrine of "infallibility," existed in its completeness, Florence said, only in the self-constituted unchecked head of an order, parish, congregation, or doctrine (she limits her critique to orders not in constant contact with secular institutions). Florence's painful relationship with Mother Bridgeman sounds through these thoughts. In obedience to her call, Florence had prepared herself for an opportunity like Scutari by applying *all* her faculties—analyzing, observing, organizing—and her skills—languages, philosophy, theology, health care, and so on—and had gone thus equipped to the Crimea, only to be opposed by a mother superior who judged her and her work inferior in the spiritual and vocational arena because she did not have a religious "office." With Florence's idea that everything was "part of God's reign" and everyone sacred because of their work,

> The election of a bishop may be a most secular thing. The election of a representative may be a religious thing. It is not the preluding such an election with public prayer that would make it a religious act. It is religious so far as each man discharges his part as a duty and a solemn responsibility. The question is not whether a thing is done for the State or the Church, but whether it is done with God or without God.[5]

The authority of the priest had long been argued on a hierarchical understanding of the Trinity—Father, Son, priest, people; but Florence had already taken a fresh look at the Trinity, opting to speak about activity and relationship rather than ontological being, satisfied not with one metaphorical description, but many. The Perfect Being *related* to other existence in three ways:

1. As *Creator* of all other existence, its purpose, and its means of fulfilling its purpose. A Being would not be perfectly omnipotent if it did not will other modes of existence with the plan of producing happiness.

2. As *partaker* in these other modes of existence. A Being would not be perfectly wise if it did not will the means to exist for fulfilling its purpose.
3. As *manifested* to these other modes of existence. A Being would not be perfect if it did not cause others to partake in that which constitutes well being.[6]

In earlier letters, she had described these three aspects in activity metaphors—Thought, Word and Hand, arranging, commanding, and actuating. We cannot assume, however, that the three are different metaphors for the traditional three of Father, Son, and Spirit. Florence thought those terms overused and limited by their anthropomorphism. She ended up, in fact, not with a *Trinity*, but an Infinity. The "Father" of traditional Trinitarian language was wisdom, goodness, love, righteousness, power, or the thought, purpose, and will that engender development. The "Son" was the manifestation of God, which is *all* humanity developing according to the will of the Father, so that the Son's (humanity's) nature actually *becomes* that of the Father. The incarnation was not an isolated act, but the "Father" at all times "making Himself the Son—God becoming human to enlighten us."[7] The "Holy Ghost" was the divine within each person through which the "Father" as Thought communicates the divine will to the "Son"—*all* of us. Since God the Father is incomprehensible to humanity, God the Holy Ghost is what we comprehend:

> The son [humanity] must work his way from ignorance and imperfection to truth and perfection before he is one in being with the father. The Holy Spirit developed within him by the law within and around him shall lead him onwards till his being is one with God. Then shall the spirit of God again set forth on the work of fresh development and manifestation.[8]

If Jesus was not the second person of the Trinity, who was he? In John's gospel, Florence found this noble human being whom the Church had "daubed over with bright colors" so no one could see the beautiful form underneath. Since the Spirit was incarnate in everyone, Jesus was not divine in the sense of being *God*. Since miracles were the language of an ancient worldview, Florence thought Jesus was the greatest religious teacher, with his focus on God's truth, God's judgment, and God's work. His uniqueness lay in his single-hearted search, the search to which all are called, and his life of self-giving. The crucifixion was the world's "most important event" as an *example* of this life of service.

I do think *that Christ on the Cross is the highest expression hitherto of God,* not in the vulgar meaning of atonement—but God does hang on the Cross *every* day in everyone of us.[9]

The cross was the tragic result of human ignorance and error, from which humanity must learn. Just as Christ voluntarily embraced the cross, despite his innocence and in order to teach the world from its dreadful mistake, so we must embrace the crosses in our daily lives so the world can continue to learn of God from mistakes, moving toward the perfection of the Perfect. Christ was thus "the way" as a type for humanity, the *practice* of the cross being better than the *doctrine* of the cross. Florence said,

> When you say that it requires "imagination" to take in such expressions as St. Paul's "I die daily—yet I live"—"yet not I, but Christ liveth in me"—I think, it requires not "imagination" but *practice.* I feel, not only that I can understand them, but that every day, every night of my life...they are the true expression of my daily, nightly practice.[10]

By calling Jesus the greatest teacher, Florence was not referring to a perfect message but his example of devotion to his task. Although the church made him a God, he said many things that were culturally bound, not fully explained, or inaccurate. Thus, he was not omniscient. The obscurity in his teaching was also not a helpful educational ploy. The *problem,* Florence argued, was that we look for all the wrong things in Jesus, demanding accuracy and supernatural knowledge rather than recognizing there was *no one* like him, no one who knew as much truth as he did, no one who lived like him—*this* was the wonder of his being!

> Many who do not believe Christ miraculously inspired do not become hardened about him; they love him more than they ever did; they admire his life and character more than those do who think him God.[11]

Florence, like her Unitarian and Broad Church peers, rejected the Church's atonement doctrine—Anselm's idea that Christ was a sacrifice to satisfy God's offense over human sin. Florence saw no need for an atonement, since humanity was not eternally damned through original sin but was working toward God's perfection with the help of the Spirit. Mistakes were not sins to be punished, but lessons to be learned.

> Trials must be made, efforts ventured—some bodies must fall in the breach for others to step upon, failure is one of the most

important elements of success—the failure of one to form a guide-post for others—till, at last, a dog comes who, having smelt all the other roads, & finding them scentless and unfeasible, follows the one which his Master has gone before.[12]

The idea that God seeks revenge by punishing eternally, needs propitiation like an offended parent, or *sent* Jesus to a torturous death were hangovers from an era that demanded such judgment and punishment.Now we think differently, we reform! Such theories concentrating on guilt and remorse turn people uselessly inward, depressing their energy for God. While we should not be *indifferent* to mistakes, we must allow them to urge us toward their elimination so that all enjoy the emerging reign of God. Florence said:

> Away with regrets which have no true foundation, empty your hearts of them! Work out the page of today with goodwill, even though the mistake of yesterday may have complicated it...There is a higher, better, truer help than those pangs—you will never rise high goaded by them. Strive to awaken the divine Spirit of love in yourself, to awaken it in doing your present work, however you may have erred in the past—this will help you far better than dwelling on your own mistakes...Turn your mistakes to as much account as you can for the gaining of experience, but, above all, work on, yield not to paralyzing, depressing retrospection. God gives us the noble privilege of working out His work. He does not work for us. He gives us the means to find the way we should go. An eternal course is before us.[13]

Jesus was therefore the perfect prototype for humanity. He harmonized his nature with God's nature and attained the level of consciousness (union with God) that is promised to us all. His divinity was his union with the Divine, the promise to all of us since Jesus said, "Those are gods or the sons of God to whom the word of God comes."[14] The term *Christ* (Messiah, Savior) indicated this idea of "divinity" rather than a unique, once-only incarnation of God. By changing the human Jesus into *God*, the Church Fathers focused on *one* incarnation and the suffering of *one* day, building all sorts of theories out of it and ignoring the suffering and passion of God over eternity.

> The true feeling of *God in us*, which led to the belief in one incarnation, ought to be extended to the incarnation *in all of us*.[15]

If people thought more about *this*, Florence says, a greater God would be found and a better gospel preached. Why is this so shocking when

Roman Catholicism teaches a continuous incarnation—man to man—through apostolic succession? Besides, *Jesus* did not preach an atonement or incarnation as we know it, nor did he teach ecclesiastical pomp, church hierarchy, or celibate orders, for that matter!

> Do we not see that God is incarnate in *every* man. We think He was only incarnate in one. We make the Trinity God, Christ and the Holy Ghost—instead of making it God and man, and such manifestation of God as man is able to comprehend.[16]

The concept of "saviors" was important to Florence's theology. God the Spirit is incarnate in each of us, encouraging us to exercise all our faculties to bring about the reign of God. This Spirit was also at work through eternity raising up saviors—people sent at different times to save humanity from particular errors.

> God's plan is that we should make mistakes, that the consequences should be definite and unvariable; then comes some Saviour, Christ or another, not one Saviour but many an one, who learns for all the world *by* the consequences of those errors, and "saves" us from them.[17]

Traditional christological arguments distorted this term, Florence said, by arguing that the salvation humanity needed was from an eternal hell— images from an earlier era when punishment was the fate of "bad" people.We know better now. We try to help people grow from their mistakes, to reform themselves, and so we need new images of salvation and saviors.

> Instead of talking about man being "desperately wicked," we should say, as we sometimes do say of great heroes, we did not know of what man was capable. Instead of that hideous, hopeless repetition every day for years of "there is no health in us," we should be living with a purpose, a purpose of moral improvement, which would be constantly realized till we were "perfect, even as God is perfect." What a difference there is between those thus living with a purpose and those who live with no purpose at all.[18]

Just as Jesus helped people see their errors in his day(and was killed for it), saviors are still sent to point out errors —intellectual (hence the rise of science), sociological (hence the rise of societal analysis), physical (hence the influence in sanitation and health), or theological (hence the challenge to the Church). While *everyone* works to discover God's laws, saviors offer special skills at critical moments, not doing the work themselves, but teaching people by pointing out their mistakes. Saviors are specialized:

> Every man is not intended to be superior in everything. But, let him organize a right life, and men superior to himself in different things (or "angels") will spring up. And mankind, not only Christ, will be the Son.[19]

Scientists Galileo, Copernicus, and Newton saved from intellectual error, but Florence also saw a desperate need for saviors from *moral* error to prevent repetition of moral mistakes, the concern of social theorists Jeremy Bentham and John Stuart Mill as well. "Eternal death" was the repeating of past mistakes—there will be no "heaven" *here* until we make it.

Florence received a second call during the time she was writing this— to be a savior. To this point, I have spoken mostly of her "call" or "vocation," but her theology of "saviors" cracks wide open the vision that drove her life. She saw *herself* as a savior—someone "called up" from the crowd of history for a special purpose at a special time. Her reclusiveness was not some selfish maneuvering but her "living sacrifice" as a savior. Her long hours of writing were no thirst for power and influence, but her urgent mission to teach the world through its mistakes. Her determination throughout life to publish her theological ideas, despite constant rejection, was not for public acclaim but was her commission as a savior to free the working class from the mistaken theology that crippled their lives and to urge them to work toward bringing in the reign of God—heaven—on earth. Many have criticized Florence's single-minded focus, excluding friendships and disdaining people who did not share her dedication to work for this reign; but having been called to be a savior, her model was *Christ*, who renounced family life and friends to walk the lonely path of service and death. She felt with Moses in his passion to help the Hebrew people despite his inadequacies. She heard Jesus' cries of desertion and abandonment at Gethsemane and knew them in her own life. With so much preventing humanity's progress toward the Perfect, and possessing so many more "faculties" to exercise than the average person, Florence simply organized her whole life around her call to be a savior.

Once we orientate ourselves to Florence's different theological perspective, so many other doctrines and ideas taken for granted in traditional theology have to be reexamined. Free will was a major debate in Victorian England. The mind consisted of intellect (knowing), sensibility (feeling), and will (acting). One could will to do something, but some actions happened without one's willing them. As Paul said,

"For I do not do what I want, but I do the very thing I hate" (Romans 7:15). To what extent, then, do humans have free will? The fatalists argued that eternal fate, God's Providence, or universal laws governed everything and humans, subject to the law of necessity, had no free will. Freedomists, at the other extreme, argued that humans had total free will. Along the continuum, people differed on the question, Is there existent such a thing as the "power to the contrary"? or is mind a power competent for either of several different results? Necessitarians denied a power to the contrary in the human will, claiming an invariable sequence in all events, psychological and physical, an unbreakable chain where every cause is potent only for one sole effect. If God put this chain of events in place, then God fore*ordained* what everyone would do, denying humans free will; or did God simply have fore*knowledge* of what would come to pass? Election was the extrapolation of this puzzle. If God fore*ordained* everything, does this mean God arbitrarily selected some for eternal bliss and others for eternal punishment, leaving humans no free will to choose? Freedomists, as opposed to Necessitarians, *affirmed* a power to the contrary, arguing that if God has this power, humanity made in God's image must have it also. The question then arose, if humans made in God's image had free will, did they lose it in the Fall? [20] Such questions had social and political as well as religious ramifications. Calvinists argued that God fore*ordained* and had fore*knowledge* of all occurrences. Thus, what *is*, is God's will. If it was not, God's special Providence would have intervened and made changes. The English class system was God's will, a theology attractive to the rich, who also saw themselves as the "elect," but disastrous for the poor, who saw themselves doubly damned, physically and spiritually. The Wesleyans, on the other hand, agreed to God's fore*knowledge* but not predestination—salvation was offered to *all*.

Florence argued that God was a Perfect Being and willed our perfection. How then, does this differ from predestination? Florence said God was the only *cause*, and the *effect* of God's laws or thoughts was the universe. A particular circumstance interacting with a certain nature will produce the same, definite effect. God does not interfere with this, and humans are predestinate in that *all* are predestinate, or heirs to, the happiness of the Creator. Any punishment not intended to improve the creature on this road to happiness is inconsistent with a Being of perfect goodness. This universal preordination to God's happiness gives each of us the power to discover God's laws leading to this happiness. While God's laws are invariable, they are general laws rather than laws predestining individual actions and maneuvering circumstances by special decree. By discovering these invariable laws and cooperating with them, we are cocreators, free to influence our progress toward the Good. Through this process, humans develop a desire for the *same* object, thought, feeling, and wish as God, thus partaking in "the omnipotence of God." We are *not*, as Calvin said, powerless to bring about our own salvation, since we can discover the laws that lead to the state of grace and pursue it. While the statistician Adolphe Quetelet had shown that human behavior could be predicted in particular circumstances, this did not mean people were *puppets* of God's laws, or that the predictions must of *necessity* happen. Rather, such predictions enabled humankind to create the circumstances that would *eliminate* a predicted evil and point people toward the right. God's laws did not *control* humanity, but taught humanity how to *take* control by changing undesirable circumstances. Florence demonstrated this with her reading rooms and schools for Crimean soldiers. While statistics showed soldiers were drunkards, they were not *necessarily* drunk if conditions were changed. Thus when bad things happened, God should not be asked to change the laws, but humankind urged to create humankind by helping the paralyzed soul out of the situation.[21]

Florence preferred the expression "*power* to will what one pleases," to "free will." What we please is shaped by our nature. Three wills are in operation—the will (ability) to do what you want, the will (characteristics) written into our nature that determines what we will *want* to will, and the will (necessity) to decide between them. You can *will* to go into a room but you will *not*, by nature, because you are shy. However, if there is another force strong enough to overcome your nature, you *could* go into the room to show yourself you *can* do it; that is the freedom (will) to go against your nature. By "perfecting" our natures, however, we exercise our free will to align our personal will with the will of God. God does not will us an imperfectible nature. Power, as opposed to free will, allows us to create the *causes* that help our character grow to reflect the Divine character. The laws of God preordain the minutest *connection* of things but not the *consequences*, and, according to these connections and our innate nature, we choose to act. If we miscalculate with unfamiliar laws at play, we learn from the mistake for the future, the process to perfection. When we finally discover *all* God's laws, we will see their full beauty and not wish them any different. We will not say, "Not my will but thine be done," but "Thy will is mine," and all we wish will be done—we will be omnipotent like God, desiring nothing but what God wills.[22]

Some might argue that this "nudging" rather than preordaining God working *with* humanity in a process toward a goal is not omnipotent, but why should omnipotence mean ability to do *everything* that can be thought of, even effect contradictions? Must God be able to make injustice appear as justice, and cruelty as mercy in order to satisfy the condition "all things are possible with God (Matthew 19:26)"? Florence asked.[23] Does not God become *imperfect* by effecting contradiction and making right wrong? If free will means the ability to choose *anything,* even evil, *God* has no free will, since God's wanting to choose evil is a contradiction of a perfect and good God. Is it not better to develop a nature that attracts only good and is not tempted by evil? The aim in rearing children is not to encourage the choice to murder, but to position the child so this would be impossible for its nature—"incline our hearts to keep the law."

> We shall not will to commit evil,—not because we shall have acquired what is called "free will" to make a choice between good and evil, but because we shall no longer be capable of willing evil.[24]

If God is not imaged as an arbitrary Providence to be enticed, praised, and appeased, but rather as the Spirit of truth and love that lures us into union with the divine self, prayer will look different, shifting from asking and pleading to communion and conversation with the Spirit of Love. Again, Florence learned this in an Egyptian hieroglyphic of the great Rameses. Rameses did not enter the temple awestruck, kneeling, beating his breast, asking for forgiveness, but stood "with face upturned and head uncovered, reverentially offering a reasonable service" (Romans 12:1, KJV).

> A mind, which does not offer praise, tiresome praise to God, but says, after its great prototype, "I and my Father are one," for his will is one with God, whatever may befall...The Rameses is that of a perfect intellectual and spiritual man, who feels his connection with that of God, whose first and last lesson through His Christ has been, "Be *one* with me," not be my instrument, nor my worshipper, nor my petitioner, but *one* with me. I am glad to have seen that representation of prayer, it has taught me more than all the sermons I ever read.[25]

What Florence learned was that prayer was the *process* of being at one with God, intercourse with God, feeling devoted to God's case, living with the God within. "To be without God in the world leaves every joy without brightness, to be with Him makes every sorrow in some sense bliss."[26]

Such communion did not need words. In many of her travel letters, Florence spoke of sitting in a sacred place communing with God, with or without words. Art and architecture were often more powerful communicators than words. Of artist Michelangelo's paintings in the Sistine Chapel of the Vatican in Rome she wrote:

> I feel these things to be part of the word of God, of the ladder to heaven. The word of God is all by which he reveals his thought, all by which he makes a manifestation of Himself to men—it is not to be narrowed and confined to one book, or one nation...no one can have seen the Sistine Chapel without feeling that he has been very near to God, that he will understand some of his words better for ever after—and that Michael Angelo...has received as much of the breath of God, and has done as much to communicate it to men, as any *seer* of old. He has performed that wonderful miracle of giving form to the breath of God, chiseling his inspiration, wonderful whether it is done by words, colours or hard stones.[27]

Breaking old models, Florence called prayer not intercession with an absent crucified Christ in heaven persuading and being persuaded, but communication with "the Son" as the divine in all humanity, the *many* Christs, the Spirit which "ever liveth to work for us." Asking for deliverance was not God's plan—those who think God works by sending miracles in response to prayers of petition should ask why there are so few! We are not paupers asking for bread, but people working to bring about the reign of God. As for those who wanted God to "speak" messages to them, we can't even *comprehend* the Eternal, let alone understand the Eternal's speech—yet God does speak through the Spirit:

> I could not understand God, if He were to speak to me. But the Holy Spirit, the Divine in me, tells me what I am to do. I am conscious of a voice that I can hear, telling me more truth and good than I *am*. As I rise to *be* more truly and more rightly, this voice is ever beyond and above me, calling to more and more good. But you have to invent what it says (put it into words and action). We believe that each man has his Holy Ghost; that is, the best part of himself inspired by God. But whether it is I who speak or whether it is God speaking to me, I do not know.[28]

Public prayer, as spelled out in The *Book of Common Prayer*, was, to Florence, dishonest and a sham. At morning prayer, we admit everything we have done is wrong and we mean to act differently. At evening prayer we say the same thing—"It is to be hoped for the sake of their sincerity that they have done something wrong between this and then, otherwise they would be telling a lie."[29]

Such prayer was seen only as one's *duty.* No one expected to meet God there, so no one was ever disappointed. If public prayer had any use, it would be about communion and communing—the celebration of our shared task in the world—not petition and penitence. "Would that our intercourse with each other could be such as that to be together *were* a means of being more, not less, in the presence of God!"[30]

The day could start with our being together, learning one another's hearts and rousing ourselves to the divine within us through words addressed to reason, and end by recounting God's work and hailing our fellow workers.

The image of a *relationship* between humanity and God also changes perceptions about human beings. How we envisage the character of God *does* matter. Responsibility or "duty" was considered an important Christian virtue in Victorian England, locking people into boxes not of their choosing—Florence was imprisoned in the drawing room for years by her duty as a daughter. How, Florence argued, can we be *responsible* to God for what we did not request? Responsibility is what someone contracts when accepting a task, yet humans did not ask to be born or to be assigned particular talents or class. Moral responsibility for what we did not request is forced on us by society under threat of punishment, and we consequently live in anxiety about failing, or need to escape. In the same way, rewards and punishment make no sense. How can those whose will is formed by the Creator be justly rewarded or punished for it? The human relationship with God is, instead, that of trainee to trainer where we are "gradually raised to share in all our Father's powers, in all His happiness, in all His truth."[31] We share a mutual goal with the Divine and, on the way to this joint goal, there are moments when we feel "I and my Father are one" (John 10:30), the ultimate state to which both the Spirit and ourselves are working. In this image, God does not seek to be praised, adored, and gloried—that would make God arrogant and vain, not *desirable*—but to work with us, to be in communion with us. God wants us to be "one with Him, not prostrate before Him."[32]

> A just and true appreciation of what we are and what we may become, of how God will help us if we take the appointed means to receive His help, what He will do for us and what we are to do for ourselves, is the state which is true to our nature, true to God's nature...If our state of mind is right, we shall press ever onward to be and to do in the infinite career before us. Such progress will be the want, the thirst of our nature—not undertaken to satisfy pride, not calling forth pride. To God we shall refer what we are, what we shall become, our means of becoming what it is fitting we should be. There will be no place in us where pride can enter. While the infinite is beyond, how can we feel proud of any step towards it?[33]

Pride and humility were ambivalent issues with which Florence struggled throughout her life. Humility was preached as a virtue checking pride, but humility is only noble if pride is a "sin." If God's laws have made us what we are, without which we can do nothing, how can we be proud *or* humble? These are two extremes *transcended* by an honest appraisal of our abilities, having more to do with concern about our "reputation" than anything. Florence had learned this through her own "mistake." For years she blamed the lack of a second call on her pride, whipping herself into false humility and self-abnegation, which trapped her in inactivity. Now she could say, in autobiographical honesty:

> We may pray for humility, but "it's no use" while there is no wind of sufficient strength to blow our thoughts away from ourselves. How many have struggled against a sin of vanity, and prayed and prayed, and gone through years of self-mortification, and self-inflicted tortures, and wondered why God was so far off, and whether "His arm was shortened that He could not save" and why He was so deaf that He would not hear, and have been brought to the very verge of despair...whereas if they had lived a life which had afforded them one interest so strong as to make them forget themselves, they would have forgotten their own puny reputation from the mere force of another interest.[34]

Pride, on the other hand, was a God-given natural desire implanted in us to be and do something. Humility, a perversion of that desire, hampers its proper exercise. Florence had watched this in orders where subordinates surrendered their own authoritative voice to a superior, becoming "dead bodies," because they believed God spoke only through the superior, not themselves. To esteem everyone superior to oneself was folly—the extrapolation would demand that the scientist Galileo give up his opinion to an "ignoramus."

> Humility is thinking meanly of ourselves, placing ourselves below others, and being willing that others should do so too. Is not this rather absurdity and untruth? What I want is a true estimate of myself, not a false one. I want to see myself as God sees me...The maxim, let a man know what he can do, and do it, is not compatible with that of humility. Humility, if logically carried into our conduct, would lead to our giving up everything we do into the hands of those whom we are to strive to think can do it better than ourselves.[35]

Renunciation of the world and ourselves was a further step on this same road. The religious goal to renounce this world for another made no sense, since *this* world and humankind is our work, and we are called to create a better world *here* as the reign of God.

> Besides, it is ungrateful to God, when He is seeking to give you pleasure, always to take the worst—*not that someone else may have the best*, but only for the sake of mortifying *yourself*, and especially, if you do this for the sake of having the best in another world. To "renounce worldly enjoyment" implies a mistake. It should *be* our enjoyment to do the world's work. It does not improve us to 'hate' anything.[36]

While St. Teresa of Avila went into raptures at a heavenly vision, we should be in *constant* rapture since God is *always* with us saying, "It is I, be not afraid" (Matthew 14:27).[37]

> "Do not regret anything that is past. It is all right. *I did it.* Do not be anxious about anything to come. It is all under my laws, in accordance with my nature." We should have perfect trust...Can we ever doubt that He exists? It seems ingratitude to do so (as if we were to doubt the goodness of the kindest friend), after such proofs as we have had of His goodness.[38]

Others promoted *self*-denial, but to seek the work you *disliked* most, to forget yourself, to despise praise, to mortify and humble yourself, was a false and unhealthy "doing of things for reward" touched with a certain "pride even in humility." Turning away from evil, and cleansing the soul of iniquity is a kind of self-seeking and self-absorption, instead of taking every means to do good. Concentrating on "burying the old man" takes time away from discovering the "new man" and calling forth our good, not our bad. In each case, Florence said, the end was better attained by going out of ourselves than by "trampling upon ourselves."[39]

Florence's theology was revolutionary for those caught in seemingly hopeless situations. Rather than being overwhelmed with guilt, remorse, and failure, especially when not the agent of one's plight, people could image instead an encouraging God struggling *with* them, urging them to learn from their situation and move toward their liberation.

> Let us rejoice and bless God, with our eyes open to the evils around and within us. All we suffer, and see suffered, all the melancholy privations we feel and see, are voices telling us these things.[40]

While *The Book of Common Prayer* continued to preach illness as God's infliction and cure as a miracle, Florence's religion in an ordered universe where nature could not be contradicted had no place for those teachings. Jesus' walking on the sea was a "paltry" part of the story, Florence thought, when Jesus *also* said, "It is I, be not afraid." The reliability of God's laws constantly speaking to us of God was a far better basis for religion than the occasional, arbitrary miracle, even though people are "terrified" at the idea of a religion without miracles—a lowering of the conception of God, Florence thought.

> We open a book of science, and we read of a God all order and beauty and goodness, and He excites no feeling. We open the life of St. Teresa, and we find a God all injustice and disorder, and we find her in a rapture about Him. The God of law is always speaking to us—always saying what is wise and good. The God of St. Teresa speaks to her sometimes, and says something which is often foolish and not good. Curious indeed, that, while the God of science never appears to have excited any feeling, the other God has excited so much![41]

This theology drove Florence's reform work. Horrific army conditions in the Crimea led her to reform the army medical services and draft the British delegation's proposals to the Geneva Conference that would produce the Geneva Convention and the Red Cross. Inhumane treatment of paupers in the workhouse impelled her to train workhouse health care givers. Deaths among soldiers in India jump-started her numerous social reforms for *all* of India. Shocking conditions in England's hospitals pushed her toward effective hospital design and sanitation. Suffering patients forced her to create new theories about health as a state humans must achieve for themselves. In *Notes on Nursing* (1860), she argued that healing, like all physical phenomena, was a lawful process regulated by God's natural laws. The caregiver's task was to discover these laws through observation—proper food, ventilation, cleanliness, and quiet—and cooperate consciously with the recovery process..."Nature alone cures, and what nursing has to do...is to put the patient in the best condition for nature to act upon him."[42]

The germ theory was not yet proven, and sanitation not widely accepted by doctors since Joseph Lister had not yet published on asepsis and bacteria and Robert Koch's germ theory was only accepted in 1879.[43] Disease, for which there was little scientific treatment, was attributed to a type of fermentation "emanating" from human and animal waste and decay in filthy, overcrowded conditions. Florence thought the suggestion of contagion was "witchcraft," believing there were no specific *diseases* but disease *conditions* to be rectified. She removed funding for a statistics chair at Oxford, afraid it would be used "to endow some bacillus or microbe." "Medicine is a mere matter of experience of which we do not yet know the rules."[44] When Koch proved the germ theory in 1879, Florence's theories as to what *caused* disease became outdated, but not her practical sanitation ideas or her theology that concentrated not on belief in certain unchangeable *facts*, but in a *process* that allowed such "facts" to change with knowledge and context:

> Sanitary Science is showing how we may affect the constitution of the living and of future lives. In one direction sanitary science is understood to apply to the physical nature; but each part of man's nature affects every other. Moreover, there is a sanitary science essential to each of man's faculties and function. To each there is an appropriate state and operation—in other words, a healthy state—and there is a science discoverable as to how, by what means to bring about the appropriate state.[45]

Florence's theology prefigured aspects of many twentieth-century theologians. Of particular interest is her anticipation of Alfred North Whitehead's process philosophy with its inclusive framework within which different sciences could operate, and of his *theological* successors who saw in this broad-based philosophy a way to *also* talk about God, including science and religion in a single vision. Whitehead's ideas emerged not from a career in philosophy, but one in mathematics, Florence's passion as well. Whitehead (1861–1947) began his Cambridge career in Mathematics and Logic, moving to the Philosophy of Science mid-career. In his later years at Harvard University in the United States, he pulled his accumulated thoughts into the most extensive philosophical cosmology of the twentieth century. In *Science and the Modern World* (1825) Whitehead argued that cosmology should be based on aesthetic, ethical, and religious intuitions as well as science, and that scientific method pointed away from a mechanistic world to an organismic worldview. Although agnostic, Whitehead's philosophy led him to affirm the *philosophical* existence of a "principle of limitation" accounting for the basic order of the world. Process *theology* emerged out of Whitehead's metaphysics by elaborating on that principle of limitation as God.

Some of process theology's basic arguments, which parallel Florence's theology, include:[46]

1. Everything, whether an eternal deity or bits of matter or molecules, is a *momentary* event with an internal process of becoming, involving some degree of spontaneity or self-determination.

2. Everything can be included under the same principles of discussion, whether scientific or religious. Nothing lies outside this scheme of analysis, even God.

3. There is no duality between humans and nature. God did not create nature as a backdrop for the human drama, but rather, each has its own integrity.

4. Everything in the universe is interconnected, affecting one another, not just in external ways but in internal relations. All things flow, and reality is relational—a social process. We experience God by the way God is present in all "others" around us. "Others" are not simply other *finite* processes in the environment, but *all* processes— God is pervasive of all nature and present in every individual, whether microbe, bird, or electron. Each is a unique mode of the divine presence in a web of relationships. God is omnipresent, with everything in every moment experiencing God as ground of both order and freedom.

5. God calls us to choose God's good vision for the world, working within the world's process by continual and universal self-revelation. This revelation is interwoven into our experience of the world, and shaped by it, therefore always somewhat ambiguous. God is also the ground of the world's *becoming*, but, since the power of God is interwoven with the power of the world, this is also open. The world may be more or less responsive to God, but there are no separate events in our world standing outside the laws of nature and history that can be pointed to as "God alone did that."

6. All individual things have "experience," not only sensory but also a nonsensory "prehension" where the prehended objects are taken into the prehending subject. This allows for religious experience to be described as God's becoming incarnate in the experiencer. The challenge for Christian theology in this infinite incarnation of God is to show how God present in Jesus was different enough to make Jesus of decisive importance.[47]

7. The world is not external to God, but God is the essential soul of the universe and has always interacted with the universe. Thus, the universe was not created from nothing. God is love, the foundation of all reality, and God's power is persuasive, not coercive. God is coeternal with the world and shares the adventure with us. There has always been some sort of realm where God has been creatively active.

8. Evil in this system exists, since creatures can both determine themselves and affect others for good or bad, influenced, but not

controlled by, God. Without evil, this could not happen. The freedom of individuals allows them to go against the divine will, which, because it is not self-limiting, cannot be revoked now and then to prevent evil. God loves perfectly, thus suffers completely in and with the world, not overruling our freedom but awaiting our response and seeking to create the best that can become from the choices we make. The future is therefore always open, not fixed and settled. God's goodness is more plausible in this system than theodicies that say God *could* or *does* control all events.

9. Creativity is the basic power within all activity. God is not creativity, but the *primordial* embodiment of creativity. There is the primordial nature of God—God in Godself—and the consequent nature of God is in process with and affected by the world. The primordial nature of God is unchanging perfection, but the consequent nature in process with the world "changes," because new things are happening, new creatures arise, new experiences occur, and thus, divine experience is *also* being enriched. To be an individual in the world is to be self-creative, but only out of what has gone before (limits) and whatever new impinges on our present, including God (possibilities for transformation).

10. We are "saved" by being taken up into God's consequent nature as a "given" of existing; yet we are also "saved" to the degree God becomes effective in our lives—becoming "deified," as the Eastern Orthodox say, as we act in harmony with God, lured on by God. This "salvation" is not an individual process, but in process with all else in the world, all influencing each moment of being and becoming. God is the initial aim of the moment luring us to make optimum choices for that moment.

11. This process of creative transformation through divine grace does not end with bodily death.

It is not hard to see the amazing similarities between process thought emerging in the early twentieth century and Florence's prior vision in the mid-nineteenth century. Whitehead and Florence, both fascinated with mathematics, wanted a "map of being" that included *all* categories of existence, including, but not limited to, science and religion. The outcome for Whitehead was a philosophical system that proved itself also able to accommodate a God-concept. The intention for Florence was a system that *did* include a God-concept from the beginning, over against Comte's elimination of God. Traditional theology argued a God over against the world and nature, interrupting its laws through special Providence. Florence sought to describe God *within* the universe, the Eternal Will beyond everything manifesting itself in laws.

"The whole universe is a single intellectual aim," we might add a *single aim* of the spirit of love, of beauty, of order, of righteousness, of benevolence, of every attribute which man can appreciate as right and good, and true; of others, it may be, which he cannot appreciate.[48]

The debates of science, geology, and biology in Florence's time had centered around matter—where it came from and when—a debate which inevitably came into collision with religion's pre-scientific ideas of creation. Florence, like her process theology counterparts, changed the focus of the argument from things or matter to events, with God the *spring* or fountain of all existence, which is eternal. All "beginnings," therefore, were simply changes from one present state to another arising from this eternal spring—all manifestations of one unvarying purpose. In this framework, we do not have to focus on whether matter exists, where it came from, when, and who created it, no more than *everything* exists as the thought of God "eternally possessing perfect goodness and wisdom." Everything springs from the same will and tends to the same purpose. The more we penetrate, whether as geologists, historians, or theologians, the character of various things and the effect they have on one another, the more traces we will find of this underlying or interconnecting Eternal Will or Thought: "The true prophet will see vistas in the eternity before us, as the eye, which penetrates into the past, sees them in the past eternity, all disclosing the same will."[49]

How then do we explain phenomena? Florence said that everything builds on the past into the future. "There is nothing final in the universe of mind or of matter—all is tendency, growth."[50] Geology and other sciences were already showing this process—how changes actually took place in things previously believed not to change—the everlasting hills, the "solid orb" of earth.

Such great and remarkable changes come to pass by small and imperceptible changes, not to be conceived, only to be expressed by saying, that all that *is*, all that has existence (except the unchanging one, whose will is the source of all other being) is always changed in time present from what it was in time past. That present time, so quickly passing, that before we can say, before we can think that it *is*, it is gone; yet has changed all existence but the One who directs *all*. Preceding, simultaneous with each individual physical phenomenon, each state of mind, there have been and are conditions without which that particular phenomenon or state of mind would not have been. It would be again—the same conditions existing. But they will never exist again *precisely*. Mark the eternal road, without beginning, without end, in which all that is, marches, ever the same *principle, tending* all the same way. In all that is now, there is repetition of what has been, but also variety; never exactly the same; never quite different. For the conditions which regulate the present are never *quite* different or *quite* the same, but enough the same, differing enough to reveal that the resemblance and the difference mark a relation, a connection, which is what we intend to express when we say that all change manifests law, as the *constitution* of each individuality manifests law. The history of each individuality, the *tendency* of that history, manifests law. If *this* has been, *that* is invariably. If *this* is, *that* will be certainly.[51]

In this explanation so accommodating with process theology, Florence credited what also became central to Whitehead's thinking as the measure of knowledge—*experience*. Florence did not argue a doctrine to be believed, but something to be examined and tested by one's own experience:

This is maintained on no man's...opinion, or belief that have been revealed by Omnipotence to men long ago departed from this world. It is open to all men to examine whether it is or is not so. Observe, examine, vast nature is before you. Your own thoughts, what you wish, what you will, the consciousness ever present to you (which *is* yourself), all this there to answer the question whether this is true or not of law.[52]

Just as process theology sees God as the initial aim, first thought, instigator or ground of each moment, luring the world toward harmony, Florence's God was also woven *with* the world, urging the exercise of all one's faculties. Each present mode of being was part of a development from a past without beginning to a future without end. The consistency of *will* or direction was the eternal Spirit, "whose thought, whose feeling, whose purpose, whose will, comprehends every other mode of being."[53] The inconsistency of will was ours. God's aim was to bring our wills into union with the divine will, so that we would will what the Perfect Good wills. This process takes time and patience since it is not coercion, but persuasion, and humans make mistakes (or choose to repeat the past moment):

The reason of our suffering and grievousness of inefficiency is the want in us of this consistency and comprehensiveness of will. If I knew how, I too would have a *single aim* of righteousness, and love, and benevolence, and beauty, and order; but I have a different aim every half-hour, without comprehensiveness, connection, consistency. In this only can I be comprehensive and consistent. I can say, "thy will be done"; I accord with that will; I acquiesce in waiting till we find out how to be comprehensive and consistent, till we attain the blessed oneness.[54]

The "blessed oneness" is in knowing that, even in suffering and ignorance and inefficiency, we shall work our way to the light at last and, by remembering these days of darkness, "wish to deliver others from sufferings and privations which we have known by experience."[55]

The more humanity advances, the more it can conceive of a spirit of perfection at work in the world, with each action part of the perfecting process. Why do we not just sit and do nothing then? Because the laws of God visit us with consequences until we do something. God's laws have provided that it is impossible for our natures to continue to do nothing. Providence then, in Florence's theological dictionary, was this working out of the laws leading to perfection through the Spirit within. God had it in the divine thought that when we act in each moment, we should do so given past events, what the plan of the event was, and its purported results, somewhat like God's "initial aim" in process theology. "The whole state of the universe at this moment is the consequence of the whole state of the universe at every past moment, both in regards its spiritual and its physical laws."[56] This is not determinism, since we could choose *not* to follow the divine thought, or may be ignorant of it as a "law." Thus, new circumstances have to arrive to induce us once more to choose that path. This is why *all* our faculties must constantly be engaged to recognize the event.

Since the eternal Spirit has always been at work, questions of beginnings and ends become less important, and the *process* becomes central. Florence said:

> Was there never a time when the spirit of love, of wisdom, of truth, of righteousness, did not exist? What is time? All that we know of it is succession of events. And is there any reason within or without us for supposing that this spirit in any succession of events did not exist? in any succession of events will not exist? And if the thought, the sentiment of right, and love, and wisdom is eternal, will not its manifestation in life, in activity, be eternal?[57]

In this developing process, individuality becomes less important because each takes up the thought of the one before and further develops it, sharing in God's whole being and purpose. Death does not bring an end to our individual affections, because the process of continued growth goes on, unaffected by the loss of physical existence—"The eternal becoming is always going on"—which makes sense, given the work toward perfection already achieved. We are contained within the nature of God:

> The Perfect thus contains in His nature all the individual affections which ever were, matured by life and work, in one. And this one, in again individualizing, according to the laws of righteousness and benevolence, contains in its nature those same individuals which may again meet as individuals, again merge into perfection—perfection of thought and feeling, now and for ever, but such thought and feeling ever anew worked out in successive phases of life. This is not pantheism, which asserts that man will be merged in God and lose his individuality...Can we suppose that God sent forth a being to suffer and struggle, merely in order that it should be re-absorbed into God's existence? Most lame and impotent conclusion. Why send it forth? To what end its suffering? Individuality appears to be sacred in the thought of God. Indeed, if we suppose man to be a modification of the attributes of God limited by the laws of physical nature, it seems natural to expect that individuality will be preserved in every instance till perfection is attained.[58]

In a world where the authority of Bible and church, so long at its zenith, was being radically challenged by scientific knowledge, sociological changes, moral questions, and political unrest, and where the space for God had become crowded or uncertain, Florence opted for an honest, experiential engagement of *all* human faculties to discover God as the "spring" in the midst of it all. With her brilliant mind and incredible breadth of knowledge in various fields, she could attempt such a task, in order to articulate a religion that might answer the questions of the age, not just for the elite, but for those whose circumstances needed it most, the working-class poor. When it came to the bottom line, *experience,* with which Florence began her theological argument, was for her the path to truth about God:

> What can we know of the Being we call God, but from the manifestation of His nature—His attributes? Look for His thought, His feeling, His purpose; in a word, His spirit within you, without you, behind you, before you. It is indeed omnipresent. Work your true work, and you will find His presence in your self—i.e., the presence of those attributes, those qualities, that spirit, which is all we know of God. If we recognize this spirit without us in the rule of the universe—if we recognize this spirit within us, whenever

man is well at work, may we not say, "He is in us, and we in Him"? We shall find this no vain or fanciful theory. If we seek Him by true work, true life, we shall find Him (i.e., His attributes which are all we know of Him) within us; limited indeed, as is right, till our life and work shall attain for us higher regions of being—i.e., greater love, greater wisdom, greater power. Well it is that power is so limited, while love and wisdom are so feeble. Blessed are the limits of humanity, till it has advanced to greater purity and truth!...And let all this be tested by the realities of life, striving to look at these comprehensively, in relation to all being and all successions of being. Thus only can we, in any degree, see as God sees, which is "truth."[59]

CHAPTER ELEVEN

A "True" Marriage

God surrounds us. His Law is ever at work, bringing about the right,
so all will be well. Without this conviction, the present world would be fearful
for, in the errors which are dying out, it is difficult to distinguish
the germs of truth which are growing up. Oh! That we could
help ourselves and each other out of the present selfish, cold, self-satisfied views,
poor and narrow, while supposed to be new and improved light.[1]

When Arthur Clough and Sir Sidney Herbert died within months of each other in 1861, another man emerged in Florence's life to whom she would pour out her intense grief and form an undying bond of friendship. She had begun corresponding with Benjamin Jowett in 1860 when Clough sent her "anonymous" manuscript to him for comment. Jowett, feeling the "impress of a new mind," was even more intrigued to hear that it was Florence Nightingale's. The two like minds instantly fused, even though they did not meet until October 1862. From then until Jowett's death in 1893, their friendship was foremost in both of their lives—a "spiritual" marriage cemented by their deep affection for each other despite very different backgrounds.

Since Florence's theology was forever evolving, *Suggestions for Thought* was not her final word. Florence's open, frank, and frequent correspondence with Jowett until his death reveals her evolving theology over the next thirty years of her life, always in a dance with her work and experience. Consequently, I have constructed the last two chapters about Florence's life and theology around Jowett's letters to her.[2] Unfortunately, Jowett obeyed Florence when she demanded he burn her letters, so we have only his, with a few of hers, and must interweave these with other material and letters Florence was writing during this time to get an expanded picture. However, Jowett's letters not only highlight their ideas and their careers, but also make Florence come alive in a way no other resource can. Through the trivia of everyday life, the teasing and affectionate banter of two people with so much in common, and the trauma of reform in which both were involved, the amazing personality of this incredible woman reaches out to grasp us and introduces us, at the same time, to the towering figure of Anglican dissent who won her heart and guided her spirit.

Three years older than Florence, Benjamin Jowett was born in 1817 at the opposite end of the social world. His father was a third-generation furrier who drove the family business into bankruptcy, obsessed as he was with producing a new metric version of the Psalms. The senior Jowett's narrow, dogmatic Wesleyan evangelicalism, with a liberal dose of William Cowper, was imposed on his wife and seven children, only two of whom lived to middle age. Benjamin's mother was of better stock and temperament but, bowed under her husband's will, focused almost completely on her *sickly* children, leaving Benjamin and sister Emily to fend for themselves. When the family business finally collapsed, Benjamin's mother took six children to Bath, leaving her husband alone in a low-paying job and eleven-year-old Benjamin to find single lodgings near his school. Alone outside of school hours and with no funds to visit his family, Benjamin grew up disgusted at both his father's failure and narrow, unreasonable religion.

Jowett set out to succeed where his father had failed. With few resources save some helpful teachers, he won a scholarship to Balliol College, Oxford, and was elected a fellow as an undergraduate—a rare feat. He became a tutor at twenty-five and, although he would have preferred otherwise, was ordained, a requirement for tutors. He thought that creeds and statements of belief were difficult to uphold, putting obstacles in thinking people's way. Nor did clergymen help people to think, creating instead great schemes "for the regeneration of mankind," and using the church as their means to do it. Remaining loyal to the Church as long as it did not require "lying to his soul," the ever-accessible Jowett excelled as a tutor, shaping a generation of devoted students to think for themselves. He was retiring, little interested in trivialities or small talk, and demanded the highest standard of himself and others. These words about him could have been written about Florence:

He had the almost preposterous belief in what men can do by hard work and self-mastery. He had little mercy on those who pleaded incapability. As a teacher and tutor he got hold of men...and persuaded them by sheer force of will to exercise their will so as to do work of which they thought themselves utterly incapable...there were hundreds of men whom Jowett convinced of the power of the human will. He himself throughout life showed resolute strength, determined, unflinching, almost autocratic strength. Yet he combined this with the most humble and child-like submissiveness to the will of God.[3]

Jowett was not without enemies—those jealous of his popularity and brilliance, those uncomfortable with his silences and undefined sexuality, and those threatened by his open-minded, liberal opinions. He never stood for any party or aligned with any cause, perhaps his greatest contribution as a tutor. One student wrote:

As to Jowett's "religion." I used to wonder what he believed. I came to the conclusion that he never put a clear and distinct issue to himself or to anyone else on any speculative subject...I doubt if any downright statement—on speculative matters—was ever true or false to Jowett. It was true "in a sense." In another generation it would have been true "in another sense"...possibly, to use Andrew Lang's simile, he found a *ledge* somewhere, where he could stand without slipping. But he was incapable by nature of taking up a pickaxe and delving out a *"hole"* in which to stand, as Newman did, or Liddon, or Calvin or Luther.[4]

At Balliol in the 1830s, the big question was, What should the Church of England be? Oxford and Cambridge educated those for Anglican Orders *and* those for government, which thus had a stake in the question. Catholics and Nonconformists now held national and municipal offices, and "subscription"—the rule that undergraduates sign the *Thirty-Nine Articles* to graduate—had become muddied, in that Anglican divines themselves did not hold with all the *Articles*. Did "orthodoxy" mean believing *all* the doctrines, even the troublesome damnation clause in the Athanasian Creed, or simply acceptance of *The Book of Common Prayer* despite one's scruples about some of it?[5] John Henry Newman further stirred the waters by claiming a Roman Catholic could sign the *Articles*, raising the specter of popery in an Anglican pulpit. Furthermore, "heretic" Renn Hampden had been made a divinity professor; redundant Anglican bishoprics in Ireland had been disbanded; electoral reform was shaking established and powerful parishes, and an ecclesiastical inquiry into church revenue was in the air. The men in the Balliol common room pitted themselves against one another. Some, like Jowett, who was more comfortable with nonbelievers than with some of his clergy colleagues, wanted the university to be as much as possible "all things to all men."[6]

Jowett had abandoned his rigid evangelical upbringing, but did not go with the Oxford Movement. Neither atheistic nor agnostic, he was a modernist and a moderate with a simple genuine piety. He read philosophy and brought Hegel's thoughts to England from Germany for the first time. As a classical scholar, he dedicated his life to translating Plato, and, as a theologian, he struggled to define the Ideal that he saw both in Plato and in Christ:

> That image which Plato saw dimly in the distance, which, when existing among men, he called, in the language of Homer, 'the likeness of God,' the likeness of a nature which in all ages men have felt to be greater and better than themselves.[7]

Jowett's "moral" religion gave him more clarity, upholding an ideal pattern exemplified by Christ and promoted by the Church, from which everyone must seek to make their own character. The reward was the fulfillment of the obligation. "We are more certain of our ideas of truth and right than we are of the existence of God, and are led on in the order of thought from one to the other."[8]

Only later in life did Jowett realize that the moral code was not as universal and obvious as he had thought. He was always a quiet reformer free of sectarian leanings, believing that if people had means and privilege, whether from inheritance or hard work, they were bound to help others and work hard. From his comfortable security at Balliol, he went to extremes to encourage working-class boys to achieve.

Jowett's tutorial years from 1842 to 1854 were his happiest ones at Oxford. He enjoyed teaching and good friends. Interested in university reform, he prepared a letter to Parliament in 1847, which, with Prime Minister Gladstone's support, became the basis of the 1854 University Reform Bill. That same year, the Crimean War began, and the Master of Balliol died. Jowett's name was put forward with others, but his friend Robert Scott was brought back for the job by Jowett's opposition.[9] In the following years, Scott did everything possible to crush all Jowett's schemes of reform and also questioned his orthodoxy. Badly hurt, Jowett removed himself from the common room and the dining hall, concentrating instead on his students and writing. He was appointed Regis Professor of Greek by Lord Palmerston in 1855 as a compensation, but this nominal Crown appointment from Henry VIII's era still carried the forty pounds a year salary, while University professors earned four hundred pounds. Jowett took his role seriously, struggling on this pittance until 1865 when a public outcry equalized his salary with University teachers. It did not help that during this time he was labeled a heretic for an essay on the Atonement.

He and his friend Arthur Stanley had begun writing a commentary on Paul's epistles. Jowett's commentaries on Thessalonians, Galatians, and Romans were published with Stanley's on Corinthians in 1855. Jowett's essay in the collection *On Atonement and Satisfaction* provoked an outcry with its claim that the Atonement doctrine as commonly expounded was "morally disgusting." A *slave* was not low enough of mind to justify such disproportionate severity, especially from the hand that gave it life.

> God is represented as angry with us for what we never did: He is ready to inflict a disproportionate punishment on us for what we are: He is satisfied by the sufferings of the Son in our stead…The imperfection of human law is transferred to the Divine…The death of Christ is also explained by an analogy of the ancient rite of sacrifice. He is the victim laid upon the altar to appease the wrath of God.[10]

So bad were theories like this, developed over a thousand years and "rooted in language, disguised in figures of speech, fortified by logic" that "they seem almost to have become part of the human mind itself…One cannot but fear whether it be still possible so to teach Christ as not to cast a shadow on the holiness and truth of God."[11]

Jowett concluded that this conception of Christ's work had no foundation in scripture, but was developed in ecclesiastical history. The only sacrifice a Christian must make was moral or spiritual, not the pouring out of blood, but a living sacrifice to do God's will, in which the believer as well as God plays a part. When the first attack on the essay came from evangelical Anglicans, the vice-chancellor ordered Jowett to resubscribe to the *Articles*, along with receiving an admonition. Jowett, disgusted by such a childish, legalistic procedure, took "the meaner part" and resigned as the only way to keep his teaching position, resolving to enlarge his Atonement essay in the second edition! High Churchman E. B. Pusey also thought Jowett's ideas heretical and dangerous, but he was honest enough to pursue the greater evil of Jowett's puny salary, proposing an increase, which was defeated. Hot on the heels of all this came the publication of the controversial collection of essays, *Essays and Reviews*.

When the idea for this volume of theological essays by Broad Church scholars was proposed to him, Jowett saw it as an opportunity to publish an important essay on the critical study of scripture he had been writing for more than ten years. Each essay was to stand alone as the individual essayist's views. The names of the essayists would be included to protest the current "abominable system of terrorism, which prevents the statement of the plainest facts, and makes true theology or theological education impossible."[12]

Everyone knew this publication would be a hot potato, and Arthur Stanley advised Jowett against contributing, having seen others who rocked the Anglican boat drown. Jowett contributed anyway, and the unexpected furor that followed discouraged him from publishing in theology ever again, despite constant promises to Florence that he would. The ideas in his essay are well accepted now, but his fate was to be ahead of his time.

Essays and Reviews appeared in February 1860—seven essays of varying merit, all from significant scholars. The goal was stated:

> The volume, it is hoped, will be received as an attempt to illustrate the advantage derivable to the cause of religious and moral truth, from a free handling, in a becoming spirit, of subjects peculiarly liable to suffer by the repetition of conventional language, and from traditional methods of treatment.[13]

Together, they covered all the controversial issues of the Church, and the religion and science debate as well. It was a best-seller! *Essays and Reviews* is important to our story because it was published at the same time as Florence's draft of *Suggestions for Thought*, dealing with the same issues, and many of its authors were her conversation partners and friends. Frederick William Temple, headmaster of Rugby, wrote the first essay on *The Education of the World*, offering a world now grown that required a "wider view" of things—science, biblical interpretation, and so on—and "fearless" study of the Bible. Temple said:

> If geology proves to us that we must not interpret the first chapters of Genesis literally; if historical investigations shall show us that inspiration, however it may protect the doctrine, yet was not empowered to protect the narrative of the inspired writers from occasional inaccuracy; if careful criticism shall prove that there have been occasionally interpolations and forgeries in that Book, as in many others; the results should still be welcome…The immediate work of our day is the study of the Bible…For we are now men, governed by principles, if governed at all, and cannot rely any longer on the impulses of youth or the discipline of childhood.[14]

Rowland Williams, professor of Hebrew, wrote on *Bunsen's Biblical Researches*. Von Bunsen, a mentor of Florence's, was dying at this time, but his book *God in History* was about to be published. Von Bunsen also had a new translation of the Bible partially completed, intended "for the people," where he made significant alterations and rearrangements of the traditional Hebrew text. Like Jowett, von Bunsen believed "the dogmatic mould into which the Church had poured belief had made belief set too hard."[15] Williams added some controversial ideas of his own, including "Why may not justification by faith have meant the peace of mind, or sense of Divine approval, which comes of trust in a righteous God, rather than a fiction of merit by transfer?"[16]

Baden Powell, an Anglican priest and Oxford Professor of Geometry contributed *On the Study of the Evidences of Christianity* from a scientist's perspective, saying that miracles must be discredited because they bore no analogy to the harmony of God's dealings in the material world, and were a violation of the laws of matter and an interruption of the course of physical laws. Were miracles really *necessary* anymore to convince believers or happenings now open to scientific explanation?

Henry Wilson, the conceiver of the project and a professor of Anglo-Saxon turned country parson, wrote *Seances Historiques de Geneve—The National Church*. Courageously argued and well written, it was probably the most shocking essay. Wilson described what a national church ought to be, and argued that God *also* favored the "neutral multitude" when called to their account after death. This went totally against the Anglican doctrine that the wicked were irretrievably damned and would be eternally punished. Wilson also argued that a national church should not insist on dogmatic positions that did not represent the beliefs of a majority, but should be broad enough to include the beliefs of most of the nation. Wilson's concern was less about Nonconformists than about retaining intelligent people in the Church who found the creeds impossible to accept. The fifth essay *On the Mosaic Cosmogony* by Charles Goodwin, a Cambridge layperson, argued that the new science, especially geology, challenged the Genesis story of creation, and that attempts to reconcile science and religion by simply calling the days "ages" were insufficient. The story of creation must be accepted as a simple Hebrew myth of human origin, used by Providence in earlier times to educate humanity, but now superseded by better facts. Essay six, *Tendencies of Religious Thought in England, 1688–1750* by Mark Pattison, Oxford Anglican divine, traced this period of history, but ended with a sentence that suggested that contemporary folk should *also* check the authority on which their beliefs rested.

Jowett's essay, *On the Interpretation of Scripture,* was the last one and the best, asking that reason be used in scriptural interpretation.

Jowett summarized his argument with a classic description of what is now the accepted biblical critical method:

> Of what has been said, this is the sum:—That Scripture, like other books, has one meaning, which is to be gathered from itself without reference to the adaptations of Fathers or Divines; and without regard to *a priori* notions about its nature and origin. It is to be interpreted like other books, with attention to the character of its authors, and the prevailing state of civilization and knowledge, with allowance for peculiarities, style and language, and modes of thought and figures of speech. Yet not without a sense that as we read there grows upon us the witness of God in the world, anticipating in a rude and primitive age the truth that was to be, shining more and more unto the perfect day in the life of Christ, which again is reflected from different points of view in the teaching of His Apostles.[17]

Jowett urged that theologians come with impartiality, not with preconceived "affections" that might disorder their conclusions. Those who reverence inquiry cannot hold the right to condemn other inquirers.

The book's popularity was increased by the ecclesiastical furor. Laity found answers to questions, and many clergy supported the essayists. However, when Bishop Samuel Wilberforce of Oxford objected, panic ensued, and archbishops were called to stand against these traitors to their calling, guilty of moral dishonesty by remaining in the Church.[18] The Positivists, followers of Comte, attacked as well, seeing a liberalized Christianity harmful to their own position. The "official" Church objected to

> the denial of the atoning efficacy of the Death and Passion of our Blessed Saviour Jesus Christ, both God and Man, for us men and for our salvation, and to the denial also of a Divine Inspiration, peculiar to themselves alone, of the Canonical Scriptures of the Old and New Testament.[19]

The essayists were disappointed in that Bishop Tait of London, who had supported their theology to their faces, secretly opposed them.[20] Jowett despaired that there would soon be "no religion in Oxford among intellectual young men, unless religion is shown to be consistent with criticism. I wish the Bishops were alive to the great and increasing evil of the want of ability among young clergymen."[21] *Essays and Reviews* was brought before the Church courts. Williams and Wilson were prosecuted, but made successful appeals to the Privy Council, who found nothing "as to require us to condemn as penal the expression of hope by a clergyman that even the ultimate pardon of the wicked who are condemned in the day of judgment may be consistent with the will of Almighty God."[22] Goodwin was beyond censure as laity, but Baden Powell was charged, dying before his trial. Temple lived under a cloud at Rugby School and withdrew his essay to become Bishop of Exeter.

Conservative High Churchman Pusey was very distraught about the essays, fearing the end of faith because nothing "keeps men from any sin except the love of God or the fear of Hell."[23] He instigated heresy proceedings against Jowett for his ideas on the atonement and scriptural interpretation, but the suit was dismissed without appeal. The whole situation made Jowett despair of taking on the Anglican establishment, and he resolved never again to speak his mind publicly on theological matters. Pusey furthered his pursuit with an alliance with evangelical Bishop Wilberforce against their common enemies, producing a declaration of belief with more than 12,000 clergy signatures. It affirmed that the Church

> in common with the whole Catholic Church, maintains without reserve or qualification the inspiration and Divine authority of the whole canonical Scriptures, as not only containing, but being, the Word of God, and further teaches, in the words of our blessed Lord, that the "punishment" of the "cursed" equally with the "life" of the "righteous" is "everlasting."[24]

Chaos ensued as bishops and archbishops took sides. When Arthur Stanley appealed to Pusey in the name of "common Christianity," Pusey denied anything in common with Jowett:

> I do not know what single truth we hold in common, except that somehow Jesus came from God, which the Mahommedans believe too. I do not think that Professor Jowett believes our Lord to have been Very God, or God the Holy Ghost to be a Personal Being. The doctrine of the Atonement, as he states it, is something wholly unmeaning.[25]

In a reply to Jowett's supporter F. D. Maurice, Pusey hit the nail on the head about the problem—"We do not believe in the same God":

> The God, whom we adore in His awful and inscrutable justice and holiness, these writers affirm to be cruel. The God whom they acknowledge we believe to be the creature of their own minds, not the God Who has revealed Himself to man.[26]

A petition from 137,000 Anglican laity arrived at Lambeth Palace opposing the heretics. The committee investigating the book condemned it, and the battle raged on. During this traumatic time, Florence Nightingale came into Jowett's life and eclipsed all others.[27]

Jowett had more to contend with growing up than his family circumstances. He was constantly described as "girlish," and was possibly gay, something unmentionable at Oxford at the time.[28] From early days, he was repelled by physical intimacy and sex, no doubt unsure of his own sexuality and horrified at his feelings toward something described as monstrous. During his lifetime, he nurtured three great friendships—with Arthur Stanley, Robert Morier, and Florence Nightingale. He loved the two men, but could never bring himself to acknowledge any erotic bent to his affection, although others saw it. A strict upholder of Victorian morals, Jowett revealed some of his inner struggle in his translation of male eroticism in his beloved Plato. Plato's description of love between males in *Phaedrus* and the *Symposium* became, in Jowett's translation, heterosexual love and *married* love at that:

> In this, as in other discussions about love, what Plato says of the loves of men must be transferred to the loves of women, before we can attach any serious meaning to his words. Had he lived in our times he would have made the transposition himself. But seeing in his own age the impossibility of woman being the intellectual helpmate or friend of man (except in the rare instances of a Diotima or an Aspasia), seeing that, even as to personal beauty, her place was taken by young mankind instead of womankind, he tries to work out the problem of love without regard to the distinctions of nature.[29]

The physical love between Socrates and Phaedrus, a man and a younger boy, was no more than kissing and embracing, according to Jowett, paralleling the union of minds in a marriage where the *best* love is holy friendship rather than sexual love—when two souls are "purified from the grossness of earthly passion."[30] The following description by Jowett of a "true" marriage bears strong resemblance to some of Florence's ideas:

> The poet might describe in eloquent words the nature of such a union; how after many struggles the true love was found; how the two passed their lives together in the service of God and man; how their characters were reflected upon one another, and seemed to grow more like year by year; how they read in one another's eyes the thoughts, wishes, actions of the other;...how after a time at no long interval, first one and then the other fell asleep, and "appeared to the unwise" to die, but were reunited in another state of being,

in which they saw Justice and holiness and truth, not according to the imperfect copies of them which are found in this world.[31]

The relationship between Florence and Jowett has been much dissected, as has their individual sexuality. Woodham-Smith's biography, which included material not available to Cook, said that friends knew of Jowett's pressure on Florence to marry him, but she refused.[32] Barbara Dossey's biography includes a conversation between an Indian student at Oxford, Cornelia Sorabji, and the aging Jowett. Jowett had arranged for Cornelia to meet Florence and later, in his office, pointed to the only picture of a woman—Florence in her younger days. He said, "When she was like that, I asked her to marry me," but then added abruptly, "It was better so." Sorabji, who went on to become "the Nightingale of India," remembered Florence's cousin showing her an entry in Florence's diary referring to that occasion: "Benjamin Jowett came to see me. Disastrous! Nothing more."[33] No doubt Jowett found in Florence this union of minds sublimating both the physical and his guilt-filled sexual ambivalence. He had, for a time in 1860, been interested in Margaret Elliott, daughter of the Dean of Bristol, but Oxford fellows had to vacate their fellowship to marry. Jowett was tempted, smarting under Robert Scott as Balliol's Master and being attacked for heresy. He could have taken a country post and *did* apply, unsuccessfully, for the position for a married fellow at Oxford. After that, Jowett gave up on Margaret and, by then, Florence had appeared on his scene.

In his later years, Jowett seemed more able to acknowledge his inner struggles of sexual identity. Reformer Josephine Butler praised Jowett's handling of an "outbreak of abnormal immorality among a few of the young men at Oxford":

> To such he was (I know) the wisest, most prudent and gentlest of counselors. He was extremely severe and tender at the same time...I got to know how implicitly such misguided or guilty creatures might confide in him, and seek and follow his advice. In these matters he was a help and blessing to many beyond what it is possible to publish...he never seemed to give any man up as hopeless, or beyond the reach of sympathy and help.[34]

Perhaps this contact with other strugglers allowed Jowett to accept himself, giving him permission to recognize Plato's love between men. He finally admitted there was a place for "passion," even in friendships, such as the love of Jonathan for David, "wonderful, passing the love of women." In a later letter to an unidentified woman, Jowett said:

You ask me where in Plato's writings the idea of Platonic love is to be found. In the *Symposium* and *Phaedrus*, two of the most wonderful of human creations. But I should explain that Platonic love in the modern sense does not exist in Plato. Women, as you rightly conjecture, were too little accounted of among the Greeks. The love of which he speaks is the mystical love of men for one another, the union of two souls in a single perfect friendship. Whether such a thing is possible, I do not say—or right. But it appears to have been a much stronger feeling than the regard of men for women.[35]

The friendship between Florence and Jowett began in 1860 when Jowett read *Suggestions for Thought,* her "stuff" as they called it.[36] Jowett was immediately intrigued with both the content and the person behind it. He did express doubt as to whether her selected audience, the working class, would enter into her broad, speculative attempts to link science and religion, but this was an even greater reason to pursue it. He also said he saw many things more clearly after reading her work. After a few months, Jowett was comfortable enough to suggest she reduce her "irreverence" in expression as much as possible while still preserving truth. Jowett was obviously stunned over "Cassandra," wondering from his limited male experience just how *widely* this was women's experience. Of interest to feminist theologians, he advised Florence against using so much of her own *experience* in the argument, lessening "the weight of what is said."[37] Jowett was at a loss for a remedy for the women's dilemma. He agreed a female Christ would help, but such a woman would need a nature "which unites all feminine sympathies & in a certain sense graces, with an heroic temper & firmness of soul."[38] He did not say whether Florence had this combination. Any action would also have to conceal its real goal because, if not, it would degenerate into vulgarity on one side (the Suffragists) or sentimentalism on the other. Jowett, in his early days of correspondence with Florence, revealed his dearth of good female role models:

> For the mass of women I doubt whether any change in the subjects of Education would do any good—a second rate mind intellectualized & crammed with information is very useless & disagreeable. The "Sweet creature" who knows nothing is far preferable. With women even more than men it seems absolutely necessary that education should bear some proportion to original power.[39]

We are at a disadvantage not having Florence's replies to Jowett, and can only surmise her response by what he then replies to her.

Florence must have assured him that "Cassandra" was not purely autobiographical, but many women's experience. As to whether he thought her egotistical in presuming to write theology, Jowett assured Florence of the value of her ideas, and offered to help rearrange and reconstruct them. His one critique of her content involved her idea that sin was simply a mistake to reveal a law. Jowett saw it as more "a species of moral deterioration" for which we must take responsibility rather than denying moral evil and one's own evil deeds as the effect of law.[40] The idea of evil as moral deterioration rather then a mistake may have been on his mind as he shared with Florence the charges against Rowland Williams for his essay. His accusers were not concerned about whether his ideas were untrue, but about "prudence and public opinion."

Sir Sidney Herbert died at this time (August 1861), and Jowett sent his sympathies to Florence, both for Herbert's death and the restrictions of her "illness," limiting her to writing rather than "the jaw"—teaching. The *Essays* outcry still weighed on him as he discussed Temple's suppression of his real views to aid his rise to a bishopric. Jowett continued to worry over Florence's assertive prose as a woman, encouraging her not to offend would-be supporters with "shocking" stray thoughts unnecessary to the argument. In response to her no doubt fiery reaction, he countered, "I don't think that all the bone & muscle of the book need be taken out."[41] He was intrigued with Florence's attempts to combine the idea of universal laws in the universe with a mysticism or reverence, agreeing there was an audience for this— "religious people who will sympathize with the practical side—scientific people to whom religion (contrary to human nature) has become a blank."[42] As well as all this, in only eight short months of correspondence, the very private Jowett was softening his formal approach and opening his soul a fraction to let out the sorrows of his past:

> Some things in your papers strike me as remarkably true to my own experience of life. 1) the unhappiness of families, which is generally, however, sealed & shrouded from the world. 2) the absolute want of discernment that parents have about the characters & tastes of their children; to which I should add their strong affection for them, & inversely the greater discernment that children have of the characters & wants of their parents together with a strong sense of duty towards them & yet a much feebler affection for them. 3) the waste of youthful talent for want of opportunity. Every year I am more & more impressed with the natural talents of young men. And I wish I could do more & more to prevent

these good blossoms from falling—some from shyness, some from ignorance of the world & of the characters of others—some from fanaticism, religious or irreligious; others from worse causes yet none of them, while young, incurable. I know some persons will say "You think young men able because they often take your opinions." That is not, I think, the case; it is not difficult to distinguish between a young man following your opinions & his real capacity. From some young men I seem to learn more than from any older friends.[43]

Two months later in 1861, Jowett penned another letter of sympathy to Florence when their mutual friend Arthur Clough died. Jowett tried to impress on her devastated soul that she should carry on alone. "If there be any way in this world to be like Christ it must be by pursuing in solitude and illness, without the support of sympathy or public opinion, works for the good of mankind."[44]

Florence in her grief had sunk back into illness, despairing whether she could go on alone. In March 1861, Jowett wrote of his concern for her condition, asking if he could help with "further sewing together" her "stuff," perhaps knowing that was one thing which might pull her out of her despair:

I should wish you every earthly good, if you were not past caring for such things. But now as years of suffering come & go & many of your friends are taken I cannot but wish you (as sincerely as I ever desired anything) unabated hope & trust & resolve to continue in your work to the end, & many rays of light to cheer the way. It is not the expedition to the Crimea so much as the patient, solitary, unknown toil which astonishes me & makes me feel grateful for your example.[45]

Florence did not reply because Jowett wrote again, four months later, on the pretext that Mary Clarke Mohl (Clarkey) said Florence wished to know the outcome of the *Essays* trials. Florence had by this time resumed her intense workload without Clough's help, analyzing the extensive data she had received from her questionnaires on Indian sanitary and health conditions. Rather than wait for the government to instigate the promised Indian Sanitary Commission, Florence had written personally to every military station in India in preparation for writing the Commission Report herself.

Jowett related to Florence the Privy Council's actions in favor of the essayists, but also the stupidity of theological questions being argued from a purely legal stance by lawyers:

The Interpretation of Scripture is left entirely open; it may be literal, allegorical, ideological—what you please—provided there is no contradiction of the letter of some Article. To speculate whether there were two Isaiahs...is no longer forbidden ground to a clergyman of the Church of England. Scripture is, or is supposed to be, the foundation of the C. of E. in popular opinion & therefore the value of this latitude can hardly be overrated...The region marked "dangers," where you are liable to fall in, is in statements of doctrine which contradict the Articles…An important point in the case is the express statement of the Judge that no Clergyman can be called to account for anything but overt acts: "The Court is not cognizant of mere opinions."[46]

Reflecting on Florence's question as to why the essayists did not leave the Church, instead of trying to reconcile their consciences to her teaching, Jowett thought that, despite everything, the Church of England still gave a greater freedom through its diverse parties than in a small, more homogenous religious community even of freethinkers. "I cannot give up the hope that this great organization may be one day used for far higher purposes...At any rate I feel that I should be denationalized & sectarianized if I separated."[47]

In a rare surviving letter to Jowett (July 1862), Florence thanked him for inquiring again about her "Stuff," telling him nothing more had been done, but that, once her Indian War Office work was finished— doing for the Army in India what was done for the Army at home—she would return to it. She bemoaned her loss of enthusiasm and feeling for her work now that her supportive men had gone:

If I were what I was 8 years ago, I would have a Working Men's Children's School to teach them all the laws of Nature (known) upon this principle, that it is a religious act to clean out a gutter and to prevent cholera, and that it is not a religious act to pray (in the sense of asking). I have such a strong feeling that he who founds a Soldiers' Club (to keep them out of vice) is doing more than he who teaches abstract religious truth, that I would not teach the "stuff" if I could do anything else practical—but I can't now.[48]

Despite Florence's conviction that mistakes are to be learned from, she was not beyond questioning God's wisdom in *some* situations, especially the "wisdom" of Sir Sidney's death.

I could not go on...if I did not believe myself part of a plan...For otherwise it would seem as if I had been trying to work for God and he to thwart my work (I have often told him so). He brought about the most extraordinary combination—one which could hardly ever happen again, by which a woman obtains all the practical knowledge of Army organization, and a Secretary of State is willing not only to listen to her, but to devote every instant of 5 years to it—and he breaks this up.[49]

In the midst of Florence's work on Indian Sanitary reform, her health deteriorated sufficiently for Florence to ask Jowett to come to London and administer the Sacrament to her. Jowett agreed, and on October 19, 1862, they met for the first time. After the visit, Jowett wrote:

Dear Miss Nightingale, I shall always regard the circumstance of having given you the Communion as a solemn event in my life, which is a call to devote myself to the service of God & men (if He will give me the power to do so). Your example will often come before me, especially if I have occasion to continue my work under bodily suffering.[50]

Jowett's concern for Florence and his interest in her family begins to sound more than pastoral. Geoffrey Faber, Jowett's biographer, says that Jowett's affections for Florence began growing in 1862, peaking in 1864, when she must have said something to discourage further hope. For the administering of that Sacrament, Jowett had asked if Uncle Sam and Aunt Mai, or any member of their family should be present. At this point, Florence was estranged from Aunt Mai, still angry that Aunt Mai had "deserted" her to return to her family. From something said to him by a family member, Jowett gently admonished Florence about her relationship with them:

You cause more pain than you are aware of by isolating yourself from them…I am aware that difficulties of character & nervous states are very great; also that your public duties leave no time for gossip & friendships. Still it seems to me that Christian love should win a way over these obstacles, so far at least as to make people who love & care for you, understand that you love & care for them…The worldliness & weakness of many of them may be the reason of such an estrangement. Still the strong should find a place in their hearts for the weak.[51]

Aunt Mai's daughter Blanche, Clough's widow, was the cause of the problem, as indicated in Jowett's next letter. Florence was obviously concerned that Blanche had said something about her to Jowett, and Florence's father had also written to him, criticizing the "terrible load" he had placed on the ailing Florence—no doubt Jowett's comments about family harmony! Jowett sympathized with Florence over a painful attack attributed to the "common misery about the death of our dear friend." Perhaps Blanche Clough was blaming Florence's work for her husband's death, or perhaps Aunt Mai had been recalled home because her daughter was not happy with her husband's infatuation with Florence's ideas and reform. Later, when Florence was editing Jowett's Plato translation, she described the perfect relationship between two people:

> One of the highest relations in life possible is friendship (not love) between a *man* and a *woman*—*not* husband & wife, that where marriage is *good* its goodness is enhanced, enlarged, by the husband having *friendship* with other women, married or not, & also, I suppose, by the wife having friends among other men. Surely marriage should enlarge & strengthen all other ties, instead of cutting them off as in England.[52]

Jowett visited Florence again in December 1862 to give her the Sacrament. He was now obviously enchanted with this soul mate, whom he chides, is in awe of, and treats as an equal, all in one letter. He continued to update her on the *Essays* trials. Another storm was brewing in South Africa, where Bishop John Colenso had adapted Christian doctrines to the native African context and had published *Critical Examination of the Pentateuch,* whose ideas, similar to the *Essays,* would generate similar shock waves. The Church tried to excommunicate Colenso, and again the Privy Council overturned the charges. Colenso insisted on continuing as Bishop, even though an "orthodox" Bishop was sent to act in his stead. As a result of this farce, by 1866 half the Balliol fellows supported Jowett and the Broad Church's belief that the church should not silence or obstruct truth.

Florence was totally absorbed in her latest call to be a savior—her "sacred mission" of Indian sanitary reform. Stories of appalling sanitary conditions in the British Army in India had surfaced during the 1859 Army Royal Commission, and a sanitary commission was established on Florence's urging. Prior to its establishment, Florence personally sent questionnaires to all the military stations in India soliciting information and requested all the government reports on India. The 2,183-page report she produced was the *only* database available on India when the sanitary commission began its work. Her concern was not only the troops but also Britain's responsibility to care for those under its control. Florence envisaged a public health department for *all* of India, since Army sanitation would not improve unless village sanitation also improved.

Florence's report, *Observations by Miss Nightingale* or *The Red Book*, illustrated by cousin Hilary, was issued in 1863 in two volumes. Once again, her statistics showed a disaster—nine per one thousand soldiers in India dying from natural causes and sixty per one thousand of causes related to poor sanitation. This mortality rate was three times greater than for troops at home prior to the Crimea. Without some action, England would not produce enough troops for India. Wise in the ways of officialdom, Florence sent a few advance copies of her report to journalists, infuriating officialdom because of its damning information, but rightly foreshadowing her fears. A lower-level clerk edited out much of her critique for the Parliamentary copies, so Florence contacted each Parliamentary member to tell him to request the original. Her privately published *"Red Book"* stood against the government's edited *"Blue Book,"* and, when asked later what brought sanitation reform to India, the Governor of Bombay said, "a certain *Red Book.*" Lord Stanley, chair of the India Sanitary Commission, wrote to Florence in 1864 attributing the rapid progress of reform in India to her almost single-handedly.

Florence did not stop with sanitation. She advocated for an administrative structure between India and Britain that could not be undermined by successive governments and a scheme to enable soldiers embarking for India to have money sent back to their families for the weeks at sea. In every case, her call was the same—to help others help themselves, "to speak for those who have no voice, to be the voluntary representative of the poor and dumb and ignorant…to make others noble we must ourselves be noble."[53]

Since any real progress in India had to come from within, Florence spent many hours encouraging key Indian individuals by letter to initiate change:

> A people cannot really be helped except through itself: a people must be *in*formed, *re*formed, *in*spired through itself. A people is its own soil and its own water. Others may plant, but it must *grow* its own produce.[54]

She was concerned that Indian people had, in the British, "an alien bureaucracy living chiefly for itself, with little or no sympathy with the people."[55] She wanted her sanitary reforms headed up by *local* people.

> If villagers are not taught the simple things they can do for themselves to promote health at home, law cannot force them, nor can funds help them. Is it not generally not so much want of money as the want of knowledge that produces bad sanitary conditions?[56]

When severe drought swept India in the 1870s, Florence turned her attention to preventive irrigation schemes. Because of the expense, this was abandoned by the government in preference of railways to deliver grain to drought-affected areas. She also wrote tracts for Indian villagers on sanitation, which were translated into many dialects and widely distributed so people could learn to help themselves. Many doctors who answered her early requests about Indian health problems stayed in touch with her. She sent a paper to the National Association for the Promotion of Social Science in 1873 on *Life and Death in India* discussing problems of deforestation, development of railways, and other Western intrusions disadvantaging the Indian. During India's 1877 famine, Florence's article *The People of India* was published, claiming that Britain did not care about India's plight and suggesting measures to help the lower classes emerge from poverty. Although she had never been to India and made mistakes in her Indian work, few English people knew India as well as she did. Biographers who criticize Florence's "use" of influential people, maneuvering behind the scenes, forget this was all she *could* do to pursue her call to be a savior. She could not sit on commissions or be a member of Parliament, and, without her Crimean fame, her writings and research would never have been taken seriously. She stepped out of her place and was not shy about using opportunities to get her message across, often at her own expense. This is why she saw the "accident" of her friendship with Sir Sidney as part of God's elaborate plan for humanity's progress.

Florence's support systems were now sparse. The remaining "war cabinet" member, Dr. Sutherland, met with her daily as personal physician and liaison with visitors. He advised her on almost every project, Florence grasping the details and doing the statistics, and Sutherland bringing it to reality. He edited her rough manuscripts, since she hated that process, always wanting to work on the next task. Their ongoing partnership gave him a way to continue his sanitation interest, though his lack of passion and drive frustrated Florence. His was a sensible, lighthearted approach, a balance to her excesses, a tonic for her stress, and a lightener of her moods with his notes to "Dear and respected enemy" or "Dear howling epileptic friend." Although cousin Hilary had been a great help to Florence, Florence sent her home in 1862, hoping she would pursue her art career. Without Hilary and Clough, Florence did all her own correspondence and final copying of reports. By the mid-1860s, she was in very poor health, doing only what was important for her work and seeing only those directly related to it.

After sharing Florence's feelings with Jowett in the summer of 1863, together with her ongoing grief over Sir Sidney's death, Jowett wrote:

It troubles me sometimes to think of your solitary sufferings—you to whom others owe so much. I cannot think there is anything wrong in your desire for death: it seems to me quite natural & not in the least degree to be made a subject of self-reproach. Only let me put the other side to you. It has pleased God to enable you to do great things for your fellow creatures. But far more may be done in the next ten years, if your life is spared, than has been already done. And you must not desert your post while anything remains to be done…I think that a blessed vision of those whose sufferings you have alleviated ought to hover around you by night or day, under the pressure of your own…It is a higher strain of faith to go on with them now when there is no human sympathy or friendship to assist in them but God only.[57]

Over the years, Jowett sometimes seemed impatient with Florence's erratic illnesses and her "near death" moments, even though he remained sympathetic. Perhaps, like others, he recognized their convenience:

I should be glad to hear that you were suffering less when I saw you. Sometimes I think that the Doctors ought to cure you; sometimes that you ought to cure yourself, or a combination of both. I wish you would try the latter process—though the age of miracles is past I think that something might be done.[58]

With the obviously deep affection between them, and the story that Jowett *did* ask Florence to marry him, perhaps her excuse against marriage had been her poor health and her imminent death!

By 1864, Florence was opposing the Contagious Diseases Act and writing long letters to Jowett about it. The Act required regular inspection of prostitutes associated with Army brothels. Florence had published an opposition paper, believing such diseases were not contagious and that inspection of prostitutes "legalized" prostitution rather than working to establish other outlets for soldiers. When her recommendations were defeated and the Act passed, Florence refused to help select medical officers for the examinations and pushed harder for diversionary avenues for soldiers. Later she saw the prostitutes' perspective. Examinations were a form of rape for women, and nothing was done to stop promiscuous men. She began to work to help prostitutes find other careers. Jowett disagreed with Florence's desire to "legislate" moral issues rather than address the practical problem of the spread of disease—"there seems to me a prior obligation to mitigate disease of so fearful a character which may affect the innocent quite as much as the vicious."[59] However, Florence's approach reflected her *medical* belief that disease came from disease *conditions* rather than being contagious.

At the same time, philanthropist William Rathbone contacted Florence about training nurses for the Liverpool Workhouse Infirmary.[60] Florence embraced this new opportunity to work on something dear to her heart—poorhouse reform:

> Whatever may be the difficulties about pauperism, in two things most people agree—viz., that workhouse sick ought to have the best practical nursing, as well as Hospital sick—& that a good, wise Matron may save many of those from life-long pauperism by first nursing them well, & then rousing them to exertion, & helping them to employment.[61]

Poorhouses or workhouses were places for the destitute and were segregated by sex and age, sick and healthy, breaking up families and causing all sorts of health problems. Florence felt workhouse patients were the "most neglected of the human race." She arranged for twelve Nightingale nurses from St. Thomas's to go to Liverpool, and her scheme for training workhouse nurses became a model for workhouse health reform. Rathbone's gratitude was so great he sent flowers *daily* to her home until his death in 1902. Not content with Liverpool, Florence entered the national Poor Law Reform debate along with Dr. Sutherland, helping tip the scales for reform. Rather than improve a few of the problems, she attacked the *intent* of the Poor Law:

> As long as a sick man, woman or child is considered administratively to be a pauper to be repressed, and not a fellow-creature to be nursed to health, so long will these most shameful disclosures have to be made…Why do we have Hospitals in order to cure, and Workhouse Infirmaries in order not to cure?[62]

Florence suggested the poor sick be separated from the general poorhouse population and placed where they could get proper health care. She also requested a central administration to monitor all poorhouses and a general tax to pay for it. The bill that passed was based on Florence's recommendations.

Florence's fame spread beyond England. British officials concerned with deaths among the indigenous people through contact with white settlers contacted her. In 1863, she convinced the Colonial Office to allow her to investigate the effect of European schools and hospitals on native populations, collecting data from Australia, Ceylon, Natal, West Africa, and British North America. Australia sought her advice on the death rate among their aboriginal people (as did New Zealand), and her response included the then-revolutionary observation that cultural beliefs must be preserved, because many customs were healthy and practical. Bringing aboriginal people to a hospital reduced their chance of recovery and, when they returned to the bush, they would become strong again. On the other hand, she was also active in emigration—"bringing the landless men to the manless lands"—because she saw this as a constructive solution for England's crowded working poor.[63] When international delegates, at the bequest of Swiss Henri Dunant (inspired by Florence's Crimea work), met in Geneva to advocate the neutralization of wounded soldiers under the Red Cross, the British War Office commissioned Florence to draft their position paper.[64] The Treaty of Geneva was passed, and Florence sent nurses to serve on both sides in the Franco-Prussian War of 1870–71, receiving medals of honor from both nations. When the National Society for Aid to the Sick and Wounded was founded in England in 1870, many hoped Florence would take command. She was not well enough, but she stayed involved. When Dunant spoke in London, he said:

> Though I am known as the founder of the Red Cross and the originator of the Convention of Geneva, it is to an Englishwoman that all the honour of that Convention is due. What inspired me to go to Italy during the war of 1859 was the work of Miss Florence Nightingale in the Crimea.[65]

Amid Florence's busyness, Jowett needed encouragement. He spoke often of writing more on theology, but his Plato translations absorbed him and gave him an excuse to avoid more ecclesiastical hostility. He planned ambitious projects—biblical commentaries, a work on Christian morals, and a life of Christ—but nothing was done after the *Essays*. Toward the end of 1864, he confided in Florence his disenchantment with the Church, and his loss of self-confidence for theological pursuits. Like her, he wanted to write a "new religion" for England:

> What seems to be wanted is a restoration of natural religion, not in the narrow, abstract sense, but as based on the past history of man, and as witnessed to by conscience & fact, & supported by our first notions of a Divine being. Natural religion should so leaven & penetrate Christianity...that the doubtful points of fact & doctrine in Christianity should drop off of themselves. Unitarianism & German theology have both of them, in different ways, a zeal for

Criticism & for truth which is very commendable. But neither of them have ever found a substitute for that which they were displacing. They have never got hold of the heart of the world. The attempt to show the true character of the Pentateuch & the Gospel History is very important negatively. But it does nothing towards reconstructing the religious life of the people...a great opportunity seems to be utterly lost in the education of the common people. Half the books that are published are religious books, and perhaps 19/20 of those which have any moral or religious purpose—And what trash this religious literature is! Either formalisms or sentimentalisms about the Atonement, or denunciations of rational religion, or prophecies of the end of the world, explanations of the man of sin, the little horn, & the number of the beast.[66]

Although many of his students badgered him to explain what he *really* thought about religion, Jowett told Florence in confidence that he doubted whether, in his present state of mind and health, he could succeed in working this through. As squabbles over Bishop Colenso continued, he despaired of where it would end:

The mere external roots of the Old Orthodoxy are so deep & tangled & knotted & widely spread, and the inner life so feeble; and so little of the appearance of a New Tree, under the shadow of which "the birds of the air" may find shelter, that one can neither believe in the present, nor conjecture what is to come.[67]

Florence encouraged him to leave Balliol and accept the deanery of Christ Church, but he would not "give up the young life of Oxford (so full of hope) for the dead men's bones of a Cathedral town"—Balliol was *his* "War Office" and he an inferior clerk, probably for life. No doubt the loss of the Master's position and his unjust salary were affecting him as well—his pay increase had just been defeated and would not be approved until the following year. Florence suggested he submit some articles for the second series of *Essays*, but he never finished them.

Instead, Jowett encouraged *Florence* to do more writing—on the Army, women, theology. Never satisfied enough to publish anything *he* wrote (except his lifelong translation of Plato), Jowett refused another request from Florence to edit her "Stuff," still concerned it was not yet at book stage. He saw her strength of thought, but was distracted by what was, in his opinion, a disorderly style. He still worried about her inclusion of personal experiences, especially such obviously autobiographical ones as in "Cassandra." Jowett made a new proposal.

Florence might either write some essays or articles, or write her letters to him with the view to their eventual publication as a dialogical book:

> What do you say to extending…your views a little more at length & with more of system—I would answer you, & we might let the thing follow the course of the winds…Only, I am quite clear that in case of this or any other remains of yours being placed under my care, if I should outlive you…they ought to appear anonymously or under the name of one of your own family.[68]

Jowett's renewed interest in getting Florence published reflected his concern about her health. While totally overworked, she had given up her opium treatments for pain because of their effects on her, and the withdrawal had taken its toll. Besides, Florence was constantly convinced she was dying, and Jowett wanted to preserve her thoughts.

Constantly in Jowett's letters, references are made to his feelings for her—"It is that which does me good—to know that you are in the world."[69] The feeling was mutual. Florence wrote in June 1865, "If you were happy, I could part good friends with life, after all."[70] As the years went on, the metaphorical images of their relationship became more and more intimate and playful. Jowett instructed Florence to "make love to" Prime Minister Gladstone rather than angering him and accused her, in her reform work with ministers, of "flirting with four gentlemen at once," knowing she "takes on so terribly when disappointed in love."[71] In this rather strange marriage of minds if not of bodies, two people, so intensely independent and ambivalent about relationships, had each found a soul mate.

CHAPTER TWELVE

Being Called

I still feel that it is such a blessing to have been called, however unworthy,
to be the "handmaid of the Lord"...I see women, so far better & cleverer than I,
wasting their whole lives, not in improving
but in deteriorating their own families—
I feel so ungrateful & so wicked not to give the return I ought to God,
the return of wishing for absolutely nothing but
the accomplishment of His holy Will...
I have never felt tempted to refuse God any thing. However unworthy,
I have always felt, I could live 1,000 lives to prove to Him how inestimable
the blessing I think it to be "called."

FLORENCE NIGHTINGALE[1]

In 1865, Florence moved to a home of her own on South Street, London. Never letting up on her single-minded call to "save" the poor, she was working on Poor Law reform, acquiring trained nurses for workhouses, and advocating for a change in land ownership policies so that the poor could own both their land and house. As Florence faced stiff opposition, especially without Sir Sidney's Parliamentary access, Jowett helped Florence put her amazing success in perspective:

> Considering what ministers are, instead of wondering at their not doing all you want, I wonder at their listening to a word you say. A poor sick lady sitting in a room by herself They have only not to

go near her, & never to read her letters, & there is an end of her. And yet you seem to draw them still by some silken cords.[2]

Jowett was always patient with Florence's ongoing grief over Sir Sidney and what it meant to her work. To encourage her, he recounted stories he heard giving Florence all the credit for improving the soldiers' lot—"to remember on lonely days and weary nights":

> There is something very soothing in knowing that a great number of persons are attached to you. And the common people would be wonderfully attached to you if you could let them know of your existence a little more.[3]

He was also a calming influence when Sir Sidney's work was criticized (and also when his widow, Liz, became Catholic). When Florence found it difficult to remain silent, Jowett reminded her of the incredible task God had given her and how it would be jeopardized if her enemies discovered her great influence behind the scenes:

> When there is so much to be done in the service of mankind, which is also the service of God, ought our feelings to be wasted in useless sorrow, especially when life is closing in upon us & the time of work is shortening & mere experience teaches us that painful things, like other things, fade into the distance?…if there is anything that will banish painful thoughts, I believe the sense that we are doing & have to do God's work is most likely to do so—"Heaven," as you once said.[4]

Indicative of their intimate relationship, Florence accepted his chiding, agreeing that she marred God's work with impatience and discontent, but blamed the circumstances of her working life and her lack of power to accomplish all she needed to do. Florence's passion and Jowett's peacemaking reflect their different approaches. Rather than seeing the *misery* of the world, Jowett celebrated what had already been "mended"—the "happy routines" of so many people. Florence, the liberation theologian, *blamed* these happy routines for the plight of the poor:

> It is because Mr. Villiers [President of the Poor Law Board] eats & drinks like other people that the Workhouses are not reformed. It is because Lord Westminster & the other great London proprietors eat & drink & don't look after their London properties, like other people, (tho' they do look after their country properties) that London dwellings are what they are. Well-meaning people are, of all others, the people I detest. If you could but exchange them for

ill meaning people, who will do the world's work, the world would be such a gainer.[5]

When Jowett wrote for advice on his dinner speech at the college about "life," Florence replied that sermons and speeches were geared for "happy people, at least for tolerably successful people, who have not to construct or alter their lives, sometimes to begin again life 'right from the bottom,' but only to make themselves and others as happy as possible in their lives." She continued:

> We are never lectured about the study of anything else in the weak, wishy-washy, womanish terms that we are preached to about life. (And this is thought Christian: as if Christ had not been the boldest preacher of all, about reforming or reconstructing life.)[6]

Perhaps Florence had accepted Jowett's suggestion that they correspond with the goal of publication, or perhaps Jowett knew the theological exchange would divert Florence from her frustrations in other areas. Whatever, he took up Florence's theodicy (God's benevolence and the problem of evil) which he had urged her to work on toward publication. A basic difference in their theological approaches shines through. While Jowett agreed that the current "sham religion" should be replaced, he differed on how this should be done. Florence wanted to begin afresh from conscience and experience to discover the nature of God and how God works in the world, looking not to past doctrines, but developing new ways of thinking. For Jowett, this was not so clear-cut. While conscience might tell us God was just, true, and good, and our experience show us that humankind had infinite power to turn evil into good personally and globally, this was too abstract and *not* the experience of the mass of humankind:

> The stream of improvement is so narrow in the whole of the world & the whole of history, & such a mere rivulet, even in the improving countries, that instead of casting your eyes far & wide over the world, you have rather to look forward to some ideal future.[7]

While God as just and true were great "types" or ideas, as Plato would say, *where* were they actually found in nature or engraved on the human heart? Jowett agreed that God's laws had been discovered over time by both Greek philosophers and Jewish prophets and continued to be discovered, but felt it better to build a new religion on *old* forms of religion, reinterpreting and critiquing them for the modern context, rather than trying to start afresh from abstract concepts of God—"The whole world & all things in it, instead of being secular & external to revelation, needs to be brought back within the sphere of revelation."[8] Instead of a New Reformation, he advocated reconstructing the truth of the Old "partly because this accidentally suits best with the position of a clergyman of the Church of England, & also because this appears to me the best way of avoiding the truth becoming sectarian."[9]

Florence must have interpreted Jowett's comments as wishing to retain the doctrines she had already relegated to the archives, because he countered her return letter arguing that many doctrines had to dissolve before the questions, What do we know? Whence do they come? What is the fact?

> I think that you are quite right in getting rid of the fictions of the origin of evil, necessity & free will, those portentous abstractions which have ever been used to terrify the more intelligent part of the world into the belief of notions & articles of faith which have no connection with them—"Pray, Sir, can you explain the Origin of Evil?"[10]

Having been reading five chapters a day of the Hebrew Bible, Jowett was increasingly amazed at its beauty and moral greatness but also at "anybody being still willing to hang the life of man on the Inspiration of Scripture."[11] He agreed with Florence's attack on Church prayer, seeing prayer rather as

> a mental, moral, spiritual process, a communion or conversation with God, or an aspiration after him & resignation to him, an anticipation of heaven, an identification of self with the highest law, the truest idea—the blending of true thought & true feeling, of the will & the understanding, containing also the recognition that we ask for nothing but to be better, stronger, truer, deeper than we are.[12]

As for the resurrection and miracles, Jowett, as already expressed in his infamous essay in *Essays and Reviews,* agreed with Florence there was little possibility of having enough evidence on such things to justify "resting upon that" in an age of reason and science. Like Florence, he preferred to see Jesus' divinity as an example of the Spirit within all of us:

> I sometimes think that the death, & not the resurrection of Christ, is the really strengthening & consoling fact—that human nature could have risen to that does show that it is divine.[13]

By the mid-1860s, the *Essays* furor had calmed, Jowett had inherited a Yorkshire property for summer escapes, and his popularity could carry

Balliol on any issue. He wrote to Florence energized when an Oriel College fellow proposed and carried a motion to admit Roman Catholics to Oriel without requiring chapel attendance:

> If these sort of young men can only be kept straight, they may do almost anything. Old staid Dons like the Provost of Oriel, whose repose they greatly disturb think them "wanting in reverence." But without irreverence to a great many things in Oxford very little would be done.[14]

Their letters at this time reveal so much history in the making, given the era in which they lived. While not Balliol's Master, Jowett had moved to implement many university reforms, opening closed awards to competition, reducing the number of clerical fellowships, suppressing catechetical lectures and remodeling divinity lectures, initiating lectures on other religions, and ending compulsory weekday chapel for undergraduates. He also became college preacher for a few years, introducing critical ideas in his sermons (which Florence helped write) that triggered new thoughts in the students. One of his favorite innovations was enabling intelligent boys to be selected by merit from parish schools and be given bursaries for school and university to live on site—a reflection of his own youthful struggles. Jowett's goal was to change Oxford from a breeding place of orthodox Anglican theology into a center of open learning where students read, not just Greek philosophers and Anglican divines, but also Modern History, Physical Science, and contemporary philosophers and social theorists, making a return to "old doctrines of authority" impossible. At this high moment after so much disappointment and persecution, Jowett also shared his personal goals with Florence, asking for her help—to finish Plato, devote a few years to preaching and publishing his sermons, and write a practical commentary on the New Testament and some "reasonable" tracts for the poor. Jowett dreamed of a revival in Anglicanism for the educated such as John Wesley had done for the poor, a religious movement for better religious teaching in schools, better preaching by clergy, and better theology.

Whatever Florence was working on surfaced for discussion in their letters—Poor Law reform, Indian villagers, poor soldiers, and emigration. Florence appreciated Jowett's calm, considered perspective and his total awareness that what she did was *God's* work, not for her own advancement. His sharp intelligence and mutual concern for religious truth, together with his influence on students who later went into church and government office, guided her in her approach to both causes and people, often forewarning her of potential clashes. For this reason they kept their friendship strictly secret, passing information like "pickpockets in a crowd" so as not to lessen their influence. Jowett encouraged Florence to see good in people she would otherwise have dismissed. While admitting the people's "failings," he urged temperance, forever assuring her that people were not as evil or obstructionist as she made out. Of one victim he said:

> Are you quite sure he is so bad as you imagine; is he a deliberate villain? I quite agree that you should be Pope…but I don't like to be wholly deaf to the voice of humanity. Why don't you humbug [expose his errors] him instead of quarreling with him? That is much better & more Christian policy.[15]

If Jowett was critical of anything, it was people's intellectual output. He demanded high standards, which is also why he was so enamored with Florence, whom he called the most intelligent woman he had ever met. In many ways, they were a pair of contented gossips, both isolated from the real world yet influential in it, and sharing many things only with each other. Jowett praised, teased, and contradicted Florence over issues and ideas—his support of the emerging germ theory she rejected became an inside joke. One of his letters to her in 1868 begins, "My dear Florence the first, Empress of Scavengers, Queen of Nurses, Maitresse of drolesses, Governess of the Governors of India, Reverend Mother Superior, Mother of the British Army &c. &c. &c."[16] Jowett worried about her drivenness and lack of interests outside of work. Writing of his exhilaration after finishing a section of Plato translation, he asked:

> Don't you admit that the world is a very interesting place in which there is so much to be done and suffered? I am afraid that you often suffer terribly but I cannot believe that you are dull. Don't you know that you are one of the Queens of the Earth & ought to wear your crown lightly, & smile sometimes?[17]

When John Stuart Mill asked Florence to support women's suffrage in 1866, she refused to become actively involved, but signed the petition. Prior to presenting the petition to Parliament in May 1868, Mill contacted Florence again for the use of her name. Once again, Jowett urged calmness, suggesting Florence not argue with Mill, or do it briefly and diplomatically, "because I think that you may get into an interminable controversy in which he will never understand your position."[18] As we have already seen, Florence had criticisms of the movement. Jowett also advised Florence to sign the petition to avoid negative press. Having done so much for women, she might otherwise appear indifferent to the reform work of others. An astute observer of human character, Jowett seemed more concerned about preserving Florence's reputation than she did herself, both in public and with her family. She had further limited contact with both in 1867, communicating with visitors through notes from her bedroom. It is hard, reading the wonderful rapport between her and Jowett in the letters, to remember that as she wrote, she was locked in her room and screening out most other people. Florence was not pleased when Fanny suggested Florence reduce her work to spend more time with the family. Surely they understood by now her difficulties?

> No woman ever before directed the labours of a Government office. She must be the judge as to the when & the how, if a woman chooses to undertake and direct men over whom she can have no legitimate or recognized control, she shall do it. No one else can judge how she shall do it.[19]

Jowett finally convinced her to visit her family again, and she met him there at Embley and Lea Hurst as well.

What should be done with the masses of poor people still displaced after the Industrial Revolution? Some thought they were best suited for farming or the mills, not in London. Jowett wanted to send them back to their parishes, or other parishes, at government expense, but others disagreed. It was suggested that children be put into private families, but many parishes refused to give them up because of their labor potential—Jowett no doubt could see the positives of poor children thus receiving an education as he had done. Others thought emigration was the solution, but only of able-bodied men and women. Florence's article on "Pauperism" published in *Fraser's* Magazine in 1869 discussed these alternatives. She argued that all people had a right to education, health care and employment, and that simply herding the poor into workhouses or leaving them to the mercy of private charity led to more pauperism. Anyone in a workhouse capable of work should be helped to find it; hence her scheme for training poor girls as nurses. Of the 100,000 homeless children in London at that time, Florence suggested putting them with cottagers in another parish and paying the cottagers to bring them up. As for poor adults, Britain should set up colonies overseas and help them emigrate to where they could find employment and a fresh start.[20]

Despite the article's important content, Jowett again critiqued Florence's style, even though *he* made little progress publishing his ideas! Florence must have objected to his comments about the argument's not being "connected," because he reread it and called it "jerky" instead, concerned at an impression of harshness and lack of sympathy. Florence again challenged him, but he persisted:

I entirely agree with you that it does not matter whether it gives offence or not, provided it produces an impression & is suggestive. But then, as a personal matter, your friends are desirous that it should produce the right impression.[21]

Florence could hold her own, however. When Jowett called a biography on the late Mrs. (Frances) Edgeworth an example of a "fine, simple nature & a charming picture of family life," Florence replied with iconoclastic sarcasm:

Sometimes a book and not even a clever book, is like a revelation [to one] of the whole of one's past life. I have lived 49 years in this world, and I never understood before, things which this Life of Miss Edgeworth makes me see quite plain...She sums up her brother's perfect wife:—"good sense, good manners, good conversation, good principles." That is like a new light to me. What a fool I have been. Now I see that that is really all that fathers want in their daughters, all that the world wants in his wife—good sense (meaning of course sense to think like him), good manners, good conversation (how enormous is the importance attached to that now-a-days—one would think the whole world was moved by talk), good principles (for they don't want their women to run away and get into the Divorce Court). And with the four g's, even the better sort of people are satisfied—they don't want any deeper feeling, any higher purpose in life, any deeper hold on things.[22]

No doubt Florence was pleased by her cumulative influence on him regarding women's issues when, in 1871, Jowett wrote to her of his plans to establish extension lectureships and colleges in small towns for *women* as well as men.

Jowett finally became Master of Balliol College in 1870 at age fifty-three, ruling for nearly twenty-five years. He still chafed under Church hypocrisy, especially its criteria for appointment of bishops. Florence thought he might have liked this honor himself, but his standard reply was Lord Melbourne's comment, "My dear fellow, would you wear such a dress as that for 10,000 a year?"[23] Jowett knew that to become a bishop at that time, one had to suppress one's real opinions, and one of Jowett's desires was to see the Church of England dis-established (separated from the State as the State church). In the Master's position, he had learned how to say what should be said without violating the *Thirty-Nine Articles.*

You may always retire in greater generalities. No Church can attack you for always teaching that God is just & true, or for calling attention to facts of experience, or urging that the facts of Scripture & Ecclesiastical history must rest on evidence. Now I do not much want to say more than this. I do not (think) that this is a desirable state of things, but making allowance for all difficulties, it does not appear to me to be dishonest.[24]

Just prior to Jowett's appointment, Florence was again frustrated at her lack of productivity and her possible death before she had finished everything. The "Stuff" was always on her mind—the religion she was called to offer the working class. Jowett, who ten years ago had refused to help, now offered to help organize it.

Yours has been the best & greatest life of any woman's in this generation, & you must not allow yourself to leave it half-finished. I only wish you would let me help you in writing. If you would write rough notes, on Education, on Sanitary improvement, on Theodice [theodicy], I feel certain that I could put them into form & prepare them for the press. When you are somewhat better, will you try?[25]

The extra responsibility he had assumed with the master's job, however, reduced even their regular correspondence, moving from weekly to often monthly. Florence reacted:

Ah, Rev Sir, it's the poor old fogey me, who's thrown overboard now by the Master who consorts with Archbishops in purple and fine linen, and Dukes, and teaches the sheep to laugh at Socrates, and goes to church on weekdays.[26]

Florence's circumstances had changed as well. Her active Army work both in India and at home was almost completed, and many contacts from Crimean and Royal Commission days had died. Although she was consulted by the Princess of Prussia about care of the wounded during the Franco-Prussian war, her influence in government waned with a new slate of players. She now turned her attention back to the nursing training she had abandoned for Army reform some fourteen years before. Although her biographers have painted her as the founder of hospital nursing, she saw hospitals as interim necessities until the sick could all be cared for by trained women at home. She wrote in 1867:

The ultimate destination of all nursing is the nursing of the sick in their own homes. I look to the abolition of all hospitals and workhouse infirmaries. But it is no use to talk about the year 2000.[27]

In 1861, Florence had actually put into practice at King's College Hospital a midwifery training school funded by the Nightingale Fund on the lines of Kaiserswerth. The graduates had no obligation to the Fund beyond serving the rural poor for four years in the parish's employ. Florence's fears were proven true, however. The superintendent Florence appointed assumed unofficial religious duties as well, introducing her Catholic bent into an Anglican environment. Annoyed at religious proselytizing of any brand, Florence and the Fund removed their support, convincing Florence never again to become involved with hospitals affiliated with religious orders. From the experiment, she did produce a book, *Introductory Notes on Lying-in Institutions,* from statistics on maternal and fetal mortality rates, finding them *higher* in hospitals. District nurses were her solution, with the poor learning moral and practical knowledge from a trained, educated woman who in turn learned from them. In characteristic fashion, she surveyed cities and towns for statistical information, asking how home nursing was currently done. She published her report in 1876, which led to the establishment of a training home for district nurses, funded initially by the Nightingale Fund. In every new project, Florence always included a retirement pension scheme for her trainees "to give an English woman that proper feeling of independence & self-help."[28]

For the first time, Florence became actively involved in the Nightingale School, working with cousin Henry Bonham Carter, secretary of the Nightingale Fund.[29] When the new St. Thomas's Hospital and Nightingale Nursing School opened in 1871, Florence began monitoring probationers and curriculum from her home, inspecting the diaries the nurses kept. She became concerned with the level of training and wrote to Dr. Whitfield, Matron Wardroper, and Bonham Carter about the need to enforce stricter rules.[30] To learn more, she invited trainees over for tea. When Whitfield complained that Florence's standards were too high, she demanded his resignation. The problem of recruiting good nurses did not improve, and many dropped out to marry, since Florence's high standards of dedication left no time for marriage or family. Other teaching hospitals had less rigorous requirements, but the better-educated women chose St. Thomas's because of Florence's name. Florence did not want nursing to be only a voluntary occupation or a task within a religious order like the self-sacrificing Sister of Charity image so fixed in the public mind. She envisaged a professional woman, thoroughly trained and spiritually committed to her profession, serving God and humanity:

> God sent them [human beings] into the world expressly for the purpose of doing the business of the world...the object of the

statesman, the lawyer, the doctor, the merchant, the shopkeeper, the day laborer are as sacred as those of the priest...when the scavenger cleans the street or the stockbroker sells shares, or the publican serves his customers, he is discharging a divinely imposed duty and playing his part—and an essential part too—in a divine scheme, as much as a priest administering the sacrament to a dying man.[31]

To instill her ideas, Florence instigated an annual address to be read to Nightingale School probationers, continuing from 1872 until 1900. Her constant theme was their work for God:

To think our own life worth nothing except as serving in a corps, God's nursing corps, unflinching obedience, steadiness and endurance in carrying out His work—that is true discipleship, that is true greatness, and may God give it to us Nurses, and make us His own Nurses.[32]

In January 1871 Jowett sent his 2,700-page translation of Plato to the binders, thanking Florence for her invaluable help. With her excellent knowledge of Greek, she had edited his manuscript, making suggestions that he adopted. He offered again to help her prepare her work for publication, suggesting the most suitable topics:

I. Theology—a) you must work out your notion of Divine perfection, especially showing that this may be consistent with the appearances of evil in the world—b) of the vanity of free thinking & criticism, & their purely negative use.

II. Social life—the ideal of the family: Education of women—Sisterhoods & their true principles, the employment of women (you might rewrite in a more consecutive manner some part of those volumes which you used to call the "Stuff").

III. The poor law—beginning with a Study of Political Economy & shewing how there is still a place for humanity.

IV. Sanitary or theological tracts for the poor—How people may live & not die.[33]

Perhaps conscious of his previous critiques, he promised to edit not to his own style, but in her better and more striking style. Again he suggested short papers or essays that depended less on form and even admitted "an imperfect expression of the idea." Above all, she should be "moderate & consecutive." Nothing further eventuated of this, and Florence complained in April 1871 of being "snubbed," again bemoaning her loss of Sir Sidney and Clough. Jowett promised to spend a week with her at Lea Hurst in the summer and asked again about her writing, suggesting she leave her other reform work with its political battles and "bring together the raveled threads, & put in some permanent form of word or act what you have been aspiring to all your life."[34] Florence's feelings of desertion could well have been fueled by Jowett's tour of the Alps with close friend Arthur Stanley, and his frequent references to his other friend Robert Morier.[35]

Interspersed with other conversations, Jowett and Florence pursued their great gift to each other—a constant sharing of books and projects. In 1871, Jowett was reading Charles Darwin's writings, together with naturalist Alfred Wallace's 1870 *Contribution to the Theory of Natural Selection* (for Wallace, see glossary note on Darwin). Jowett wrote a sermon about Darwin, urging that he be treated civilly despite religious opposition to him, because he was a very ingenious observer and a good man. Of interest today, Jowett did wonder aloud to Florence whether "this bubble supported by so much genius & careful observation, [will] break!"[36] In turn, Florence lent Jowett *The Modern Buddhist; Being the View, of a Siamese Minister of State on His Own and Other Religions,* by Chao Phya Praklang, translated by Henry Alabaster (London, Trubner & Co., 1870), which Jowett enjoyed:

> The writer has more conception of true religion than all the Bishops put together. His difficulty is our difficulty, the amount of evil in the world, & this seems to lead him to the rejection of the Being of God.[37]

They both read George Eliot's *Middlemarch*. Jowett decided it would be a failure, and Florence called it a "novel of genius," writing to Jowett:

> I think that you are very intolerant & persecuting to George Eliot. She has painted—what often takes place in real life—the failure of an ideal. Why should not this be described as well as any other chapter in the life of a family?[38]

Later, when Jowett met Eliot (Mary Ann Evans) and urged her to work further on writing about women and moral philosophy, as she wished to do, Florence appeared jealous. Not eager to reprove Florence, which was like "pouring cold water upon a red hot iron & makes a terrible hissing," he assured Florence that apart from *her,* George Eliot was the only woman of her generation who could accomplish much.

In August 1871, Jowett consulted Florence about two writing projects, the *Children's Bible* and his essay on "Religions of the World." Of the essay, Florence was overjoyed, telling him to let all the religions come out as a common search after a Perfect God, the search after Truth. When Jowett sent her the draft of the *Children's Bible*, he received the opposite response—Florence was appalled at his selection of stories:

> The story of Achilles and his horses is far more fit for children than that of Balaam and his ass, which is only fit to be told to asses. The stories of Samson and Jephthah are only fit to be told to bulldogs; and the story of Bathsheba to be told to Bathshebas. Yet we give all these stories to children as "Holy Writ." There are some things in Homer we might better call "Holy" writ—many, many in Sophocles and Aeschylus.[39]

Jowett accepted Florence's critique and, when the *Children's Bible* was finished, wrote, "I blessed you every time I took the papers up, especially in the Prophets. I have adopted your selection almost entirely, with a slight abridgement."[40] At the same time as writing the *Children's Bible*, Jowett was passed over for the committee for the revision of the *King James Version* of the Bible, no doubt because of his "radical" ideas.

Florence was apparently reworking some of her "Stuff" at this time. Ever the strict teacher urging the best from a pupil, Jowett pressed her on her notion of "the character of God" known from both nature and inner experience. What, Jowett asked, do we actually *learn* from these; on what grounds should we believe it is God; on and how do we reconcile the God revealed in nature with the God experienced? Jowett had not been impressed with attempts by his colleague Henry Mansel to make this connection. Florence replied that knowledge of God through God's laws (thoughts) in nature was an ongoing process through history to which *everyone* contributed, not, as had happened to this point, just the Church with its doctrines. Pushing Florence further, Jowett asked how one then distinguished between true and false witness of nature, when what seemed *physically* right was not *morally* right— such as disposing of sickly or deformed infants. Florence, again foreshadowing feminist theology, was "scandalized" at his dualism— there was more to the universe than just matter.

> I believe that the laws of nature all tend to improve the whole man, moral and physical, that it is absurd to consider man either as a body to be "improved," or as a soul to be '"improved" separately.[41]

A railway accident reveals more information than simply facts about steel and friction—it also reflects whether the employees were properly paid or overworked. Arguing against those such as Thomas Henry Huxley (whom Jowett quoted), who believed that what we knew through our senses was more real than "inferences and imaginations,"

Florence saw the *finest* human powers as those that enable us to infer, from what we see, what we *cannot* see, lifting us into a higher level of learning and truth than from the senses alone.[42] While the law of physical improvement might require that we get rid of sickly children, Florence pointed to a larger lesson from the situation, which involved more than the physical problem—to prevent or improve, or, if not possible, to have patience and heroism in caring for them. Jowett was still not satisfied with Florence's term "character of God." He thought it anthropomorphic and, picking up on her own argument about metaphors for God, argued that terms should be changed frequently in theology so that they would not become the reality:

> "Nature" is both better & worse than "character:" better because it is not affected by human associations, & worse because it is more dead & impersonal. No word will at all express the "nature," "being," "substance," "character" of God. We must describe it under many figures of speech, as well as we can.[43]

From 1872 onward, Florence turned more and more attention to writing. When she reported plans for a book on medieval mystics to Jowett, he was encouraged because she had just endured yet another bout of despair over her life, even threatening to check herself into St. Thomas's Hospital for her "last days." Jowett challenged her to come up with a mysticism for contemporary society, one as intense as early mysticism, but with a fusion of faith and reason—"reason in religion and religion in reason."[44] Florence also worked on articles on India and continued the eternal edit of Jowett's Plato, giving him a taste of his own frank critique. While he thought her writing too confrontational, she thought his introduction to *Phaedrus* "lame." While admitting she was his best critic, he did not leave it at that. "What you suggest is always most useful to me: I mix it with water & make it drinkable for the English public."[45]

They were soul mates in their commitment to *work,* always making resolutions about how to do better and measuring what they did against Christ's example. Florence sent Jowett the first draft of her translations of the mystics, some of which had not been translated before. Jowett was still wary of any talk about inner *experience,* wanting less of Teresa's repetition, explanations, and allusions to herself and her feelings—"I should like better to have the impersonal soul rising to God." Jowett also suggested Florence cease calling the soul *it*— no doubt Florence's astute feminist recognition of the decidedly female nature of Teresa's encounters with Christ and thus her decision not to resort to male pronouns for her soul. Obviously uncomfortable with mysticism, Jowett suggested a preface to explain how popular mystical writings had been used in their time so as not to appear "unreal."

> I do not say what may be the case with great saints themselves, but for us I think it is clear that this mystic state ought to be an occasional & not a permanent feeling—a taste of heaven in daily life. Do you think it would be possible to write a mystical book, which would also be the essence of common sense?[46]

In 1873, Florence published two articles from her "Stuff' in *Fraser's* Magazine, a progressive literary journal. The first one, "Note of Interrogation," dealt with Florence's concept of God and God's laws, and attacked both traditional Christian theology and positivism. Jowett thought the article too crowded, but recognized she "had poured her heart into it." He questioned, however, whether her "perfect God" who governed the worlds did so with the least pain possible, consistent with her idea that the purpose of pain and suffering was to educate humankind. How did Florence reconcile this "perfect education" with many appearances of "wasteful evil" in the world? The second paper was "A Sub-note of Interrogation: What Will our Religion be in 1999?" with a subheading "The Indian's Estimate of Our Religion." This article focused on Florence's belief that history was progressing through the discovery of the invariable laws of the universe and their application. Given this, she asked, "What will this world be on August 11 at 10 a.m. in 1999 [the estimated time for the total eclipse of the sun in England]?" She answered her own question, "What we have made it."[47] Florence introduced into the discussion various areas of reform needs but concentrated on reform of religion. God, she said, had become nothing, or simply the "God of Sundays"

> ... not the God of our weekdays, our business and our play, our politics and our science, our home life and our social life, our House of Commons, our Government, our Post Office and correspondence ... our Foreign Office, and our India Office.[48]

Religion needed to become, not belief in a Creed or doctrines but God as "a real presence among us" that would challenge our ideas of the "social contract"—the immutability of the state of life into which we have been born—and lead us to the "reconstitution of society":

> The Kingdom of Heaven is within, but no one laboured like Christ to make it without. He actually recommended people to leave their own lives to do this, so much was he penetrated by this conviction, filled by the enthusiasm, that we MUST ALTER the "state of life,"

(NOT conform to it…) into which we are born, in order to bring about a "kingdom of heaven."[49]

The paper is rather disjointed in its argument, but Florence finished with a challenge:

> Let us press on so that 1999 shall have as much more truth than 1873 as it should have; much more advance of truth than 1873 has over 1746; for truth should advance by geometrical, not arithmetical progression, or rather by progress which cannot be measured or fettered by numbers.[50]

Florence received many letters, pro and con, about the articles, some promising to pray for her conversion! Jowett once again had something to say, finding it "very able & striking" but in "scream style." He was still concerned with her passion and appeal to experience, neither very acceptable in the theology of her day.

Jowett took on too much as Master of Balliol. His biographers believe he finally suffered a breakdown from this. Florence had detected his overwork and offered health advice, receiving an appreciative letter back in May 1873, also telling her he had reread *Notes on Nursing*, one of the "most interesting books" he had ever read. His letters became less regular, and Florence chided him for this, but also for remaining in a Church that troubled him without speaking out like he had in the *Essays*. Jowett gave his reasons:

> We & all Liberal Theologians are really on sufferance in the Church of England: we have to repeat services of which about one half appear to us to be monstrous & superstitious, like some parts of all the Creeds: although we are in a false position in the Church we should be in a still more false position out of the Church…I suppose that the only way is to leaven the existing Church & the existing Creed, with a higher truth & a higher morality, & gradually change public opinion. That is why I want to write…You must help me; though I have great doubt whether I can do any good…you & my other friends will have good reason to say that I have utterly failed if the "Essays & Reviews" are to be my last word on Theology.[51]

The difference between Jowett and Florence was that the Church, in the form of Balliol College, was the *only* home Jowett ever had—to leave was to once more be an orphan. Florence, on the other hand, had longed for that same Church to "mother" her and be a home for her, but it would not.

Florence's situation changed again in January 1874 when her father died at age eighty. Florence was distraught that she had not said good-bye to him, hinting at what had also played into her relationship with her father. His lack of a son denied WEN a larger family inheritance early in life and once again denied that inheritance to his daughters—Lea Hurst went to Aunt Mai's son. WEN had trained Florence "like a son," and her early responsiveness to him had something to do with her consciousness of his lack of a male offspring. Jowett wrote to her:

> I am very much grieved to hear of what has happened to you…He was a fine old gentleman, full of liberal feelings, though he could not have been made to walk either in my ways or in yours. He simply would not have understood what we were doing or thought we were doing…Your father was very proud & pleased about your work—though he did not understand it. I told him once that to have a daughter who would keep alive his name was better than to have many sons. He was greatly taken by this. And no doubt many persons will ask & talk about him, because he was your father. It is painful (as I suppose that Christ found) that when a person undertakes an extraordinary work the family can do so little for them. The family is meant for ordinary life.[52]

WEN's death signified the breakup of the family roots at Lea Hurst and reminded Jowett of women's disadvantages—"It is one of the greatest of women's wrongs that they do not succeed to estates."[53] Realizing the awkwardness for Florence, now without her family properties, Jowett suggested she spend her free time with him at his preferred vacation spots. They did occasionally still meet at Lea Hurst—Clarkey told her husband of meeting Jowett there in 1875: "He is a man of mind; I think he would suit you…He is very fond of Florence, which would also suit you. She is here, and her conversation is most nourishing."[54] Not only did Florence mourn the one family member who had always supported her, she also had to take responsibility for her mother and settle the transfer of the estates, since Parthe was bedridden with rheumatism. For the next five years, Florence shuttled between London and Embley, diverted from reform and writing and trapped again by her increasingly senile mother who, ironically, had cared so little for her. Florence struggled to remind herself that this "utter ship wreck" was part of God's scheme. "I *must* believe in the plan of Almighty Perfection to make us all perfect…I must remember God is not my private secretary."[55]

In March 1874, three months after WEN's death, Jowett again offered to work on Florence's "Stuff," but this time *all* of it. His previous reticence now becomes obvious—it was *Cassandra* and Florence's other comments on the family that troubled him, but now WEN was gone and Fanny was senile. Writing had become a priority for both of them, though Jowett's published output was slim compared with Florence's, partly because of different ideas about when something was finished. Florence's writings were passionate and urgent, flowing from her in the way she thought and talked; Jowett was almost paralyzed with "reputation" and the perfect product. Critiquing Florence's latest article on India, he still did not let up, confident Florence would not be angry because of some pact they had made to improve each other's work. Anticipating the smoke arising from her ears, Jowett preempted her comment, "What does the man mean by talking to me about style, when I am thinking only of the sufferings & oppression of 100,000,000 of Ryots [Indian peasants]?"[56] The pamphlet should be *perfect,* he advised, so that her work would be taken seriously, especially by those ready to pounce if she took too many liberties *as a woman.* Although he loved her wit, he was not always sure it was appropriate—she should focus more on the flow of paragraphs than on writing clever sentences. At one point, he did try a different approach with her, praising the style of *Notes on Nursing* and its consequent successful influence, and suggesting that "if cleaning out the drains is doing the will of God, may we not feel this also in turning a sentence, i.e., in writing well & clearly about some truth that will be for the good of mankind?"[57] As one biographer said of Jowett's ruthless pursuit of excellence:

> A friendship once established, meant for him that his friend should have no rest while any fault remained, unreproved, any defect uncorrected. And if that friend's position in life were such as to give opportunities for influence or distinction, Jowett was never weary of inciting to fresh exertions, nor would desist from the attempt because of advancing age, although he was well aware that "miracles are only wrought upon the young."[58]

Jowett was interested in India himself. However, he was caught in England's colonial arrogance, though more progressive than most. In condemning the Indian caste system, which had outlived its usefulness and ruined the lives of so many peasants, he was unable to understand how "respectable classes" should be so proud and disdainful of others, even though it played out daily in his own context in England. His racist solution was "civilization" and emigration—an Indian labor force for the Western world, as had been perpetrated with indigenous African people:

> The East to be civilized, partly by the west going to it, partly by its going to the West. A black footman, if you contemplate him, if not

a very *magnificent* is a very *real* product of civilization. Think of him quietly standing behind his master's chair & of his grandfather a savage…(This) shows what can be done by individual European influence. And the Hindu is probably not less amenable to such influence.[59]

Jowett did express concern, however, as to whether Florence was equal to writing a book on the Indian Ryots, because of her lack of personal experience of this complex situation. A rash or inaccurate book would destroy not only her influence in the Indian office but also the credibility of her other work and writings.

Jowett's own problem was the opposite—never feeling his work was good enough to publish. Of all his plans to write down his Moral Theology, only his Plato translations were published. In Florence's reminiscences for Jowett's biographer, she wrote:

I used to bother him and remember once saying to him that the services of the Church of England and still more of the Church of Rome were like old clothes dropping off in rags bit by bit, and that soon, if he and others did not make haste, the Churches would be naked. Of course I only mention this because he always agreed, and would say, "As soon as I have done 'Plato' (and he would often add: which will be 'in six months') I will set about it."[60]

Although always being re-edited, Jowett's literary legacy was his Plato translations. When he realized he couldn't accomplish what he wanted to write in theology, Jowett began including his religious thoughts in his Plato introductions. Florence felt he put too much of his genius into Plato, and Plato took too much of him. His constant critique of his own work and Plato's thought made his basic approach to scholarship negative. As Florence told him, there is nothing inspiring about denying miracles and a Moral Governor simply for the sake of shocking good people trying to be Christians. One must offer something definite to take the place of what was taken away. Jowett's (and others') valid criticisms of church and theology had helped create a spiritual void, but Jowett was unwilling to refill it by writing on theology. Pontius Pilate, Florence said, did not answer the question, "What is truth?" because he didn't care—Jowett should have "because I *did* care."[61] With *her* passion for a reasonable religion for the artisans, she was frustrated that he never encouraged his students to develop a theology of God's moral government (theodicy), the major problem of the day.

However Jowett *did* establish Toynbee Hall for working-class students and gave them practical assistance, and he did strive to connect university education with *life*. Before his time, the rich were spoiled and the poor ignored in terms of education. At Balliol, Jowett made room for everyone, rich and poor, ensuring all had a good education *and* access to jobs afterward. H. W. Carless Davis, in his history of Balliol, wrote of Jowett:

> He held that the only results of value are those which a man reaches for himself. Truth cannot be seen with the eye of another; the most that a teacher can do is to indicate the road which leads to the vision. He had his own beliefs and held them fast; but he knew that no good would come of dictating them into notebooks...the work of a tutor in that age was much more to clarify ideas than to impart them.[62]

John Henry Newman and others had been dismissed from Oriel College in 1831 for trying to indoctrinate students, but Jowett believed young men should not be prematurely forced into beliefs that marked them for life before they learned how to make their own judgments. Rather than negative, Jowett was realistic, struggling *with* them over the difficulties of faith and trying to preserve faith by not pitting it *against* reason. And his methods contributed to change. In 1888, he wrote to Florence of the sermons at Balliol over the last few years:

> They are not on "miracles" or on Atonement or on Everlasting Damnation, deathbeds...Chiefly on reconciling Science with Religion or Philosophy with Religion, or on good works, like Toynbee Hall, among the working class.[63]

Despite her frustrations with his omissions, Florence respected Jowett's tremendous influence, saying, "He was always finding the better part" of people:

> (He) lived the greatest life in this century. He created many a Statesman, many an Educator, many a devoted man and really religious man. And he did not feel, himself, the want of anything more definite, because as he always said: 'The man is greater than the doctrine."[64]

From 1880 onward, only a few letters remain from Jowett to Florence, though they obviously continued corresponding. Those that remain exude the quieter comfortableness of two people facing their aging with both contentment and regret. Jowett wrote in that year:

> There is in these latter years from 60–70 & from 70 to 80, an extraordinary power latent, if we only knew how to call it forth. Greater experience, fewer mistakes, less personal antagonism, a more comprehensive view of the world.[65]

In February 1880, Florence's mother died at age ninety-two. Florence was finally free, not only because Fanny was dead, but because she was also reconciled with Parthe and spent time with Parthe's family. Florence went out more, no longer needing an excuse not to be disturbed. In 1882, she inspected the Nightingale School of Nursing at St. Thomas's for the *first* time! Uncle Sam died, and Florence made peace with Aunt Mai in 1881 after not addressing her directly for twenty years. By 1890, almost all her friends were dead. Her eyesight began to fail in the 1880s, but she continued to write to Nightingale School nurses serving in several countries. She also became involved in the conditions of the Army Medical Service in South Africa and Egypt, and spent three years compiling an exhaustive syllabus on what village health educators should be taught. Her last nursing battle was against standardization of nurse training and registration exams. Nursing was a calling, not something verified by examination. The *character* of the nurse was judged against *Christ's* example, not a written test.

> Christ was the author of our profession. We honor Christ when we are good nurses. We dishonor Him when we are bad or careless nurses...when we do not do our best to relieve suffering—even in the meanest creature.[66]

Jowett, after ten years as Master of Balliol, became more self-reflective and despondent at lost opportunities. He regretted a "great want of life," possibly marriage. The Church and its prayers had become difficult for him. He tried to wrestle more with his theological ideas, but bemoaned his wandering thoughts. His goal was mostly to fulfill his college duties and devote his remaining years to God's service, going on to perfection:

> Is it possible to feel inspired by the "great power of God"; to live altogether above human thoughts and opinions, out of self, meditating on the means and ways of perfection; to live together for others and for the highest, not for gain or honour or self-satisfaction? Is it possible to attain a divine force? I hardly know. Sometimes I feel as if old things had passed away and all things had become new. Then again, I relapse through some weakness...Yet upon the whole I certainly make progress.[67]

Through him, Balliol had flourished. Jowett made the master's position terminable, removed the requirement that the master be in holy orders, allowed fellows to marry, made Balliol an education for *life*, changed it from a clerical establishment to one for professional education, and provided opportunities for poor students. From 1882 to

1886 he was vice-chancellor, a post which hastened his death. He revised Plato's *Republic* in 1888 and wrote the third edition of *Dialogues of Plato* in 1892. Had he given to theology what he gave to Plato, he might have left, beside his Balliol legacy, a theology that reformed his age.

After 1880, the letters became more reflective on Jowett and Florence's past together, and on present, practical support of each other, revealing more than ever their deep feelings and the "true marriage" they had achieved in their own way. At the beginning of 1888, Jowett told Florence of his great debt to her:

> It is about 18 years since you first sent me the "Stuff" to read, and about 17 years since we first became friends. How can I thank you properly for all your kindness & sympathy—never failing? I have not been able to do so much as you expected of me, & probably never shall be, though I do not give up ambition. But I have been too much distracted by many things, and not "strong enough for the place." I shall go on as quietly & industriously as I can. If I ever do much more, it will be chiefly owing to you; your friendship has strengthened & helped me, & never been a source of the least pain or regret.[68]

Seven years later, his sentiments had not abated on the twenty-fifth anniversary of their first acquaintance:

> I may venture, perhaps, to call ours a silver friendship. It has been a great blessing to me: one of the best things in my life. I do not believe in going downhill; the truer, the safer, the better years of life are the later ones.[69]

Always one of Florence's greatest supporters, Jowett constantly reminded her in her failing years of how much good she had done in the world:

> Nobody knows how many lives are saved by your nurses in hospitals (you have introduced a new era in nursing); how many thousand soldiers, who would have fallen victims to bad air, bad water, bad drainage & ventilation, are now alive owing to your forethought & diligence; how many natives of India (they might be counted probably in hundreds of thousands) in this generation & in generations to come, have been preserved from famine & oppression & their load of debt, by the energy of a sick lady who can scarcely rise from her bed...you are a Myth in your own life time. Do you know that there are thousands of girls about the ages of 18 to 23 named after you?[70]

While Jowett regretted what he had not achieved, he always struggled more with Florence's inability to acknowledge *her* tremendous achievements, dwelling on what was *not* done and the opposition she had experienced from her family and others. "I want to see you at peace in the years which remain to both of us," he wrote.[71] He always listened, the one friend to whom she could reveal everything, even her dark side, but he sometimes scolded. On New Year's Day, 1886, he wrote:

> Most persons are engaged in feasting & holiday making amid their friends & relations. You are alone in your room, devising plans for the good of the natives of India or of the English soldier, as you have been for the last thirty years, and always deploring your failures as you have been doing for the last thirty years, though you have had a far greater & more real success in life than any other lady of your time...will you not thankfully & cheerfully acknowledge how much God has done by your means? It would be happier for you & better for your work.[72]

Education was an ongoing passion they shared until the end, whether for India, in elementary schools, or at Oxford. When in 1867 Lord Russell announced a priority for education, Jowett produced the paper advocating secular instruction and schools funded by taxes. The Endowed School Act of 1869 came from Jowett's suggestions. Under Florence's influence, Jowett pushed for women's education in schools and colleges, and in 1878 women attended lectures at Oxford for the first time. Florence's passion for statistics fueled another Jowett-Nightingale alliance, a jointly endowed Chair in Statistics at Balliol. Jowett was eager for this to eventuate, but Florence stalled as interest in the germ theory grew and finally withdrew her bequest because she was afraid it would be used to endow some microbe! They worked together to bring Indian students to Balliol to study agriculture, and by 1884, Jowett was working on a School for Indian Studies in Oxford. In 1886, he wrote to Florence:

> I want to prove to you that your words do sometimes affect my flighty or stony heart, & are not altogether cast to the winds; & therefore I send you the last report of the Indian students, in which you will perceive that Agricultural Chemistry has become a reality & that owing to you (though I fear that like so many other of your good deeds this will never be known to man) Indian students are reading about Agriculture, & that therefore Indian ryots may have a chance of being somewhat better fed than hitherto.[73]

Florence was by now using her writing skills to promote Indian nationalism and the Indian National Congress, which would eventually emerge with Mahatma Gandhi. She was especially pleased when Cornelia Sorabji trained with Jowett at Oxford and returned to India as a lawyer to become known as "the Nightingale of India."

In the 1890s, Florence became more serene and a favorite with her young relatives. Parthe died in 1890, and her husband Sir Harry Verney in 1893. Aunt Mai's son William ("Shore"), who inherited the Nightingale property, died in 1894, and Embley was sold. Florence had outlived them all, but she could now look back more peacefully on life, knowing she had responded to God's call to the best of her ability. She still responded to any emerging situation as a savior to the poor and disadvantaged, defending pregnant, poor single women who were at risk of being thrown, with their families, out of their homes. In 1893, she said her final public word on nursing in a paper at a health congress in connection with the Chicago World's Fair. Remarkable and surprisingly modern, the paper summarized her lifelong reflections on health:

> Sickness or disease is nature's way of getting rid of the effects of conditions which have interfered with health. It is nature's attempt to cure. We have to help her. Diseases are, practically speaking, adjectives, not noun substantives. What is health? Health is not only to be well, but to be able to use well every power we have. What is nursing? Both kinds of nursing are to put us in the best possible conditions for nature to restore or to preserve health, to prevent or to cure disease or injury. Upon nursing proper, under scientific heads, physicians or surgeons must depend partly, perhaps mainly, whether nature succeeds or fails in her attempts to cure by sickness. Nursing proper is therefore to help the patient suffering from disease to live, just as health nursing is to keep or put the constitution of the healthy child or human being in such a state as to have no disease. No system can endure that does not march. Are we walking to the future or to the past? Are we progressing or are we stereotyping? We remember that we have scarcely crossed the threshold of uncivilized civilization in nursing; there is still so much to do. Don't let us stereotype mediocrity...In the future, which I shall not see, for I am old, may a better way be opened! May the methods by which every infant, every human being, will have the best chance of health, the methods by which every sick person will have the best chance of recovery, be learned and practiced! Hospitals are only an intermediate stage of

civilization, never intended, at all events, to take in the whole sick population.[74]

In his last years, Jowett expressed his feelings more directly. In 1892, he wrote, "I want to send you my love on New Year's Day if you won't think this language is too sentimental. I often think of the long years in which we have known one another & of the great piece in my life which this friendship has been." Later that year, he wrote,

> You are never out of my mind for long. I remember your extraordinary kindness to me during my illness and before when I was ill five years ago & for more than thirty years before that. You have taken an interest in the College & my work. I have never come to you for sympathy & failed to receive it. And how little or nothing have I done in return for all this! I want to hold fast to you, dear friend, as I go down the hill. You and I are agreed that the last years of life are in a sense the best and that the most may be made of them of them even at the time when health & strength seem to be failing.[75]

In a much weakened state, his last note in September 1893 reiterated his love for her in a few, formal words, "How greatly I am indebted to you for all your affection. How large a part has your life been of my life."[76] Jowett died soon after at seventy-six. One of his students who was also a friend of Florence's wrote to her in her grief of his influence on so many:

> His religion always seemed to me nearer to that which the Master taught his followers than that of any other man or woman whom I have met, and I doubt whether any one of our time has done so much to spread true religion and Christianity in the best sense of the word.[77]

To the end of their days, their theological conversation had never waned, nor did their ongoing debate about what we can know and how we know it. On his first reading of her work, Jowett had accused Florence of trying to merge Enlightenment rationalism with medieval mysticism. In 1887, they were still debating this! When Florence asked, "What is truth?" Jowett responded, "Let me try & answer it still for *my* own satisfaction rather than yours."

> Truth is the sense of the highest within us: God the Good, the idea true conceived under many names & in various forms, personal & impersonal, intensive and extensive, acknowledged in some germ or seen in some ray of light, and capable of being developed by

reason, from all regions and all the parts & infinitesimal particles of nature. Truth is the sense of the Unity of God & nature which the true intelligence refuses to divide, a circle necessarily continuous, & necessarily vague & abstract, which we slowly fill up with a few particulars of knowledge. Truth is the application of these two principles to our own lives that we may habitually dwell in them & appropriate them and become one with them.[78]

Having said that, Jowett bemoaned the difficulty of knowing this ideal in real life and so approached truth instead from the human direction—truth is the *refusal* to believe speculations and fancies about those things we can never know, which waste our time and divert us from our duty. As for Florence's mysticism, he conceded in 1889 that, if it be true enlightenment, it was important and good. However, as someone whose simple piety was expressed in duty, he was still not convinced, given the variety of human nature, that a mystical experience was attainable or necessary for everyone:

I cannot see why persons should not be satisfied with devoting their lives to God in some very simple form. Provided the devotion is entire they will have no fears or doubts. If they have, let them increase their self-devotion. I cannot see how they can find a further safeguard or comfort in taking upon themselves the lies & the crimes of the Roman Catholic Church. Why contaminate themselves with these when they can keep clear of them? I can compare it only to a pious and really good young lady falling in love with a man who she knows to be a scamp.[79]

The following year, on her seventieth birthday, Florence summed up her life in the words with which this book began. Having now witnessed her amazing life, the reader may find them much more profound:

You say that "mystical or spiritual religion is not enough for most people without outward form." And I say I can never remember a time when it was not a question of my life. Not so much for myself but for others. For myself, the mystical or spiritual religion as laid down by John's Gospel, however imperfectly I have lived up to it, was and is enough. But the two thoughts which God has given me all my whole life have been…First, to infuse the mystical religion into the forms of others (always thinking they would show it forth much better than I), especially among women to make them the "handmaids of the Lord." Secondly, to give them an organization for their activity in which they could be trained to be the"handmaids of the Lord"…When very many years ago I planned a future, my one idea was not organizing a hospital but organizing a religion.[80]

Epilogue

By the turn of the century, many honors had been showered on Florence, but her memory was failing. She died in her sleep from old age and heart failure on August 13, 1910. Overflowing crowds packed St. Paul's Cathedral for her memorial service, but Florence was buried where she wanted to be—in the small churchyard with her family in East Wellow, Hampshire. Her casket was lowered into the ground by six of her "children" drawn from various regiments of the British Army. Her grave is marked simply "F. N. Born 12 May 1820. Died 13 August 1910."

Glossary

Arminius, Jacobus (1560–1609), Dutch Reformed theologian who rejected Calvinism's deterministic arguments on predestination and insisted that divine sovereignty was compatible with human free will and that Christ died for all, not just the elect. These views were condemned by the Synod of Dort (1618–19), and adherents banished or persecuted. John Wesley espoused these ideas in the eighteenth century.

Arnold, Thomas (1795–1842), headmaster of Rugby School (1828–41) and member of the Broad Church movement. He became famous for the education system he developed at Rugby.

Ashley, Lord (Anthony Ashley Cooper Shaftesbury, later Lord Shaftesbury) (1801–1885) entered Parliament in 1826 and is best known for his reform of factories, mental institutions, and child labor. He was also involved in Ragged Schools, YMCA, and several missionary societies.

Bentham, Jeremy (1748–1832), English scholar of jurisprudence, political philosophy, sociology, and ethics, and founder of utilitarianism, the belief that society should aim at the greatest good for the greatest number. This principle opposed the traditional idea promoted, by church and state, of the "social contract"– that God ordained each to his or her place or class with its resulting benefits and power. His book *Fragments on Government* challenged the social contract and led to an overhaul of English law and government.

Blackwell, Elizabeth (1821–1910), an Englishwoman who emigrated to the United States and became the first woman doctor to graduate in the United States. Elizabeth became friends with Florence while studying in London, and they shared many hopes for the training and professionalism of women. Elizabeth and her sister established a Women's Hospital and Medical College in New York in 1868.

Bonham Carter, Henry (1827–1921), son of Fanny Nightingale's sister Joanna and John Bonham Carter, was Florence's cousin and brother to Hilary. He was secretary of the Nightingale Fund from Arthur Clough's death (1861) until 1899 while also acting as managing director of Guardian Assurance Co. He remained on the Nightingale Fund Council until 1914.

Bonham Carter, Hilary (cousin Hilary) (1821–1865) was Henry Bonham Carter's sister and Florence's favorite cousin. Florence and Mary Clark encouraged Hilary, an accomplished artist caught in the extended family as the unmarried "available" help, to pursue her art in Paris, but she was recalled home to the family. Hilary helped Florence with her reform work after the Crimea, but died young.

Bracebridge, Charles (Mr. B.), and Selena (Sigma), friends of the Nightingales, were ardent travelers but in delicate health. Charles was a businessman with a passion for Greece, and Selena became Florence's close friend and mentor. Childless, they took Florence with them on trips to Rome, Greece, and Egypt, and went with her to the Crimea.

Bridgeman, Rev. Mother Mary Frances, of Kinsale, Ireland, was selected by Rev. Henry Manning and the Vatican to lead a second group of Catholic nuns to the Crimea without Florence's permission. She and the fifteen Irish "Kinsale" nuns from different convents refused to submit totally to Florence's authority and became Florence's opposition throughout the Crimea, siding with Army officers also opposed to Florence. Mother Bridgeman had extensive experience working with the sick and poor in Ireland and so offered a strong challenge to Florence.

Brontë, Charlotte (1816–1855), famous English novelist, daughter of an Anglican clergyman and sister of novelist Emily Brontë. Never leaving her widowed father's home, Charlotte wrote *Jane Eyre*, *Shirley*, and *Villette*, and finally in 1754, married her father's curate who moved in with them. Charlotte died the following year, aged thirty–nine.

Butler Josephine (1828–1906), social reformer and women's advocate, with her clergyman husband George befriended prostitutes in Liverpool, England, horrifying her neighbors. She led the fight against the Contagious Diseases Act aimed at controlling venereal disease in the Army by arresting prostitutes and subjecting them to degrading medical examinations. Josephine's lobbying led to the Act's repeal in 1886. She also worked for the abolition of child prostitution, higher penalties for child abuse, and the raising of the age of consent from twelve to sixteen.

Calvin, John (1509–1564), French lawyer, reformer, and theologian whose theological treatise *Institutes of the Christian Religion* (1536) became the basis of the Protestant church and theocracy he developed in Geneva, Switzerland. His followers, Calvinists, took his ideas on predestination and election to extremes, resulting in many of the theological and social doctrines Florence and her friends would challenge.

Canning, Lady Charlotte (1817–1861), a Board member of the Harley Street institution where Florence worked, helped Liz Herbert with the selection of Florence's nurses for the Crimea and continued corresponding with Florence, even when her husband was the first Viceroy of India (1856–62).

Catherine of Genoa, Saint (1447–1510), a noblewoman whose call to religious life was thwarted by an arranged marriage at sixteen. She converted her husband and they lived together in celibacy until his death, working with the sick and poor. Catherine then became a Franciscan tertiary and a Directress in 1490. She died in 1510, was canonized in 1737, and is the patron saint of brides, childless couples, difficult marriages, victims of unfaithfulness, and widows. Her writings were to be included in Florence's book on medieval mystics.

Catherine of Siena, Saint (1347–1380) became a Dominican tertiary at sixteen. In 1376, she went to Pope Gregory XI in Avignon (France) to persuade him to return to Rome and stabilize the Church again. Her following in Siena were attracted to her spirituality, ecstatic prayer, and writings.

Chadwick, Edwin (1800–1889), a disciple of philosopher Jeremy Bentham, was the secretary of the Poor Law Commission and, seeing links between poverty, illness, and slums, crusaded for improved sanitation. His 1842 report to Parliament on working-class sanitary conditions was monumental, even though it greatly upset the establishment. Florence supported his views, both of them suspicious of the emerging germ theory.

Church of England, Anglican Church, Established Church ("the Church") emerged as the Catholic Church's expression in England when King Henry VIII declared himself head of the English church over the Pope, severing financial, judicial, and administrative bonds with Rome. Monasteries were dissolved, and *The Book of Common Prayer*, produced by Archbishop T. Cranmer, became the official service book of the English Church. After Elizabeth I, the Crown assumed the title of "Supreme Governor" and another edition of *The Book of Common Prayer* emerged, together with the *Thirty-Nine Articles* summarizing the Church's essential doctrinal beliefs. Relations between church and state have historically been turbulent but, at the turn of the 1800s, bishops sat in the British Parliament's upper house, the House of Lords (the lower house is the House of Commons) and non-Anglicans could not hold public office or be elected to Parliament. Both clergymen and political figures graduated from the established Church's universities, Oxford and Cambridge, which demanded allegiance to the *Thirty-Nine Articles* for graduation; hence the protests in Florence's time for political enfranchisement of non-Anglicans (Nonconformists, Jews, and Catholics). Within these universities, numerous colleges functioned as residences and places of learning. Oxford's Balliol College was Benjamin Jowett's home for most of his life, and Oxford's Oriel College spawned the Oxford Movement. The Church of England prided itself as a middle way, holding within itself in Florence's day, with various degrees of tension, a High Church (stressing historical continuity with Catholic roots), a Low Church (evangelicals stressing spiritual experience and conversion with little sacramental emphasis) and a Broad Church (demanding freedom of thought in theological and scientific inquiry).

Clark, Sir James, physician to Queen Victoria, was also physician and friend to the Nightingales. His home in Scotland was near Balmoral Castle and, through him, Florence met the Queen after the Crimea.

Clarke, Mary (Clarkey) (1793–1883), a year older than Florence's father, left England for Paris as a young girl. Through her grandmother, she retained contacts with England's intellectual life and also became a success in Paris through her individuality and intelligence, her literary salon attracting Paris' intellectual elite. Florence met "Clarkey" in Paris in 1838 and was inspired by her rapport with the great (male) minds of Europe. Mary married oriental scholar Julius Mohl, also a lifelong friend of Florence's.

Clough, Arthur (1819–1861) moved beyond traditional religion at Oxford to become, through his poetry, a voice for Victorian theological skepticism. He visited America and taught with Ralph Waldo Emerson, married Aunt Mai's daughter Blanche, and became attracted to Florence's reform work and theological ideas on her return from Crimea, becoming her secretary and also secretary for the Nightingale Fund. In 1860, he encouraged Florence to publish her draft of *Suggestions for Thought* and introduced her to Jowett as a result. Florence was devastated at Clough's death from tuberculosis the following year, aged forty-two.

Colenso, Bishop John (1814–1883), Bishop of Natal, South Africa, from 1853. He published a commentary on Romans in 1861 denying eternal punishment; published papers on the Pentateuch and Joshua challenging their authorship and accuracy; and adapted Christian ideas to South African indigenous traditions. In 1863, he was deposed as bishop for his ideas, but England's secular Privy Council reversed the decision. Another bishop was appointed, but Colenso maintained his position alongside the new appointment. Both Florence and Jowett supported his cause.

Comte, Auguste (1798–1857), French philosopher and founder of the philosophical school of Positivism, which allowed knowledge gained from observable phenomena only and was suspicious of theology and metaphysics. Comte's practical concerns were social reform and societal harmony, and he was supported in this by John Stuart Mill. Comte coined the term *sociology* for the systematic study of unifying principles in society.

Cook, Sir Edward T. (1857–1919), noted biographer commissioned by the Nightingale family to write the official biography of Florence, *The Life of Florence Nightingale*, first published in 1913 in two volumes and later condensed into one volume in 1942.

Cowper, William (1731–1800) was called to the Bar in 1754, but suicidal mania sent him into a psychiatric institution in 1763. Later, he became a lay assistant to Calvinist preacher and former slave runner John Newton and began writing hymns. His psychiatric problems continued, despite the fine hymns he composed between bouts of illness.

Darwin, Charles (1809–1882), English naturalist whose theory of evolution by natural selection revolutionized science, offended the Church, and changed assumptions about the human being forever. After studying medicine at Edinburgh University, Darwin quit his studies for the ministry at Cambridge and became the naturalist for a five-year survey expedition on the H.M.S. *Beagle* (1831–36). The voyage allowed him to study plant and animal life worldwide and ask questions about their origins. He developed his theory of evolution long before its publication, realizing the controversy it would produce against the biblical account of creation. Only when naturalist Alfred Wallace began suggesting similar ideas did Darwin publish *On the Origin of Species by Means of Natural Selection* in 1859, and the rest is history.

Dunant, Henri (1828–1910), Swiss humanitarian who helped the wounded at the Battle of Solferino in 1859 and realized the need for an international organization to alleviate suffering in war and peace. His efforts culminated in the Geneva Convention of 1864 and the formation of the Red Cross, for which he credited Florence as his inspiration. Although business failures bankrupted him, he continued his humanitarian causes, receiving the first Nobel Peace Prize in 1901.

Eliot, George (Mary Ann Evans) (1819–1880), famous essayist and novelist who translated into English the German theologian Ludwig Feuerbach's *Essence of Christianity*, representative of her own theological ideas. Having abandoned her strict evangelical upbringing, she lived an unconventional lifestyle by Victorian standards and wrote such novels as *Mill on the Floss*, *Adam Bede*, and *Middlemarch*.

Essays and Reviews (1860), a controversial collection of seven essays published by adherents of the Church of England's Broad Church Movement, challenged the Church's resistance to new scholarship, both German biblical criticism and scientific inquiry. The essayists were Frederick Temple, Rowland Williams, Baden Powell (father of Boy Scouts founder), Henry Wilson, Charles Goodwin, Mark Pattison, and Benjamin Jowett. An outcry followed their publication, and the ordained among them were brought to Church trial. They were later acquitted by a secular Privy Council, causing additional waves through Anglican circles.

Farr, Dr. William (1807–1891), a pioneer in medical statistics and member of the Army Health Board. Farr was assistant Commissioner for Census

Returns in 1851 and 1861, and Commissioner in 1871. He advised Florence on the analysis of her Crimean mortality figures and continued with her in later reforms.

Fliedner, Pastor Theodore, a Protestant pastor from Kaiserswerth near Dusseldorf, Germany, went to Holland and England in 1823–24 to raise funds for his struggling Protestant parish after the failure of its silk mill. He met prison reformer Elizabeth Fry and was impressed with her work, visiting Dusseldorf's prisons on his return. There he discovered a need for a home for discharged women prisoners, and the Kaiserswerth Institute was born in his back garden, spreading across the world with its deaconess training for work in prisons, education, and hospitals. Florence first fulfilled her dream to work for the poor at Kaiserswerth.

Fowler, Dr. Richard, of Salibury Hospital, and his wife were friends of the Nightingale family. Knowing Florence's wish to learn hospital work, Fowler invited her in 1845 to work with him, much to the family's horror. The plan fell through, but Dr. Fowler later took Florence to a Medical Conference in Dublin, Ireland, so she could spend time training with Irish nursing Sisters.

Franco–Prussian War (1870–71) between France's Napoleon III and Prussia's Otto von Bismarck was fueled in general by Prussia's increasing power in Europe. Its immediate cause was Prussia's attempt to put a Prussian royal on the Spanish throne. France declared war on Prussia and was crushed in six weeks. After Napoleon III's surrender and the collapse of France's Second Empire, revolution broke out in Paris. The Peace of Frankfurt gave Alsace and part of Lorraine to Prussia, and France was required to pay heavy indemnity.

Fry, Elizabeth (1780–1845), an upper-class Quaker woman who committed herself to prison reform after visiting London's Newgate Prison. She founded an industrial school in 1819 for female prisoners and was the inspiration for Pastor Fliedner of Kaiserswerth.

Gaskell, Elizabeth (1810–1865), leading Victorian novelist and social commentator, married Unitarian minister William Gaskell in 1832 and worked with him in the industrial north against social inequities resulting from the Industrial Revolution. These problems informed her novels, including *North and South* and *Wives and Daughters*. She wrote a biography of Charlotte Brontë (1857) and contributed regularly to the periodical *Household Words*.

Germ theory. The germ theory of disease, first proposed by Louis Pasteur in 1862, argued that certain diseases were caused by microorganisms invading the body. The theory was accepted slowly, since many, like Florence, thought contagious diseases were caused by "miasma" or bad air. Robert Koch from Berlin finally proved the theory in 1876 by demonstrating a bacillus causing anthrax in animals, and later identified microbes responsible for tuberculosis and cholera.

Gladstone, William Ewart (1809–1898), four times Prime Minister of Great Britain as well as other parliamentary posts, entered Tory politics in 1833. The old Tory and Whig parties declined in the 1840s and 1850s as more people gained suffrage, and Gladstone joined the Liberals in 1859, becoming their leader in 1866. A student of Homer, he translated the *Iliad* and wrote books about Homer. Devoutly religious, he was responsible for disestablishing the Church of England in Ireland in 1869 and freeing Irish Catholics from its allegiance, but also expressed concern in an article entitled "Vaticanism" that British Catholic civil obedience might be subordinated to papal command.

Hall, Sir John (1795–1866), a surgeon with forty-two years' experience in Army Medical Services, was reassigned from Bombay at sixty–three to become Inspector-General of Hospitals for the Crimean campaign. From the moment of Florence's arrival, the two clashed, given her political influence, his ambivalence toward women nurses, and the ambiguity of Florence's authority. They remained antagonists throughout the war and afterward.

Hampden, Renn Dickson (1793–1868), Anglican theologian who, in his Bampton lectures in Oxford in 1832, offered a less traditional and more scientifically accommodating view of Christianity that challenged the dominant Anglican theology of William Paley. Supporters of the Oxford Movement tried to block Hampden's appointment as Regius Professor of Divinity at Oxford (1836) and his appointment as Bishop of Hereford (1848) because of his "liberal" tendencies.

Herbert, Sir Sidney ("Sir Sidney") and Elizabeth (Liz). Sir Sidney (1810–1861), a landlord from Wiltshire, entered Parliament at twenty-two and served in different roles under Prime Minister Peel. He was Secretary at War from 1845 to 1846 and from 1852 to 1855, initiating Army reform. His wife, Liz Herbert, served on the Harley Street committee where Florence was working when the Crimean War began, and Sir Sidney was responsible for sending Florence to the Crimea. Afterward, he and Florence worked tirelessly on Army reform until his early death in 1861. Liz, a close friend of Florence's, was also involved in social reform.

Hill, Frances, and John Henry, American missionaries working in a school and orphanage in Athens, whom Florence met on her visit there in 1851. Florence spent long hours discussing her call with Mrs. Hill.

Howe, Dr. Ward, and Juliet. American social reformer and philanthropist, Dr. Ward Howe was involved in nursing and health reform in his own country when he visited the Nightingale home in England. Florence consulted with him many times about her plans to work with the poor. Juliet Howe wrote the words for "The Battle Hymn of the Republic." Laura Richards, one of Florence's biographers, was their daughter.

Huxley, Thomas Henry (1825–1895), a surgeon in the Royal Navy, studied marine life, and his work became the basis for some of its classification, especially jellyfish and squid. Huxley keenly promoted Darwin's ideas, debating Bishop Samuel Wilberforce at the Oxford meeting of the British Association for the Advancement of Science in 1860. While Darwin had not specifically applied his evolutionary theories to the human species, Huxley did in his 1863 *Man's Place in Nature*. He also argued during the 1860s that there was no evidence for racial superiority and coined the word *agnostic* to describe his theological position.

Jowett, Benjamin (1817–1893) was educated at Balliol College, Oxford, and stayed on its faculty for life, becoming Master of Balliol in 1870. Liberal in theology, he was an important member of the Anglican Broad Church Movement, writing a controversial essay on "The Interpretation of Scripture" for *Essays and Reviews* (1860). As a result of the controversy, Jowett stopped writing on theology, concentrating on his major contribution, his translations of Plato. He became acquainted with Florence in 1860 when Clough sent Florence's *Suggestions for Thought* to him for comment. Their intimate friendship continued until Jowett's death.

Kaiserswerth (see Fliedner, Pastor Theodore)

Keble, John (1792–1866), clergyman and Professor of Poetry at Oxford who, concerned with challenges to the Church of England from reforming and liberal forces, preached a sermon at Oxford in 1833 on "National Apostasy." John Henry Newman heard it and, together with other supporters, formed the Oxford Movement.

Kinsale Sisters (see Bridgeman, Mother)

Lefroy, Colonel John Henry (1817–1890) was advisor on scientific matters to Secretary for War Lord Panmure. Sent to the Crimea by Panmure in October 1855 to report on the state of the hospitals, Lefroy was impressed with Florence's achievements and abilities, remaining her close friend and advisor after she returned from the Crimea. Lefroy's endorsement of her to Panmure secured her General Orders as Head of all nurses in the Crimea, a position Sir John Hall had opposed.

Madre (Mother Santa Colomba), Mother Superior of the Sisters of the Sacred Heart at St. Trinita di Monta in Rome, where Florence took a retreat in 1847. The Madre taught Florence her spiritual disciplines and remained Florence's spiritual director.

Manning, Rev. Henry Edward (1808–1892), an ordained Church of England priest, became a Roman Catholic through the influence of the Oxford Movement and John Henry Newman. He was appointed (Catholic)

Archbishop of Westminster in 1865 and became involved in social reform. A friend of Florence's, he supported her efforts to serve God among the poor.

Mansel, Henry Longueville (1820–1871), Dean of St. Paul's Cathedral from 1868, argued in his Bampton Lectures at Oxford in 1858 on *The Limits of Religious Thought* that the mind can intuit an Absolute Being and that which is intuited must be the God of Scripture. Although trying to reconcile Christianity with an age of science, Mansel thus made no challenge to supernatural revelations and evoked much criticism. (The Bampton Lectures were eight lectures delivered annually on the exposition and defense of the Christian faith).

Martineau, Harriet (1802–1876), famous theological writer, political journalist and social critic, promoted Florence's reform ideas in the popular press after the Crimea and also wrote a book on the soldiers' plight in the Crimea, using Florence's findings.

Martyn, Henry (1781–1812), the distinguished Victorian "scholar missionary," was educated at Cambridge, experiencing a religious conversion there and emerging with highest academic honors. After ordination, he went to India and later to Persia as a missionary, translating the New Testament into the languages of both the Hindus and the Persians.

Maurice, Frederick Denison (F. D.) (1805–1872) was Professor of Theology at King's College, London, from 1846 until the publication of his *Theological Essays* (1853), which denied endless punishment in hell and argued that "Eternity" in the New Testament had nothing to do with time or place, but existed already in the present. In 1866, he became Knightsbridge Professor of Moral Philosophy at Cambridge, and his lifelong interest in social reform led to the formation of the Christian Socialists.

McNeill, Sir John (1795–1883), began his career as a surgeon in the East India Company in Bombay, rising quickly in the Foreign Service. On returning to Scotland from a post in Persia, he served as Chairman of the Poor Board, averting a potato famine that swept Ireland. An expert on Russia and the Middle East, he was appointed, with Colonel Alexander Tulloch, to investigate Army supplies and operations in the Crimea. Their McNeill-Tulloch report exposing the fiasco was whitewashed for political reasons. McNeill met Florence in the Crimea and remained her close friend and advisor, receiving a draft of her *Suggestions for Thought* for comment.

Mill, John Stuart (1806–1873), philosopher, political economist, and reformer, was the son of philosopher James Mill (1773–1836), an early Utilitarian. John was rigorously educated from childhood and worked for the

British East India Company until its demise in 1858. He wrote many books with his wife, Harriet Taylor Mill—*A System of Logic* (1843), *Principles of Political Economy* (1848), *On Liberty* (1859), *Utilitarianism* (1863) and *The Subjection of Women* (1869), which alludes to the writings of a celebrated woman, namely Florence. Mill was elected to Parliament in 1865 and fought for Irish land reform and women's rights.

Mohl, Julius (see Clark, Mary)

Monckton Milnes, Richard (1809–1885), poet, politician, scholar, and reformer, proposed to Florence after seven years of courting, but she refused him in order to pursue her call. They remained good friends throughout life, Monckton Milnes serving on the Nightingale Fund and supporting her reform.

Moore, Mother Mary Clare (1814–1874), founding Mother Superior of the Bermondsey Sisters of Mercy, London, was born Protestant in Ireland but joined the Catholic Sisters of Mercy at nineteen. In 1837, she helped found the Sisters of Mercy in Cork, Ireland, and from there founded the Bermondsey Order responsible for visiting the sick, educating the poor, and preparing children for their first communion. From there, she took four sisters to the Crimea. Florence formed a close friendship with her, spiritually identifying herself with the Order and with Mother Mary Clare as her Mother Superior. On returning to London after the Crimea, Florence went first to Bermondsey and corresponded with Mother Mary Clare throughout her lifetime.

Muller, Friedrich Max (1823–1900), comparative philologist at Oxford, edited a 51-volume translation of religious classics, *The Sacred Books of the East*, and wrote on comparative religion, appealing to religious liberals.

Mysticism reached new heights in the twelfth to sixteenth centuries, especially among women, as a way to approach God without ecclesiastical mediation. Florence described it thus:

> What is this but putting in fervent and the most striking words the foundation of all real Mystical Religion?—which is that for all our actions, all our words, all our thoughts, the food upon which they are to live and have their being is to be the indwelling Presence of God, the union with God, that is, with the Spirit of Goodness and Wisdom. Where shall I find God? In myself. That is the true Mystical Doctrine. But then I myself must be in a state for Him to come and dwell in me. This is the whole aim of the Mystical Life, and all Mystical Rules in all times and countries have been laid down for putting the soul into such a state (Sir Edward T. Cook, *The Life of Florence Nightingale*. 2 vols. in 1 [New York: Macmillan, 1942], vol. 1: 223).

Newman, John Henry (1801–1890), born Low Church Evangelical, became High Church at Oxford and the instigator and leader of the Oxford Movement, a holiness movement that sought to return the Church of England to its roots in the primitive church and its creeds. Castigated for a tract declaring the *Thirty–Nine Articles* no different from Catholic teaching, Newman converted to Catholicism. His ideas found more followers at the time of Vatican II (1960s) than when first written.

Nicholson, Hannah (Aunt Hannah), unmarried sister of George Nicholson, who married Fanny Nightingale's sister Anne, lived with George and his family in close contact with the Nightingales. A mystic, she encouraged the young Florence to sublimate her frustrations in mystical experience and accept her lot in life.

Oxford Movement (see Newman, John Henry; Keble, John; and Pusey, E. B.)

Paley, William (1743–1805), Anglican divine whose 1794 *View of the Evidences of Christianity* returned Enlightenment debates to the traditional doctrines of the Church of England. His work became popular in England's uncertainty during the French Revolution and was compulsory reading for all students at Oxford and Cambridge in the early 1800s.

Palmerston, Lord Henry (1784–1865) entered Parliament in 1807, was Secretary of War (1809–1828) and twice Prime Minister (1855–58 and 1859–65). He first became Prime Minister after the government resigned over the mismanagement of the Crimean War.

Panmure, Lord (The Bison) (1801–1874) was secretary of State for War (1855–1858) when Florence returned from the Crimea. On the Queen's instruction, Panmure requested a formal report of Florence's experiences with suggestions for army reform. He approved a Royal Commission into the Army and consulted Florence on plans for England's first general military hospital at Netley. Florence was frustrated with his rejection of her Netley suggestions and his delays with the Royal Commission—they were both enemies and friends. She wrote at his death, "He used to call me 'a turbulent fellow.'"

Pantheism holds that all things are modes, attributes, or appearances of a single reality or being. Therefore, nature and God are identical—two names for the one reality. *Deism*, at the other end of the spectrum, says that God and the world are totally separate entities, and that God as creator does not guide or interfere in any way with the world's subsequent course or destiny. Christian theologians have positioned themselves at various points between these extremes. *Panentheism*, the position of process theology, argues that the world (nature) is included in God's being as cells are included in a larger organism, but the world does not exhaust God's being or creativity. God includes nature within the divine Self but exceeds or is more than nature.

Positivism (see Comte, Auguste)

Priestley, Joseph (1733–1804), an important scientist of his day, rejected Christianity's supernatural claims, including Christ's divinity and the Atonement, in favor of a religion based on reason. In his *The Doctrine of Philosophical Necessity* he argued, not for a unique divinity in Jesus, but God's Spirit incarnate in everyone. Priestley campaigned for religious and social reform and for non-Anglicans in public office. In 1791, he and his followers formed the Unitarian Society, but people favored his reform ideas more than his theological ones, and he later fled to America under persecution.

Pusey, Edward Bouverie (1800–1882) was educated at Oxford and, after exposure in Europe to German biblical criticism, returned as Regius Professor of Hebrew. The early death of his wife sent him back to traditional High Church theology and the Oxford Movement. When John Henry Newman became Roman Catholic, Pusey took over its leadership, defending the High Church against liberals and evangelicals (Puseyism). He desired reunion of the English church with Rome and was disappointed when this did not happen at Vatican I (1869–70) when the Roman Church defined Papal Infallibility.

Quetelet, Adolphe (1796–1874), Belgian astronomer, meteorologist, and statistician, impressed Florence with his statistical ideas, especially when applied to social dynamics. They met during the International Statistical Congress held in London in 1860.

Rathbone, William (1819–1902), a wealthy Liverpool shipowner and a Unitarian, approached Florence in 1860 for her advice and assistance in setting up a district-nursing scheme in Liverpool. He later offered to finance a nurse training scheme for a Liverpool Workhouse Infirmary. In 1868, he became a Liberal Member of Parliament.

Savior. When Florence speaks of her call to be a Savior, she does not mean in the traditional understanding of Jesus as a divine Savior and an atonement. Like her Unitarian heritage, Florence did not believe in the divinity of Christ, seeing the task of Christ and many others in the Hebrew sense of a messiah or Plato's idea of "guardians"—people called by God at various times in history to lead the people from error.

Smith, Mai (Aunt Mai) (1798–1889), WEN's sister and Florence's Aunt. Mai married Samuel Smith, Fanny's brother, and their son William Shore Smith inherited the Nightingale estates from WEN, since WEN had no sons. Aunt Mai's eldest daughter, Blanche, married Arthur Clough, secretary to Florence and the Nightingale Fund. Aunt Mai and Florence were close during Florence's childhood, and Mai accompanied Florence to the Crimea and stayed with her in London after the War.

Smith, Samuel (Uncle Sam) (see Smith, Mai)

Smith, William (1756–1835), Fanny Nightingale's Unitarian father, was a Member of the House of Commons in Parliament for forty-four years, campaigning against religious intolerance and political and social inequities. He worked with William Wilberforce to outlaw slavery and sponsored the 1813 Unitarian Toleration Act, which removed Unitarian beliefs (denial of Christ's divinity) from the criminal list. His father, Samuel Smith, made his fortune in the grocery business and supported the American colonies in their War of Independence against the British crown.

Stanley, Arthur Penrhyn (1815–1881), an intimate friend of Benjamin Jowett's and a member of the Broad Church, collaborated with Jowett on commentaries of the New Testament epistles. Stanley became Dean of Westminster in 1864 and tried to make the Abbey a national shrine for all, irrespective of creed. His sister Mary was in the Crimea with Florence.

Stanley, Lord, Earl of Derby, was Secretary of State for India (1858–1859), Foreign Secretary (1867–68; 1874–78), Colonial Secretary under Gladstone (1882–85), and a supporter of Florence's India work as Chair of the Indian Sanitary Commission after Sir Sidney.

Stanley, Mary, daughter of the Bishop of Norwich and sister of Rev. Arthur Stanley, was a friend of the Herberts. Florence met her first in Rome in 1847. Later, Mary led a second team of nurses, all Irish Catholic sisters, to the Crimea against Florence's will, and converted to Roman Catholicism.

Strachey, Lytton (1880–1932), Cambridge educated biographer, critic, and member of the Bloomsbury Group, is credited with revolutionizing the writing of biography after the dull and hagiographic two-volume Victorian tomes. His biographies were swift, selective, critical, witty, and artistic and included *Eminent Victorians* (1918), a volume of short biographical studies, *Queen Victoria* (1921), and *Elizabeth and Essex* (1928). Florence is one of his eminent Victorians.

Strauss, David Friedrich (1808–1874), a German theologian, wrote *Das Leben Jesu* (1835–36), which denied the historical foundation of supernatural events in the gospels, arguing that they emerged in a developing "myth" in the community after Jesus and before the gospels were written down. Christianity must therefore recognize them as such by trying to reconstruct their origins in the evolving church. Strauss lost his position at Tubingen, but his ideas fueled the German biblical criticism that would change Protestant theology.

Sutherland, Dr. John (1809–1898), a leading sanitary expert and sanitary inspector under the first Board of Health, headed many Government inquiries, including one sent by Lord Palmerston in 1855 to the Crimean War. Appalled by the conditions, Sutherland set to work making improvements in Scutari Hospital, dropping its mortality rates from 42.7 to two deaths per 1,000 patients. Florence, who met and worked with him there, claimed that his Report "saved the British Army." They remained close friends and colleagues, Sutherland working almost daily with Florence on all aspects of her reform until his retirement in 1889. He was also her personal physician and protector from the public.

Temple, Frederick (1821–1902), an *Essays and Reviews* essayist, was headmaster of Rugby School (1857–69), Bishop of Exeter (1869–85), Bishop of London (1885–97) and Archbishop of Canterbury from 1897. He withdrew his essay from the second edition to become Bishop of Exeter, much to Jowett's disappointment.

Teresa of Avila, Saint (1515–1582), a Spanish Carmelite nun and mystic who entered the convent in 1535 but began her mystical life in 1555 with divine voices, visions, and ecstatic experiences. She founded a convent, wrote extensively, and combined her mystical life with ceaseless activity.

Theodicy (theodike) is the theological attempt to defend the goodness and omnipotence of God in face of the existence of evil in a world of God's creation and providence. Either God is able to prevent evil and will not, or willing to prevent evil and cannot. If the former, God is not merciful; if the latter, God is not omnipotent.

Tulloch, Colonel Alexander (1801–1864), an Army internal affairs investigator who instituted major reforms in the Indian Army. This experience and his legal background were put to use in the Crimea, both through the McNeill–Tulloch report he helped produced and also through the practical improvements he introduced there. Less politically experienced than his colleague Sir John McNeill, Tulloch was devastated when their report was scuttled (see McNeill).

Underhill, Evelyn (1875–1941), English exponent of mysticism whose book *Mysticism* (1911) remains a classic.

Verney, Sir Harry (1801–1894), Member of Parliament for Buckinghamshire for over fifty years and a widower with children, married Florence's sister Parthe in 1858, and they resided at Claydon. He became involved in Florence's reform work, chairing the Nightingale Fund until 1890. Claydon became a second home for Florence in her later years, and Sir Harry made daily visits to Florence when they worked together on the Fund after 1870.

von Bunsen, Christian (1791–1860), theologian, scholar, and Prussian Ambassador to the Court of St James's (1842 to 1854), helped introduce German biblical critical scholarship into England and was a leader in the Broad Church Movement. Florence visited his home in London many times for discussion, and he guided her early reading in theology and Egyptology.

Wesley, John (1703–1791), founder of the Methodist Movement within the Church of England, gathered a group together at Oxford which became known as the "Holy Club" or "Methodists." He later experienced a heart-warming conversion and espoused Arminius' doctrine of universal salvation against Calvin's "election." These convictions sent him into the countryside of England, offering a universal gospel and establishing covenant groups with lay leaders for the poor and unchurched. Methodists separated from the Church of England after Wesley's death.

Whitehead, Alfred North (1861–1947) began his Cambridge career in mathematics and logic, moving later to philosophy of science. In his later years at Harvard, he arranged his thoughts into the most extensive philosophical cosmology of the twentieth century, known as process thought. In *Science and the Modern World* (1825), Whitehead argued that cosmology should be based on aesthetic, ethical, and religious intuitions as well as science, and that scientific method pointed away from a mechanistic world to an organismic worldview. Agnostic himself, Whitehead affirmed the *philosophical* existence of a "principle of limitation" accounting for the basic order of the world. Process *theology* elaborated on that "principle of limitation" as God.

Wilberforce, Samuel (1805–1873), Bishop of Oxford (1845–69) then of Winchester, attacked *Essays and Reviews* for its liberalism and led the condemnation of the essayists. He was also responsible for initiating the revision of the Authorized Version of the Bible.

Wilberforce, William (1759–1833), lay evangelical Churchman and philanthropist, focused his parliamentary energies on the abolition of the slave trade, the bill becoming law in 1807. He achieved the abolition of slavery in 1833, supported by Florence's maternal grandfather, William Smith. Wilberforce helped form the Church Missionary Society and the British and Foreign Bible Society.

Williams, Rowland (1817–1870), Anglican divine and Broad Church adherent, was condemned for heresy in 1860 after his essay in *Essays and Reviews*, a charge later removed by the Privy Council. He also wrote a comparative Christian-Hindu study, which talks of humankind's unity through one supreme soul (God) made distinct in various forms.

Woodham-Smith, Mrs. Cecil (Blanche), an expert on the Crimean War, was the author of *Florence Nightingale 1820–1910* (London: The Reprint Society, 1952). Woodham-Smith had access to papers not available to Sir Edward Cook, Florence's earlier biographer. This book won the James Tait Black Memorial Prize.

Notes

Preface

[1]William Zinsser, ed., *Extraordinary Lives: The Art and Craft of American Biography* (New York: American Heritage, 1986), 18.

[2]Barbara Montgomery Dossey, *Florence Nightingale: Mystic, Visionary, Healer* (Springhouse, Pa.: Springhouse Corp., 2000), 399.

[3]William Zinsser, ed., *Extraordinary Lives*, 10.

[4]Ibid., 13.

[5]Lytton Strachey, *Eminent Victorians* (New York: The Modern Library, 1918), viii.

[6]In this book, "Church" used with no further qualifiers refers to the Church of England, and "church" with no other qualifiers is a generic term for all such Christian institutions.

[7]Florence Nightingale, *Suggestions for Thought: Selections and Commentaries*, ed. Michael D. Calabria and Janet A. Macrae (Philadelphia: University of Pennsylvania Press, 1994), 7.

[8]Florence Nightingale, *Cassandra: An Essay* (New York: The Feminist Press, 1979), 25.

[9]Mrs. Cecil (Blanche) Woodham-Smith, *Florence Nightingale* (London: Constable, 1950. First ed. New York: McGraw-Hill Book Co., 1951), 67.

[10]Sir Edward T. Cook, *The Life of Florence Nightingale*, 2 vols. (1913–14; reprint, 2 vols. in 1, New York: Macmillan, 1942), v.

[11]"God-intoxicated" is Bishop John Shelby Spong's term, in John Shelby Spong, *Why Christianity Must Change or Die: A Bishop Speaks to Believers in Exile* (New York: Harper SanFrancisco, 1998), 3.

Chapter 1: Biographies—Fact and Fiction

[1]Lytton Strachey, *Eminent Victorians* (New York: Modern Library, 1918), 131.

[2]Hugh Small, *Florence Nightingale: Avenging Angel* (New York: St. Martin's Press, 1998), 20. The Crimean War (1853–56), one in a series of Russo-Turkish Wars (1676–1878) spawned by Russian expansion against the weakening Ottoman Empire, pitted Russia against the Ottoman Empire and its allies Great Britain, France, and Sardinia. The Crimean War began when the Turks refused to allow Czar Nicholas of Russia to establish a protectorate over Orthodox Christians in Turkish borders. Russia invaded the Turkish-controlled territories of Moldavia and Wallachia in Romania, bringing France, Britain, and later Sardinia to Turkish aid. France and Britain were concerned about Russian expansion. Russia abandoned the Romanian territories, but Britain and France pursued the war to Sebastopol (Sevastopol), Russia's naval base on the Black Sea coast of the Crimean peninsula. In September 1854, allied forces landed north of Sebastopol and the Battle of Alma River forced the Russians into a yearlong siege in Sebastopol. The Battle of Balaclava (October 25, 1854) was a costly allied victory remembered for the disastrous cavalry charge made famous by Tennyson's poem "The Charge of the Light Brigade." The Battle of Inkerman, just days after Florence and her nurses arrived in Scutari, was also victory with a high human price. A cruel winter decimated the remaining British soldiers through cholera, cold, and starvation. Russia finally evacuated Sebastopol in September 1855, and the Treaty of Paris in 1856 ended the hostilities. More than 21,000 British troops had been lost, 16,000 from disease.

[3]Sidney Godolphin Osborne, "An Eye-Witness Account," in Raymond G. Hebert, ed., *Florence Nightingale: Saint, Reformer or Rebel?* (Malabar, Fla.: Robert E. Kreiger, 1981), 96.

[4]Mrs. Cecil (Blanche) Woodham-Smith, *Florence Nightingale 1820–1910* (London: The Reprint Society, 1952), 99. This book won the James Tait Black Memorial Prize.

[5]Sir Sidney Herbert's wife, Liz, was on the organizing committee of this institution.

[6]Daniel 12:1.

[7]Evert A. Duyckinck, *Portrait Gallery of Eminent Men and Women of Europe and America*, vol. 2 (New York: Johnson, Wilson and Company, 1873), 535.

[8]Florence Nightingale, *Ever Yours, Florence Nightingale—Selected Letters*, ed. Martha Vicinus and Bea Nergaard (Cambridge, Mass.: Harvard University Press, 1989), 138.

[9]Monica Baly, "Florence Nightingale and the Establishment of the First School at St. Thomas's—Myth Versus Reality," in Vern L. Bullough, Bonnie Bullough, and Marie Stanton, eds., *Florence Nightingale and Her Era: A Collection of New Scholarship* (New York and London: Garland Publishing, 1990), 7.

[10]*Notes on Matters Affecting the Health, Efficiency, and Hospital Administration of the British Army* (1857), *Mortality of the British Army* (1858), *Notes on Hospitals* (1859), and the famous *Notes on Nursing* (1860).

[11]The germ theory of disease, first proposed by Louis Pasteur in 1862, said that certain diseases were caused by microorganisms invading the body. The theory was accepted only slowly since many, like Florence, thought contagious diseases were caused by "miasma" or bad air. Robert Koch from Berlin finally proved the germ theory in 1876 through experimentation with anthrax in animals.

[12]Sir Edward T. Cook, *The Life of Florence Nightingale*, 2 vols. (1913–14; reprint, 2 vols. in 1, New York: Macmillan, 1942).

[13]Laura E. Richards, *Florence Nightingale* (New York and London: D. Appleton & Co., 1909, 1927), 1.

[14]Small, *Avenging Angel*, 53.

[15]Ibid., 53.

[16]Strachey, *Eminent Victorians*, 160.

[17]Martha Vicinus, "What makes a Heroine? Girls' Biographies of Florence Nightingale," in Bullough, Bullough, and Stanton, *Florence Nightingale and Her Era*, 90.

[18]Amy Steedman, *When They Were Children: Stories of the Childhood of Famous Men and Women* (London and Edinburgh: T. C. & E. C. Jack, n.d.), 312.

[19]Duyckinck, *Portrait Gallery*, 536.

[20]Steedman, *When They Were Children*, 310.

[21]Ibid., 314. The story of Jairus' daughter—Mark 5:21–43; Luke 8:40–56.

[22]Ibid.

[23]W. J. Wintle and Florence Witts, *Florence Nightingale and Frances E. Willard: The Story of Their Lives* (London: Sunday School Union, n.d., around 1897), 13–14.

[24]Ibid., 24.

[25]Elmer C. Adams and Warren Dunham Foster, "Heroine of Modern Progress," in Hebert, *Saint, Reformer or Rebel?* 105.

[26]Wintle and Witts, *Florence Nightingale and Frances E. Willard*, 94.

[27]Strachey, *Eminent Victorians*, 160.

[28]Elmer C. Adams and Warren Dunham Foster, "Heroine of Modern Progress," Hebert, *Saint, Reformer or Rebel?* 107.

[29]Mrs. E. J. Richmond, *Woman, First and Last, and What She Has Done*, vol. 2 (New York: Phillips & Hunt, 1887), 251.

[30]Ibid., 253.

[31]Wintle and Witts, *Florence Nightingale and Frances E. Willard*, 55.

[32]Richmond, *Woman, First and Last*, 257.

[33]Wintle and Witts, *Florence Nightingale and Frances E. Willard*, 56.

[34]Ibid., 133.

[35]Nancy Boyd, *Three Victorian Women Who Changed Their World: Josephine Butler, Octavia Hill, Florence Nightingale* (New York: Oxford University Press, 1982), 187.

[36]Yvonne Ffrench, *Florence Nightingale, 1820–1910* (London: Hamish Hamilton, 1954), 8.

[37]Cook, *The Life of Florence Nightingale*, 2:424.

[38]Strachey, *Eminent Victorians*, vii.

[39]Lytton Strachey, quoted in Richard Rees, *For Love or Money: Studies in Personality and Essence* (London: Secker & Warburg, 1960), 25. Strachey is using the Victorian convention of the generic "he."

[40]Lytton Strachey, quoted in Hebert, *Saint, Reformer or Rebel?* 151.

[41]Natalie N. Reigler, "Lytton Strachey's Biography of Florence Nightingale: A Good Read, a Poor Reference," in Bullough, Bullough, and Stanton, *Florence Nightingale and Her Era*, 62.

[42]Raphael Sabatini, *Heroic Lives* (Boston and New York: Houghton Mifflin Company, 1934), 363.

[43]Barbara Montgomery Dossey, *Florence Nightingale: Mystic, Visionary, Healer* (Springhouse, Pa.: Springhouse Corp., 2000), 164.

[44]Sabatini, *Heroic Lives*, 380.

[45]Ibid., 414.

[46]Mrs. Cecil (Blanche) Woodham-Smith, *Florence Nightingale 1820–1910* (London: Constable, 1950).

[47]Elvi Waik Whittaker and Virginia Olesen, "Why Florence Nightingale?" in Hebert, *Saint, Reformer or Rebel?* 203.

[48]See Bullough, Bullough, and Stanton, *Florence Nightingale and Her Era;* and Hebert, *Saint, Reformer or Rebel?*

[49]F. B. Smith, *Florence Nightingale: Reputation and Power* (New York: St. Martin's Press 1982), 12.

[50]Nancy Boyd, *Three Victorian Women,* xvii.

[51]Web site: http://www.sociology.uoguelph.ca/fnightingale

[52]I. B. (Ida Beatrice) O'Malley, *Florence Nightingale, 1820–1856: A Study of Her Life Down to the End of the Crimean War* (London: Thornton Butterworth, 1931), 120.

Chapter 2: Nurturing a Call: 1820–1849

[1]Sir Edward T. Cook, *The Life of Florence Nightingale,* 2 vols. (1913–14; reprint, 2 vols. in 1, New York: Macmillan, 1942), 2:434.

[2]Mrs. Cecil (Blanche) Woodham-Smith, *Florence Nightingale* (New York: McGraw-Hill, 1951), 14.

[3]David L. Edwards, *From the 18th Century to the First World War,* vol. 3 of *Christian England* (Grand Rapids, Mich.: William B. Eerdmans, 1984), 30.

[4]Nonconformist (or Dissenter) was the term used for those who refused to conform to the doctrines, polity, or discipline of the established Church of England, especially those of Protestant sympathy.

[5]Aunt Mai—Mai Smith (1798–1889)—was WEN's sister. She married Samuel Smith, Fanny's brother, and their son William Shore Smith inherited the Nightingale property since WEN had no sons. Aunt Mai and Florence were very close. Aunt Mai accompanied Florence to the Crimea and stayed with her in London during her reform work after the Crimea. Great Aunt Elizabeth Evans was WEN's single aunt, and Grandmother Shore was WEN's mother Mary.

[6]Florence Nightingale, *Florence Nightingale Curriculum Vitae: With Information about Florence Nightingale and Kaiserswerth,* ed. Anna Sticker (Dusseldorf-Kaiserswerth: Diakoniewerk, 1965), 4. In Greek mythology, Circe, daughter of Helios (Sun), tempted men with an irresistible magic cup containing a potion that a turned them into swine. Ulysses, fortified against such magic, drank without harm.

[7]Florence Nightingale, in Barbara Montgomery Dossey, *Florence Nightingale: Mystic, Visionary, Healer* (Springhouse, Pa.: Springhouse Corp., 2000), 264.

[8]Margaret Lesser, *Clarkey: A Portrait in Letters of Mary Clarke Mohl (1793–1883)* (Oxford: Oxford University Press, 1984), 150.

[9]Cook, *The Life of Florence Nightingale,* 1:15.

[10]Ibid., 30.

[11]I. B. (Ida Beatrice) O'Malley, *Florence Nightingale, 1820–1856: A Study of Her Life Down to the End of the Crimean War* (London: Thornton Butterworth, 1931), 128. Later, Florence would see that her mother had also been trapped in the limitations imposed on women against which Florence rebelled.

[12]Nightingale, *Curriculum Vitae,* 3.

[13]Cook, *The Life of Florence Nightingale,* 1:11.

[14]J. A. Froude, *The Nemesis of Faith* (London: Chapman, 1849), 7.

[15]Ibid., 4–5.

[16]Cook, *The Life of Florence Nightingale,* 1:14–15.

[17]Nightingale, *Curriculum Vitae,* 4.

[18]Woodham-Smith, *Florence Nightingale,* 14.

[19]Giuseppe Mazzini (1805–1872) was an Italian nationalist agitator who supported Italian independence from Austria. A few years before Florence's visit to Italy, Mazzini formed his own nationalist organization, Young Italy, and plotted against the Piedmontese monarchy. He went first to Switzerland then England in 1836, where he continued to work for Italian reunification and write on Italian nationalism.

[20]Dossey, *Florence Nightingale: Mystic, Visionary, Healer,* 39. Sismondi married a niece of Fanny's friend, and Florence was enthralled by both his knowledge and compassion.

[21]Ibid., 38.

[22]Mary Clark (1793–1883) was a year older than WEN, and had left England for Paris as a young girl. Through her grandmother, she had contacts with the intellectual life in England and became a great success in Paris through her individuality, intelligence, and gift for languages. Her literary salon attracted the best of Paris intellectual life. Mary later married oriental scholar Julius Mohl, who also became a lifelong friend of Florence's.

[23]Lord Palmerston (1784–1865) was Secretary of War from 1809–1828, and twice Prime Minister (1855–58 and 1959–65). He first became Prime Minister after the government resigned over the mismanagement of the Crimean War. Lord Ashley (Shaftesbury) (1801–1885) entered Parliament in 1826 and is best known for his social reform—in factories, mental asylums, child labor, Ragged Schools, and the YMCA.

[24]Cook, *The Life of Florence Nightingale*, 53–54.

[25]John Calvin, *Institutes of the Christian Religion*, ed. John T. McNeill (Philadelphia: The Westminster Press, 1960), 1.2.1; 1.16.1, 4.

[26]Woodham-Smith, *Florence Nightingale*, 36.

[27]Nightingale, *Curriculum Vitae*, 3–4. This should not be read as an early call to *nursing*, as Florence at other times talked of not knowing to what she was called. Nursing was one aspect of her wider call to serve the poor.

[28]Dossey, *Mystic, Visionary, Healer*, 55–56.

[29]Fanny's sister Anne married George Nicholson. Hannah was George's unmarried sister, who lived with George and his family.

[30]Cook, *The Life of Florence Nightingale*, 1:1, 52

[31]Ibid., 52.

[32]Dossey, *Mystic, Visionary, Healer*, 52.

[33]Natalie Riegler, "Lytton Strachey's biography of Florence Nightingale: A Good Read, a Poor Reference," in Raymond G. Hebert, ed., *Florence Nightingale: Saint, Reformer or Rebel?* (Malabar, Fla.: Robert E. Kreiger, 1981), 68. Florence's conversation with Dr. Howe was described both by Mrs. Howe in her *Reminiscences* and in the life of Dr. Howe by his daughter, Mrs. Laura E. Richards.

[34]Woodham-Smith, *Florence Nightingale*, 40.

[35]Charles Dickens' *Martin Chuzzlewhit* (1843) stereotyped the status of nursing with his characters Sarah Gamp and Betsey Prig.

[36]Hilary Bonham Carter (1821–1865) was the daughter of Fanny's sister Joanna and John Bonham Carter, and Florence's favorite cousin. An accomplished artist, she was trapped in the extended family as the single woman and "available" help. Florence and "Clarkey" encouraged Hilary to pursue her art in Paris, but she was recalled to the family. She helped Florence with her reform after the Crimea, but died young.

[37]Cook, *The Life of Florence Nightingale*, vol. 1, 44–45.

[38]O'Malley, *A Study of Her Life Down to the End of the Crimean War*, 120.

[39]Dossey, *Mystic, Visionary, Healer*, 52.

[40]Woodham-Smith, *Florence Nightingale*, 48.

[41]Ibid., 51.

[42]Cook, *The Life of Florence Nightingale*, vol. 1, 66. Sappho, a lyric poet and native of Mytilene was said to be in love with Phaon, a Mytilene boatman who, after carrying Aphrodite across the sea, was changed from an ugly man to a beautiful youth. When Sappho's love was not returned, she leapt down from the Leucadian rock—the leap to which Florence is referring.

[43]Woodham-Smith, *Florence Nightingale*, 51.

[44]Charles (Mr. B.) and Selena (Sigma) Bracebridge were childless and in delicate health. They took Florence with them on many overseas trips and also accompanied her to the Crimea. Charles Bracebridge was a businessman with a passion for Greece, and Selena became Florence's close friend and mentor.

[45]O'Malley, *A Study of Her Life Down to the End of the Crimean War*, 125.

[46]Woodham-Smith, *Florence Nightingale*, 54.

[47]Mary Keele, ed., *Florence Nightingale in Rome: Letters Written by Florence Nightingale in Rome in the Winter of 1847–1848* (Philadelphia: American Philosophical Society, 1981), 146.

[48]Henry Edward Manning (1808–1892) was ordained a Church of England priest but, through the Oxford Movement and John Henry Newman, became Roman Catholic and was made Archbishop of Westminster in 1865.

[49]Ibid., 87.

[50]Ibid., 28.

[51]Ibid., 88.

[52]Ibid., 101.

[53]Ibid., 220.

[54]Ibid., 155.

[55]Ibid., 61.

[56]Ibid., 198.

[57]Dossey, *Mystic, Visionary, Healer,* 60.

[58]Nightingale, *Florence Nightingale in Egypt and Greece: Her Diary and 'Visions,'* ed. Michael D. Calabria (New York: State University of New York, 1996), 44.

[59]Ibid.

[60]Keele, *Florence Nightingale in Rome,* 244.

[61]Woodham-Smith, *Florence Nightingale,* 58.

[62]Ibid., 59.

[63]Cook, *The Life of Florence Nightingale,* 1:100

[64]Dossey, *Mystic, Visionary, Healer,* 62.

[65]Cook, *The Life of Florence Nightingale,* 1:101.

[66]Donald R. Allen, "Florence Nightingale: Toward a Psychohistorical Interpretation," in Hebert, *Saint, Reformer or Rebel?* 70.

[67]Woodham-Smith, *Florence Nightingale,* 67.

[68]Dossey, *Mystic, Visionary, Healer,* 119.

Chapter 3: Finding God in Egypt: 1849–1850

[1]Florence Nightingale, *Florence Nightingale: Letters from Egypt: A Journey on the Nile,* ed. Anthony Sattin (New York: Weidenfeld & Nicholson, 1987), 77.

[2]Florence Nightingale, *Florence Nightingale in Egypt and Greece: Her Diary and "Visions,"* ed. Michael D. Calabria (New York: State University of New York, 1996), 5. I am indebted to Michael Calabria's edition of Florence's diaries. Her diary is located in the British Museum.

[3]Nightingale, *Letters from Egypt,* 145.

[4]Ibid., 161.

[5]Ibid., 48.

[6]Nightingale, *Diary and "Visions,"* 18.

[7]Nightingale, *Letters from Egypt,* 24.

[8]Ibid., 22.

[9]Ibid., 87–89.

[10]Ibid., 81.

[11]Ibid., 152. Thebes was ancient Egypt's magnificent capital city on the Nile, the home of the Pharaohs' monumental temples, including Luxor and Karnack.

[12]Ibid., 73–74.

[13]"PreAdamite," in The Rev. John M'Clintock and James Strong, *Cyclopaedia of Biblical, Theological and Ecclesiastical Literature,* vol. 8 (New York: Harper & Brothers, 1894), 484–92.

[14]Ibid., 485–86.

[15]Ibid., 486.

[16]In the 1990s, the High Court of Australia officially rejected *terra nullius* and declared the aboriginal people the owners of the land at the time of the arrival of the First Fleet in Australia. This action opened the door for aboriginal claims to land that had been taken from them.

[17]Nightingale, *Letters from Egypt,* 207.

[18]Ibid., 188.

[19]Florence Nightingale, "Who is the savage?" in Social Notes concerning social reforms, social requirements, social progress, May 11, 1878, vol 1: 10, 145–47, in Vol 1., March–August 1878, ed. S.C. Hall, barrister-at-law (London: Simpkin Marshall & Co., Stationer's Hall Court), 146. Copy in Florence Nightingale British Library collection.

[20]Ibid., 74.

[21]"Vision of Temples" is reproduced in Nightingale, *Diary and "Visions,"* 124–33.

[22]Ibid., 124.

[23]Ibid., 125.

[24]Nightingale, *Letters from Egypt,* 146–47.

[25]Ibid., 147.

[26]Nightingale, *Diary and "Visions,"* 126.

[27]Ibid., 126.

[28]Nightingale, *Letters from Egypt,* 144–45.

[29]Ibid., 142.

[30]In Florence's day, there was debate as to the dating of Sethos I, whether he was the Pharaoh under whom Joseph was Premier. Lepsius thought so, but Bunsen thought he was earlier. Florence, however, warmed to the idea that Joseph had walked those wonderful halls.

[31]John L. Stoddard, *John L. Stoddard's Lectures: Constantinople, Jerusalem and Egypt,* vol. 2 (Chicago and Boston: Geo. L. Shuman & Co, 1897; 1911), 305.

[32]Nightingale, *Letters from Egypt,* 145.

[33]Ibid., 161.

[34]Nightingale, *Diary and "Visions,"* 129.

[35]Nightingale, *Letters from Egypt,* 153.

[36]Theodicy (theodike) is the term used for the theological concern to defend the goodness and omnipotence of God against the challenges of the existence of evil in a world of God's creation and providence. This will be discussed more fully later in the book.

[37]When Florence found this same idea at Ipsambul's temple of Athor, she asked the family to tell Aunt Mai she had seen the idea in the Egyptian temples: "Tell Aunt M I thought of her when I looked at him and of all she had taught me, and rejoiced to think how the same light dawns upon the wise from the two ends of space and of time." (Nightingale, *Letters from Egypt,* 96).

[38]Ibid., 154.

[39]Ibid.

[40]Ibid., 96.

[41]Nightingale, *Diary and "Visions,"* 130.

[42]Ibid., 130.

[43]Ibid., 131.

[44]Nightingale, *Letters from Egypt,* 140.

[45]Nightingale, *Diary and "Visions,"* 40.

[46]See Jack Miles, *God: A Biography* (New York: Alfred A. Knopf, 1995); Karen Armstrong, *The History of God* (New York: Ballantine Books, 1993); Marcus Borg, *The God We Never Knew* (New York: HarperSanFrancisco, 1997).

[47]Nightingale, *Letters from Egypt,* 34.

[48]Ibid., 168.

[49]Ibid., 74.

[50]Nightingale, *Diary and "Visions,"* 30.

[51]Nightingale, *Letters from Egypt,* 54.

[52]Ibid., 99.

[53]Ibid., 104.

[54]Ibid.

[55]Ibid., 109.

[56]Ibid., 208. Circassian was the term for the people inhabiting mountain valleys in the northern regions of the Caucasus mountains. Their religion was a mix of Islam, Christianity, and indigenous traditions.

[57]Ibid., 117.

[58]Ibid., 139.

[59]Ibid., 28.

[60]Ibid., 39.

[61]Ibid., 207.

[62]Ibid., 205. Ragged Schools were established in Victorian times by private charities to provide basic and religious education for poor "ragged" children. The diverse institutions were brought together under Lord Shaftesbury (son of Lord Palmerston, Florence's neighbor) in 1844. By the 1850s some 300,000 children were educated this way. The schools disbanded when the Education Act of 1870 introduced compulsory government education for all children.

[63]Ibid., 105.

[64]Nightingale, *Diary and "Visions,"* 25.

[65]Ibid.

[66]Ibid.

[67]Ibid., 31; and Nightingale, *Letters from Egypt,* 114.

[68]Nightingale, *Letters from Egypt,* 119.

[69]Nightingale, *Diary and "Visions,"* 30.

[70]Ibid., 31–32. In Rome in 1848, Florence had made a retreat with her spiritual director Madre Santa Columba, who gave her the spiritual disciplines she was following in her silent moments in Egypt.

[71]Ibid., 33.

[72]Ibid.

[73]Nightingale, *Letters from Egypt*, 134.

[74]Nightingale, *Diary and "Visions,"* 39.

[75]Ibid., 42.

[76]Ibid., 43.

[77]Ibid., 45.

[78]Ibid.

[79]Ibid., 46.

[80]Ibid.

[81]Ibid.

[82]Nightingale, *Letters from Egypt*, 169–70.

[83]Nightingale, *Diary and "Visions,"* 47.

[84]Nightingale, *Letters from Egypt*, 172.

[85]Nightingale, *Diary and "Visions,"* 47.

[86]Nightingale, *Letters from Egypt*, 184.

[87]Ibid.

[88]Nightingale, *Diary and "Visions,"* 38.

[89]Nightingale, *Letters from Egypt*, 187.

[90]Ibid., 200.

[91]Nightingale, *Diary and "Visions,"* 50–51.

[92]Barbara Montgomery Dossey, *Florence Nightingale: Mystic, Visionary, Healer* (Springhouse, Pa.: Springhouse Corp., 2000), 66.

Chapter 4: From Dreaming to Action: 1850–1851

[1]Monica Baly, ed., *As Miss Nightingale Said; Florence Nightingale through her Sayings: A Victorian Perspective* (London: Scutari Press, 1991), 19.

[2]Florence Nightingale, *Florence Nightingale in Egypt and Greece: Her Diary and "Visions,"* ed. Michael D. Calabria (New York: State University of New York, 1996), 56.

[3]Ibid., 59.

[4]Catherine of Genoa, the daughter of a religious nobleman, felt called to religious life as a child but, on her father's death, was married at sixteen to Julian Adorno. They were childless and he was unsuccessful, cruel, and unfaithful. After Catherine converted him, they lived together in celibacy till his death in 1497, working with the sick and poor. Catherine became a Franciscan tertiary, and a Directress in 1490. She died in 1510 and was canonized in 1737. Her writings form part of the literature of medieval mystics.

[5]Nightingale, *Diary and "Visions,"* 61–62.

[6]Ibid., 63.

[7]Ibid., 61.

[8]Ibid., 64.

[9]Ibid.

[10]Ibid.

[11]William Cowper (1731–1800) was called to the Bar in 1754, but suicidal mania sent him to a psychiatric institution in 1763. Later, he became a lay assistant to Calvinist preacher and former slave runner John Newton, and began writing hymns. His psychiatric problems continued to assail him through his life.

[12]Val Webb, *In Defense of Doubt: An Invitation to Adventure* (St. Louis: Chalice Press, 1995), 51.

[13]Nightingale, *Diary and "Visions,"* 66.

[14]Ibid., 67.

[15]Ibid., 67– 68.

[16]Charlotte Brontë, *Shirley* (Hertfordshire: Wordsworth Editions Limited, 1993), 70.

[17]Ibid., 132–33.

[18]Ibid., 133.

[19]Florence Nightingale, *Suggestions for Thought: Selections and Commentaries,* ed. Michael D. Calabria and Janet A. Macrae (Philadelphia: University of Pennsylvania Press, 1994), 107.

[20]Nightingale, *Diary and "Visions,"* 70.

[21]Sir Edward T. Cook, *The Life of Florence Nightingale,* 2 vols. (1913–14; reprint, 2 vols. in 1, New York: Macmillan, 1942), 1:92.

[22]Nightingale, *Diary and "Visions,"* 70.

[23]Ibid., 70.

[24]Ibid.

[25]Ibid., 78.

[26]Ibid., 79.

[27]Mrs. Cecil (Blanche) Woodham-Smith, *Florence Nightingale* (New York: McGraw-Hill, 1951), 64.

[28]Raymond G. Hebert, ed., *Florence Nightingale: Saint, Reformer or Rebel?* (Malabar, Fla.: Robert E. Kreiger, 1981), 5. The Kedron (Kidron) is a river and valley east of Jerusalem, mentioned in the Hebrew Bible (2 Samuel 15:23) and the New Testament (John 18:1).

[29]Nightingale, *Diary and "Visions,"* 81.

[30]Ibid., 145.

[31]Cook, *The Life of Florence Nightingale,* 1:59.

[32]Florence Nightingale, *Ever Yours, Florence Nightingale—Selected Letters,* ed. Martha Vicinus and Bea Nergaard (Cambridge, Mass.: Harvard University Press, 1989), 44–45. The Roman Emperor Domitian (51–96 C.E.) was famous for his persecution of the Christians.

[33]Ibid., 45.

[34]Ibid., 46–48.

[35]Woodham-Smith, *Florence Nightingale,* 67.

[36]Ibid., 68.

[37]Nightingale, *Ever Yours,* 48.

[38]Ibid., 50.

[39]See this discussion on treating doubts about inadequate doctrines as nudges of God in Webb, *In Defense of Doubt.*

[40]Florence Nightingale, *Florence Nightingale Curriculum Vitae: With Information about Florence Nightingale and Kaiserswerth,* ed. Anna Sticker (Dusseldorf-Kaiserswerth: Diakoniewerk, 1965), 7.

[41]William J. Bishop, "Florence Nightingale's Message for Today," in Hebert, *Saint, Reformer or Rebel?* 193.

[42]W. J. Wintle and Florence Witts, *Florence Nightingale and Frances Willard: The Story of Their Lives* (London: Sunday School Union, n.d. [around 1897]), 31.

[43]Nightingale, *Curriculum Vitae,* 16.

[44]Cook, *The Life of Florence Nightingale,* 1:112.

[45]Ibid., 114.

[46]Nancy Boyd, *Three Victorian Women Who Changed Their World: Josephine Butler, Octavia Hill, Florence Nightingale* (New York: Oxford University Press, 1982), 180.

[47]Barbara Montgomery Dossey, *Florence Nightingale: Mystic, Visionary, Healer* (Springhouse, Pa.: Springhouse Corp., 2000), 78.

[48]Nightingale, *Ever Yours,* 311–12.

[49]Dossey, *Mystic, Visionary, Healer,* 19–20.

[50]Lytton Strachey, *Eminent Victorians*(New York: The Modern Library, 1918), 20.

[51]The *Thirty-Nine Articles* summarized the essential doctrinal beliefs of the Church of England, receiving their final form in 1571. Prior to 1865, Anglican clergy had to affirm all sections in detail. After this date, only a general assent was required for ordination. The Council of Trent reaffirmed orthodox Catholic belief and practice after challenges from Luther and other Protestant reformers.

[52]David L. Edwards, *From the 18th Century to the First World War,* vol. 3 of *Christian England* (Grand Rapids, Mich.: William B. Eerdmans Publishing Company, 1984), 194.

[53]Benjamin Jowett (1817–93) was educated at Balliol College, Oxford, remaining on its faculty for life. He became Master of Balliol in 1870. Liberal in theology, he was an important member of the Anglican Broad Church Movement, writing a controversial essay on "The Interpretation of Scripture" for their explosive book *Essays and Reviews* published in 1860. After this experience, he stopped writing on theology, concentrated on his major contribution, his translations of Plato. Jowett became acquainted with Florence in 1860 when Clough sent him a draft of Florence's *Suggestions for Thought* for comment. Their deep friendship and correspondence continued unabated until Jowett's death.

[54]Nightingale, *Suggestions for Thought,* 5.

[55]William Ewart Gladstone (1809–98) was four times Prime Minister of Great Britain. When the old Tory and Whig parties declined in the mid-1800s, he joined the new Liberals and became their leader in 1866. Devoutly religious, and responsible for disestablishing the Church of England in Ireland in 1869, freeing Irish Catholics from its allegiance, he did express concern in *Vaticanism*.

[56]Woodham-Smith, *Florence Nightingale*, 74.

[57]Nightingale, *Ever Yours*, 58–59.

[58]Nightingale, *Diary and "Visions,"* 148.

[59]Florence Nightingale, *Cassandra and Other Selections from Suggestions for Thought*, ed. Mary Poovey (New York: New York University Press, 1993), xvii.

[60]Margaret Lesser, *Clarkey: A Portrait in Letters of Mary Clarke Mohl (1793–1883)* (Oxford: Oxford University Press, 1984), 141.

[61]Cook, *The Life of Florence Nightingale*, 1:117.

[62]Ibid.

[63]Sir James Clark was a physician to both the Nightingale family and Queen Victoria. His home in Scotland was near Balmoral Castle and through him, Florence was invited to meet the Queen after the Crimea.

[64]Lesser, *Clarkey*, 132.

[65]Ibid., 131.

[66]Dossey, *Mystic, Visionary, Healer*, 84.

[67]Nightingale, *Ever Yours*, 56–57.

[68]Ibid., 61.

[69]Ibid., 64.

[70]Woodham-Smith, *Florence Nightingale*, 84.

[71]Dossey, *Mystic, Visionary, Healer*, 84.

Chapter 5: A Scream of Pain—*"Cassandra"*: 1852

[1]Florence Nightingale, *Suggestions for Thought: Selections and Commentaries*, ed. Michael D. Calabria and Janet A. Macrae (Philadelphia: University of Pennsylvania Press, 1994), 108.

[2]In Homer's *Iliad*, Paris of Troy, Cassandra's brother, eloped with or abducted the beautiful Helen of Sparta, wife of King Menelaus, starting the war between Greece and Troy. Helen helped the Greeks in the battle, betraying Troy. Troy fell when a hollow wooden horse filled with Greek soldiers was brought into the city and the soldiers opened the gates at night to the Greek army.

[3]I will use the edition edited by Myra Stark, *Florence Nightingale's Cassandra* (New York: Feminist Press, 1979). "Cassandra" was also published separately in 1928 as an appendix to Ray Strachey's *The Cause: A Short History of the Women's Movement in Great Britain* (London: G. Bell and Sons, 1928).

[4]Vincent Quinn, and John Prest, *Dear Miss Nightingale* (Oxford: Oxford University Press, 1987), 4.

[5]Christology is the study of the person and work of Christ, traditionally the union of the divine and human natures in the one person and the saving work of Christ.

[6]Mrs. Cecil (Blanche) Woodham-Smith, *Florence Nightingale* (New York: McGraw-Hill, 1951), 71.

[7]Sir Edward T. Cook, *The Life of Florence Nightingale*, 2 vols. (1913–14; reprint, 2 vols. in 1, New York: Macmillan, 1942), 1:270.

[8]Stark, *Cassandra*, 4–5.

[9]Woodham-Smith, *Florence Nightingale*, 72.

[10]Stark, *Cassandra*, 25.

[11]Ibid., 27.

[12]Ibid., 27–28.

[13]Nightingale, *Suggestions for Thought*, 111–13.

[14]Stark, *Cassandra*, 30–31.

[15]Ibid., 29.

[16]Ibid., 32.

[17]Ibid., 34.

[18]Ibid., 35.

[19]Nightingale, *Suggestions for Thought*, 110. John Stuart Mill used this example from Florence's writing in his 1869 book *The Subjection of Women*.

[20]Virginia Woolf, *A Room of One's Own* (New York: Harcourt & World, 1929), 69–70.

[21]Stark, *Cassandra*, 37.

[22]Florence Nightingale, *Cassandra and Other Selections from Suggestions for Thought*, ed. Mary Poovey (New York: New York University Press 1993), 131.

[23]Stark, *Cassandra*, 38.

[24]Ibid.

[25]Ibid., 39.

[26]Ibid., 40.

[27]Nightingale, *Cassandra and other Selections*, 188.

[28]Margaret Lesser, *Clarkey: A Portrait in Letters of Mary Clarke Mohl (1793–1883)* (Oxford: Oxford University Press, 1984), 164.

[29]Stark, *Cassandra*, 49.

[30]Ibid., 49–50.

[31]Ibid., 50–51. The Castel Saint'Angelo, a squat round building dominated by a huge statue of an angel, began as an imperial Mausoleum. In 590 c.e., when Pope Gregory the Great led a procession against a devastating plague in the city, an angel appeared on top of the mausoleum sheathing his sword, a sign the plague would cease, hence the statue.

[32]Ibid., 52.

[33]Ibid., 53.

[34]Ibid., 50.

[35]Ibid., 54.

[36]Cook, *The Life of Florence Nightingale*, 1:485.

[37]Stark, *Cassandra*, 55.

[38]Nightingale, *Suggestions for Thought*, 100.

[39]Ibid., 101.

[40]Ibid., 102.

[41]Ibid., 103.

[42]Ibid., 104.

[43]Ibid., 104–5.

[44]Nancy Boyd, *Three Victorian Women Who Changed Their World: Josephine Butler, Octavia Hill, Florence Nightingale* (New York: Oxford University Press, 1982), 221.

[45]Nightingale, *Suggestions for Thought*, 104–5.

[46]Rafael Sabatini, *Heroic Lives* (Boston and New York: Houghton Mifflin Company 1934), 406.

[47]Ibid., 412. Lord Stanley, Earl of Derby, was Secretary of State for India (1858–59), Foreign Secretary (1874–78; 1867–68), Colonial Secretary under Gladstone (1882–85), and a great supporter of Florence and her work. He became Chair of the Indian Sanitary Commission after Sir Sidney.

[48]Nightingale, *Suggestions for Thought*, xix.

[49]Sue M. Goldie, ed., *I Have Done My Duty: Florence Nightingale in the Crimean War, 1854–56* (Iowa: University of Iowa Press, 1987), 289. Lady Charlotte Canning (1817–1861) was a member of the Board of the Harley Street institution where Florence worked. She helped Liz Herbert with the selection of nurses to go with Florence to the Crimea and continued corresponding with Florence, even from India where her husband was the first Viceroy (1856–62).

[50]W. J. Wintle and Florence Witts, *Florence Nightingale and Frances Willard: The Story of Their Lives* (London: Sunday School Union, n.d. [around 1897]), 58.

[51]Ibid., 140.

[52]Goldie, *I Have Done My Duty*, 281–82.

[53]Monica Baly, ed., *As Miss Nightingale Said; Florence Nightingale through Her Sayings: A Victorian Perspective* (London: Scutari Press, 1991), 60.

[54]Not until 1888 could some English women vote and be elected to office in county and municipal races, and 1894 in local government races. Women over thirty gained the full vote in 1918 and women over twenty-one in 1928.

[55]For this discussion, see my book *Why We're Equal: Introducing Feminist Theology* (St. Louis: Chalice Press, 1999), chapter 5.

[56]Sir Theodore Martin, quoted in Lytton Strachey, *Queen Victoria* (New York: Harcourt, Brace and World, 1921), 409–10.

[57]W. J. Bishop, comp. (completed by Sue Goldie), *A Bio-bibliography of Florence Nightingale* (London, Dawsons of Pall Mall for the International Council of Nurses, 1962), 47.

[58]Vincent Quinn and John Prest, *Dear Miss Nightingale* (Oxford: Oxford University Press, 1987), 322.

[59]Wintle and Witts, *Florence Nightingale and Frances Willard*, 153.

[60]Ibid., 142.

[61]Ibid., 143.

[62]Josephine Butler (1828–1906), social reformer and women's advocate, came from a politically powerful family and married George Butler, academic and clergyman. In Liverpool, she befriended prostitutes, horrifying her neighbors, and led the fight against the Contagious Diseases Act aimed at controlling venereal disease in the Army by arresting prostitutes and subjecting them to degrading medical examinations. Her lobbying led to the Act's repeal in 1886. She also attacked child prostitution, achieving higher penalties for child abuse and the raising of the age of consent from twelve to sixteen.

[63]Nightingale, *Cassandra and Other Selections*, 156.

[64]Ibid., 158.

[65]Ibid., 163.

[66]Ibid., 159.

[67]Ibid., 166.

[68]Ibid., 170.

[69]Ibid., 159.

[70]Nancy Victorin-Vangerud, *The Raging Hearth: Spirit in the Household of God* (St. Louis: Chalice Press, 2000), 211–12.

Chapter 6: Harley Street and the Crimea: 1853–1856

[1]Florence Nightingale, *Ever Yours, Florence Nightingale—Selected Letters*, ed. Martha Vicinus and Bea Nergaard (Cambridge, Mass.: Harvard University Press, 1989), 136.

[2]Margaret Lesser, *Clarkey: A Portrait in Letters of Mary Clarke Mohl (1793–1883)* (Oxford: Oxford University Press, 1984), 139.

[3]Quoted in Sir Edward T. Cook, *The Life of Florence Nightingale*, 2 vols. (1913–14; reprint, 2 vols. in 1, New York: Macmillan, 1942), 1:139.

[4]Barbara Montgomery Dossey, *Florence Nightingale: Mystic, Visionary, Healer* (Springhouse, Pa.: Springhouse Corp., 2000), 90.

[5]Ibid., 94.

[6]Ibid., 98.

[7]Elizabeth Gaskell (1810–1865), leading Victorian novelist and social commentator, married Unitarian minister William Gaskell in 1832 and worked with him in the industrial north amongst the social inequities resulting from the Industrial Revolution. These problems informed the novels for which she is famous. She also wrote a biography of her friend Charlotte Bronte (1857) and contributed regularly to the periodical *Household Words*.

[8]Ibid., 99. Elizabeth of Hungary (1207–1231), daughter of the King of Hungary, was married at fourteen to Ludwig IV, Landgrave of Thuringia. When he died six years later, she was driven from court because her charitable works were bankrupting State finances. In Marburg, she gave up her children and lived a life of austerity and charity.

[9]Ibid., 96.

[10]W. J. Wintle and Florence Witts, *Florence Nightingale and Frances Willard: The Story of Their Lives* (London: Sunday School Union, n.d. [around 1897]), 48.

[11]Cook, *The Life of Florence Nightingale*, 1:184.

[12]Dossey, *Mystic, Visionary, Healer*, 114.

[13]Zachary Cope, *Florence Nightingale and the Doctors* (Philadelphia: J. B. Lippincott, 1958), 18.

[14]Nightingale, *Ever Yours*, 138.

[15]Sue Goldie, ed., *I Have Done My Duty: Florence Nightingale in the Crimean War, 1854–56* (Iowa: University of Iowa Press, 1987), 206. Dr. John Hall (1795–1866) had forty-two years in the Army's Medical Services when reassigned from Bombay at sixty-three to become Inspector-General of Hospitals for the Crimean campaign. From the moment of Florence's arrival in the Crimea, the two clashed, given their senior roles and the ambiguity of Florence's authority. They remained antagonists throughout the war and beyond.

[16]Ibid., 179.

[17]Lesser, *Clarkey*, 187. The Franco-Prussian War (1870–71), fueled by Prussia's increasing power in Europe, began with Prussia's attempt to put a Prussian on Spain's throne. France

declared war on Prussia and was crushed in six weeks. After Napoleon III's surrender and the collapse of France's Second Empire, revolution broke out in Paris. The Peace of Frankfurt gave Alsace and part of Lorraine to Prussia with France paying heavy indemnity.

[18]Mary C. Sullivan, ed., *The Friendship of Florence Nightingale and Mary Clare Moore,* (Philadelphia: University of Pennsylvania Press, 1999), 58.

[19]Hugh Small, *Florence Nightingale: Avenging Angel* (New York: St. Martin's Press, 1998), 26.

[20]This is part of a long poem, "The Nightingale in the East," written in 1853 and published by Lyle & Co. Printers, 2 & 3 Monmouth Ct., Seven Deals, London (British Library, Cup. 400. K. 20 (4).

[21]Lesser, *Clarkey,* 144.

[22]Dossey, *Mystic, Visionary, Healer,* 129.

[23]Florence Nightingale, *Florence Nightingale Curriculum Vitae: With Information about Florence Nightingale and Kaiserswerth,* ed. Anna Sticker (Dusseldorf-Kaiserswerth: Diakoniewerk, 1965), 15–16.

[24]Mrs. Cecil (Blanche) Woodham-Smith, *Florence Nightingale* (New York: McGraw-Hill, 1951), 105.

[25]Dossey, *Mystic, Visionary, Healer,* 167.

[26]Ibid.

[27]Cook, *The Life of Florence Nightingale,* 1:255–56.

[28]Monica Baly, ed., *As Miss Nightingale Said; Florence Nightingale through Her Sayings: A Victorian Perspective* (London: Scutari Press, 1991), 23.

[29]Jacobus Arminius (1560–1609), Dutch Reformed theology professor at Leyden, rejected the deterministic arguments of Calvinism on predestination and insisted that divine sovereignty was compatible with human free will and that Christ died for all, not just the elect. These views were condemned at the Synod of Dort (1618–19) and their adherents banished or persecuted. Later, they were espoused by people like Wesley as an alternative to Calvinist predestination.

[30]Dossey, *Mystic, Visionary, Healer,* 22.

[31]Vincent Quinn and John Prest, *Dear Miss Nightingale* (Oxford, Oxford University Press, 1987), 201. Of course, such transformation did not include Florence's gender. Degrees at London University were first opened to women in 1878, but not until 1920 at Oxford and 1921 at Cambridge.

[32]Wintle and Witts, *Florence Nightingale and Frances Willard,* 82.

[33]Baly, *As Miss Nightingale Said,* 27.

[34]Rev. Mother Mary Clare Moore (1814–1874), founding mother superior of the Sisters of Mercy, Bermondsey, London, became a Sister at nineteen in Ireland. She helped found the Sisters of Mercy in Cork, Ireland, then founded the Sisters of Mercy in Bermondsey, London. The Sisters' work was multifaceted, sick-visiting, education, and religious instruction. From Bermondsey, Mother Mary Clare took four sisters to the Crimea. Florence became close to Mary Clare, spiritually identifying herself with her Order. On returning to London after Crimea, Florence went straight to Bermondsey, and corresponded with Mother Mary Clare throughout Clare's lifetime.

[35]Mother Mary Frances Bridgeman of Kinsale, Ireland, was selected by Rev. Henry Manning, in discussion with the Vatican, to take a second group of Catholic nuns to the Crimea against Florence's wishes. Mary Stanley, a friend of Florence's and sister of Rev. Arthur Stanley, accompanied them as a secularly "neutral" Anglican person, although about to convert to Catholicism herself. The fifteen Irish nuns came from different convents, Mother Bridgeman having authority over them independent of Florence. Mother Bridgeman became Florence's opponent from the start, siding with Army officers who opposed Florence. Since Mother Bridgeman had extensive experience working with the sick and poor in Ireland, she offered a strong challenge.

[36]Goldie, *I Have Done My Duty,* 56.

[37]Evelyn Bolster, *The Sisters of Mercy in the Crimean War* (Cork, Ireland: The Mercer Press, 1964), 76.

[38]Ibid., 52.

[39]Ibid., 68.

[40]Ibid., 111.

[41]Ibid., 112.

[42]Ibid., 162.

[43]Cook, *The Life of Florence Nightingale,* 1:299.

[44]Nightingale, *Ever Yours,* 156.

[45]Ibid., 134.

[46]Bolster, *The Sisters of Mercy in the Crimean War,* 136–37.

[47]Nightingale, *Ever Yours,* 149.

[48]Ibid., 152. The priests mentioned by name were Roman Catholic chaplains to the Army.

[49]Ibid., 167.

[50]Ibid., 112.

[51]Bolster, *The Sisters of Mercy in the Crimean War,* 287. Sairy Gamp was a character in Charles Dickens's writings that caricatured the standard of nursing in that day.

[52]Ibid., 142.

[53]Ibid., xx.

[54]Nightingale, *Ever Yours,* 194.

[55]Cook, *The Life of Florence Nightingale,* 1:57.

[56]Baly, *As Miss Nightingale Said,* 76.

[57]Ibid.

[58]Elvi Waik Whittaker and Virginia L. Olesen, "Why Florence Nightingale?" in Raymond G. Hebert, ed., *Florence Nightingale: Saint, Reformer or Rebel?* (Malabar, Fla.: Robert E. Kreiger, 1981), 205.

[59]Baly, *As Miss Nightingale Said,* 75.

[60]Wintle and Witts, *Florence Nightingale and Frances Willard,* 141.

[61]Sir Zachary Cope, *Florence Nightingale and the Doctors* (London: Museum Press, 1958), 84.

[62]W. J. Bishop, comp. (completed by Sue Goldie), *A Bio-bibliography of Florence Nightingale* (London: Dawsons of Pall Mall for the International Council of Nurses, 1962), 38.

[63]Florence Nightingale, "Notes on Nursing," in Hebert, *Saint, Reformer or Rebel?* 148.

[64]Baly, *As Miss Nightingale Said,* 64.

[65]Nightingale, "Notes on Nursing," 148–49.

[66]Baly, *As Miss Nightingale Said,* 66.

[67]Bishop, *A Bio-bibliography,* 17.

[68]Ibid., 39–40.

[69]Ibid.

[70]Ibid., 39–40.

[71]Ibid. David Livingstone (1813–1873), famous Scottish doctor, missionary, and explorer in Africa, first described the Victoria Falls (1855) and led expeditions in search of the sources of the Nile, Zambesi, and Congo Rivers. Fearing him lost, the *New York Herald* sent journalist Henry Stanley to find him. Livingstone refused to return to England and died in Africa. His body was returned to Westminster Abbey, London.

Chapter 7: Loving God and the World: 1856–1910

[1]Sir Edward T. Cook, *The Life of Florence Nightingale,* 2 vols. (1913–14; reprint, 2 vols. in 1, New York: Macmillan, 1942), 1:309.

[2]Barbara Montgomery Dossey, *Florence Nightingale: Mystic, Visionary, Healer* (Springhouse, Pa.: Springhouse Corp., 2000), 143.

[3]Lord Panmure (1801–1874) was Secretary of State for War (1855–58) when Florence returned from the Crimea. On the Queen's instruction, Panmure requested a formal report of Florence's experiences with suggestions for army reform. He approved a Royal Commission into the Army and consulted Florence on plans for England's first general military hospital at Netley. Florence was frustrated with Panmure's rejection of her Netley alterations and also his delay on the Royal Commission.

[4]Sir John McNeill (1795–1883), a Scot, began as a surgeon in the East India Company, rising quickly in the Foreign Service. On returning to Scotland from a post in Persia, he served as Chairman of the Poor Board, averting a Scottish crisis during the potato famine. An expert on Russia and the Middle East, he was appointed, with Colonel Alexander Tulloch, to investigate Army supplies in the Crimea. Their report exposing the fiasco was white-washed for political reasons. McNeill, who met Florence in the Crimea, remained her close friend and advisor, receiving a draft of her *Suggestions for Thought* for comment.

Colonel Alexander Tulloch (1801–1864), an Army internal affairs investigator, had instituted major reforms while serving the Army in India. His experience there and his legal background were put to use in Crimea, both through the McNeill-Tulloch report they produced and also through practical improvements he introduced. Less politically experienced and more eager to lay blame than his colleague Sir John McNeill, Tulloch was devastated when their report was scuttled.

[5]Dr. John Sutherland (1809–1898), a leading sanitary expert and sanitary Inspector under the first Board of Health, led a Sanitary Commission inquiry to the Crimea in 1855. Appalled by conditions in Scutari Hospital, he set to work making improvements, which dropped mortality rates from 42.7 to 2 deaths per 1,000 patients. Florence claimed Sutherland's Report "saved the British Army." They remained close friends, Sutherland working almost daily with Florence on all aspects of her reform until his retirement in 1889. He was also her personal physician and protector from the public.

[6]Colonel John Henry Lefroy (1817–1890) was adviser on scientific matters to Secretary for War Lord Panmure. Sent to the Crimea by Panmure in October 1855 to report on the state of the hospitals, he was impressed with Florence's achievements and abilities, remaining her close friend and advisor in reform after she returned from the Crimea. Lefroy's endorsement of her to Panmure led to her General Orders as Head of all nurses in the Crimea, a position Sir John Hall had opposed.

[7]Sue Goldie ed., *I Have Done My Duty: Florence Nightingale in the Crimean War, 1854–56* (Iowa: University of Iowa Press, 1987), 204.

[8]Thomas à Kempis, *Imitation of Christ* (London: Burns & Lambert, 1851), 58. Florence Nightingale Museum, St. Thomas's Hospital, London.

[9]Florence Nightingale, *Florence Nightingale in Egypt and Greece: Her Diary and "Visions,"* ed. Michael D. Calabria (New York: State University of New York, 1996), 152.

[10]Monica Baly, ed., *As Miss Nightingale Said; Florence Nightingale through Her Sayings: A Victorian Perspective* (London: Scutari Press, 1991), 32.

[11]Dossey, *Mystic, Visionary, Healer*, 179.

[12]Goldie, *I Have Done My Duty*, 166.

[13]Ibid., 182.

[14]Ibid., 184.

[15]Ibid., 206.

[16]Ibid., 212.

[17]Ibid., 268–69. Sir Benjamin Hawes was at this time Permanent Undersecretary at the War Office.

[18]Baly, *As Miss Nightingale Said*, 32. Magic Lanthorns were the forerunners to kodachrome slide shows.

[19]Mary C. Sullivan, ed., *The Friendship of Florence Nightingale and Mary Clare Moore* (Philadelphia: University of Pennsylvania Press, 1999), 176.

[20]Ibid., 24.

[21]Dossey, *Mystic, Visionary, Healer*, 182.

[22]Florence Nightingale, *Ever Yours, Florence Nightingale—Selected Letters*, ed. Martha Vicinus and Bea Nergaard (Cambridge, Mass.: Harvard University Press, 1989), 171.

[23]Lytton Strachey, *Eminent Victorians* (New York: Modern Library, 1918), 162.

[24]Nightingale, *Ever Yours*, 160.

[25]Ibid., 161.

[26]Goldie, *I Have Done My Duty*, 285.

[27]Ibid., 286.

[28]Ibid.

[29]Nightingale, *Ever Yours*, 171.

[30]Ibid., 5.

[31]Cook, *The Life of Florence Nightingale*, 1:318.

[32]Ibid, 499.

[33]Dr. William Farr (1807–1891), a pioneer in medical statistics and a member of the Army Health Board, was assistant Commissioner for census returns in 1851 and 1861, and Commissioner in 1871. Farr helped Florence analyze her Crimean mortality figures.

[34]Strachey, *Eminent Victorians*, 171. Panmure's great interest outside of politics was the Free Church of Scotland which had been formed in 1843 when 474 out of 1203 ministers of the Established Church of Scotland broke away. The dispute centered on the laity's demand for a voice in matters of patronage.

[35]Dossey, *Mystic, Visionary, Healer*, 206.

[36]W. J. Bishop, comp. (completed by Sue Goldie), *A Bio-bibliography of Florence Nightingale* (London: Dawsons of Pall Mall for the International Council of Nurses, 1962), 53.

[37]Ibid. Florence had been consulted by the founders of Johns Hopkins prior to its establishment.

[38]Cook, *The Life of Florence Nightingale,* 1:372.

[39]Nightingale, *Ever Yours,* 189–90.

[40]Ibid., 172.

[41]Dossey, *Mystic, Visionary, Healer,* 212.

[42]Nightingale, *Ever Yours,* 190.

[43]Arthur Clough (1819–1861) moved beyond the traditional religious teachings at Oxford, becoming a voice for the theological skepticism of the time through his poetry. He visited America and taught with Ralph Waldo Emerson, married Aunt Mai's daughter Blanche, and became attracted to Florence's reform work and theological ideas. He became her secretary and also secretary for the Nightingale Fund. In 1860, he encouraged Florence to publish the draft of *Suggestions for Thought.* Florence was devastated when he died the following year of tuberculosis, aged forty-two. It was Clough who introduced Florence to Jowett.

[44]Sir Harry Verney (1801–1894) was a Member of Parliament for Buckinghamshire almost continuously for more than fifty years. A widower with children, he married Florence's sister Parthe in 1858, and they resided at Claydon. He was interested in Florence's reform work and became chair of the Nightingale Fund until 1890. Claydon became Florence's second home, and Sir Harry made daily visits to Florence during their work together on the Fund after 1870.

[45]Adolphe Quetelet (1796–1874), Belgian astronomer, meteorologist, and statistician, made a great impression on Florence with his statistical calculations, especially when applied to social dynamics. They met during the International Statistical Congress held in London in 1860.

[46]Sir Zachary Cope, *Florence Nightingale and the Doctors* (London: Museum Press, 1958), 107.

[47]Edwin Chadwick (1800–1889), a disciple of Jeremy Bentham and Poor Law Commission secretary, crusaded for improved sanitation, seeing links between poverty, illness, and slums. His 1842 report to Parliament on sanitary conditions in the working class was monumental, even though he greatly upset the establishment. Florence agreed with him and corresponded with him, both suspicious of the emerging germ theory.

[48]Florence Nightingale, *A Note on Pauperism,* British Library, Cup.401 h 4 (8) March 1869, 281–90.

[49]Baly, *As Miss Nightingale Said,* 40.

[50]Florence Nightingale, "A Subnote of Interrogation — what will our religion be in 1999?" *Fraser's* Magazine, July 1873, 29. British Library.

[51]Ibid., 39.

[52]F. B. Smith, *Florence Nightingale: Reputation and Power* (New York: St. Martin's Press, 1982), 90.

[53]Ibid.

[54]Margaret Lesser, *Clarkey: A Portrait in Letters of Mary Clarke Mohl (1793–1883)* (Oxford: Oxford University Press, 1984), 160–61.

[55]Florence Nightingale, *Florence Nightingale Curriculum Vitae: With Information about Florence Nightingale and Kaiserswerth,* ed. Anna Sticker (Dusseldorf-Kaiserswerth: Diakoniewerk, 1965), 3.

[56]Cook, *The Life of Florence Nightingale,* 1:43.

[57]Evert A. Duyckinck, *Portrait Gallery of Eminent Men and Women of Europe and America,* vol. 2 (New York: Johnson, Wilson, 1873), 534.

[58]W. J. Wintle and Florence Witts, *Florence Nightingale and Frances E. Willard: The Story of Their Lives* (London: Sunday School Union, n.d., around 1897), 138.

[59]Ibid.

[60]Dossey, *Mystic, Visionary, Healer,* 427.

[61]Ibid., 426.

[62]Sidney Godolphin Osborne, "An Eye-Witness Account," in Raymond G. Hebert, ed., *Florence Nightingale: Saint, Reformer or Rebel?* (Malabar, Fla.: Robert E. Kreiger, 1981), 100–101.

[63]Hugh Small, *Florence Nightingale: Avenging Angel* (New York: St. Martin's Press, 1998), 2.

[64]Dossey, *Mystic, Visionary, Healer,* 209.

[65]Nightingale, *Ever Yours,* 177.

[66]Ibid., 178.

[67]Dossey, *Mystic, Visionary, Healer*, 208.

[68]Nightingale, *Ever Yours*, 179.

[69]Ibid.

[70]Bram Dijkstra, *Idols of Perversity: Fantasies of Feminine Evil in Fin-de-Siècle Culture* (New York: Oxford University Press, 1986), 25.

[71]Ibid., 26.

[72]Cook, *The Life of Florence Nightingale*, 2:431.

[73]Rafael Sabatini, *Heroic Lives* (Boston & New York: Houghton Mifflin, 1934), 373.

[74]Dossey, *Mystic, Visionary, Healer*, 260.

[75]Sullivan, *The Friendship of Florence Nightingale and Mary Clare Moore*, 182.

[76]Lesser, *Clarkey*, 150–51.

[77]Ibid., 177–78.

Chapter 8: Liberation Theologian and Mystic

[1]Florence Nightingale, *Suggestions for Thought: Selections and Commentaries,* ed. Michael D. Calabria and Janet A. Macrae (Philadelphia: University of Pennsylvania Press, 1994), 116.

[2]Florence Nightingale in Mary C. Sullivan, ed., *The Friendship of Florence Nightingale and Mary Clare Moore,* (Philadelphia: University of Pennsylvania Press, 1999), 20.

[3]Barbara Montgomery Dossey, *Florence Nightingale: Mystic, Visionary, Healer* (Springhouse, Pa. : Springhouse Corp., 2000), 343–44.

[4]Nightingale, *Suggestions for Thought*, 120.

[5]Nancy Boyd, *Three Victorian Women Who Changed Their World: Josephine Butler, Octavia Hill, Florence Nightingale* (New York: Oxford University Press, 1982), 233.

[6]Florence Nightingale, *Cassandra and Other Selections from Suggestions for Thought,* ed. Mary Poovey (New York: New York University Press 1993), 63.

[7]Nightingale, *Suggestions for Thought*, 116.

[8]Gnosticism was a complex religious movement in the second century C.E. that also entered Christianity with the formation of separate sects. It was declared a heresy because of its claims for "gnosis"—special revealed knowledge about God—and its teachings about the world as evil and humans as souls trapped within it.

[9]Oxford's Max Muller was a comparative philologist who edited a fifty-one-volume translation of religious classics, *The Sacred Books of the East,* and wrote on comparative religion. Rowland Williams, a Broad Church essayist condemned for heresy in 1860, wrote a comparative Christian–Hindu study that talks of humankind's unity through one supreme soul (God), made distinct in various forms.

[10]Nightingale, *Suggestions for Thought*, 119.

[11]Ibid., xxix.

[12]In my book *John's Message: Good News for the New Millennium* (Nashville: Abingdon Press, 1999), I develop this further. The relationship between the Father and Son is that of a shared task, a shared "family business" as it were, and the "oneness" of the Father and Son is oneness in a task rather than ontological categories—an originator and a deputy.

[13]Sir Edward T. Cook, *The Life of Florence Nightingale*, 2 vols. (1913–14; reprint, 2 vols. in 1, New York: Macmillan, 1942), 1:223.

[14]Sullivan, *The Friendship*, 178.

[15]Nightingale, *Suggestions for Thought*, xiii.

[16]Boyd, *Three Victorian Women*, 228.

[17]Florence Nightingale, *Florence Nightingale in Egypt and Greece: Her Diary and "Visions,"* ed. Michael D. Calabria (New York: State University of New York, 1996), 10.

[18]Boyd, *Three Victorian Women*, 217.

[19]Ibid., 229.

[20]Evelyn Underhill, *Mysticism: A Study in the Nature and Development of Man's Spiritual Consciousness* (1911; 12th ed., New York: Doubleday, 1988). Evelyn Underhill (1875–1941) was an English exponent of the mystical life. Her book *Mysticism* is a classic.

[21]Nightingale, *Diary and "Visions,"* 9.

[22]Nightingale, *Suggestions for Thought*, xiii.

[23]Nightingale, *Diary and "Visions,"* 148.

[24]Boyd, *Three Victorian Women*, 231.

[25]Thomas à Kempis, *Imitation of Christ* (London: Burns & Lambert, 1851), 244. Florence Nightingale Museum, London.

[26]Underhill, *Mysticism*, 81.

[27]St. Catherine of Siena (1347–1380) became a Dominican tertiary at sixteen. In 1376, she went to Pope Gregory XI in Avignon (France) to persuade him to return to Rome. She had a following in Siena of people attracted to her spirituality, ecstatic prayer, and writings.

St. Teresa of Avila (1515–1582) was a Spanish Carmelite nun and mystic. Although she entered the convent in 1535, her mystical life did not begin until 1555 with divine voices, visions, and ecstatic experiences. She founded a convent, wrote extensively, and combined her mystic experience with ceaseless activity.

[28]Boyd, *Three Victorian Women*, 227.

[29]Florence Nightingale, *Ever Yours, Florence Nightingale—Selected Letters*, ed. Martha Vicinus and Bea Nergaard (Cambridge, Mass.: Harvard University Press, 1989), 310.

[30]Sullivan, *The Friendship*, 16.

[31]Ibid., 23.

[32]Ibid., 106.

[33]Ibid., 128.

[34]Ibid., 172.

[35]Ibid., 26–27.

[36]James R. Price III, "Mysticism," in Donald W. Musser and Joseph L. Price, eds., *A New Handbook of Christian Theology* (Nashville: Abingdon Press, 1992), 320.

[37]"The Poor," in Paul J. Achtemeier, general ed., *Harper's Bible Dictionary* (New York: HarperSanFrancisco, 1985), 807–8.

[38]"Liberation Theology," in Musser and Price, *A New Handbook of Christian Theology*, 290.

[39]Ibid., 291–92.

[40]Ibid., 292.

[41]Ibid., 293.

[42]Ibid., 287–88. Paulo Freire, born in Brazil in 1921, experienced hopeless poverty when his middle-class parents fell into debt. He vowed, at age eleven, to give his life to the struggle against poverty and hunger so other children would not experience his agony. He became a Professor of Education in the University of Recife, his home-town. His educational methods for the poor and illiterate, outlined in his classic *Pedagogy of the Oppressed*, so threatened the old dominant order that he was imprisoned in 1964, then encouraged to leave the country.

[43]These people and events will be discussed later.

[44]Florence's theology will be discussed in depth later.

[45]Vincent Quinn and John Prest, *Dear Miss Nightingale* (Oxford: Oxford University Press, 1987), 213.

[46]Sullivan, *The Friendship*, 21.

[47]Nightingale, *Suggestions for Thought*, 9. Comte's ideas will be discussed later.

[48]Nightingale, *Cassandra and Other Selections*, 132.

[49]Lytton Strachey, *Eminent Victorians* (New York: The Modern Library, 1918), 11–12.

[50]Jeremy Bentham, a scholar and philosopher in the areas of jurisprudence, political philosophy, sociology, and ethics, was the "father" of utilitarianism, the belief that society should operate on the greatest good for the greatest number. This idea opposed the traditional idea, promoted by church and state, of the "social contract," and led to the overhaul of English law and government.

[51]Joshua Watson, a wine merchant who retired from business in 1814 to devote himself to good works in the name of the Church of England, was instrumental in forming the National Society for Promoting the Education of the Poor in the Principles of the Established Church, which educated in the first part of the Nineteenth Century, without church or government funds, the majority of primary school children. Watson also formed an Incorporated Church Building Society, which built six hundred new churches by the time of his death, in areas without churches.

[52]Auguste Comte (1798–1857), French philosopher, was the founder of the philosophical school of positivism, which sought knowledge gained from *observable* phenomena only, especially science. Comte's practical goals were social reform and a harmonious society, and he was supported in this by John Stuart Mill. Comte coined the term *sociology* for the systematic study of unifying principles in society.

[53]John Stuart Mill was the son of philosopher James Mill (1773–1836), an early Utilitarian. Rigorously educated from childhood, John worked for the British East India Company until its demise in 1858. During this time, he wrote many books with his wife, Harriet Taylor Mill, and was elected to Parliament in 1865, fighting for Irish land reform and women's rights.

[54]John Stuart Mill, *The Subjection of Women* (1869; New York: Dover Publications, Inc., 1997), 74.

[55]Cook, *The Life of Florence Nightingale,* 1:471.

[56]Ibid., 473.

[57]Dossey, *Mystic, Visionary, Healer,* 243.

[58]Cook, *The Life of Florence Nightingale,* 1:476.

[59]Dossey, *Mystic, Visionary, Healer,* 243.

[60]Nightingale, *Suggestions for Thought,* xxxviii.

[61]Cook, *The Life of Florence Nightingale,* 1:474.

[62]Ibid.

[63]Nightingale, *Ever Yours,* 211.

[64]Cook, *The Life of Florence Nightingale,* 1:470.

[65]Strachey, *Eminent Victorians,* 189.

[66]Margaret Lesser, *Clarkey: A Portrait in Letters of Mary Clarke Mohl (1793–1883)* (Oxford: Oxford University Press, 1984), 169.

[67]Lytton Strachey, quoted in Raymond G. Hebert, ed., *Florence Nightingale: Saint, Reformer or Rebel?* (Malabar, Fla.: Robert E. Kreiger Publishing Co., 1981), 155.

[68]Mrs. Cecil (Blanche) Woodham-Smith, *Florence Nightingale* (New York: McGraw-Hill, 1951), 290.

[69]Dossey, *Mystic, Visionary, Healer,* 245.

[70]Cook, *The Life of Florence Nightingale,* 1:407.

[71]Ibid., 1:412.

[72]Nightingale, *Ever Yours,* 228.

[73]Nightingale, *Cassandra and Other Selections,* 148.

[74]Dossey, *Mystic, Visionary, Healer,* 248.

[75]Nightingale, *Ever Yours,* 229.

Chapter 9: A Religion for the Working Class

[1]Florence Nightingale, *Suggestions for Thought: Selections and Commentaries,* ed. Michael D. Calabria and Janet A. Macrae (Philadelphia: University of Pennsylvania Press, 1994), 150.

[2]"Radical," in Jean L. McKechnie, ed., *Webster's New Universal Unabridged Dictionary,* 2d ed. (New York: Dorset & Baber, 1983), 1486.

[3]Nightingale, *Suggestions for Thought,* 10.

[4]Florence Nightingale, *Cassandra and Other Selections from Suggestions for Thought,* ed. Mary Poovey (New York: New York University Press, 1993), 3.

[5]Ibid., 4.

[6]Nightingale, *Suggestions for Thought,* 10.

[7]Nightingale, *Cassandra and Other Selections,* 114.

[8]David L. Edwards, *From the 18th Century to the First World War,* vol. 3 of *Christian England* (Grand Rapids, Mich.: William B. Eerdmans Publishing Company, 1984), 132.

[9]Ibid., 143.

[10]Ibid., 149.

[11]Ibid., 307.

[12]Ibid., 308.

[13]Ibid., 311.

[14]Ibid., 300.

[15]Ibid., 303.

[16]Paley's (1743–1805) *A View of the Evidences of Christianity* returned the Enlightenment debates to the traditional doctrines of the Church of England. His book became popular during English uncertainty over the French Revolution and, by the early 1800s, was compulsory reading for all students at Oxford and Cambridge.

[17]Charles Darwin (1809–1882) studied medicine at Edinburgh University and, after quitting his theological studies in Cambridge, obtained a job as naturalist for a five-year expedition on the H.M.S. *Beagle.* The voyage (1831–36) gave him the opportunity to study the world's plant, animal, and human life and ask questions about origins. He developed his theory of evolution long before its publication, realizing the controversy it would produce against the biblical account of creation. Only when naturalist Alfred Wallace began working on a similar theory did he publish *On the Origin of Species by Means of Natural Selection.*

[18]Edwards, *From the 18th Century,* 297.

[19]Florence had read works by German orientalist and theologian Heinrich Ewald (1803–1875) and others, along with French philosophers Auguste Comte and Victor Cousins. Nightingale, *Suggestions for Thought*, xxiii.

[20]Renn Dickson Hampden (1793–1868), Anglican theologian, in his Bampton lectures in Oxford in 1832, offered a less traditional and more scientifically accommodating view of Christianity, challenging the established theology of William Paley. Supporters of the Oxford Movement tried to block Hampden's appointment as Regius Professor of Divinity at Oxford in 1836 and his appointment as Bishop of Hereford in 1848 because of his "liberal" tendencies.

[21]Henry Longueville Mansel (1820–1871) was Dean of St. Paul's Cathedral from 1868. In his Bampton Lectures at Oxford in 1858 on *The Limits of Religious Thought*, Mansel began from human capacity. The mind can intuit an Absolute Being, and that which is intuited must be the God of the scriptures. Mansel made no challenge to supernatural revelations, evoking criticism in an age of science.

[22]Frederick Denison (F. D.) Maurice (1805–1872) was Professor of Theology at King's College, London, from 1846 until his Theological Essays (1853) attacked the idea of endless punishment in hell, and argued that "Eternity" in the New Testament had nothing to do with time or place, but existed already in the present. He was dismissed from King's College, and in 1866 became Knightsbridge Professor of Moral Philosophy at Cambridge. His interest in social reform led to the formation of the Christian Socialists.

[23]F. G. Hamish, *Ideas of Order: Anglicans and the Renewal of Theological Method in the Middle Years of the Nineteenth Century* (Assen, The Netherlands: Van Gorcum & Comp. B.V., 1974), 136.

[24]Ibid., 161.

[25]Ibid., 168. Nicene refers to the first ecumenical Church Council in Nicaea (325 C.E.), called by Emperor Constantine, to settle the debate as to the divine and human natures of Jesus. The Nicene Creed came from this Council. Jowett is arguing that what was metaphorical for Paul in terms of who Jesus was became literal at Nicaea.

[26]Nightingale, *Suggestions for Thought*, 22. Patristic theology deals with the writings of the Church Fathers between the end of the First Century and the close of the Eighth Century, the "Patristic Age."

[27]For details of these people, see Glossary.

[28]Nightingale, *Suggestions for Thought*, xxxii.

[29]Ibid., xxxiii.

[30]Frederick Temple (1821–1902) was headmaster of Rugby School (1857–69), Bishops of Exeter (1869–85), Bishop of London (1885–97) then Archbishop of Canterbury from 1897. Arthur Penrhyn Stanley (1815–1881) was an intimate friend of Benjamin Jowett's, and a member of the Broad Church. He became Dean of Westminster in 1864 and tried to make the Abbey a national shrine for all, irrespective of creed. His sister Mary was in the Crimea with Florence and later converted to Catholicism.

[31]Friedrich Schleiermacher (1768–1834), a Reformed theologian from Berlin, published in 1799 his famous *Religion: Speeches to Its Cultured Despisers* aimed at disenchanted intellectuals. He argued that religion was a feeling of absolute dependence rather than doctrines. The diversity of this feeling accounted for different religions, of which Christianity was the highest but not the only true one. Schleiermacher had considerable influence on Protestant thought.

[32]Nightingale, *Suggestions for Thought*, xxxv. John Colenso (1814–1883), Bishop of Natal, South Africa, from 1853, published a commentary on Romans in 1861 denying eternal punishment; published papers on the Pentateuch and Joshua challenging their authorship and accuracy; and adapted Christian teachings to African indigenous traditions. In 1863, he was declared deposed as Bishop, but the Privy Council reversed the decision. Another Bishop was appointed by the Church, but Colenso maintained his position alongside the new appointment.

[33]"Providence," in the Reverend John M'Clintock and James Strong, *Cyclopaedia of Biblical, Theological and Ecclesiastical Literature*, vol. 8 (New York: Harper & Brothers, 1894), 707–11.

[34]Ibid., 709.

[35]Sue Goldie ed., *I Have Done My Duty: Florence Nightingale in the Crimean War, 1854–56* (Iowa: University of Iowa Press, 1987), 17.

[36]"Providence."

[37]Nightingale, *Cassandra and other Selections*, 57.

[38]I. B. (Ida Beatrice) O'Malley, *Florence Nightingale, 1820–1856: A Study of Her Life Down to the End of the Crimean War* (London: Thornton Butterworth, 1931), 130.

[39]Nightingale, *Suggestions for Thought*, 136.

[40]Hugh Small, *Florence Nightingale: Avenging Angel* (New York: St. Martin's Press, 1998), 90.

[41]Nightingale, *Suggestions for Thought*, 9.

[42]Ibid.

[43]Ibid., 10.

[44]Ibid., xiv.

[45]Nancy Boyd, *Three Victorian Women Who Changed Their World : Josephine Butler, Octavia Hill, Florence Nightingale* (New York: Oxford University Press, 1982), 203.

[46]Ibid., 202.

[47]Ibid., 200.

[48]Nightingale, *Suggestions for Thought*, 13.

[49]Nightingale, *Cassandra and Other Selections*, 10.

[50]Nightingale, *Suggestions for Thought*, 121.

[51]For current books dealing with the evolving idea of God, see footnote 46 in chapter 3.

[52]Nightingale, *Suggestions for Thought*, 28.

[53]Ibid., 16.

[54]Nightingale, *Cassandra and Other Selections*, 13.

[55]Ibid., 9.

[56]Ibid., 14.

[57]Nancy Boyd, *Three Victorian Women*, 203.

[58]Ibid., 204.

[59]Nightingale, *Cassandra and Other Selections*, 6.

[60]Val Webb, *In Defense of Doubt: An Invitation to Adventure* (St. Louis: Chalice Press, 1995), 3–4.

[61]Nightingale, *Suggestions for Thought*, 23.

[62]Ibid., 28.

[63]Nightingale, *Cassandra and Other Selections*, 15.

[64]Ibid., 29.

[65]Nightingale, *Suggestions for Thought*, 30.

[66]Nightingale, *Cassandra and Other Selections*, 10.

[67]Ibid., 173.

[68]Ibid.

[69]Ibid., 202–3.

[70]Florence Nightingale, *Ever Yours, Florence Nightingale–Selected Letters*, ed. Martha Vicinus and Bea Nergaard (Cambridge, Mass.: Harvard University Press, 1989), 209.

[71]Nightingale, *Suggestions for Thought*, 5.

[72]Nightingale, *Cassandra and Other Selections*, 11–12.

[73]Nightingale, *Ever Yours*, 209.

[74]Nightingale, *Cassandra and Other Selections*, 12.

[75]I am indebted to Patricia Wismer for her discussion of evil in Donald W. Musser and Joseph L. Price, eds., *A New Handbook of Christian Theology* (Nashville: Abingdon Press, 1992), 174.

[76]Florence Nightingale, *Florence Nightingale in Egypt and Greece: Her Diary and "Visions,"* ed. Michael D. Calabria (New York: State University of New York, 1996), 23.

[77]Mary C. Sullivan, ed., *The Friendship of Florence Nightingale and Mary Clare Moore* (Philadelphia: University of Pennsylvania Press, 1999), 187.

[78]Nightingale, *Suggestions for Thought*, 80.

[79]Ibid., 81.

[80]Ibid., 83.

[81]Nightingale, *Cassandra and Other Selections*, 81.

[82]Ibid., 78.

[83]Ibid., 105.

[84]Ibid., 103.

[85]Ibid., 24.

[86]Ibid., 113.

[87]Small, *Avenging Angel*, 193.

[88]Ibid., 192.

[89]Nightingale, *Suggestions for Thought*, 11.

[90]Ibid., 144.

[91]Ibid.
[92]Ibid., 154.
[93]Ibid., 146.
[94]Ibid., 73.
[95]Small, *Avenging Angel*, 196.
[96]O'Malley, *Florence Nightingale, 1820–1856*, 116.
[97]Nightingale, *Suggestions for Thought*, 152.

Chapter 10: Creating Heaven Here and Now

[1]Florence Nightingale, *Suggestions for Thought: Selections and Commentaries*, ed. Michael D. Calabria and Janet A. Macrae (Philadelphia: University of Pennsylvania Press, 1994), 8.
[2]Florence Nightingale, *Cassandra and Other Selections from Suggestions for Thought*, ed. Mary Poovey (New York: New York University Press 1993), 169.
[3]Ibid., 94.
[4]Florence Nightingale, *Florence Nightingale: Letters from Egypt: A Journey on the Nile*, ed. Anthony Sattin (New York: Weidenfeld & Nicholson, 1987), 160–61. A Hierophant was the high-priest of Demeter who conducted the celebration of the Eleusinian Mysteries, always a citizen of Attica. In the Greek Church, the hierophant is the prior of a monastery.
[5]Nightingale, *Suggestions for Thought*, 136.
[6]Nightingale, *Cassandra and Other Selections*, 63.
[7]Nightingale, *Suggestions for Thought*, 130.
[8]Ibid.
[9]Nancy Boyd, *Three Victorian Women Who Changed Their World : Josephine Butler, Octavia Hill, Florence Nightingale* (New York: Oxford University Press, 1982), 218.
[10]Mary C. Sullivan, ed., *The Friendship of Florence Nightingale and Mary Clare Moore* (Philadelphia: University of Pennsylvania Press, 1999), 184.
[11]Nightingale, *Suggestions for Thought*, 29.
[12]Florence Nightingale, *Ever Yours, Florence Nightingale—Selected Letters*, ed. Martha Vicinus and Bea Nergaard (Cambridge, Mass.: Harvard University Press, 1989), 30.
[13]Nightingale, *Suggestions for Thought*, 96.
[14]Ibid., 30.
[15]Ibid., 15.
[16]Ibid., 13.
[17]Nightingale, *Cassandra and Other Selections*, 79.
[18]Nightingale, *Suggestions for Thought*, 27.
[19]Ibid., 13.
[20]"Will," in The Rev. John M'Clintock and James Strong, *Cyclopaedia of Biblical, Theological and Ecclesiastical Literature*, vol. 8 (New York: Harper & Brothers, 1894), 989–94.
[21]Nightingale, *Suggestions for Thought*, 64.
[22]Nightingale, *Cassandra and Other Selections*, 44.
[23]Ibid., 44.
[24]Ibid., 50.
[25]Florence Nightingale, *Florence Nightingale in Egypt and Greece: Her Diary and "Visions,"* ed. Michael D. Calabria (New York: State University of New York, 1996), 23–24.
[26]Nightingale, *Cassandra and Other Selections*, 60.
[27]Mary Keele, ed., *Florence Nightingale in Rome: Letters Written by Florence Nightingale in Rome in the Winter of 1847–1848* (Philadelphia: American Philosophical Society, 1981), 111.
[28]Nightingale, *Cassandra and Other Selections*, 61–62.
[29]Ibid., 64.
[30]Ibid.
[31]Ibid., 40.
[32]Ibid., 54.
[33]Nightingale, *Suggestions for Thought*, 136.
[34]Ibid., 132–33.
[35]Ibid., 133.
[36]Nightingale, *Cassandra and Other Selections*, 95.
[37]Ibid., 86.
[38]Ibid., 90.
[39]Ibid., 91– 93.
[40]Ibid., 168.

[41]Nightingale, *Suggestions for Thought*, 50.

[42]Ibid., xvii.

[43]Joseph Lister (1827–1912), a surgeon in Glasgow, studied Louis Pasteur's germ theory and applied carbolic acid (phenol) directly to wounds rather than spraying the air, thus founding antiseptic surgery. Robert Koch (1843–1910), a German physician, demonstrated bacillus spores responsible for anthrax in animals in 1876, giving support to Pasteur's germ theory. He later identified the bacilli causing tuberculosis and cholera.

[44]Sir Zachary Cope, *Florence Nightingale and the Doctors* (Philadelphia: J. B. Lippincott, 1958), 24.

[45]Boyd, *Three Victorian Women*, 209.

[46]I am indebted for this discussion of process thought and process theology to David Ray Griffin's entry in Donald W. Musser and Joseph L. Price, eds., *A New Handbook of Christian Theology* (Nashville: Abingdon Press, 1992), 383–88; and Robert C. Mesle, *Process Theology: A Basic Introduction* (St. Louis: Chalice Press, 1993).

[47]This argument is addressed in John B. Cobb, Jr., *Christ in a Pluralistic Age* (Philadelphia: Westminster Press, 1975).

[48]Nightingale, *Cassandra and Other Selections*, 26.

[49]Ibid., 27.

[50]Nightingale, *Suggestions for Thought*, 145.

[51]Nightingale, *Cassandra and Other Selections*, 37–38.

[52]Ibid., 37–38.

[53]Nightingale, *Suggestions for Thought*, 151.

[54]Nightingale, *Cassandra and Other Selections*, 26.

[55]Ibid., 26.

[56]Nightingale, *Suggestions for Thought*, 43.

[57]Ibid., 152.

[58]Ibid., 153.

[59]Ibid., 143.

Chapter 11: A "True" Marriage

[1]Florence Nightingale, *Cassandra and Other Selections from Suggestions for Thought*, ed. Mary Poovey (New York: New York University Press 1993), 156–57.

[2]The first and commissioned biography of Benjamin Jowett was by L. Campbell and E. Abbott, *Life and Letters of Benjamin Jowett*, 2 vols. (London: J. Murray, 1897). A biography by Geoffrey Faber, drawing on material not included in Campbell and Abbott, was published in 1957 (Geoffrey Faber, *Jowett: A Portrait with Background* [Cambridge, Mass.: Harvard University Press, 1957]).

[3]Faber, *Jowett: A Portrait*, 169.

[4]Ibid., 170. Andrew Lang (1844–1912) was a famous Scottish writer; Newman is John Henry Newman; and Henry Liddon (1811–1898), canon of St. Paul's, was a supporter of High-Churchman E. B. Pusey and Catholic principles.

[5]The "troublesome damnation clause in the Athanasian Creed" began the recitation of the Athanasian Creed for Morning Prayer in the *Book of Common Prayer*:

Whosoever will be saved: before all things it is necessary that he hold the Catholic Faith. Which Faith except everyone do keep whole and undefiled: without doubt he shall perish everlastingly. And the Catholic Faith is this ...

Many doctrines under dispute at this time were listed as the "Catholic Faith" outlined in this Creed.

[6]Jowett would spend much of his life working for the disestablishment of Oxford as an Anglican institution and the secularization of university studies in general.

[7]Faber, *Jowett: A Portrait*, 143.

[8]Ibid., 144.

[9]Robert Scott (1811–1887) was Master of Balliol from 1854 to 1870 when he became Dean of Rochester and Jowett succeeded him at Balliol. Scott collaborated with H. G. Liddell on a well-regarded Greek Lexicon.

[10]Faber, *Jowett: A Portrait*, 219.

[11]Ibid.

[12]Ibid., 231.

[13]Ibid., 234.

[14]Ibid., 235.

[15]Ibid., 236.

[16]Ibid.

[17]Ibid., 245.

[18]Samuel Wilberforce (1805–1873), Bishop of Oxford (1845–69) then of Winchester, attacked *Essays and Reviews* for its liberalism and led its condemnation amongst the bishops. He was also responsible for initiating the revision of the Authorized Version of the Bible.

[19]Faber, *Jowett: A Portrait*, 252.

[20]Bishop Archibald Tait (1811–1882) was one of four tutors at Oxford who protested against John Henry Newman's *Tract 90*, arguing that the Church of England was a version of the Church of Rome. However, although Tait had supported the Broad Church movement, he opposed the *Essays* as Bishop of London, much to the essayists' disappointment. Tait became Archbishop of Canterbury in 1868.

[21]Faber, *Jowett: A Portrait*, 259.

[22]Ibid., 275. Williams died prematurely, and Wilson's health and spirit were broken.

[23]Ibid., 273.

[24]Ibid., 278.

[25]Ibid., 280.

[26]Ibid., 281.

[27]Campbell and Abbott's biography made absolutely no mention of Florence or her and Jowett's friendship and correspondence. She had ordered that he destroy all her letters and not mention their friendship. Woodham-Smith's biography of Florence was the first to note their relationship.

[28]The word *homosexuality* did not replace the whispered description of *bestiality* at Oxford until 1897, and in the 1890s, Oxford's Oscar Wilde was charged with homosexual offenses under an 1885 Criminal Law Amendment Act, and jailed for two years. Tom Stoppard's play *The Invention of Love* (1997) deals with the issue of homosexuality at Oxford during this period, with A. E. Houseman, Oscar Wilde, and Benjamin Jowett as characters in the play.

[29]Faber, *Jowett: A Portrait*, 96. The women mentioned were both famous in Greek literature as wise, educated women.

[30]Ibid., 98.

[31]Ibid., 98–99.

[32]Mrs. Cecil (Blanche) Woodham-Smith, *Florence Nightingale* (New York: McGraw-Hill, 1951), 280. Although it has been suggested by some that Florence was lesbian because she did not marry, I have found nothing in my research to suggest that conclusion and much that would challenge it.

[33]Barbara Montgomery Dossey, *Florence Nightingale: Mystic, Visionary, Healer* (Springhouse, Pa.: Springhouse Corp., 2000), 373.

[34]Faber, *Jowett: A Portrait*, 92.

[35]Ibid., 90–91.

[36]I am indebted for this discussion to Jowett's edited letters by Vincent Quinn and John Prest in their *Dear Miss Nightingale* (Oxford: Oxford University Press, 1987). Jowett left instructions for his letters from Florence to be burned, so most of her letters to him were lost, except for a small packet. When Abbott and Campbell were commissioned to write Jowett's biography, they asked Florence for his letters to *her*. She refused, saying they had been written with the conviction that they were sacred to the receiver. She eventually sent a few, but even then, nothing was published without her consent. Some of the letters that finally surfaced were polished or condensed. Florence insisted she not be mentioned anywhere in Jowett's biography, with any letters to her quoted as "to a friend." No letters of Florence's were included in *Letters of Benjamin Jowett* published in 1899. After Florence's death, Cook used some of the letters, but not extensively. Faber also made scant use of them in his biography on Jowett, most appearing for the first time in Quinn and Prest's collection, with some representative letters from Florence to give the flavor of her writing.

[37]Quinn and Prest, *Dear Miss Nightingale*, 4.

[38]Ibid., 6.

[39]Ibid., 7.

[40]Ibid., 10.

[41]Ibid., 12.

[42]Ibid.

[43]Ibid.

[44]Ibid., 13.

[45]Ibid., 14.

[46]Ibid., 15.
[47]Ibid., 17.
[48]Ibid., 18.
[49]Ibid.
[50]Ibid., 23.
[51]Ibid., 23–24.
[52]Ibid., 245–46.
[53]W. J. Bishop, comp. (completed by Sue Goldie), *A Bio-bibliography of Florence Nightingale* (London: Dawsons of Pall Mall for the International Council of Nurses, 1962), 79.
[54]Ibid., 80.
[55]Ibid., 82.
[56]Ibid., 85.
[57]Quinn and Prest, *Dear Miss Nightingale, 29.*
[58]Ibid., 81.
[59]Ibid., 30.
[60]William Rathbone (1819–1902) came from a line of wealthy Liverpool shipowners. A Unitarian, he approached Florence in 1860 for her advice on setting up a district nursing scheme. He later offered to finance a nurse training scheme for a Workhouse Infirmary. In 1868, he became a Liberal Member of Parliament.
[61]Florence Nightingale, *Ever Yours, Florence Nightingale—Selected Letters,* ed. Martha Vicinus and Bea Nergaard (Cambridge, Mass.: Harvard University Press, 1989), 246.
[62]Dossey, *Mystic, Visionary, Healer,* 296.
[63]Bishop, *A Bio-bibliography,* 89.
[64]Jean-Henri Dunant (1828–1910), Swiss humanitarian, helped the wounded at the Battle of Solferino in 1859 and saw the need for an international organization to alleviate suffering in war and peace. His credited his efforts, culminating in the Geneva Convention of 1864 and the Red Cross, to Florence's inspiration. He received the first Nobel Peace Prize in 1901.
[65]Dossey, *Mystic, Visionary, Healer,* 324.
[66]Quinn and Prest, *Dear Miss Nightingale,* 35–36.
[67]Ibid., 39.
[68]Ibid., 53.
[69]Ibid., 55.
[70]Ibid., 60.
[71]Ibid., 80.

Chapter 12: Being Called

[1]Mary C. Sullivan, ed., *The Friendship of Florence Nightingale and Mary Clare Moore* (Philadelphia: University of Pennsylvania Press, 1999), 183.
[2]Vincent Quinn and John Prest, *Dear Miss Nightingale* (Oxford: Oxford University Press, 1987), 71.
[3]Ibid., 66.
[4]Ibid., 51.
[5]Ibid., 69.
[6]Ibid., 214.
[7]Ibid., 41.
[8]Ibid.
[9]Ibid., 68.
[10]Ibid., 46.
[11]Ibid., 47.
[12]Ibid., 50.
[13]Ibid., 52.
[14]Ibid., 52–53.
[15]Ibid., 133.
[16]Ibid., 153.
[17]Ibid., 120.
[18]Ibid., 141.
[19]Florence Nightingale, *Ever Yours, Florence Nightingale—Selected Letters,* ed. Martha Vicinus and Bea Nergaard (Cambridge, Mass.: Harvard University Press, 1989), 240.
[20]Florence Nightingale, "A Note on Pauperism," *Fraser's* Magazine, (March 1869), 281– 90. Cup.401 h 4 (8) British Library, London.

[21]Quinn and Prest, *Dear Miss Nightingale,* 163.

[22]Ibid., 168.

[23]Ibid., 183.

[24]Ibid., 174.

[25]Ibid., 188.

[26]Ibid., 202.

[27]Barbara Montgomery Dossey, *Florence Nightingale: Mystic, Visionary, Healer* (Springhouse, Pa.: Springhouse Corp., 2000), 298.

[28]Nightingale, *Ever Yours,* 248.

[29]Henry Bonham Carter (1827–1921), Florence's cousin and brother of Hilary, was secretary of the Nightingale Fund from 1861 (after Clough's death) to 1899 while full-time managing director of the Guardian Assurance Co. He remained on the Nightingale Fund Council until 1914.

[30]Medical officer Dr. Whitfield organized the establishment of the Nightingale School of Nursing at St. Thomas's and was the first appointed lecturer. Matron Wardroper was the School's first matron.

[31]Dossey, *Mystic, Visionary, Healer,* 300.

[32]W. J. Bishop, comp. (completed by Sue Goldie), *A Bio-bibliography of Florence Nightingale* (London, Dawsons of Pall Mall for the International Council of Nurses, 1962), 43.

[33]Quinn and Prest, *Dear Miss Nightingale,* 206.

[34]Ibid., 208.

[35]Stanley and Morier were the two men most intimately connected with Jowett throughout his life.

[36]Quinn and Prest, *Dear Miss Nightingale,* 219.

[37]Ibid., 207.

[38]Ibid., 237.

[39]Dossey, *Mystic, Visionary, Healer,* 341. The non-Biblical characters here are from classical Greece.

[40]Quinn and Prest, *Dear Miss Nightingale,* 281.

[41]Ibid., 220.

[42]Thomas Henry Huxley (1825–1895), a surgeon in the Royal Navy, studied marine life during his travels, and his work became the basis for future classification of much sealife. Huxley promoted Darwin's ideas and writings, debating Bishop Samuel Wilberforce at the Oxford meeting of the British Association for the Advancement of Science in 1860. While Darwin did not apply his evolutionary theories to the human species, Huxley did in his 1863 *Man's Place in Nature.* Huxley also argued that there was no evidence for racial superiority, and coined the word 'agnostic' to describe his theological position.

[43]Quinn and Prest, *Dear Miss Nightingale,* 235.

[44]Ibid., 233.

[45]Ibid., 246.

[46]Ibid., 239.

[47]Florence Nightingale, "A subnote of Interrogation — what will our religion be in 1999?" *Fraser's* Magazine (July 1873, 25–36), 25.

[48]Ibid., 27.

[49]Ibid., 33.

[50]Ibid., 36.

[51]Quinn and Prest, *Dear Miss Nightingale,* 249.

[52]Ibid., 251.

[53]Ibid., 255.

[54]Margaret Lesser, *Clarkey: a Portrait in Letters of Mary Clarke Mohl (1793–1883)* (Oxford: Oxford University Press, 1984), 202.

[55]Mrs. Cecil (Blanche) Woodham-Smith, *Florence Nightingale* (New York: McGraw-Hill Book Co., 1951), 390.

[56]Quinn and Prest, *Dear Miss Nightingale,* 261.

[57]Ibid., 280.

[58]Geoffrey Faber, *Jowett: A Portrait with Background* (Cambridge, Mass.: Harvard University Press, 1957), 374.

[59]Quinn and Prest, *Dear Miss Nightingale,* 262.

[60]Ibid., xxxiii.

[61]Ibid., xxxiv.

[62]Faber, *Jowett: A Portrait with Background*, 355.

[63]Quinn and Prest, *Dear Miss Nightingale*, 308.

[64]Ibid., xxxv.

[65]Ibid., 281.

[66]Dossey, *Mystic, Visionary, Healer*, 404. Florence opposed the three-year training and registration until her death. It was finally put into place in 1919.

[67]Faber, *Jowett: A Portrait with Background*, 408.

[68]Quinn and Prest, *Dear Miss Nightingale*, 281.

[69]Ibid., 308.

[70]Ibid., 280–81.

[71]Ibid., 283.

[72]Ibid., 301.

[73]Ibid., 305.

[74]William J. Bishop, "Florence Nightingale's Message for Today," in Raymond G. Hebert, ed., *Florence Nightingale: Saint, Reformer or Rebel?* (Malabar, Fla.: Robert E. Kreiger Publishing Co, 1981), 199–200.

[75]Quinn and Prest, *Dear Miss Nightingale*, 320.

[76]Ibid., 323.

[77]Dossey, *Mystic, Visionary, Healer*, 396.

[78]Quinn and Prest, *Dear Miss Nightingale*, 305.

[79]Ibid., 310. At this time, mysticism was considered by Protestants as the exclusive property of the Roman Catholic Church.

[80]Dossey, *Mystic, Visionary, Healer*, 395.

Index